W9-BLZ-296

THE S. MARK TAPER FOUNDATION

IMPRINT IN JEWISH STUDIES

BY THIS ENDOWMENT

THE S. MARK TAPER FOUNDATION SUPPORTS

THE APPRECIATION AND UNDERSTANDING

OF THE RICHNESS AND DIVERSITY OF

JEWISH LIFE AND CULTURE

The publisher gratefully acknowledges the
generous contribution to this book provided by
the following organizations and individuals:

DEBORAH LOW DOPPELT
THOMAS J. FLEISH
DAVID B. GOLD FOUNDATION
LUCIUS N. LITTAUER FOUNDATION
JOSEPH LOW
SKIRBALL FOUNDATION
S. MARK TAPER FOUNDATION
EVAN AND TERRI WEIN

THE SABRA

The Sabra

The Creation of the New Jew

Oz Almog

TRANSLATED BY

Haim Watzman

UNIVERSITY OF CALIFORNIA PRESS

Berkeley · Los Angeles · London

*The author gratefully acknowledges the generous
contributions to this book provided by the
Sacta-Rashi Foundation and the Yad-Hanadiv
Foundation.*

University of California Press
Berkeley and Los Angeles, California

University of California Press, Ltd.
London, England

© 2000 by Oz Almog

Translated and abridged from *The Sabra: A Profile*
[Hebrew], published by Am Oved Publishers, Ltd.,
Tel Aviv, 1997.

Library of Congress Cataloging-in-Publication Data

Almog, Oz.
   [Tsabar. English]
   The Sabra : the creation of the new Jew /
Oz Almog ; Haim Watzman, translator.
         p.   cm.—(S. Mark Taper Foundation
   imprint in Jewish studies)
   Includes bibliographical references and index.
      ISBN 0-520-21642-3 (cloth : alk. paper)
      1. National characteristics, Israeli.   2. Sabras.
   3. Jews—Israel—Identity.   I. Title.   II. Series.
   DS113.3.A5613   2000
   305.892'405694—dc21   00-042613

Manufactured in the United States of America

09   08   07   06   05   04   03   02   01   00
10   9   8   7   6   5   4   3   2   1

The paper used in this publication meets the
minimum requirements of ANSI/NISO Z39.48-1992
(R 1997) (*Permanence of Paper*). ♾

To my late grandparents,

Asher and Sarah Kantor

and

David and Miriam Lichtshine

Contents

Illustrations

Translator's Note

It is difficult enough to explain a subculture to people who share the same language and country. To make it comprehensible to speakers of another language is a daunting task—so much depends on nuances and connotations and dialect that it hardly seems possible. Americans, whose own subcultures—thanks to television—have achieved worldwide currency, at least in watered-down versions, can count on foreigners knowing something about rednecks and hippies and rappers and generation X-ers. But Americans, even American Jews with close ties to the State of Israel, have little idea what the word "Sabra" connotes to Israelis. Even those who recognize the word generally take it to be synonymous with "native-born Israeli."

In fact, as Oz Almog states in his introduction, most native-born Israelis were never Sabras in the real sense of the word. The Sabras were a small, homogeneous group who had influence far beyond their numbers because they carried the standard of labor Zionism and became the reference group by which the rest of Israeli society, in the country's early years, measured itself. In this they were one of Zionism's great myths. I should emphasize here that Almog does not use the word "myth" in its popular connotation of something false. A myth is a concept, a set of associations and beliefs, a view of reality that serves as a dramatic mechanism for expressing or explaining a basic set of values, the self-image and social goals of the society. Every culture has its myths, and these myths are often accepted uncritically, but this does not mean they are false. On the contrary, Almog musters evidence to show that much of the mythological image of the Sabra was true.

As is the case with any subculture possessing such a sense of identity and mission, the Sabras developed their own lifestyle, their own way of dressing, their own music and literature, and their own language. Like any language that is specific to a particular time, place, and culture, it is almost impossible to translate the Sabra idiom without losing its uniqueness— the essence that Almog has gone to such pains to convey in his Hebrew manuscript. So, in consultation with the author, I have decided to impose some Hebrew terms on the reader, especially in instances when the book addresses Sabra slang and customs. Although most of these terms are restricted to the small sections of the text where they are defined and discussed, a few appear throughout the book. I therefore offer here a crash course in Zionist terminology and Sabra slang to prepare the reader. There is also a glossary of Sabra terms at the back of the book to serve as a ready reference when memory fails.

First, however, a note on transliteration, in which consistency must sometimes bow to culture. I have used *ch* to designate the guttural *h*, which is similar to the *ch* in the Scottish "loch." It represents both the Hebrew letters "chaf" and "chet," since Sabras did not generally differentiate between these letters—except when they borrowed words from Arabic. In such Arabic borrowings "chaf" remains *ch* but "chet" is represented by *h*. To complicate things, the *ch* in *chizbat* is pronounced in the normal English way—as in "church." Likewise, *tz* has been used to designate the Hebrew "tzadi"—sounding more like *ts,* but the *z* avoids confusion with plurals.

Also, it should be noted, the Hebrew version of this book contains extensive quotations from Sabra writings, making it a fairly long work. In order to pare the book down for English readers, Almog reluctantly decided to remove a great deal of this material.

A Narrative Glossary

The early Zionists came almost entirely from the Jewish communities of Eastern and Central Europe, the ASHKENAZIM (sing. ASHKENAZI). The Jews of the Islamic world (with a few outposts in Europe) are called ORIENTAL or SEPHARADI (pl. SEPHARDIM) Jews. Traditional Jewish life revolved around religious practices and religious study. The YESHIVA was an institution for religious studies (for men—women did not study). One branch of traditional Judaism, emphasizing spiritual ecstasy, song, and dance was HASIDISM, whose adherents are called HASIDIM.

The first Zionist settlers came to Palestine in the late nineteenth century with the object of reestablishing a Jewish nation in the land of their fathers. They left the Diaspora—the Exile—behind them and sought to create a new kind of Jewish life and a new kind of Jew. The Zionist movement sought to buy up land in Palestine and settle Jews on it. The standard measure of land used in Palestine is the DUNAM, which is now standardized at one-quarter of an acre but varied widely in the Turkish and British periods.

The traditional Hebrew word for immigration to the Holy Land— ALIYA (pl. ALIYOT), or "ascent"—was adopted by the Zionists. In addition to applying it to the act of immigration, they used it to designate each of the successive waves of Zionist immigration. So the FIRST ALIYA comprises the immigrants who came during the last two decades of the nineteenth century, preceding the establishment of the Zionist movement by Theodor Herzl. Most of these immigrants settled in the cities, but they also created the first type of Zionist farming village, the MOSHAVA (pl. MOSHAVOT). Furthermore, they set up the first Zionist paramilitary organization, HA-SHOMER, "The Guard," whose members became legendary figures and gave the term GUARD the special connotation of a free-spirited warrior who wandered the Galilee hills on his horse, often dressed like an Arab.

The SECOND ALIYA, during the decade following 1904, and the THIRD ALIYA, of 1919 to 1923 brought, among others, Zionists influenced by socialist ideas and Russian revolutionaries—including the future leaders of the Zionist labor movement, which would become the dominant Zionist tendency. Those among them who sought to settle on the land established two new forms of agricultural settlement: the MOSHAV (pl. MOSHAVIM), where farmers tilled individual plots but cooperated to varying extents, and the KIBBUTZ (pl. KIBBUTZIM), where work and living were communal. A member of one of these settlements was a MOSHAVNIK or a KIBBUTZNIK.

These three waves of immigrants, specifically those who worked the land, are collectively referred to as the PIONEERS. They also established one of the most important Zionist institutions in Palestine, the HISTADRUT, a labor federation that also ran businesses and provided social, health, and educational services to its members. The entire sector of society affiliated with the Histadrut was often referred to as the LABOR MOVEMENT.

The FOURTH ALIYA and FIFTH ALIYA of the late 1920s and the 1930s have often been labeled the "bourgeois aliyot" because they included a large number of middle-class Jews who arrived with some money and property and settled in the cities.

The entire Jewish community in Palestine during the pre-state years is referred to as the YISHUV. Many in the Yishuv, especially in the labor movement, tended to avoid calling themselves "Jews." They preferred the term HEBREWS, which emphasized, they believed, a national affiliation rather than a religious one.

While the Zionist farmers were a minority of the Yishuv, they were regarded, even by the urbanites, as fulfilling the Zionist mission in its fullest form. They were "realizing" or "consummating" Zionism—engaging in HAGSHAMA. Hagshama thus became the ideal to which the younger generation was educated, and a loyal young Zionist was expected to aspire to it. (Construction, road work, and other forms of nonagricultural manual labor could also be acceptable forms of hagshama.)

The younger generation—the Sabras—that grew up in Palestine was socialized through a series of frameworks and organizations. If the Sabra man or woman came of age on a kibbutz or a moshav, this socialization was part of daily life. In the kibbutzim, where children lived in separate children's houses, the young people were called the YOUTH DIVISION and enjoyed a large measure of independence.

In the cities many young people joined a PIONEER YOUTH MOVEMENT, one of several organizations whose declared ideal and goal was hagshama. Almost all of them were of explicitly socialist orientation. Many teenagers participated, through their schools, in the GADNA (an outgrowth of the earlier CHAGAM, a premilitary group), the youth corps associated with the HAGANAH, the military defense organization sponsored by the Zionist self-governing organizations. Kibbutz children had a similar framework called the KIBBUTZ BRIGADE.

The elite strike force of the Haganah—to a large extent independent of it and associated specifically with the socialist Zionist movements and settlements—was the PALMACH. Palmach units, which included both men and women, split their time between military training and action and work on kibbutzim. The time they spent working on the kibbutzim, as well as the group of men and women participating in it, was called HACHSHARA (pl. HACHSHAROT). A member of the Palmach was a PALMACHNIK.

After the State of Israel was founded the Palmach was disbanded, but a unit of the Israeli army (officially the Israel Defense Forces, or IDF), called the NACHAL, was organized along the same lines, combining military service with agricultural labor, and was itself later an important Sabra socialization framework. One of the Palmach's units operated within the Arab population by dressing up in Arab clothes and adopting Arab speech and ways. These were the MISTARABIM, important because they exemplified the Sabra link with Arab culture. A young man who sought out a noncombat position in the army, a desk job or support role, was a JOBNIK. The collective legends of the operations and battles of the IDF and its predecessors, passed on to young soldiers to educate and motivate them, were called MORESHET KRAV, combat heritage.

The Zionist movement also organized groups of young people who immigrated to Palestine, and later to Israel, without their parents. This was the YOUTH ALIYA. Such children, along with some city children, were sent to live on kibbutzim in a kind of boarding school arrangement called a YOUTH SOCIETY.

Common Sabra terms that appear throughout this work are DUGRI, the direct, frank, no-holds-barred Sabra way of talking, and CHIZBAT (pl. CHIZBATIM), a tall tale or humorous anecdote. A Sabra boy generally sported a BLORIT, forelocks, that tuft of hair over the forehead that was always uncombed and wafted in the wind.

I have largely preserved Oz Almog's practice of using the masculine form as generic. While this is more acceptable in Hebrew than in English, it is, in this case, more than a matter of convention. The fact is that Sabra society was very much based on masculine ideals. Of course there were Sabra women, and they played an important role in Sabra society, culture, and even in the military. But the classic, influential, and familiar Sabras were men, and the mythic Sabra ideal of the farmer, military commander, and adventurer, as well as the poet and writer, was explicitly a male one. The great majority of the products of Sabra culture were men, and the characters they portrayed were masculine.

Women existed in Sabra folklore less as individuals than as part of the group, in which the men dominated. There were many reasons for this, in particular the importance that the military unit and the experience of battle played in the formation of the Sabra character. For this reason, the use of the masculine gender provides a more accurate representation of how this society viewed itself.

Haim Watzman

Introduction

When blond, handsome, fearless Yaron Zehavi, commander of the Hasamba gang, defied the evil British policeman Jack Smith, who threatened to throw him and his valiant comrades in jail, how different he seemed from the cowed and pious Diaspora *yeshiva* boy in Europe! Here was the new Jew, born and bred on his own land, free of the inhibitions and superstitions of earlier ages; even his physique was superior to that of his cousins in the old country. Zehavi, the hero of the most popular series of children's books produced by the new State of Israel, was the classic Sabra, a native-born Israeli modeled on the ideal that the books' author, Yigal Mosinzon, himself exemplified. Zehavi represented what has been described as a sudden and nearly total sociocultural revolution that, in a historical instant, produced a new society and culture with its own customs and codes and a new language and literature. Yet in important ways, many of which they would have vehemently denied, the Sabras were embedded in the Jewish culture that preceded them and can be understood only in its context.

This book is about the second generation of Zionist Israelis, the first generation to be educated and socialized within the Yishuv—the Jewish community in Palestine. It portrays them and tries to understand them and their influence on the society around them largely through an analysis of the writings they produced.

The Sabras were a product of what historians call the Hebrew revolution. That revolution's first generation has generally been called the pioneer generation, while the second generation has been called the Sabra generation. The Sabra generation includes the Jews born in Palestine toward the end of World War I through the 1920s and 1930s who were educated in social frameworks belonging, formally or informally, to the labor movement of the Yishuv, as well as immigrants who arrived in Palestine as youngsters (alone or with their families) and were assimilated into the same milieu. These social institutions included the *kibbutzim,* the *moshavim,* and their schools; the Hebrew gymnasiums (academic high schools) in the large cities; the agricultural youth villages (agricultural vocational boarding schools); the pioneering youth movements; the premilitary corps such as the Chagam and the Gadna; the Palmach and its brigades in the War of Independence and, after the founding of the state, the Nachal and the first elite units of the Israel Defense Forces (IDF)—Commando Unit 101, the paratroopers, the marine commandos, and the pilots—who continued the Palmach tradition.

This book's definition of the Sabra is thus not biological (someone born in Palestine) but cultural—a generational unit identified not by country of birth, but rather by affiliation to the institution that imprinted a specific culture on these young people. As already indicated, the term includes immigrants who came to Palestine as children and whose personalities were shaped in the melting pot of Sabra socialization. They were generally considered full-fledged Sabras by both themselves and their comrades, as well as by the older generation.

The Sabra generation's beliefs were molded by the Hebrew-Zionist educational system in Palestine. This was a generation for whom Hebrew was the language of conversation and of reading, and who were educated under the mythical aura of the pioneer settler and defender. They studied in schools and boarding schools affiliated with the labor movement—the socialist Zionist political parties united under the aegis of the Histadrut labor federation—or schools belonging to the general educational system sponsored by the Jewish Agency. They spent many of their adolescent hours in youth movement chapter houses and volunteered after completing high school to work in agricultural settlements (those who grew up in moshavim and kibbutzim did so as a matter of family duty, while young people from the cities arrived in the settlements under the sponsorship of the youth movements and as part of Palmach's agricultural-military training units, the *hachsharot*). The Sabras fought in the Haganah, the Palmach and, during World War II, in the British army, as well as in IDF combat units in the War of Independence and in the Sinai Campaign.

The Sabra generation's temporal boundaries are generally set at 1930 and 1960. In other words, we are concerned with a group of people whose formative years coincided with the formative years of the new Israeli society.[1] The generation began when solid foundations were laid for the pioneer youth movements, the kibbutzim and moshavim, the Jewish urban centers (largely Tel Aviv, Jerusalem, and Haifa), and the Hebrew educational system, and it ended in the period of the Sinai Campaign, the absorption of the massive immigration from the Islamic world, and the establishment and institutionalization of the new state's organs of government.

There is reasonably accurate data enumerating those who belonged to these Sabra institutions over a period of years, meaning those who were guided by the model of Sabra behavior. This leads to an estimate that the Sabra generation numbered in the area of 5,000 to 8,000 in the 1930s and about 20,000 at the time the State of Israel was established. In other words, we are talking about a group that was no larger than 10 percent of the total population of the Yishuv. Since the Sabra generation is a sociological and not a biological group, it is hard to compute precisely how many young people fit the Sabra profile perfectly or nearly perfectly. Even the Palmach had a heterogeneous membership. It included high school graduates, working youth who had not completed their schooling, Holocaust refugees, and volunteers from overseas. Many of the young people who passed through the Sabra melting pot lacked some of the classic traits discussed in this book. For example, they might not have looked like Sabras, they might not have spoken with a Sabra accent, and they might not have had Hebraicized names. The conversations I conducted with members of the generation and my examination of the primary and secondary sources have led me to the conclusion that the classic Sabras— those who matched the profile presented in this work perfectly, or nearly so—were a minority within a minority. They numbered no more than a few hundred and comprised the counselors and commanders who were what sociologists call the "generational nucleus." They were the leading group that served as a behavioral model for the entire generation. This book focuses on the nucleus, not on the entire generation. The great gulf between the Sabras' low representation in the population at large and their huge cultural influence is perhaps the secret of their fascination and their importance in the history of Israeli society and culture.

The Term "Sabra"

Ironically, the *tzabar*, or prickly pear cactus, is not native to Israel. It was introduced from Central America some two hundred years ago, but quickly acclimatized. In fact, it took hold so well in Palestine that it became one of the country's best-known features. Even before it became a symbol for the country's Jewish natives, the *tzabar*, or "sabra," cactus appeared in paintings, stories, and songs of local artists and was cited by visitors as one of the outstanding visual elements of the Palestinian landscape.

The widespread use of the word "Sabra" as a generic term for the generation of native-born Israelis began in the 1930s, but the first glimmerings of a generational term can be seen forty years earlier in the use of the Biblical term "Hebrew." This term spread through the Jewish community in Europe at the end of the nineteenth century and became one of the key words of the Zionist movement.[2] It was very common during the period of the pre-state Yishuv, especially in reference to the younger generation. Both "Hebrew" and "Sabra," which was used alongside "Hebrew" in the thirties and forties and replaced it in the fifties, were meant to denote the growing distinction that the Zionists made between the Jew of the Diaspora and the "new Jew"—the native Jew of Palestine.[3]

Some trace the source of the term "Sabra" to the use of the same word, with a Yiddish inflection, by the immigrants of the Second and Third Aliyot in the 1920s and 1930s. They used it to refer to the first natives produced by the Zionist movement—the young people whose parents had come to Palestine during the last two decades of the nineteenth century as part of the First Aliya. Whether or not this etymology is correct, we know that these young natives referred to themselves not as Sabras but as *etrogim* ("citrons")—another term taken from the local flora—or by the Biblical term "Gideons."[4]

In time—during the 1930s, and even more clearly in the 1940s—"Sabra" changed from a derogatory term to one of endearment. The emphasis was no longer on the cactus's sharp spines but rather on the contrasting sweet pulp of its fruit. This was taken as a metaphor for the native Israeli, whose rough, masculine manner was said to hide a delicate and sensitive soul. The appellation contained another symbolic comparison—just as the prickly pear grew wild on the land, so were the native-born Israelis growing, so it was said, naturally, "without complexes," in their true homeland.

Credit for the transformation of the term "Sabra," now with a modern Hebrew pronunciation, into a generic term for the native-born Israelis was claimed (rightfully, as far as I have been able to discover) by the journalist Uri Kesari. On 18 April 1931, the newspaper *Do'ar Ha-Yom* published an essay by Kesari titled "We Are the Leaves of the Sabra!" It charged that the Zionist institutions were discriminating against the native-born Jews, the Sabras, and giving preference to Russian and German Jews "and the rest of the Ashkenazim."[5] Kesari's contemporaries, especially the artists among them, quickly began using the term and the symbol of the sabra, and slowly inculcated them into the collective consciousness, as Dan Almagor relates:

> Less than two weeks after the appearance of Kesari's essay, the publisher . . . produced a new humorous pamphlet named *Tzabar*. On 19 April 1932— precisely a year and a day after the birth of the new epithet—the poet Yehuda Karni published, in the illustrated newspaper *Kolnoa* in Tel Aviv, a poem entitled "In the Homeland of the Sabra," in which he told of an encounter with a young Sabra. On that very same day there appeared, under an article by the Jewish-Polish film director Alexander Ford in the literary weekly *Ketuvim*, the following note: "The cinema director is currently preparing a film on life in Palestine—*The Sabra*." Two months later the editors of *Ketuvim* reiterated, under another piece by Ford, that he was "preparing in Palestine the movie *The Sabra*." The production of the Israeli film *The Sabra* was not completed for various reasons, but the new term had already taken root, even among educators. When the first issue of *Ofakim*, the newspaper of the Ha-Shomer Ha-Tza'ir movement devoted to problems of education and society, first appeared in December 1932, the introductory editorial already referred to the "Sabra spirit."[6]

The Sabra as a Cultural Archetype

The burgeoning popularity of the term "Sabra" in the 1930s and the beginning of the 1940s reflected the rising prestige of the second generation of the labor movement, which in those years was achieving political and cultural hegemony in the Yishuv. (An example of the link between the ensconcement of the labor movement as the leading social and political movement and the transformation of the Sabra into a cultural hero can be seen in a 1943 advertisement for Sabra Shaving Cream produced by the Histadrut's Shemen factory. It shows a picture of a smiling prickly pear spread with shaving foam and the slogan "Even the stubborn Sabra beard surrenders to Shemen.")

As the Sabra archetype and stereotype took shape, the students at the Hebrew gymnasiums, the young people of the kibbutzim and moshavim, and the members of the youth movements and the Palmach began developing a consciousness about their cultural uniqueness. They also produced and honed native status symbols and a peculiarly native Israeli style in language, dress, and collective leisure culture. Novelist Moshe Shamir, a Sabra who followed the typical socialization path of the members of his generation, was apparently the first to express this consciousness in writing. In an article he published in one of the *Yalkut Ha-Re'im* pamphlets (anthologies written and edited by Sabra writers, produced at the beginning of the 1940s), he wrote: "I am a member of the revolutionary generation, and I feel a sense of collaboration with all those who were born [with me]."[7] But the first to express this generational consciousness through the concept of the Sabra and with an emphasis on the Sabra style as distinct from that of the pioneer was the journalist Uri Avneri. Perhaps not coincidentally, Avneri was not a native-born Israeli but had immigrated from Germany as a boy. He was assimilated into his new country via the Sabra institutions, losing all signs of his Diaspora origins except for his accent.[8] In September 1946 Avneri published two articles on Sabraism in the periodical *Ba-Ma'avak:* "The Floor to the Israeli Generation!" and "Who Are These Sabras?" These articles sang the praises of the *Yalkut Ha-Re'im* collections and identified them as the manifestations of a healthy and welcome rebellion against the older generation, which was depicted as a band of old and degenerate men and women holding sway over Jewish society in Palestine. Avneri considered Sabraism the culmination of the anti-Diaspora vision and made one of the most extreme cultural distinctions of that period between the Jew and the Israeli. "Moshe Shamir," he wrote in reference to Shamir's article in *Yalkut Ha-Re'im,* "views the Diaspora in all its bleakness—as a proud, healthy Israeli man. . . . This is the most glorious victory of the Israeli generation— to see the sons of the Diaspora cured and made upright as they are absorbed and assimilate into his way of life."[9]

Avneri's words were an indirect echo of the view that a new Israeli or Hebrew nation had come into being. This proposition was in the air among Tel Aviv youth at the beginning of the 1940s and produced the Canaanite circle led by the poet Yonatan Ratosh.[10] It was no coincidence that Yitzchak Yatziv, journalist and editor of the children's newspaper *Davar Le-Yeladim,* attacked the Canaanite phenomenon in an article entitled "Sabraism as an Ideology,"[11] published in the Histadrut daily newspaper, *Davar,* close to the time that Avneri's article appeared. The Canaanite view was in fact an extreme and somewhat simplistic ideological expression of a spontaneous cultural process that had begun within the Yishuv as early as the 1920s—the creation of a local native culture cut off from the traditional Jewish way of life and influenced by the ecological and cultural environment of Palestine and by the ideology of the Yishuv's labor movement.[12] A radical expression of this view was presented in an essay, "Hebrews and Not Sabras," published in October 1949 by Amos Keinan in *Bamat Elef,* a periodical put out by the Canaanite group at the end of the War of Independence. In Keinan's opinion, the Sabras of his generation (the fighters of 1948) had not yet liberated themselves from their roots in the Diaspora:

> The spiritual image of the Sabra is not the product of a natural and continual development. The Sabra is the outgrowth of an extremely strange adulteration. There are two worlds here. Our parents who are not Sabras, with all their years in this country—and us. . . . The renaissance that we await is not Zionist and is not Jewish. It is Hebrew.[13]

Keinan, with the naiveté of the revolutionary, erred in not identifying the umbilical cord linking Judaism and Zionism. The Canaanite vision of "the land of the Hebrews, the land of the Euphrates" in which the Jew would be transformed into the Hebrew, has not been realized to this day. But he was correct to point out that a new nation had come into being in Palestine and that a new Israeli national image had been fashioned, completely different from the image of the Jew who lived outside Palestine.

The cultural phenomenon called Sabraism, the authentic culture of native Israeli youth, ostensibly appeared even earlier, during World War I, among the children of the First Aliya, the young people who had broken away from the established pre-Zionist Jewish community in Jerusalem and Jaffa, and the members of the first graduating class of the Herzliya Gymnasium in Tel Aviv. Avshalom Feinberg—who would later be called the first Sabra—and Aharon Aharonson were the prototypes of the Sabra who had been born in the *moshavot,* while Eliahu Golomb, Dov Hoz, Shaul Avigur, David Hakohen, and Moshe Sharret were to a large extent the prototypes of the Sabra graduate of the gymnasium.[14] These young people already had Sabra characteristics, such as a rough and direct way of expressing themselves, a knowledge of the land, a hatred of the Diaspora, a native sense of supremacy, a fierce Zionist idealism, and Hebrew as their mother language. Nevertheless, most scholars of the origins of Zionism agree today that these were no more than the first glimmerings of the Sabra phenomenon. It came into its own only in the 1930s and 1940s, when there was for the first time a large group of native-born Israelis in the kibbutzim, moshavim, and established neighborhoods of the cities. This was the period that saw the development of the youth movement and Palmach cultures and the artistic, ideological, and linguistic expressions of the Israeli natives. Only then did Sabraism become a fully elaborated phenomenon.

The Sabra's prestige, the consensus about how the Sabra should look, and the use of the term itself peaked during, and especially after, the 1948 War of Independence. The Israeli public, in particular the older generation, tended to attribute the war's achievements to the native-born Sabras and "Sabraized" immigrants; they minimized the role played, for example, by those new immigrants who had entered combat immediately upon their arrival in the country.[15] Examples may be found in the official army newspapers as well as in the unofficial newsletters put out by the battalions and regiments during and after the war. Many of their pages (especially their front and back covers) are illustrated with drawings and photographs of male and female combatants of a typical Sabra appearance, wearing the characteristic Palmach garb (stocking cap, Arab headdress, etc.). The Palmach-Sabra experience—the native slang, the campfires, the sing-alongs—was stressed in these newspapers. Another reason why the fighting Sabra was prominent in the national saga of 1948 was that most of the victory albums and war literature recounting the impressions of the fighters from the front were written by Sabra writers, most of whom had served in the Palmach.[16]

The culture of memorialization that developed after the war played a central role in mythologizing the native Israeli and fixing the term "Sabra." The victory's heavy price in lives lost left the older generation with a sense of guilt intermingled with deep gratitude for the younger generation—especially for the Palmach, the "favorite son" of the Yishuv leadership, which had lost many of its fighters. This feeling found expression in the press, in art, and especially in the wide-ranging memorial literature. The term "Sabra" appeared over and over again in the memorial anthologies for the fallen of 1948, including the official anthologies put out by the Ministry of Defense.[17] It turned into something of a linguistic code for expressing the nation's love for its loyal youth.

During that same period the stereotypical Sabra appeared as a cultural hero in the arts—in fiction, poetry, songs, painting, sculpture, cinema, theater, and entertainment.[18] The war albums gave prominent placement to photographs of Sabras, especially Palmach fighters with—as a well-known song described—their "handsome forelocks and countenances." A photograph of Avraham Eden ("Bren"), a good-looking Palmach commander of typical Sabra appearance, raising an "inked"

Israeli flag (an improvised flag painted onto white fabric with ink) in Eilat, became the symbol of the young nation and reflected the symbolic-mythological parallel between the beauty of the ancient country and the youthful beauty of its Sabra sons. Young people who resembled Eden began to appear prominently as heroic Sabra characters in cinema, theater, and advertisements.

An especially important contribution to grounding the mythological image of the Sabra was made by the artists and cartoonists, for example Arieh Navon, Shmuel Katz, and Dosh (Kriel Gardush), whose drawings illustrated articles on the war and on the IDF that appeared in the daily press, especially the military press (some cartoonists also published collections of their drawings). "We were then sort of journalist-artists," related Yossi Stern:

> There was a common concept then of putting a journalist and an illustrator together. The illustrator was like a news photographer. We would be given a jeep and would travel into the hot areas. Many of my Palmachniks were walking around the streets of Jerusalem. They were our heroes, the liberators of the city. Heroes from our mythology. They jumped off jeeps—red-haired kibbutzniks with stocking caps or Arab headdresses on their heads, the city favorites. . . . From the dust and the stocking cap we tried to create something new.[19]

These artists, who had a very sharp "cultural eye," memorialized the image of the Sabra in his shorts and sandals, with his slipshod appearance and his hair falling over his forehead, in drawings and cartoons. They brought out the stereotypical Sabra charm—youth, roguishness, self-confidence, boldness, and common sense. In some of the drawings the Sabras appear next to a prickly pear cactus as a kind of generational marker.

The Sabra dialect and slang, which took form in the youth movements, the youth villages, the military organizations, and the kibbutzim in the 1930s and 1940s, began to spread in the 1950s to larger social circles, in response to the joy that the rest of Israeli society took in the bristly younger generation. The disseminators of Sabraism were largely young writers, journalists, and artists (some of them former Palmachniks) with good eyes and ears who documented and spread the young folklore and humor. Native Sabra Hebrew, with its experiential layers and its fine cultural distinctions, became very common in the newsletters of the youth movements, the Gadna, and the army. It appeared in songs, in skits performed by army entertainment groups like the Chizbatron and the Nachal Troupe, in plays for children and adults (the most notable examples being Yigal Mosinzon's *On the Negev Plains* and Moshe Shamir's dramatization of his novel *He Walked in the Fields),* and in literature for children and teenagers. In 1951 the term "Sabras" appeared in the satirical lexicon *The Laughter of Our Mouths* by humorist Efraim Davidzon. In the margin of the page, under "notes and clarifications," the author wrote: "The unique Sabra language and their style in life and literature, heralding a refashioning of the Hebrew language, have spurred debates in the press and in literature. The Sabras have created new concepts and terms and stylistic elements that were not known to previous generations. . . ."[20]

The daily press also began to grant entry to Sabra style, fawning over the spoken Hebrew of the natives, the first fruits of Zionism. A humor column called "Those Sabras," which quoted the linguistic gems of Sabra children, was published in the weekly supplement *Davar Ha-Shavua* from 1951 onward, and a similar column appeared in *Ha-Olam Ha-Zeh* four years later. The innovative personal column "Uzi and Co.," written by Amos Keinan (who inherited it from Benyamin Tammuz) and published in the paper *Ha'aretz* from 1950 to 1952, was written wholly in colloquial conversational Hebrew and was widely imitated.

An important contribution to the assimilation of Sabra culture and the Sabra spirit into Israeli life in the 1950s was made by *Ha-Olam Ha-Zeh,* under the editorship of Uri Avneri and Shalom Cohen. These two veterans of the Givati Brigade tried, with no small success, to fashion a young, playful, and rebellious magazine in the spirit of the Palmach. Along the same lines was the "What's New" column written by Dahn Ben-Amotz, which appeared in *Davar Ha-Shavua* and in which the characteristic direct, frank language of the native—what the Sabras called talking *dugri*—was prominent.[21]

The early 1950s also witnessed the growth of a documentary and nostalgic literature on the period of the underground movements and the War of Independence, with the fighting Sabra as its focus. This included stories for children and teenagers produced by such Palmach veterans as Yigal Mosinzon, O. Hillel, and Yisrael Visler (Puchu). This literature also contributed to ensconcing and exalting the Sabra mythological image and heightened the identification of the hero of 1948 with the Sabra. The most important anthology of that time was *The Palmach Book,* edited by Zerubavel Gilad and Matti Megged, which appeared in 1953.[22] The book was a nostalgic summary of the Palmach-Sabra life and indirectly a collective declaration by the members of the Palmach generation of their historic place in the Israeli epic.

Among the books for children and teenagers that contributed to the glorification of and fondness for Sabra culture, three in particular deserve mention. The first is Yemima Tchernovitz-Avidar's *Eight on the Heels of One* (1945), a spy story of adventure and heroics that takes place on a kibbutz and is connected to the Haganah's activity. The second, by Puchu (Yisrael Visler), is *A Gang Like This,* published in 1950, which tells the youthful experiences of a group of Palmach enlistees. The third is Yigal Mosinzon's Hasamba series, which began to appear in 1950 and garnered a huge readership. The heroes of the series, who play pranks on the British and Arabs, are Sabra figures whose very names testify to their Sabra identity (especially Yaron Zehavi, the commander of the Hasamba gang, and Tamar, his deputy). The three works have common elements: Sabra heroes; their linguistic style (colloquial Hebrew in the youth movement and Palmach idiom); the youthful way of life in the kibbutz, the youth movement, and the Palmach; and the integration of suspense and humor, appropriate to the spirit of the times. Sabras of several decades avidly devoured these books and internalized their cultural messages.[23]

An example of the waxing popularity of the Sabra image in the 1950s can be found in a review of the play *On Children and Adults,* staged by the Ha-Matateh Theater in 1953:

> A "Sabra" play written by a writer who is almost "Sabra," directed by a born "Sabra" and presented by a theater that has the right to call itself a "Sabra" theater (Ha-Matateh) in a hall with typical "Sabra" conditions (nail heads in the chairs) and before a "heterogeneous" audience ("Sabra" and not "Sabra") that laughs without stopping and enjoys a pleasant show that, despite its many shortcomings, is quite charming.[24]

In the 1950s the Palmach humorists, led by Chaim Cheffer, Didi Manosi, Shaul Biber, and Dahn Ben-Amotz, succeeded in turning the Palmach experience into a flourishing (for that period) entertainment industry. Chaim Cheffer's book of songs *Light Ammunition,* published in 1949, was very popular. So was Didi Manosi's 1951 book of rhymed satires, *Vacation without Pay,* epitomizing Palmach slang and wit. Both these books were important milestones in the dissemination and institutionalization of the Palmach experience. Another such work is the 1956 bestseller *Pack of Lies,* a collection of Palmach and youth movement anecdotes and jokes—what were called *chizbatim*—by Dahn Ben-Amotz and Chaim Cheffer, which had been published in 1953 in *Masa,* the literary magazine of the Ahdut Ha-Avodah party. This small book had a red cover displaying a drawing of a steaming *finjan,* or Arab coffee pot, one of the Palmach's symbols. Its protagonists were the amiable Ofer, Musa, and Fat Chaim—Palmachnik Dennis the Menaces who created a new fashion of stinging local-native-nostalgic humor. At parties, at youth movement activities, even on the Voice of Israel and on IDF Radio, everyone started telling jokes and *chizbatim* according to this model. The army magazine *Ba-Machaneh* had a regular department for *chizbatim* called "When the Coins Had Holes in Them," by Shaul Biber, and the Gadna magazine, *Ba-Machaneh Gadna,* had a similar department called "The Association of Truthtellers, Inc." by Yossi Rimon.

In the middle of the 1950s Yossi Gamzo began publishing rhymed burlesques in *Ba-Machaneh Gadna* under the pen name Yossi Ein Manosi. These starred the lovable image of the Sabra and were illustrated with caricatures by Shmuel Katz. The poems, written in the spirit of Didi Manosi and Chaim Cheffer, represented the voice of the Sabras of the 1950s—called "the generation of the decade"—who imitated the Palmach Sabras of the 1940s and expanded Sabra culture.[25]

In the mid-1950s the Voice of Israel began broadcasting the satirical program "Three in a Boat" with Shalom Rosenfeld, Gabriel Tsifroni, Amnon Ahi Na'ami, Dahn Ben-Amotz, and their guests. The program was broadcast once a month on a Saturday morning and was hugely popular. Ben-Amotz, a former Palmachnik and a young writer, quickly became the unchallenged star of the program. After immigrating to Palestine alone at a young age, he had been "Sabraized" in the melting pot of the youth village at Ben Shemen and became one of the most important disseminators of Sabra culture. His biographer, Amnon Dankner, terms him "a symbol of the Israeli Sabra," and notes that the country's public relations officials used Ben-Amotz to represent Israeli culture to the world.[26] The program was based on an undercurrent of confrontation between Diaspora and native Israeli culture, especially via the witty dialogue between Shalom Rosenfeld (the parliamentary correspondent for the daily newspaper *Ma'ariv*) and Ben-Amotz. "Rosenfeld," Dankner writes, "was a representative—a shining one, it should be said—of the old-time humor, of the world that was beginning to pass on, very Jewish, very Diaspora-Polish, full of puns, one word falling upon another. He was the diametric opposite of Dahn, who was outspoken and sometimes rude—such an Israeli original. The boat rocked between these two poles, and roughly one could say that Dahn drew the young people and Shalom drew the adults among the program's huge audience."[27] With his Sabra jokes, the cynical short skits he wrote and performed, his pointed retorts, and his sharp Sabra accent and diction (nothing of the kind had ever been heard, at least with this frequency, on the national radio station before), Ben-Amotz contributed to the dissemination of Sabra humor, language, and image, and to the rising popularity of the Palmach generation.

The Sabra Writers
as Generational Spokesmen

A decisive role in shaping the Sabra stereotype, myth, and concept was played by the literary elite of the Palmach generation. This group of writers and poets, most of whom had been members of pioneering youth movements, began publishing their works at the end of the 1930s and, especially in the 1940s and the beginning of the 1950s, slowly made their way into the literary establishment as the "young guard" of Israeli writers.[28] Gershon Shaked, scholar of Hebrew literature, identifies the first appearance of native Israeli fiction with the publishing of S. Yizhar's first story, "Efraim Returns to the Alfalfa" in 1938 in the periodical *Gilyonot*. "Yizhar," Shaked writes, "published his works before all his literary fellows as a kind of elder brother, and many followed after him in any number of areas."[29] At the end of the 1940s several writers and poets of Yizhar's generation began publishing their works, first in the youth movement newspapers (*Al Ha-Choma, Ha-Shomer Ha-Tza'ir, Ba-Mivchan*) and afterward in the labor movement newspapers and journals (*Dapim Le-Sifrut, Ba-Sha'ar, Masa, Davar, Mishmar*). These writers and poets were influenced a great deal by two prominent authors of that time—Avraham Shlonsky and Natan Alterman. Shlonsky and Alterman, in turn, took great interest in the up-and-coming Sabra culture, fostered and disseminated the young literature, and drew public attention to the younger generation.

Some consider the four issues of *Yalkut Ha-Re'im*, which came out between 1943 and 1945 (edited by Moshe Shamir, Shlomo Tanai, and Ozer Rabin), to be the first manifesto of the literary, and indirectly generational, independence of the Sabras. These issues included stories, poems, translations, and essays, all by Sabra writers in their twenties.[30] Moshe Shamir's own essay "With the Members of My Generation" expresses his generation's sense of uniqueness and destiny. "All of them— they are members of my generation. There is nothing that unites us more than the feeling of responsibility to the generation. Above and beyond the hesitations of creativity and the trappings of modernism, the shades of independent personality, there beats within us a feeling of absolute belonging, one hundred percent, to the human revolution."[31]

Another literary anthology, *A New Page for Literature, Art, and Criticism,* appeared in the wake of *Yalkut Ha-Re'im,* in September 1947. Edited by Chaim Glickstein, Moshe Shamir, and Shlomo Tanai, this was intended to be a monthly, but only one issue was published. It included poems, stories, critiques, articles on theater, and "meditations" by the younger generation. In 1948 the Neuman Press put out a first collection of stories by young Sabra fighters: *In the Front Position: Stories from the Campaign.* Soon thereafter came three others—*The Bow of the Writers: A Literary Collection of Soldier Writers,* put out by the IDF Cultural Service; *In the Test of the Battles;* and an anthology of articles by military correspondents from the War of Independence, *In the Footsteps of the Fighters,* published by Sifriat Po'alim. The war experiences that were at the center of these stories reinforced the perception of their authors as having an independent generational identity. At the same time, the first books of Sabra poetry, songs, and prose, expressing the native's worldview and emotions, began to appear. These elicited enthusiastic public response. The Sabra literary guard reached the height of its popularity, especially among the young second generation of Sabras,[32] at the end of the 1950s with the appearance of the anthology *A Generation in the Country* (edited by Ezriel Ochmani, Shlomo Tanai, and Moshe Shamir), containing the works of thirty-three young writers and poets, and S. Yizhar's *Ziklag Days.* In fact, a literary "opposition" was already emerging at this time but was still in its infancy.

The Sabra writers and poets could be distinguished by four trademarks, other than their young age: (1) Hebrew was their native language, or at least the language of their childhood; (2) they wrote about Sabra life and the daily routine of life in the Palmach, the youth group, the kibbutz, the agricultural training groups, and the battlefield, and identified with it utterly; (3) many of the protagonists of the stories were typical Sabras; (4) their writing was seasoned, in greater or lesser measure, with Sabra slang and style and with the characteristic humor of the native Israelis.[33]

In the public eye, however, these writers and poets portrayed the new generation not only in their style of writing and in the content of their stories and poems, but also in their own biographies, which were similar to those of their protagonists. The Sabra biographies that characterized both the young writers and their writings were also among the reasons for the warmth, and sometimes even enthusiasm and wonderment, with which they were usually received by the literary establishment (the publishers, literary supplements, and established literary journals). In 1950, a few years after the new guard entered public consciousness, literary scholar Ezriel Ochmani described the response among critics and scholars: "They made a place for themselves. . . . The new names broke through one after another. It was visible: an entire unit had set out to conquer Hebrew prose, taking upon itself the great responsibility of meeting expectations that had been in the air for many years, potent and demanding—the expectation of an Israeli prose."[34]

From the time they were first published, the Sabra writers stressed their uniqueness, which reinforced the Israeli public's view that what had arisen was not only a new literary generation, but a new cultural generation with an authentic "Land of Israel" style. In his introduction to the anthology *Spectrum of Writers*, Moshe Shamir wrote: "This band of creative artists, whose works are given in the book before you, are united not only by a uniform, but also by the melody of their accents; they have a common denominator and it shows itself in their words—today and tomorrow as well. The year 1948 is the common denominator."[35]

Indeed, the experience of the War of Independence became the most important trademark of this young literary guard and, indirectly, of the Sabra generation it represented. It was not for nothing that this generation would later be called the "1948 generation."

The social importance of the works of these writers and poets was much greater than their artistic importance, though they had artistic value. With their typical Sabra biographies and typical Sabra experiences at kibbutzim, in youth movements, and in the Palmach, they felt the spirit of the era "in real time" and committed it to paper in their works. In the poem "Here Lie Our Bodies," for example, Chaim Guri expressed the shock his generation felt at the massacre of a detachment of thirty-five soldiers, even though he did not know most of them personally and was, in fact, not even in the country when they were killed. He was able to do this because the fallen were his contemporaries, had grown up in the same environment he had, and had been educated with the same values that had been instilled in him. Guri may not have intended it, but his special talent made him a voice of his generation. Furthermore, the Sabra writers and poets were not merely "cultural sponges," instruments for memorializing Sabra experience and folklore as they collected them from lives. Their works influenced those lives. With their genius for invention and their sensitivity, these authors reinforced the emotions and moral worldview of the members of their generation, codified their values, and rooted them firmly in the consciousness of both the Sabras and the public at large.

The Sinai Campaign at the end of 1956, in which the Israeli army dealt a humiliating defeat to the Egyptian army, was perceived by the Israeli public as the victory of the Sabra, and especially of the paratrooper and the pilot. Admiration for the fighting Sabra, exemplified in the romantic figure of Chief of Staff Moshe Dayan, then reached its climax. The term "Sabra" made many appearances in the tales of the war that appeared in the press, albums, and songs, all of which waxed ecstatic over the wondrous younger generation produced by Zionism and the IDF. Sabra folklore became one of the trademarks of the IDF's combat units, especially the paratroopers, the pilots, and the naval commandos.

The Study: Background and Documentary Material

At the end of the 1960s and the beginning of the 1970s, at the time of the War of Attrition with Egypt, a new generation (not necessarily in the biological sense) of writers, poets, playwrights, and literary and social scholars rose to challenge the Sabra generation, chiding them for their ideological derivativeness and their one-dimensional view of reality. They criticized with increasing stridency the mobilized writing of the 1948 circle with its focus on the world of the collective, while celebrating critical, anti-establishment writing that focused on the world of the individual and in particular on his distress and alienation. Implied also was criticism of the Sabra character and of the writers who represented it. This period saw the first waves and then a rising tide of secularizers of the Zionist canon, and an antiheroic and critical genre began to appear in the press, in literature, and in film, steadily displacing the mobilized Zionist genre.

Criticism of Sabra literature and the myth it represented intensified in the mid-1970s after the trauma of the Yom Kippur War, when the role of the Sabra as a social model was weakened and his aura dimmed. The Israeli intelligentsia began to see the Sabra in a less heroic light that brought out his human failings and even presented him as a pathetic and ridiculous figure.[36] The accounting demanded of the Sabra by these practitioners in different creative fields was part of the intelligentsia's withdrawal from its infatuation with Israeli power and revolutionary naiveté. It was also part of a campaign of censure against the labor movement, which the public perceived as having degenerated. A satiric television show, "Head Cleaning," heralded a change of era by directing many of

its barbs at Prime Minister Yitzchak Rabin, one of the outstanding heroic Sabra figures of 1948.

The trend to secularize Zionist ethoses and myths played itself out at the end of the 1970s and the beginning of the 1980s for a range of social reasons and as the result of historical processes. Among these were the political upset of 1977, which marked the waning of the labor movement and the culture it represented, and the peace treaty with Egypt, which transformed the mythological image of the Arab "Amalek" and so also the Israeli self-image. Then came the Lebanon War (the first war over which the Israeli public was deeply divided), the expansion of the Israeli media (which broke out of the bounds of Israeli culture), and the growing influence of critical postmodern thinking on educated Israelis. During this period, which some refer to as "post-Zionist," newspaper articles and scholarly books appeared that dealt with what was called, derisively and critically, the "myth of the Sabra."[37]

A transmutation of the heroic image of the Sabra occurred in drama as well. The satiric play *Charly Kecharly* by Daniel Horowitz, staged at the end of 1977 at the Khan Theater to mark the country's thirtieth anniversary, portrayed the Sabra in unflattering terms and caused a controversy.

A similar secularization and examination of the Sabra myth with less subjective eyes took place during these same years in the academic community. The growing distance between Israeli society's formative and current periods gradually removed the ideological boundaries that earlier historians and sociologists had accepted, consciously or unconsciously. The current scholars' point of view was more detached and less ethnocentric. The fissures in the once-firm national consensus concerning young Israel and the growing challenges to the status of the political and military establishment, especially after the Lebanon War and the Intifada, were a psychological and intellectual substrate on which dozens of scholarly studies on the Palmach, the War of Independence, and the youth movements quickly sprouted. This research was carried out in a variety of fields—sociology and anthropology, literary studies, history, cinema, psychology, linguistics, education, Middle East studies, and art history. Scholars came to recognize—first largely in the fields of literature and history and later in sociology—that the second generation of the Zionist revolution had unique characteristics, and the term "Sabra" turned from a mythological designation into a scholarly analytical label referring to the elite of Israeli youth in Israel's formative period.

One reason for the present study is the wealth of publications touching directly and indirectly on Sabra culture—the hundreds of editorials, biographies, autobiographies, and scholarly and popular books and articles—that have been written in recent years. It seems to me that the time has come to bring together and synthesize all these works and to delineate, as far as possible, a coherent sociological picture of the generation that was so important in shaping Israeli experience.

Another reason is that, until now, the texts written by the Sabra generation have not been analyzed in a methodical way. I believe that an analysis of the rich documentary material that the Sabras produced can complete the piecing together of the generational mosaic that other scholars have begun. These are texts in which the Sabras expressed their aspirations, their feelings, and their positions on a broad range of matters. This material is referred to by the general rubric "Sabra texts."

The Sabra as a "Secular Yeshiva Student"

The Zionist revolution is generally presented as a revolution against the traditional Jewish world. Dozens of articles and books, both scholarly and otherwise, have been written on the cultural metamorphosis that Zionism wrought on the Jewish people, a process summed up as "the rejection of the Diaspora." The Sabra son of the revolution was, in terms of his image, the realization of the aspirations of the generation of the fathers. He was a "gentile" Jew—secular, a skilled farmer and heroic fighter, "worthy of being counted," finally, among the family of nations. But was Zionist culture really no more than an antithesis of religion? Did the native-born Sabra really become a secular Jew, lacking all religion?

The answer lies in the structural similarity between nationalist ideologies and traditional religions. This similarity can be seen in six principal traits. The first is the striving for a future utopia. Instead of a divine paradise, believers—in communism, fascism, and capitalist liberalism, for example—are offered a social paradise in this world. The second is the mystification and glorification of leaders, sometimes to the point of a cult of personality (largely in extreme, fascist nationalism). The political and ideological leaders of the national movement take the place of the prophets and ecclesiastical hierarchy of traditional religion. The third is the perception of the nation as an exemplary, chosen society that is fulfilling an ancient prophecy under divine supervision. The fourth is the formulation of social ideas in metaphysical and religious terms, such as "redemption," "covenant," and "sacrifice." The fifth is the viewing of reality in terms of absolute values—total identification with the ideology, often to the point of fanaticism; willingness to make huge personal sacrifices for that ideology; and sharp condemnation of those who diverge from it. The sixth is the institutionalization of nationalist ideas by insinuating them into every area of individual and communal life through taboos, cyclical ritual, symbols, an institutionalized clergy, and places of study.

In the nineteenth century, a number of European thinkers identified the emergence of a type of socio-nationalist revolution that becomes a religious crusade and produces a kind of "secular religion." Fascinated and troubled by the new relation created in their time between the modern state and traditional religion, they took stock of romantic patriotism, the definition of life goals, the nature of government, and the moral system of a society in which traditional religion was becoming detached from the state. One of the most prominent among these thinkers was French historian Alexis de Tocqueville. He considered the French Revolution "a political revolution that acted as a religious revolution and in a certain sense took its character." Furthermore, he wrote, "The revolution became a kind of new religion . . . a religion that, like Islam, flooded the country with soldiers, apostles, and martyrs."[38]

In 1967 American sociologist Robert Bellah published an article in the journal *Daedalus* entitled "Civil Religion in America."[39] Bellah examined the tight cultural linkage between American nationalism and religion. He was not the first scholar to point out the close cultural tie between American nationalism and Calvinist Christianity,[40] and the metaphysical character of values in secular American culture, but he was the first who identified religious elements in a culture that had been perceived up until then as secular by its very nature. He created a general theoretical framework for understanding secular symbols, ceremonies, ideals, and myths. Civil religion (there are those today who prefer the terms "national religion" or "secular religion") is, according to his definition, a religious dimension that exists in the life of every nation through which it interprets its historical experience in the light of a transcendental reality. According to Emile Durkheim, on whose ideas Bellah based his thinking, all social cohesion is founded on a common moral denominator that derives from religious sources. Bellah argues that civil religion is vital to modern society because it creates a prophetic consciousness—a kind of pillar of fire that leads the camp. On one hand, it grants moral legitimacy to the social order; on the other, it establishes moral criteria according to which the society endlessly examines and criticizes itself. It is both a tool to preserve the existing order and a mechanism for constant social change.

The view that links revolution and nationalism to religion has also influenced the study of the Zionist movement. Many historians and sociologists have noted the religious aspect of the pioneer experience and have analyzed the para-religious deep stratum of Zionist culture. The most notable of these are Charles Liebman and Eliezer Don Yehiye,[41] who examined the link between the Zionist movement and religion through a methodical use of Bellah's theory of civil religion. The Zionist revolution, they argue in their study, created a kind of civil religion in Israel, a political and ideological structure that drew its legitimacy from traditional Jewish sources. Traditional Jerusalem, which was molded into new pioneer forms, granted legitimacy to the common Zionist values, united Israeli society under a common identity and a sense of a common fate, and granted depth and significance to the enterprise of the national renaissance.

Zionism, like other national movements that appeared in Europe, America, South Africa, and Australia, quickened hearts, swept along the masses, and grew from a small movement into a national religion that displays all the basic traits enumerated above. The Jewish foundation that preceded Zionism and the ancient, organic link between religion and nation in Judaism strengthened the para-religious dimensions of Zionism and differentiated it from other national religions. The Zionist movement enveloped the Jewish Yishuv in Palestine in a kind of bubble, gave life profound meaning, and included a complex mechanism of commandments, ritual, symbols, mission, and social supervision. The tinder for the new faith was provided by the ancient Jewish yearning for Zion, while the oxygen needed for the fire was provided by European nationalism, modern anti-Semitism, and socialist utopianism. As with other nations, the Jews partially exchanged the transcendental God for the nation, the state, and the homeland, and considered the land they had come to live in as the "promised land."

The pioneer was a devout believer who observed the precepts of patriotism with physical and spiritual valor. He did not simply prepare the soil for commercial exploitation in the Holy Land; he "made the desert bloom" and "drained swamps"—tasks that became a holy and ascetic labor. The soldier who fell defending the Yishuv was a martyr who died sanctifying the homeland (instead of sanctifying God). And the memorials and monuments that were planted in every corner of the country—in numbers that cannot be found in other cultures—became icons and altars on which the cyclical ritual of the national holidays were celebrated. Young people were sworn in year after year at these memorial sites with an oath committing them to carrying on the sacrifice, because in their deaths the fallen willed the generations that followed not only life but also the sanctity of the national land "on whose altars they fell." The Yizkor, or memorial prayer, became Zionism's declaration of faith, and the widely circulated memorial anthologies served as national prayer books, while the memorial siren sounded at the end of Israel's Memorial Day (a custom instituted after the state was founded and abolished just a few years ago) was like the *shofar* blast at the end of the final Yom Kippur service, making every fiber of the soul tremble and separating the holy from the profane.

The traditional Jewish holidays of Pesach, Hanukkah, Lag Be-Omer, Shavuot, Sukkot, and Purim were refashioned in a way that reduced, and sometimes even eliminated, the religious observances attached to them, while emphasizing their links to the agricultural cycle of planting and harvest. Myths portraying the power of God and the benefits of faith in him were exchanged for historical myths recounting the nation's strength and heroism and its struggle to escape slavery and achieve political freedom. The traditional holidays were supplemented by days commemorating events in the new Zionist history and holidays deriving from the socio-national ideology of the labor movement (May Day, Balfour Declaration Day, Jewish National Fund Day, Tel Chai Day), and these were celebrated with ceremonies and symbols exemplifying service to the homeland. The plaintive and sentimental "homeland songs" (later called "Land of Israel songs"), sung in mellow, close-knit groups in a nostalgic atmosphere, filled the same function as prayers chanted in the synagogue. After the state was founded, they became the new Jewish liturgy— what writer Amos Oz called the "tom-toms," urging the tribe to battle. The Zionist religion even created its own version of Hasidic dance—the *hora,* danced by a circle of hand-holding believers in an infectious religious ecstasy.

Like every other religion, Zionism condemned those who deviated from its precepts and castigated schismatics and heretics—in this case, Jews who chose to remain in the Diaspora. The young man who evaded service on the front line, for example, was branded a counterfeit and a degenerate, and the young boy or girl who, voluntarily or involuntarily, did not join a youth movement was dismissed as a "homebody" and perceived as someone who had not been educated properly or who had some sort of character failing. The young person who did not seek out an agricultural or military life was labeled a careerist, and the person who emigrated from the country was called a *yored,* or "descender," that is, an apostate and a traitor. The immigrant to Israel, in contrast, was honored with the moral term *oleh,* an "ascender" (note the symbolic use of the concepts of ascent and descent, which recur in various contexts in Jewish religion).

The moshavim and kibbutzim became the sanctuaries of the new national religion. The holy Zionist service was performed there in its purest form—cultivating the nation's land, settling the country's distant frontiers, guarding it against attackers, and living a life of cooperation and communal solidarity. The fathers of the kibbutz necessarily became the revered priests of the new religion, and their Sabra children were the novitiates. Many young people volunteered or were sent by educational institutions or youth movements to perform manual labor in the kibbutzim and to establish new settlements, just as young Jewish boys in the Diaspora had been sent to *yeshivot* to study before settling into secular careers. The Sabra was the disciple who was anointed by the pioneer rabbis, the boy serving in the Zionist sanctuary, and the proud and beloved yeshiva student. He was brought up to assume the yoke of the commandments in the high Zionist yeshiva—the youth movement, the Palmach, and the elite units of the Israel Defense Forces—and faithfully met the high expectations of his parents and teachers.

The concept of civil or national religion is no mere metaphor or intellectual plaything. Its purpose is not to cynically compare the present to the past. I agree with other scholars that viewing Israeli society in its formative period as a religious community conducting a total way of life is the best way of understanding the social forces that produced Sabra culture and personality. This book is meant to present the visible as well as the latent elements of the Zionist secular religion and to reveal the deep psychosociological link between this religion and the Sabra, who is its product.

This book is a sociohistorical portrait of the Israeli elite at its origins. It does not deal with the chronology of historical events and does not focus on organizations, institutions, and ideologies. Rather, it seeks to find the common ground underneath the diversity and to present a sociological overview, in an effort to grasp the spirit of the time in which Zionist idealism was at its peak.

CHAPTER 1

Idealistic Euphoria

How the Sabra Was Socialized

Spontaneity initially dominates social revolutions. But history shows that after the revolutionaries carry out their program they no longer seek innovation. Generally, when the second generation arrives, the revolutionaries seek to ensure the continuity and stability of the new society they have created by shoring up the revolution's foundations and pressing it into institutional molds.[1] The ideological "cult" strives to establish itself and to become a kind of "church," and its "prophets" seek to become "priests." The principal means of achieving this is education of the younger generation in the new values.

Leaders of the Yishuv imputed great importance to the education of their children, the Sabras, and kept a vigilant and concerned eye on how the young natives developed and behaved. The success of the entire enterprise, they realized, depended on this. "In every aspect of our lives it is our practice to give preference to the needs of the younger generation. This is not simply a matter of parental love for their children. All the investment in our children's education derives in a decisive measure from the sense and the awareness that the test of the project is its future," wrote one of the founders of Kibbutz Mishmar Ha-Emek.[2] Many of the articles, speeches, and discussions from this period deal with the younger generation and its future. The collective terms "continuing generation," "generation of the children," "second generation," and "younger gen-

23

eration," were routinely used by political leaders, educators, journalists, and intellectuals to express the importance they attached to the character of the young people. The Sabra was expected to solidify and broaden the achievements of the first generation, yet remain loyal to its values.

STORIES AND SONGS
FOR CHILDREN AND ADOLESCENTS

The Sabra was indoctrinated in Zionist ideology from the cradle. The pioneers sang lullabies charged with the pioneering ethos—though, ironically, some were sung to traditional Jewish melodies, and some were even sung in Yiddish.

Most of the songs, as one writer has noted, "promoted pride in Hebrewness, a sense of purpose, and an injunction to pioneer, fight, and conquer. The persecutions by the gentiles, the wanderings over the face of the earth, the unremitting aggression were conveyed to the young person [through the songs, which fostered] hope and faith in redemption and rebirth, the conquest of the land and its development by its returning Jewish sons."[3]

Many songs and stories for children and teenagers, published in private editions, in school readers, in yearbooks put out by such bodies as the Jewish National Fund (JNF), and in children's periodicals, explicitly and implicitly exalted the beauty of Zionist ideals and heroes and the achievements of the pioneer, the Ha-Shomer guardsman, and the soldier.[4] In inspiring language they glorified the settlement enterprise (especially in the outlying regions of the Negev Desert and Galilee), the defense of the settlements and of the Yishuv by the Ha-Shomer organization and Orde Wingate's Night Squads, the illegal immigration operation, the establishment of the State of Israel, and the War of Independence.[5] For example, Little Dani, protagonist of Miriam Yellen-Shtaklis's poem "Prayer," on his eighth birthday asks God to make him a "valiant hero" because he needs "to build an airplane . . . with guns" and "to bring immigrants to the Land of Israel"—two classic Zionist objectives.[6]

IDEOLOGICAL EDUCATION IN THE SCHOOLS

The educational system was the Yishuv's most important and most effective arena for Zionist socialization. Zionist education in Palestine was initiated at the end of the nineteenth century and reached the height of its development at the end of the 1920s, when it split into four major ideological systems of education. (These were the ultra-orthodox, the religious-Zionist, the system run by the Jewish Agency, and the labor approach under the direction of the Histadrut. In 1948, 27 percent of all elementary-school-age Jewish children were enrolled in labor-oriented schools, mostly in the kibbutzim and in the large cities.) In fact, it grew at an unprecedented rate. Employing as teachers new immigrants and young natives committed to Zionism, the educational system was the right hand of the political establishment, which set up, funded, and supervised it.[7] The educational system in Israel was influenced by the educational systems of Europe, which put a great deal of emphasis on the national language, the history of the people, the nation's creative output, physical fitness, and the citizen's duty to obey the regime. However, the focus in Israel was on the concepts of the "new world" and the "new man."

No attempt was made to conceal that the goal was to cast the Sabra's consciousness in the monolithic molds of Zionist ideology. Curriculum planners and, in their wake, teachers declared this quite openly. "There is no education without an idea," wrote Zvi Zohar, one of the founding fathers of Israeli pedagogy and a leading figure in the education establishment. "The value of every great historical epoch is that it raises an idea to the level of a movement among the people, in society—and in so doing turns the idea into an educational goal."[8]

The exceptional success of the Hebrew educational system in shaping the Sabra character lies in the educators' sense of mission. Historian Muki Tzur commented: "The teachers were not professors of the history of the revolution—they were its spokesmen."[9]

This attitude was expressed in the distinction between "teacher" and "educator" in modern Hebrew. A teacher conveys knowledge, while an educator instills ideals and values in students. In the Zionist school system, and in Israeli schools to this day, the word "teacher" is reserved for instructors of specialized subjects. The primary classroom teacher is referred to as the "educator."

Teachers from the preschool level on up saw their jobs in religious terms. By treating the values of pioneerism as sacred they determined not only the way they instilled these values in their students, but also the way they perceived themselves. "Teaching is like standing at Mt. Sinai each day anew, a giving of the Torah in miniature!" wrote teacher Y. Halperin, adding that "the teacher is not a priest but a prophet; action and vision work in harmony within him."[10]

This perception of themselves as acolytes of a sacred cause is evident in the field reports teachers sent to coordinating committees, in the minutes of the Pedagogical Council proceedings, and in articles published by educational leaders during this period. Words from the vocabulary of Jewish religion were applied to education—"values" was frequently used, as was the expression "observing the commandments."

Since education was considered an essential part of the revolutionary process, the prestige of the teaching profession soared in the Yishuv. Its practitioners had the status of pioneers and helmsmen, especially in the labor movement schools. To teach was a calling. The best of the veteran settlers and new immigrants—among them some truly exceptional people—were drawn to the profession. Many of them loved their pupils like their own children and devoted themselves heart and soul to teaching. They won the affection and admiration of their students, and some became well-known public figures.

IDEOLOGICALLY DIRECTED TEXTBOOKS

A large part of ideological Zionist education in Yishuv and Israeli schools was disseminated through lessons in Jewish history. Significantly, the subject was not called Jewish history, but "history of the Israeli nation." More textbooks were written for this subject than for any other— by 1948, thirty-two had been published.[11] Most were intended not only to teach history but also, explicitly and implicitly, to inculcate Zionist values. Until 1930 most of the history textbooks used in Yishuv schools were written in Eastern Europe and were designed for Jewish schoolchildren of the Diaspora. After 1930 most of the books used were written by teachers—of Eastern European origin—in Palestine for students in Palestine. The authors were generally teachers of history or people for whom education was of special importance. In addition to textbooks, these writers produced a wide-ranging literature of auxiliary history books, ideological in character, in the form of guidebooks and pamphlets. These were published largely on the initiative and with the support of the Council of Israeli Teachers for the Jewish National Fund, the central educational-ideological body of the Yishuv period. Especially notable is the series of booklets *To Youth: The Israeli Library*, which was something like an ideological encyclopedia, very popular as supplementary material for teaching the history of Zionism and the Yishuv in the schools. The purpose of the booklets, according to their authors and publishers, was "to demonstrate to the Hebrew nation and its youth, in Palestine and in the Diaspora, the great national and human progress of our enterprise in the Land of Israel, throughout all the pioneer periods from the First Aliya to Palestine up to our day."[12]

The number of educational periodicals was large, relative to the size of the population, and they devoted much space to ideological education. There were also many teacher conferences on the subject of Zionist education (many of them sponsored by the Council of Israeli Teachers for the Jewish National Fund), and their proceedings were published and distributed as supplementary materials for schoolteachers and principals.

The educational system omitted from textbooks and from the curriculum all beliefs and positions that might challenge, even slightly, the fundamental assumptions of Zionism. Even beliefs and ideologies that were simply different from Zionist ones were left out.[13] The textbook writers set themselves the goal, as one of them remarked, of using the books to integrate the pupil into Zionist society "in a way that will never allow him to detach himself from this fabric of the common destiny."[14] This goal was achieved in two fundamental ways.

The first way was by the presentation of the pioneer enterprise as an epic, a thrilling drama, by placing it on a historical continuum together with ancient Jewish deeds of heroism. One of the central pedagogical tools for linking the nation's mythological past to its pioneer present was the study of the Bible—one of the principal subjects in the otherwise secular schools. In the high schools of the general system of education, for example, four out of the thirty-five weekly hours of instruction were devoted to the Bible.[15] "Any Zionist structure not founded on this base of Bible," said educator Baruch Ben-Yehuda, "will be a structure made of matchsticks that the most casual breeze can knock down."[16]

The Bible was thus studied in school from a new, secular, nationalist perspective, not as a source of religious faith or as a work of philosophy; its tales served to instill Zionist ethics and to familiarize students with the glorious past of the Israeli people. The symbolic connection between Biblical mythology and modern reality in the Yishuv and in Israel was accomplished through actualization of the Biblical stories. So, for example, the educator Urinovsky recommended presenting the story of Jeremiah's opposition to a Jewish rebellion against the Babylonians (Jeremiah 24–42) in this way:

> Jeremiah the prophet opposed the Judean movement for rebellion against Babylonia out of ethical, religious considerations. . . . But worthy of special emphasis is his uncompromising, tragic struggle for his people's existence in their land. He preferred the shame of surrender and temporary enslavement to utter political destruction with honor, which leads to exile, to the uproot-

ing of the tree from the place it sprouted and grew. . . . Jeremiah, the rational, practical prophet, fearful for the fate of the homeland and the existence of the nation, the remnant in Judea, and the exiles in Babylonia, should serve as a guide to us in these frenzied times, so that we do not exchange our homeland for an imaginary policy or proclaim empty slogans, but rather strive to gain a foothold on the soil of our fathers.[17]

The second way the textbooks conveyed Zionist ideology was through cultural ethnocentrism. Hebrew culture was glorified and made central to world culture; it was the standard against which all other cultures were compared. Ethnocentrism is especially characteristic of religious societies, which organize their lives around religious doctrine and disallow information from outside that could endanger it. Writer Arthur Koestler, who served as a foreign correspondent in Palestine at the end of the 1920s, wrote of this sarcastically in his diary after a visit to the Herzliya Gymnasium:

History is taught by an equally egocentric system. For the study of antiquity the Bible serves as the main source, and Israel as the hub of the ancient world. The confused events of the Dark and Middle Ages are summed up as a series of migrations by barbarian tribes anti-clockwise round the Mediterranean, while the Jews in the same period migrated clockwise in the opposite direction. And so on.

All this reminds me of the first school I went to in Budapest. The Hungarians too, as a small nation wedged precariously between the Slavonic and Germanic worlds, were inclined toward this kind of mystical ultra-chauvinism.[18]

Although the history and culture of other nations were studied in the schools in a fragmentary way, they were not a top educational priority and were generally presented in relation to the fate of the Jews, especially their persecution. Chaim Arieh Zuta and Y. Spibak noted in the introduction to their book *The History of Our People:*

We have integrated the history of the nations into the history of our nation in a restricted and concentrated way, so as not to distract the student from the main part of his study of our people's history. . . . We have made room for the history of different nations at those junctures in which they came into contact with our nation.[19]

Cultures that did not come into contact with Jews—such as those of Africa and Eastern Asia—were shunted into a far corner of the curriculum. In this, of course, Zionism was no different from other Western cultures of the same period, much less other national religions.

As a result of this ethnocentrism, the history of humanity was perceived by Israeli youth as "the history of Jewish pride, the history of the

Jewish martyrology, the history of the Israeli people's eternal war for its existence," as Baruch Ben-Yehuda put it.[20]

Literature was also studied from an ethnocentric point of view, though one less stark than that applied to history. The focus was the literature of the national revival and the writers and poets with links to Zionism. Most of the works were studied in the context of nationalism, with stress on the importance of socialism and the pioneer epic and rejection of the Diaspora.

Teaching history and literature through an ethnocentric prism achieved three important ideological goals with regard to the younger generation. First, it magnified the importance of the Jewish people in human history and their intellectual and moral primacy in the family of nations. Second, it illustrated the logic and necessity of the Zionist solution to the persecution of the Jews. Third, it amplified implicitly the awareness that the Jewish people's survival despite the persecutions they had endured over the ages was miraculous.

The general press, which educated young people also read, was also characterized by cultural ethnocentrism. Much space was devoted to local news and little to events around the world—a result of both provincialism and the character of a revolutionary society, which tends to be preoccupied with itself. The most extreme example of this was the sparse coverage given to World War II in general (at least relative to its importance) and to the Holocaust in particular. (This was also a result of the ethos of rejection of the Diaspora, which will be discussed later.)

The person produced by the Zionist educational system was thus someone who viewed the world through the contracting lens of his ideological faith. He had limited capacity to observe his culture "from the outside" and a limited critical faculty, especially with regard to politics and society.[21]

UNCONSCIOUS IDEOLOGICAL INSTRUCTION

Zionist ideals were instilled in schoolchildren not only through ideological material in textbooks, but also through the creation of an ideological atmosphere in the schools—what Chaim Nachman Bialik called "unconscious ideological instruction."[22] The settlement enterprise was one of the common subjects in classes on painting, crafts, singing, and especially composition. Teachers encouraged their pupils to write on Zionist themes, and writing contests were conducted on subjects dealing with the Zionist epic. For example, an essay contest for schoolchildren organized in 1930 by the periodical *Lu'ach He-Chaver* and the Council of Israeli Teachers for the Jewish National Fund defined as its goal: "to receive some idea of the attitude of the Hebrew pupil in Israel toward all that is taking place here at this critical time, a time of building and creating."[23]

The student essays in school bulletins and collections testify to the success of preschool and school teachers in instilling in their charges the tendency to see even the most prosaic of subjects through Zionist spectacles.[24] Even brushing one's teeth was a service to the nation, one child proclaimed, for it produced a "healthy and fit generation" that could continue to shoulder the burden of the Zionist enterprise:

> Each and every day more bacteria enter the mouth and endanger our well-being, so we brush our teeth every day. Let us hope that by brushing our teeth and keeping clean in general a healthy and fit generation will grow up in our land that will be able to continue the growth and development of the Israeli people in our land.[25]

According to the instructions from their supervisors, teachers used contemporary examples from Yishuv life in teaching general subjects. For example, in the 1933 weekly teaching plans for third grade the following activities in natural history and geography were recommended: "A walk in the field addressing the question: Why do we fertilize? . . . How and with what do we fertilize in the Land of Israel? . . . Land improvement by the JNF." For teaching Hebrew, "stories on the life and work of the farmer in the autumn . . . work songs, children and their chores during vacation" were prescribed. In drawing, the suggested subjects were "the farmer at work, children working the earth, work in the garden, implements for working the land." In the area of "games and celebrations," the teacher was encouraged to use "Israeli songs, appropriate verses from the Bible," and the "costume of land-working pioneers."[26]

Even arithmetic was given an ideological cast. Educator Zvi Zohar suggested to arithmetic teachers that they build lessons around "the income and outlays of the farmer in the Land of Israel; the reckoning of tree plantings in Herzl Forest; money children collect for the JNF during vacations."[27] Pioneer sayings and Zionist maxims displayed prominently on posters that decorated the classrooms intensified the ideological atmosphere that enveloped the Hebrew pupil.

Preschool and school teachers were the principal transmitters of the ideological message not only because they were charged with educating children in Zionist values but also because they taught Hebrew, the reborn national language, with all the value-laden connotations and ideological and emotional overtones it had assimilated. "[The language] was the basic foundation of all education, but together with bestowing the language we enriched the children with many concepts and values," relates Zivia Katarbursky, who taught in Jerusalem and was one of the country's first preschool teachers.[28] Children's compositions during the thirties and forties in fact show the assimilation of Zionist concepts, aphorisms, and characteristic modes of expression into the public discourse—including the frequent use of the first-person plural in the future tense: "we will build," "we will plant," "we will establish."

SCHOOL PROGRAMS
AND MEMORIAL CEREMONIES

All religious societies recognize that the child is taught to accept the yoke of religion not only by winning his mind but also, and principally, by winning his heart. "Zionist education will be achieved not by explanation and persuasion alone," stated educator Baruch Ben-Yehuda, "but rather . . . by a relation to Zionism through emotion."[29]

The pedagogical means for achieving this "relation through emotion" was for current events of national importance to reverberate through morning inspections and assemblies in the schools and preschools. Another instrument was a special lesson devoted to social interactions—a kind of social dynamics class in which the teacher led a discussion of problems in interpersonal relationships and the relation between the individual and society. This brought the pupil into adult society, made him a partner in its joys and sorrows, and quickened his emotional and intellectual involvement in the national experience.

Schools and teachers also interested the children in national events and intensified their emotional participation in the national experience by assigning pupils to write letters to soldiers at the front (Yishuv soldiers volunteering in the British army during World War II and IDF soldiers during the War of Independence and the Sinai Campaign). The fate of the soldiers to whom the letters were addressed was in this way linked in the children's mind to the fate of the nation as a whole, strengthening their awareness that they lived in a fateful time that demanded national solidarity. The participation of the entire class in writing these letters made the children feel as if they themselves were taking part in a military operation and led them to value and admire the soldiers at the front all the more.

The children's sense of involvement in the Zionist enterprise was also reinforced through school assemblies conducted on special days, such as Balfour Declaration Day, JNF Day, and memorial days for Zionist leaders and graduates of the school who had fallen in battle. A student wrote in 1941 of the deep impression made by one such ceremony:

> Today is the thirtieth day since Ussishkin's death. . . . There was a memorial service in the gymnasium that I will never forget as one of the most moving moments: a few words by a friend . . . honor for the gymnasium flag: to the blast of the trumpets and the thunder of the drums the flag appeared, and the majesty of the return [to Zion] enveloped us . . . the raising of the national flag . . . our principal's speech . . . the lowering of the flag to half-mast . . . the placing of the symbol of mourning on the institution's flag . . . and "Ha-Tikva" . . . —these were moments that will not be forgotten . . . moments in which the soul is prepared to sacrifice itself for the nation—and to die peacefully.[30]

With the establishment of the state all these ceremonies and assemblies were set aside and replaced by Independence Day. The national rite was from then on celebrated on this day, as in other national religions.[31] Not by coincidence, it was also called State Day. In 1951 the Ministry of Defense initiated a memorial day for fallen IDF soldiers on the day before Independence Day, and in 1954, after a three-year trial, it became an official national memorial day. Over the years this has become Zionism's most sacred day. The frightening siren (reminiscent of the blowing of the *shofar* in synagogue on the high holidays), the moment of silence (recalling the silence of the Amida prayer, the central part of the Jewish service), and the laments and litanies recited in schools and settlements (recalling the Yom Kippur service) moved both young people and adults and intensified the national commitment of Israel's youth.

SYMBIOSIS BETWEEN CIVILIAN AND MILITARY STRUCTURES

The Sabra's socialization process can be described as the center from which organizational and ideological "sub-socializations" branched out—the kibbutz and moshav, the school, the youth movement, and the military. All of these flowed from a single source: the political establishment of the labor movement.

Chagam, the Expanded Physical Education program, was established in 1939 at the initiative of Arthur Biram, principal of the Reali High School in Haifa. Like the Gadna and the Youth Battalions that succeeded it, Chagam provided preliminary training for military service, functioning under the sponsorship of the Haganah and later the IDF. Both structures prepared adolescents for the military and taught them Zionist military history, love of the land, and the values of agriculture and volunteerism. The social activities in the Gadna clubs, which had the character of youth movement chapter houses, included public readings on Friday nights and on other days. These were generally selections from the Ha-Shomer Ha-Tza'ir newspaper, *Al Ha-Mishmar,* and from the military periodical *Ba-Machaneh,* as well as from Gadna publications. Notably, this was mostly general ideological material not addressed specifically to young people.

The youth movements also preached the pioneer creed and prepared their urban members for life on a kibbutz and for military service in the Palmach or the Nachal corps. Some youth movements received financial support and guidance from the schools. For example, the Scouts were organizationally linked to the Reali school, and Ha-Machanot Ha-Olim was connected to the Herzliya Gymnasium. Another example of the ideological symbiosis between the schools, the settlements, and the army was the volunteer work performed by urban school students on kibbutzim and moshavim; this eventually became an eleventh-grade requirement. Still another was the requirement, imposed in 1942 as a condition of receiving a high school graduation certificate, that one must perform national military service after the completion of high school.

The kibbutz movements of the early 1940s (especially Ha-Kibbutz Ha-Me'uchad) also contributed to the symbiosis between the civilian and military educational structures. They believed that preference should be given to building an independent Hebrew military force rather than to participation in the war against the Nazis, even though some of their members enlisted in the British army. In August 1942 the Ha-Kibbutz Ha-Me'uchad council decided to allow the Palmach to maintain itself by arranging for its members to work at kibbutzim. The decision was a financial solution to the continued existence of the Palmach while integrating it organizationally into the economic-social-cultural system of the kibbutz movement. Another impetus for the decision was the labor shortage that the collective farms were beginning to face. Kibbutz movement leader Yitzchak Tabenkin was responsible for the decision, seeing it as a way of consummating the idea of a "workers' army." Later on the other kibbutz movements joined the arrangement. The decision in fact saved the Palmach from being dismantled after the British ended their support for it.[32] In 1944 the Palmach headquarters signed an agreement with the pioneer youth movements (Ha-Machanot Ha-Olim, Ha-Noar Ha-Oved, the Scouts, Ha-Shomer Ha-Tza'ir, Makabi Ha-Tza'ir, and Ha-Tenu'ot Ha-Me'uchadot), according to which each group of youth movement graduates that was sent for agricultural training at a kibbutz would automatically enlist in the Palmach. Quotas of work days for the kibbutz and training days for the Palmach were set, and each group gave fifteen percent of its members to serve as commanders and pursue military specialties. This arrangement was continued with the Nachal corps after the state was established.

The Palmach and Nachal recruits absorbed the kibbutz atmosphere, and some of them chose, in the wake of this experience, to live on a kibbutz or moshav. Many young Palmachniks agonized over how to divide their time between kibbutz work and military training—a dilemma that testifies to the strong link between the two activities and to their ideological equivalence. The kibbutz movements also contributed their own resources to support the cultural activities of the youth movements associated with them.

The defense organizations did not limit themselves to military affairs; they also engaged in educational and ideological activity. The Palmach command, for example, supported the publication of two book series called *Heroic Heritage* and *Undercover Defense,* which served as didactic texts in the schools and youth movements. The Palmach integrated informational programs and seminars into its training and brought in guest lecturers (generally party leaders and activists) who preached the Zionist creed. Zionist policy, knowledge of the land, the Zionist movement, and international questions relevant to the Zionist enterprise were the preferred subjects for discussion in these forums.[33]

The role of the Palmach's political officer, whose place was taken by the regiment and battalion education officers when the IDF was established, demonstrates the importance of ideological education in combat organizations. These officers, who had exceptional speaking skills— Benny Maharshek, Yizhar Smilansky, and Abba Kovner, for instance— were responsible for spurring on the young people and fostering "combat heritage"—battle stories that illustrated a moral point or military principle. The term "combat heritage" became an identifying marker of the IDF. Some officers wrote stories about battles and their experiences in their regiments, transforming these units into the subjects of new symbols and legends. These legends were eventually adopted by the civilian populace, becoming new Land of Israel folklore.

The organizational links and the mutual spiritual feedback between military and civilian socialization is reflected in the circulation of *Alon*

Ha-Palmach, the Palmach's newsletter. *Alon Ha-Palmach,* which had a clear ideological line, served not only the members of the Palmach but also the youth movements. The latter used Palmach material in their activities and frequently reprinted texts from *Alon Ha-Palmach* in their own newsletters and publications. The national Gadna command purchased hundreds of copies of each issue for its own units, and the guidance office of its national headquarters supplied copies to the Haganah's central national schools.[34] In this way, *Alon Ha-Palmach* became the voice of the Sabra generation and a model for other periodicals for youth and the army.

THE ZIONIST MYTHS

The way an individual comprehends his nation's history, and so his national identity, depends in large measure on the national myths he was educated in while young. The principal myths that the Sabras were taught and that appear in their own writings may be identified as deliverance, the few facing the many, the binding of Isaac, the redemption of Israel, and the right to the Land of Israel.

Deliverance (in Old Times and New)   Even though the Zionists rebelled against the traditional Judaism of the Diaspora, in practice Zionism's relation to tradition was a complex and convoluted combination of rejection and acceptance; in many ways a partial cultural continuity was in fact preserved. A classic example of this continuity is the myth of Israel's deliverance from its enemies—a foundation myth of Judaism and, as it turns out, of Zionism as well. At the basis of traditional Jewish belief and central to the chronicle of Jewish history as told in the Bible is the concept that God saves Israel over and over again from its adversaries. The Jewish people rise up from the dust and are redeemed at the last minute, while their enemies are doomed to destruction.

The main pedagogical tool through which the Sabra internalized the myth of deliverance was the emphasis placed on the Jewish victory over the foe who tries to destroy Israel. This concept was clearly present in the folklore of the holidays—Pesach, Purim, Lag Be-Omer, and especially, Hanukkah. It was emphasized in stories and songs learned in preschool and school and was woven into many of the holiday songs written for preschool children. The intention was to teach children that the miracles of the present day (the victory over the Arabs and the expulsion of the British) were replays of the miracles performed by Moses and Joshua, Mordechai and Esther, Bar Kochba and his legions, and the Maccabees.

The success of the educational system in inculcating this deterministic view of Jewish history into Sabra consciousness can be gleaned from student compositions written at one of the kibbutz movement schools. At the height of World War II (1940) teachers asked students to write about the war. Here is one nine-year-old girl's vision of its outcome:

> And all the nations and all the children of Israel went out to battle with Hitler, and he fell in that war and died. And the next day the children of Israel numbered themselves and verily not one was lacking, and they came to the battlefield and looked, and here was Hitler fallen dead and his horse by him. And they rejoiced and were happy. And while they were still gazing at the body here came an army of horsemen. And they fell upon the Jews, but the Jews were victorious and destroyed all the bad people in the world. And a new generation rose, a young generation, a fresh generation, that did not know evil and cruelty, and never did another bad man rise up in the world. So will it be, so will it be done, so will it befall. Our hope is not yet lost.[35]

This girl's confidence in the myth of deliverance instilled in her the faith—even at the height of Nazi successes on the battlefield—that Hitler's end would be like those of the Jewish people's other enemies. For her and other schoolchildren to have written in this vein, the war had to be seen as part of a continuity whose end was predestined—as implied by the Biblical style in which she described Hitler's death. The myth of deliverance made the Jewish people's metaphysical power tangible to the schoolchild. The struggle for the establishment of the Jewish state was depicted as an almost religious struggle—and therefore victory was assured.

The Few Facing the Many   The myth of the few facing the many is derived to a large extent from the myth of deliverance. The theme of the victory of those who are inferior in number and weapons but superior in courage, faith, and moral values appears over and over in Jewish history, in Biblical commentaries, and in Jewish prayer. The drowning of Pharoah's army at the Red Sea, the victory over Amalek at Refidim, the conquests of Joshua, Gideon's victory over the Midianites, Barak's victory over Sisera, David's defeat of the Philistines, the Maccabees' rebellion against the Greeks, and Bar Kochba's rebellion against the Roman legions all reprise this theme.

The central elements of this myth are the boldness and craftiness ("For by deceptions thou shalt make thy war," as the Book of Proverbs advises) of the commander of the Hebrew army, whose spirit does not fail when he encounters an enemy force stronger and more numerous than his own. David, who defeats the heavily armed Philistine Goliath with a slingshot and stone, is the shining example. In the period of the Yishuv and in the first years of the state, emphasis on the numbers of the enemy is frequent in references to how Israeli forces had battled "the seven Arab nations."

Another element in this myth is the power of the Jewish God, who can overcome any other power in the universe "with a mighty hand and an outstretched arm" and who shelters the apple of his eye, Israel, under his paternal protection. The verse from the Haggadah of Pesach: "He who protected our fathers and us, when not just one has risen up on us to destroy us . . . and the Holy One, Blessed Be He, delivers us from their hands" is one of the many verses that express the secret of Jewish strength—divine providence. An evil and cruel power—Pharaoh, Midian, Amalek, or Goliath—stands against and wishes to attack Israel, and indirectly its God, yet in the end is beaten to a pulp and scattered before Israel in shame. Superiority in spirit (Jewish faith and ethics) defeats the gentile's evil—"Not by might, nor by power but by spirit, says the Lord of Hosts." The equivalent phrase in modern Israel is "the superiority of human quality over quantity."[36] Official Zionist ideology did reject the dependence on God and emphasized faith in physical strength in its stead. However, the concept that a higher power saved the people of Israel from danger was implied in the words of the pioneers—especially in the way they celebrated the traditional holidays, particularly after the War of Independence.

The uniqueness and superiority of the Jewish people as set forth in the myth of "the few facing the many" can explain why this myth became one of the most important of the Zionist religion.[37] It stands out in particular in the interpretation and emphases that Zionism gave to the Jewish holidays, especially Hanukkah (the Maccabees versus the Greeks) and Lag Be-Omer (Bar Kochba and the Jewish rebels versus the Roman armies).

The "few facing the many" myth received a contemporary pioneering cast in the sub-myths of Masada and Tel Chai. The Masada myth is not in any way a part of traditional Judaism. It is the story of a handful of fighters who fiercely defended their desert fortress against a large Roman army and chose to kill themselves rather than be taken prisoner and live as slaves. In this way the fighters were triumphant, winning a moral victory over the enemy, the Roman Amalek. (The doubtful historicity of the myth has been much written about in recent years.)[38] The Masada myth was fixed so deeply in Sabra consciousness that youth movement members, schoolchildren, and Palmach soldiers would make ritual hikes to the desert site, climaxed with an ascent on foot to the "Zionist sanctuary," where they swore an oath to the nation and the homeland. At twilight, on the peak of Masada, amid ancient Jewish remains, in the heart of a wild desert that sounded a distant echo of days of grandeur, the young Israelis saw themselves as the heirs of the ancient heroes of the Hebrew kingdom, as they lit letters wrapped in fabric and watched as slogans seemed to write themselves, burning in the fire ("Masada will not fall again" [from Yitzchak Lamdan's 1927 poem "Masada"]).

The Tel Chai myth was a story of contemporary pioneer heroism. At its heart was a group led by Yosef Trumpeldor, a one-armed Hebrew hero, battling courageously against a gang of Arab outlaws that outnumbered and outgunned it. In an essay in memory of Trumpeldor, labor-Zionist author Yosef Chaim Brenner wrote: "The small clutch of people who devoted their lives to guarding the north, alone and neglected, tattered and ragged, hungry and frozen won the right from Hebrew history to be honored after their deaths with the aura and the glory of the nation's heroes."[39]

The myth of Tel Chai encoded a symbolic element of great importance to Zionism—reinstating the Jewish people's lost honor. By the very act of fighting the Tel Chai martyrs became a symbol of what distinguished Zionism from the Diaspora Jewish tradition of bowing one's head before the gentile.

Another element of the Tel Chai myth, and perhaps its central element, was the change that Zionism made in the traditional Jewish myth of sacred martyrdom—from willingness to die to sanctify God's name to willingness to die to sanctify the homeland. Trumpeldor's last words, according to the account disseminated immediately after his death, were "It is good to die for our country." This became a slogan of Zionist martyrdom and earned Trumpeldor a place in the Zionist pantheon.[40]

A memorial in the shape of a roaring lion was erected at Tel Chai in memory of those who died in the battle. This became a site of pilgrimage for youth movements. In fact, it was at Tel Chai that the still-current Israeli tradition of pilgrimage to the graves of fallen Hebrew soldiers began. Tel Chai Day, observed on the eleventh day of the Hebrew month of Adar, integrated messages of labor, bravery, love of the land, and devotion to the Jewish settlements. An educational tradition of dramatic readings and public singing was woven around Tel Chai, and it became, in the eyes of young people, a symbol of resolute resistance and sacrifice of one's life for the homeland, as well as a symbol of the entire pioneer enterprise.

The depth to which the Tel Chai myth penetrated and was internalized in the Sabra soul can be seen in the writings of young people of all ages, from every movement and institution and in every period. An especially telling example can be found in a letter by one Sabra in which he censures his girlfriend for daring to imagine that he might settle in another country. He uses Trumpeldor's motto: "And you well know the program I have set for myself, so how can you even think of settling in a gentile country? Am I the man who would do such a thing? I have but one homeland, and it is Israel. It is good to die for it and—even more so—to live in it."[41]

The crushing defeat of the Arab armies, which had been considered well armed and numerous, in the War of Independence was perceived, even if not openly, as the finger of God, and as another link in the historical chain of deliverances from the enemies who wished to destroy Israel. The consummation of the myth in this victory honed and intensified the national feeling that the process of returning the nation to its land had "divine sponsorship," and that the IDF's victories were also achieved with divine guidance.

The Sinai victory led the public to feel the force of the "few facing the many" myth all the more intensely. Another ostensible miracle had taken place, and the small, weak Israeli nation had emerged from the battle with the upper hand. The wretched and grotesque performance of the enemy soldiers—who fled en masse from the battlefield despite Egypt's prewar boasts—fit well with the David versus Goliath legend. Here was young Srolik, the typical Sabra figure made famous by editorial cartoonist Dosh, just like David the shepherd, "ruddy, with fine eyes," innocent and moral, triumphing over the boastful Arab Goliath, heavily armed and clumsy. David was victorious because of his heroism, dexterity, and moral robustness, despite his inferior size and weaponry. He defeated Goliath, as European depictions of the scene show, by aiming precisely at the giant's single vulnerable point, his bare forehead.

The Binding of Isaac   The myth of the binding of Isaac, which interprets the fallen soldier as Isaac bound on the altar of the nation and the homeland, is not unique to the Zionist nation. It made an appearance in Europe in the nineteenth century with the rise of the national movements and became a more substantive and important element in the cult of war and the nation in Western culture in the wake of World War I, in which soldiers were killed by the millions.

The Israeli myth of Isaac as the one who falls in battle appeared initially in the first memorial anthology, *Yizkor*. From that time onward it made ever more frequent appearances in the commemorative literature, as well as in Hebrew poetry and prose.[42] Recast as a sacrifice, the fallen Hebrew soldier was transformed from an unlucky young man who had lost his life into a martyr who had willingly given it up.

Since the Hebrew fighter's death was viewed as voluntary and altruistic, it was perceived in the nation's consciousness as an expression of sublime patriotism. The martyred Hebrews—from Trumpeldor and Hannah Szenes to Dani Mas and Uri Ilan—were viewed as new incarnations of great figures of the past: the Hasmonean rebels, Hannah and her seven sons from the Book of the Maccabees, the ten rabbis led by Rabbi Akiva who were executed by the Romans after the Bar Kochba revolt, and the World War II partisans and Warsaw ghetto fighters. All were Jews who, according to legend, died sacrificing their lives to save their nation.

Parents who lost their sons in war were also glorified by the myth. They were presented as having heroically accepted the sacrifice of their most cherished possession for the sake of the nation and were praised for gritting their teeth and holding back their grief when they learned of the death of their beloved child. "At your orders he went, at your orders he fell. May you be blessed," wrote poet Re'uven Grossman, editor of *Scrolls of Fire,* to Zionist patriarch Ben-Gurion when his son had fallen in the War of Independence. His letter, which moved "the old man," was published and became a symbol of the heroic acceptance of death.

Zionism made three substantive changes in the classic, traditional myth of Isaac. First, the binding of Isaac by his father was replaced by the son volunteering to be bound. Instead of an act of submission to the divine will, it became a deed of heroism—not spiritual heroism, however (the willingness to die to sanctify God) but a physical act of heroism. No longer would heroes accept divine judgment and die reciting "*shma yisrael.*" They would now fight valiantly to the last bullet and, their heads held high, die on the altar of their homeland.

The second change was that the sacrificial victim was not sacrificed for some unknown purpose (God does not tell Abraham why he must sacrifice his son) or as a test of faith in God. Rather, his sacrifice was perceived as an important means to realizing the Zionist ideal and as a test of tribal loyalty.

The third and probably most important change was switching the story's center of gravity from the relationship between Abraham and his God (metaphorically, between the patriot and his homeland) to that between Abraham and Isaac (metaphorically, the intergenerational relation between the pioneer and his Sabra son).[43] This emphasis on the acquiescence of the son rather than the zealous faith of the father can also be found in the writings of traditional Jewish commentators, but during the formative period for the culture of loss in the Yishuv it became central to the myth. The intergenerational meaning was furthered by two complementary concepts, the "generation of the sons" and the "generation of the fathers," which appeared frequently in the commemorative literature.

Shifting the emphasis from the binding father to the voluntarily bound son gave a metaphorical tinge to the special relationship between the generation of the founding pioneer fathers and their Sabra sons. It expressed the sons' fidelity to pioneer values and to fulfillment of their parents' high expectations.

The voluntary binding of the generation of the sons on the altar of the homeland is one of the most prominent motifs of the memorial books. "Happy are the parents who were privileged to raise a son like this! Happy is the nation whose sons sacrifice themselves on its altar!"[44] proclaims a memorial book for one of the graduates of Ha-Noar Ha-Oved.

The Redemption of Israel   Even though Zionism was a fundamentally secular movement, it did not repudiate the myth of the redemption of Israel. The Zionists rejected the passive expectation of a redemption that would come with the arrival of the Messiah and advocated a national, secular redemption in which the nation would rise up and redeem itself from slavery. However, they did not deny the metaphysical and deterministic elements of Jewish existence. On the contrary, in many senses they accepted them as fundamental and used them as emotional engines to motivate the masses—especially after the establishment of the state. One demonstration of this is the presence of the God of Israel in the traditions of the holidays. Though most of the holidays in their Zionist form—Pesach, Purim, Hanukkah, Lag Be-Omer—emphasize national liberation and human heroism, they do not omit the part played by God in the national epic.[45]

In the Zionist view, the history of the Jewish people is fundamentally directed toward the goal of Zionist settlement in the Land of Israel. The Jewish people grew into maturity during their two-thousand-year exile. Always longing for the homeland, they prepared themselves for "the return home" during many years of suffering, war, and slavery. The return to Zion is a miracle, or a miraculous stage in history, that has happened to the Jewish people. Modern anti-Semitism is nothing but a catalyst for the consummation of the redemption, as were the harsh measures imposed by Pharaoh prior to the Exodus.

The "law of redemption" was a substantive element in the worldview of the Yishuv leadership; it was considered an actual law of nature according to which Jewish history progressed. Most Zionist spiritual and political leaders perceived the renewal of the Jewish people's national life not only as a practical solution to the problem of anti-Semitism, but also as an epic, a Biblical story full of miracles. Many of them sincerely believed that the Zionist enterprise was a kind of "building of the Third Temple"—in the political, rather than the religious and traditional sense. Expressions like "rebirth," "renaissance," "the dawn of redemption," "going from slavery to freedom," and "the last generation of slavery and the first of the redemption" recurred in their writings and speeches.

Faith in the myth of Zionist redemption was inculcated in students largely through the study of Jewish history. The textbooks of the Sabra era presented this history as a story of the Jews being saved from their afflicters. The return to Zion, or the establishment of a Jewish state, was viewed as the climax of the process—as the victory of the unending striving for Zion. So, for example, in the textbook *History of Zionism: The Movement for Renaissance and Redemption in Israel,* a book whose very title testifies to belief in the myth of redemption, educator Baruch Ben-Yehuda wrote: "Israel has, during its long years of exile, tried in three ways to realize the Zionist dream: messianism, political activity, and immigration to its country. The entire chronicle of the Jewish people in the Diaspora is full of great and frequent events that testify to the unceasing striving to achieve the Zionist aspiration."[46]

Holocaust Day, established after the War of Independence, was a hugely powerful pedagogical tool for instilling the myth of redemption in Sabra consciousness. The horrors of the Holocaust, the defeat of the Nazis, and the euphoria of the establishment of the state, whose inception just after the end of World War II was itself a symbol, drove the messianic conception of Zionism deeper into the consciousness of the public, especially the younger generation. Now more than ever before, Zionism seemed the fulfillment of a prophecy, the climax of a deterministic evolutionary process. Once again, although this time with unprecedented evil and cruelty, an oppressor had appeared to destroy Israel. And again, exactly according to the mythological scenario, the anti-Semitic Amalek had collapsed and the Jews had risen out of the ashes like the phoenix. Following these convulsions and catastrophes came a quasi-miraculous stage—after the destruction of the Nazi nemesis came the rebirth of the Hebrew state.

Because of the myth of redemption, Holocaust Day was not just a national memorial day for the victims of the Nazi horror but also a holy day, implicitly celebrating the myth of Zionist redemption and the victory of Zionism (the common Zionist expression "Holocaust and rebirth" testifies to this). The establishment of the state was regarded as part of a series of miracles performed for the Jews. Horrible Jewish suffering led to the longed-for redemption as ship after ship brought Jews from the hell of their Exile to the Holy Land—the land of freedom. Yosef Tabenkin's proposal to add the story of the Holocaust as an additional chapter in the Pesach Haggadah—a Haggadah devoted entirely to the myth of Jewish redemption—exemplifies this symbolic interpretation.

The Sabra was thus taught from a young age that "every man should see himself as if he came out of Egypt." Though the teaching was now detached from the context of Jewish tradition, the Sabra, like the Jews of the Diaspora, was educated in Jewish metaphysics, even if a different version. This new metaphysics took the eternity of Israel as an axiom, so the Zionist struggle was but one more stage in an ongoing chain of Jewish national struggles for renewed independence.

The myth of redemption played an important role in molding the Sabra's self-image. Perceiving the reality of Israel as a decisive stage in the realization of an ancient dream of redemption imbued the Sabras with a sense of mission. They felt as if they were meant to "liberate and purify the Temple" (in the metaphoric sense), and this feeling enhanced their self-image.

The myth of redemption seems to have played a decisive role in the fierce and determined fighting of the Sabra in the War of Independence. The myth instilled in him a feeling that he was participating in the climax of a historical process, and that his duty was not only to his pioneer fathers but also to generations of Jewish warriors who had fought for the same ideas as he. As one boy wrote in a letter: "And now, war has again come and again in this land, and again Amalek and Assyria have ranged themselves against us. We have entered this war, and again Jews are falling on the mountains of the homeland in defense of besieged Jerusalem, in defense of all the Galilee and the Negev, and we must accustom ourselves to sacrifice even if it is great."[47]

The myth of redemption made the Sabra certain of victory in the War of Independence. Its optimism was vital to the soldier on the battlefield, because it motivated him and made it easier to cope with uncertainties.

"A momentous faith in the eternity of Israel, in the victory of Israel, in the redemption of Israel lies within us all," said a member of Ha-Machanot Ha-Olim, "and that is a great force, such faith by masses of Jews."[48]

The Biblical Right to the Land of Israel   The need for a refuge for a persecuted nation and the right of the Jews to self-determination are indeed cornerstones of Zionist ideology, but from a symbolic point of view their importance was secondary. Paramount to the moral justification of the Zionist enterprise was the notion of historic justice. The term "exile" served the Zionists not only as a means of rejecting the past, but also as a way of presenting Jewish existence outside the Land of Israel as a temporary reality and, even more, as something that had been imposed.

The moral right of the Jews to immigrate to and settle in the Land of Israel was never the subject of debate in the political and ideological forums of the Yishuv, not even on the theoretical-juridical level. This right, which was at the foundation of Zionism, was taken for granted; it was expressed in the very term "Land of Israel," which implied ownership by linking a geographical place, "the land," with the Jewish people, "Israel." Even those delegates to the Zionist Congress who advocated acceptance of the British offer of Uganda to the Jews did not deny the moral right of the Jewish people to return to their own land; they merely believed that the Uganda proposal was a more practical one. Their view failed because they did not properly appreciate the force and the symbolic importance of the Land of Israel in the Jewish ethos. The right to the land was never seriously questioned in Israeli society until the period after the Six Day War—and even then the right to the land within the pre-1967 borders was never challenged.

The myth of "our right to the Land of Israel," including the right to establish an independent state in the land, was based on a mixture of justifications. There were practical and moral arguments (according to Western secular moral principles), such as the need to solve the problem of anti-Semitism, the right of the conquering defender to the land of the Arab aggressor, the settlers' rights to virgin land they had domesticated ("making the desert bloom"), and the right to land purchased legally at market prices. But there were also justifications of a mythological and metaphysical nature—first and foremost the divine promise given to the forefathers.

Along with the myth of redemption and the myth of deliverance, the myth of the right to the land was one of the most prominent in the Jewish history textbooks. This was because even nonreligious Jews needed a divine promise to justify the Jewish people's right to the Land of Israel.[49] So, for example, the textbook *Our People in the Past and Present* states:

> The chronicle of our people comforts the exiled and informs them that the land from which they were exiled is theirs forever; God promised it to our fathers—to Abraham, Isaac, and Jacob; on more than one occasion the forefathers left the bounds of the land, but they did not forget it and did not leave it for good; even after four hundred years of Egyptian slavery, the nation succeeded in liberating itself and returning to its land, the land flowing with milk and honey, which God swore to give to his people for eternity.[50]

The myth of the right to the land influenced the Sabra's worldview in two ways. First, it strengthened his feeling that Israel could justifiably annex territories that had been abandoned by the Arabs in the War of Independence. This sentiment was expressed in the widespread use of the term "liberation" to describe the battles of that war.[51]

Second, the myth influenced the Sabra's historical role (which affected his self-image). If the territories conquered were liberated lands of the forefathers, then the Sabra warrior who freed them was not simply a second-generation immigrant from Europe, but the successor to the Biblical boy who walked in his sandals over the mountains of Canaan, as the poet Ze'ev described: "Mount Gilboa's in his eyes / The Bible lilt is in his voice."[52] The myth gave the Sabras a sense of ownership, of being natives, even though they were in fact immigrants or the sons of immigrants. If the pioneers felt at home in the land from the moment they arrived, their Sabra children thought of themselves as if they had been living in the country for generations, like the trees and wildlife.

IDEOLOGICAL TRAINING

The Sabra's ideological commitment was imbued in him by the mechanisms just presented through several techniques, both overt and covert. The most important of these were exposure to Sabra ideology on a daily basis, Zionist bar mitzvahs, swearing-in and "pledge" ceremonies, reverence for national "saints," holiday ceremonies, the ritual of tree planting, and "offerings" to the "priests" of Zionism.

Daily Assimilation of Ideological Messages   The transformation of a social ideology into a "secular religion" may be gauged by its pervasiveness—that is, its ability to seep into many corners and areas of cultural life. And in fact, during the Yishuv and early state periods, pioneer ideology penetrated into the smallest capillaries of the social circulatory system to such an extent that it became, as noted earlier, a kind of all-embracing religious experience. The symbols, the connotations, the motifs, and the ideological messages found their way into many verbal and visual expressions, even if the Sabras were not always consciously aware of this. They appeared on banners, in music, in art, in radio broadcasts, in plays, in the handful of films produced then, in editorials, and even in the way people dressed and in children's toys and games.[53]

The uniform worldview held by the molders of public opinion in the press, in literature, and in advertising was a product of not only their emotional identification with the Zionist message but also the small numbers of the Yishuv population and the concentration of capital in national institutions. These last two factors enabled efficient propagandizing. The penetrative nature of the ideological messages and the close and largely unseen institutional supervision of them spread them everywhere, confirming and reconfirming the Sabra's worldview. The young Sabra lived in an "ideological bubble," where he was subjected to a constant barrage of propaganda.

The Zionist Bar Mitzvah   In S. Shalom's poem "Voices in the Night," which was frequently recited at ceremonies, a process similar to a rite of passage is described through a dialogue between an anonymous voice (as if the voice of God) and a Hebrew youth:

> Are you prepared? / asked the voice / in silent night.
> I am prepared / the voice replied / in silent night.
> And can you leave / your home and street / your friend and brother?
> Yes, I can leave / my home and street / my friend and brother.
> And can you march / so very far / and tremble not?
> Yes, I can march / so very far / and tremble not.[54]

This poem describes a covert Zionist socialization technique—imbuing national responsibility in a boy at a young age. The youth is called on to leave his home and "march so very far"—that is, to serve his people and homeland. He accepts the call, just as the young prophet Samuel accepted the call of God. In this way, the Sabra is baptized, as it were, into pioneerism and becomes an adult.

The rites of passage practiced in tribal cultures and closed communities, including the bar mitzvah in traditional Judaism, denote the acceptance of the young person as an adult member of the community of believers. Two educational goals are thus achieved. First, the youngster is given no time for doubts or for examining other options (in psychology, this transition period between childhood and adulthood is called the moratorium). He is drawn into the organized rite before he has had time to develop his own worldview.

Second (and perhaps the more important goal, connected to the process of "inner conversion"), assigning adult responsibility to a boy flatters him and inspires him to justify the faith and confidence that the community has expressed in him by proving that he is indeed a worthy member of the community of believers.

In the Zionist religion this mechanism functioned quite well. The linkage between adulthood and acceptance of the yoke of national precepts was one of Zionism's most effective techniques of ideological socialization. In the moshavim and kibbutzim children participated in the work of the adults, developing a profound commitment to the sanctity of labor and the socialist ethos. Life in a kibbutz children's house was conducted on the principle of communal self-management, which also imposed adult responsibility on the youngsters. In the pioneer youth movements children were made counselors at a young age and were charged with the care of groups of children only a few years younger than they. From a sociological and psychological point of view, this responsibility resembled that of a junior officer in the army or an educator. The young charges assigned to an adolescent counselor absorbed the ideological material he conveyed to them via their identification of him as a "big brother" figure. Even more important, the counselor himself came to identify more strongly with the ideological material he conveyed to his charges. In the Palmach and later in the IDF, young people received commands at a very young age (battalion commanders were in their twenties), and this authority imbued them with a fierce sense of duty to the organization that had demonstrated its confidence in them.

A similar educational effect was created by involving young people in Haganah missions—a necessity because of the lack of manpower. Fifteen-year-olds were called on to join the Gadna, where they assumed active roles in the underground, such as pasting up posters and serving as couriers.

The trips, hikes, and work camps in distant and unsettled areas undertaken within the framework of the Gadna, the youth movements, and the youth divisions in the kibbutzim were also an early exercise in responsibility, tightly binding young people to the ideology.

Swearing-In and "Pledge" Ceremonies   Swearing-in ceremonies directed to the youth movement, the Palmach, the country, and the IDF, practiced in all public organizations, also served as a kind of covert ideological rein to which the public was tied. The social mechanism of the oath, practiced in most achievement-oriented societies, was intended to create awe of the organization into which the inductee was being sworn, and to present social deviation as a breach of faith, and so as a sin. It symbolized eternal duty to the community and to the land—a kind of unseverable tie. The oath added drama to the rite of passage and imbued it with sanctity.

The oath to the homeland was also taken by swearing loyalty to the flag, to the rifle, or to a young seedling, all of which symbolized the national ethos. An implied pledge of loyalty can be found in the Palmach oath of the rifle. This included, in addition to a declaration of responsibility for carefully guarding this precious piece of equipment, a declaration of willingness to give one's life: "With this weapon, put in my hands by the Haganah organization in the Land of Israel, I will fight my people's enemies for my homeland—without surrender, without being deterred, and with self-sacrifice."[55]

The frequent use of the word "covenant" in its various forms in the texts of the Ha-Machanot Ha-Olim movement was also a kind of implicit oath, and it is no coincidence that an anthology of works by its members, published at the end of the 1930s, was called *In Your Covenant*. The title testified to the contents of the book, indicating the importance of the covenant with the land.

The swearing-in ceremonies were prepared and conducted with great care in order to make the maximum impression. They made every fiber of the young people's souls tremble and tied them strongly to the national organization, and indirectly also to the homeland.

The Cult of the National Saints   Creation of an ever-growing pantheon of leaders and heroes is a process that characterizes many revolutionary societies. These exemplary figures are for the most part leaders who formulate the revolution's ideological platform—men of action who stand out not only for their devotion to the revolution's ideals, but also for their moral values, and especially for their willingness to sacrifice everything, even their lives, for the realization of the revolutionary idea. They are models to be imitated.

These leaders reinforce the metaphysical image of the revolution. Superhuman traits are ascribed to many of them, and these powers make them into legendary figures and saviors who help turn the revolutionary drama into high epic. Their cult inculcates in the believer awe for the values they represent.

The Zionist pantheon included the harbingers and formulators of Zionism (Pinsker, Herzl, and others); the heroes of the Bilu movement of the First Aliya; the members of the early military organizations, Ha-Shomer and Nili; the pioneers of the labor settlements; the leaders of the labor parties; the poets and writers of the national renaissance; and later, the heroes of the wars of 1948 and 1956. These people won fame by the force of their thinking, their leadership, their vision, and their bravery in settlement and defense. Most were portrayed as giants and wonders in the literature, textbooks, children's songs, and press of the Yishuv period. Some were described in Biblical language and depicted as heirs of the Jewish people's great spiritual shepherds, such as Abraham, Moses, and Mattathias, or as successors to Hebrew military commanders such as Joshua, David, Gideon, Judah Maccabee, and Bar Kochba. People such as Chaim Nachman Bialik, Berl Katznelson, Yosef Chaim Brenner, Alexander Zeid, A. D. Gordon, David Ben-Gurion, Yitzchak Tabenkin, and Meir Ya'ari became mythological figures in life, not to mention after their deaths. They were regarded, in a way, as Hasidic rabbis. They were held in awe and their pronouncements were deemed holy; people attended to every word that came out of their mouths.

The cult of the Zionist "saints" was observed in Zionist houses of study and taught to children from a young age. Preschool children sang songs of praise to the great men of Zionism and schoolroom walls were hung with placards bearing their sayings. The schools also observed the anniversaries of the deaths of important Zionist leaders, and children were assigned to write compositions about them. One boy described his impressions of a visit with poet Chaim Nachman Bialik:

> My heart overflowed with happiness, I shook the hand that wrote so many poems. . . . His eyes glowed with a wonderful light, a shining precious light. I gazed into his eyes. I gazed well into the inner recesses of his soul, the soul of a poet. When I reached his soul, a sacred shiver ran through my body, and I cast my eyes down from the holy place.[56]

Children of all ages had a special liking for courageous heroes like Sarah Aaronsohn, Alexander Zeid, and Hannah Szenes and, more than any other, Yosef Trumpeldor, Zionism's most revered martyr. The tale of how he died, resolutely defending a border settlement on the redeemed land of the nation, fascinated children and frequently appeared in their compositions.

One of the interesting phenomena of the Israeli pantheon was the short time in which Hebrew heroes, soldiers in particular, became exemplars and the stories of their heroism became legends. "At times," historian and scholar of education Rachel Alboim-Dror has noted, "[this was] even to the point of an overlap between the current active figures and the legends woven around them, which had an imaginary dimension magnifying them far beyond the reality of their deeds."[57] This phenomenon was promoted by the rapid production of memorial books, histories, and literature based on recent events. Young people read these books and frequently quoted them in their writings and even in their diaries.[58] The great speed with which culture heroes became "larger than life" is characteristic of many revolutions, which seek to create almost instantly not only a new future but also a new history. In the Zionist revolution, however, because of the long and bloody conflict with the Arabs, a well-developed culture of memorialization, and a strong historical consciousness, this process seems to have been accelerated. (Also relevant is a well-developed culture of documentation, from which many historians today benefit.) Moreover, the best artistic talents were involved in memorialization. Poets and writers of all generations played a decisive role in the glorification of national heroes; their poems and stories turned into cultural assets and became "active monuments" or "moral signals."

Holiday Ceremonies   Holidays and ceremonies add color to life and provide emotional experiences that punctuate the day-to-day routine. Holiday customs unite the generations in a family or in an extended family (such as a village, a movement, or a nation) in pleasant and uplifting moments. United societies are generally societies with a well-developed culture of celebrations in which everyone takes part, both physically and spiritually. The educational leaders of the Yishuv understood the psychological value of holidays very well and exploited holidays as an important ideological tool in the education of the Sabra. "The Hebrew holiday" is "the starting point for all education," wrote Baruch Ben-Yehuda. "Our goal . . . is to exploit holidays and memorial days . . . in the school as moments of optimism, to plant these experiences in the children's hearts, and to dedicate them to the needs of Zionist education."[59]

The educational system was astute enough to give young people an important place in their rituals—as is common practice in the Jewish religion. The child and the adolescent were at the center of the torchlight processions, the choral singing, the marches, the dances, the public recitations, the tree plantings, and the bringing of the first fruits. In the settlements the finest talents were enlisted in preparing and conducting the ceremonies, which moved the children as much as theater performances and films did (it should be recalled that during this period professional entertainment—films, plays, and radio—was very limited). The combination of elements of the ancient Jewish tradition (especially Biblical symbols) and the new national-pioneer tradition, which so characterized the Zionist holidays (especially the agricultural ones celebrated in the kibbutzim, moshavim, and agricultural boarding schools), gave the holidays a cast of Biblical romanticism, reinforcing the link between the Zionist present and the Biblical past and infusing the holidays with an atmosphere of holiness characteristic of a religious-traditional holiday.

Moreover, Zionist holidays were observed according to their date on the traditional Jewish calendar. Due to Western influences, the Hebrew calendar fell out of use for day-to-day affairs, but it was institutionalized as the Zionist holiday calendar. This practice also preserved the traditional distinction between the Jews and the gentiles.

The education of the Sabra in Zionist values was accomplished through cyclical duties that demanded regular expressions of belief. Contributing to the JNF was one of these duties.[60] Preschools and elementary schools had a "JNF corner" for the "blue box" in which contributions were collected. The box was surrounded by the pictures of the organization's founders, directors, and officials. On Fridays, during the ceremony of welcoming the Sabbath, on the eve of holidays, and on the first day of each Hebrew month, children would, one after another, approach the table on which the blue box stood, slip in small coins, and sing Y. Friedman's song "A Dunam Here, a Dunam There" ("A *dunam* here, a *dunam* there / Three clods of earth, a fourth / So we redeem our nation's land / From Negev to the north") and A. Ashman's song "The Blue Box Anthem" ("A new month has come, a new month has come / This day is sanctified / Let us be happy and rejoice / To the box we give our tithe").[61]

At the Herzliya Gymnasium during the 1940s, a school-wide Sabbath-welcoming ceremony was celebrated in the school auditorium every Friday during the last hour of classes.[62] Each time, a boy or girl was appointed "cantor," or leader of the gathering. He or she would welcome the audience: "Welcome dear teachers, welcome dear parents, let us greet the Sabbath." The children would sing the traditional "Shalom Aleichem" hymn, and the cantor would invite one of the girls to light the candles. First, the girl would put a coin into the JNF box and say, "Sanctified for the redemption of the land, as our mothers did," and then bless the candles. As she lit the candles, all the children would light their own candles on the tables in front of them. One child would read a section from the weekly Torah portion, and in the end they would read "Borchi Nafshi," an early Hebrew nature poem that is part of the traditional Sabbath morning service. In the summers they would also read from the Mishnaic "Pirkei Avot." The ceremony would conclude with the singing of the Zionist anthem, "Ha-Tikva." This common school practice of melding the welcoming of the Sabbath ceremony with the ceremony of contributing to the JNF was another example of how the shapers of Zionist culture and education used elements of Jewish tradition that had motivated Jews for thousands of years to design a new tradition emphasizing Jewish nationalism on a Zionist foundation.

Contributing to the JNF was practiced within the family as well. On birthdays it was customary to contribute a portion, or all, of one's gift money to the JNF. In response, the JNF would send the child a certificate of appreciation, illustrated with pictures of agricultural pioneers at work, which read: "To ———, who has in good time entered his ———th year. You have remembered the JNF on your birthday and have contributed to the redemption of the land. Take this blessing from us: may you grow up into Torah, labor, and good deeds and be a delight to your parents and a blessing to your people. Amen."[63]

For teenagers, the duty to contribute was replaced by the duty to collect contributions. On what was called "ribbon day" (after the paper ribbon with the JNF symbol that the donor would receive), high school students and members of youth movements would position themselves with blue boxes on city streets and solicit passersby. Youth movement members would also empty the blue boxes that hung in public institutions and pass the money on to the JNF. The JNF would, in turn, grant certificates to the best collectors and plant trees in their name. Members of youth movements would paste JNF stamps (whose purchase was also considered a donation) on every outgoing letter and on every notice that appeared on the chapter house bulletin board. Likewise, a self-imposed tax was instituted, collected in the blue box at the beginning of every party.[64] The youth movements maintained a steady correspondence with the JNF on the matter of their contributions. Much of the youth movement's internal correspondence dealt with the issue of JNF contributions, including questions about how much the chapter house had collected and why the chapter house had stopped collecting donations.

The blue box thus became a national charity box and a Zionist sacred object. The important element in the ceremony of donating was not the actual money but rather the active and voluntary participation in building the land and the Israeli nation, symbolized by the blue and white of the box and the map of the country imprinted on it. "The coin that the child gives or that he collects for the redemption of the land is not important in and of itself, . . ." said Menachem Ussishkin, one of the JNF's best-known leaders, "but it is important as a foundation of education— it is not the child who gives to the JNF, but the JNF that gives him . . . a hold on a sublime ideal for all the days of his life."[65]

Contributing to the JNF taught the Sabra to put the noble Zionist ideal above his private needs. Saving for the common future bolstered the Sabra's orientation to a future utopia. When the contribution came from the young person's own money (sometimes the painful surrendering of allowance money or even birthday presents), it tested the expectations that the national collective made of him. This symbolic first sacrifice was meant to develop in the child the willingness to make many other sacrifices that would be demanded of him in the future for the rebirth of the Jewish people. The blue box filled gradually with small coins, not bills, which symbolized for the child the ongoing nature of the redemption of the country and the need to keep contributing to the general good over a long period of time. According to the Zionist ethos, the Land of Israel was "ransomed" coin by coin, "a *dunam* here, a *dunam* there, three clods of earth, a fourth."

The coins that piled up in the blue box also symbolized the partnership and traditional solidarity of all Jews everywhere. Every Jew, even the Jew in the Diaspora, made his modest contribution to help his brothers, thus inscribing another letter in the scroll of Zionist redemption.

The Precept of Tree Planting   The ceremony of planting trees on Tu Be-Shevat, the fifteenth of the Hebrew month of Shevat, was an impressive communal festival that symbolized the conquest of the land and an eternal covenant with the soil of Israel. A small child, dressed in a white shirt, blue pants, and a cloth cap and planting a sapling, was performing the primary precept of making the wilderness bloom. He thus entered the covenant with the land and with the pioneer community.

These tree-planting ceremonies made a powerful impression on young people, and especially on small children. A fourteen-year-old boy living on a kibbutz wrote to his parents in the city:

> Yesterday was the Tu Be-Shevat plantings. It was wonderful. We arranged ourselves in groups. One group went to Sha'ar Ha-Amakim to plant a new vineyard. I was given two three-year-old toddlers—sweet, innocent—and we were the recipients of the sapling in the planting ceremony. They held the sapling with such great respect, with such great appreciation, feeling that they held something precious. We returned crowded and packed together, sweaty and soiled with clods of earth, our song bursting forth, "nevertheless and despite it all."[66]

Offerings to the Zionist Priest   The Festival of the First Fruits—the traditional holiday of Shavu'ot—was a classic example of the integration of ancient Jewish symbols into Zionist ideology. The ceremony was generally held out in the open. The members of the moshava, moshav, or kibbutz would gather in front of a platform decked with bales of hay and agricultural implements. Decorated wagons bearing children and the farm's first fruits would pass by in a procession, and the master of ceremonies would announce each wagon as it passed. The ceremony included the reading of verses from the Torah describing the ancient ceremony of bringing in the first fruits, as well as dances and holiday songs with a Biblical cast to them. The Festival of the First Fruits was the holiday of agricultural produce, expressing Zionism's success in putting down roots and the country's economic growth. The basket, full of the settlement's produce and borne by its children, symbolized the plenty that the Zionist enterprise had brought to the country and to its pioneers and the transformation of the country into "a land flowing with milk and honey."

In the cities, the children in the preschools and schools of the general and labor styles tended a small garden in their playgrounds. On the Festival of First Fruits they and their teachers would bring a basket full of "the fruit of our garden" to the festival organized by the JNF for city and kibbutz children. The children dressed in white and wore garlands of flowers or stalks of grain. (Sometimes, instead of fruits and vegetables, the children brought work they had done—another kind of first fruits.) The ceremony, conducted on a large stage, was generally preceded by a long procession in which the children would march in pairs, joyously singing, with bands and choirs accompanying them along the way.

The link between the JNF and the Festival of First Fruits was not just organizational, but symbolic as well. The ancient rite of bringing the first fruits to the Temple was replaced by the procession with the basket laden with first-harvest produce, and the priest who received the offering was replaced by the priests of pioneerism—the representatives of the Jewish National Fund or the kibbutz and moshav elders.

Expressions of Love for the Homeland

PATRIOTIC RHETORIC

Scholars have noted that in the pre-institutional stage of the development of a religious movement adherents tend to have a single-minded commitment to the creed.[67] This certainly describes the writings of adolescent Sabras. In fact, such commitment to the Zionist national cause is the most salient element of their writing.

Writings on ideological and national issues that appeared in the newsletters of schools, youth movements, the Palmach, and the army, as well as in the letters, songs, prose, and poetry produced by young people, are more numerous than those on any other subject. While no precise count has been made of the subjects appearing in these writings, one figure can serve to illustrate: some half of the 270 poems included in the *Scrolls of Fire* anthology are idealistic works dealing directly or indirectly with topics such as the homeland, the landscape, loss, war, and the Jewish people. While this no doubt derives from the institutional nature of the anthology, it also reflects the inclinations of the young people themselves. The large proportion of nationalist subjects in the writings testifies to their prominence in the consciousness of the Sabra. He devoted himself to the nation just as a believer devotes himself to his religion.

The experiences related in many of the writings are placed not just in a personal context but also within the context of the nation and the movement. The internal prism unites with the national prism. So, for example, a Palmachnik wrote to a comrade:

> Our land is fair and there is nothing to be ashamed of. I have decided with Philon that we will open a sanatorium on a hill next to the Hatzbani [Creek] and we have made great plans—undoubtedly it will capture the hearts of the patients. . . . Gritting our teeth and choking back tears, we eulogize our fallen comrades.[68]

The sentence about the nation (the beauty of the homeland) precedes the sentence about the personal (the aspiration to build a sanatorium), and that is immediately followed by another sentence about the nation (loss and its national implications). Another Sabra expressed in his diary his sense of guilt for being too involved in his private, quotidian matters—

like a religious believer whose conscience is tortured because he does not serve his God with sufficient devotion:

> I was examining my diary today and I saw the view of the individual— memories of private events—while the national historical background is almost entirely lacking! Where is that background? It is sunk deep in my heart— and where is it? Why is it not visible in this notebook? . . . I will now correct this imbalance and write about enlistment and those who evade it, about the death of Ussishkin and the death of Brandeis, about the wars of Russia. . . . Why should I not write about these things in my diary? These facts are history and will always be remembered, while the details of individuals go astray and get lost in oblivion. Get lost and vanish.[69]

THE IDEOLOGICAL CHORUS

Sabra writings are similar not only in their content—their preoccupation with ideological and national issues—but also in their style. This is especially obvious in letters, particularly in the letters of young people from kibbutzim and moshavim. The stylistic resemblance—up to and including the use of precisely the same words—is so great that it sometimes seems as if a single person wrote them all.

The similarity among Sabra writings extends to what is left out— criticism, sarcasm, despair, and doubt. True, with regard to the lack of criticism, one has to take into account the young age of some of the writers and the filtering of the texts through editors or family members before their publication. However, comparison with original letters gives the impression that there was very little filtering on an ideological basis and that most of the deletions were aimed at respecting the privacy of the people involved. Even in the internal publications of youth movement chapters and agricultural training groups, where the discourse was freer, as well as in diaries written for the desk drawer and in letters to acquaintances, friends, and lovers, it is hard to find expressions of discontent or questioning of the principles of Zionist ideology, the duty of national service, or the actions of the political establishment.

The same is true in the literary creations of the Sabras preserved in archives (largely in the kibbutzim), some of which were published in the memorial anthologies. Here and there one can find expressions of dissatisfaction with local social phenomena—often the waste of resources— or with the establishment for not being aggressive enough toward the Arabs or the British. But expressions of nonconformism and anti-establishment discontent are almost completely absent, and there is certainly no challenge to the principles of Zionism, such as doubts about the duty to serve in the army, the moral right to the country, or the confiscation of home and land from the Arabs.

The almost complete absence of criticism of the Zionist program or how it should be accomplished testifies not only to the second generation's profound identification with Zionist ideals, but also to their reluctance to challenge them. Any expression of doubt would have been considered heresy. One may suppose that Zionist values received the force of a holy writ and had a kind of absolute validity for the Sabra elite, as if they were the Ten Commandments and thus inviolable.

This unitary voice in the youth media both reflected and reinforced the homogeneity of thinking in that period. (It was most likely bolstered not only by editors at newspapers and publishing houses in their selection of material for publication, but also by the young people themselves, who read each other's works.) The uniformity of expression formed an ideological chorus, where the vocal and emotional power of the common voices hid and masked the voice of the doubting individual. The common ideological subject drew everyone together; the common voice created a generational "stream of consciousness" that expressed the common pulse of a collective mobilizing itself as a single body to achieve common goals. The poem, stories, compositions, letters, and diaries published in the memorial anthologies, in the general press, in internal newsletters, and in the young literature became something like an oral law or an idealistic colloquy that again and again defined and reinforced a common identity.

SABRA WRITERS AS PUBLIC CLARIONS

Unity of idea and of style is also evident in the literary works by well-known Sabra writers and poets.[70] Most of them, with a few exceptions, depicted an Israeli reality with which they identified ideologically and were involved emotionally. They were strongly influenced by—and indeed often imitated—the preceding generation of Zionist writers and also the heroic and idealistic American and European, especially Russian, literature that the previous generation had translated into Hebrew.[71] With just a handful of exceptions, there is almost no social irony or ideological criticism in the prose of the younger generation, and only minimal anarchistic and anti-establishment elements. "Everything is right and clear, and there is no place for conflict and for upsetting the balance," wrote literary scholar and critic A. B. Yaffe as early as 1950 on the works of the Sabra writers.

In the 1950s, as the Sabra writers matured, the homogeneity of their works declined and complexity as well as criticism increased. But as regards ideological orientation, Yaffe's statement applies for these years as well. Not only is it difficult to find any challenge to the ruling ideology, there is also little evidence of doubt about the wisdom of the country's leaders. "This is a literature that sought to be non-Oedipal, which tried to describe a kind of ideal relation between the generations," wrote Gershon Shaked. "The conflicts of the protagonists are among themselves or between them and their times more than they are between them and their fathers."[72]

This literature was commonly a documentary-journalistic reflection of Jewish life in the Land of Israel, in particular the life of the veteran Ashkenazi elite. (The style was influenced a great deal by Hemingway's novels, which were popular at that time.) The Israeli experience is generally described against the backdrop of armed conflict with the Arabs and the British, and from the Jewish point of view. The stories are not shallow or vulgar in their form and content, despite the relatively young age of the writers; their language is rich, mature, and polished, even if highly ornate and overly literary. However, these youthful works have a kind of emotional sterility and an overdose of the author's self-conscious choice of words, granting them an almost slogan-like quality. A methodical reading reveals a nearly uniform linguistic and moral code according to which the plots and protagonists are crafted (principally in the war stories written after 1948). The writers examine reality through a single interpretive prism. The stories are schematic and provide little to surprise, amaze, or anger the reader. Plots are typically straightforward and contain no suspense-creating tension, no apprehension, and no small ironies. The comic relief that appears here and there is generally of the Palmach buddy-humor type.

This serious atmosphere is characteristic of all Sabra writing, not just that intended for publication. The same is found in the stories and poems not published in literary platforms (those published in *Scrolls of Fire* and in private memorial anthologies, or never published) and in letters to family and friends. The seriousness of these private writings was, of course, a product of existential anxiety and sorrow over the death of relatives and comrades. Yet it was also a manifestation of the solemnity and weightiness characteristic of religious and ideological societies.

Sabra literature does not have much of a psychological dimension, perhaps in part because of the spirit of the times. Most of the writing is highly realistic, although not anthropological; it does not aim to simplify reality and provide profound expression of the inner workings of the individual. In most of the stories only the "upper layer" of the protagonists' souls is described, and the dialogues between the characters are in many cases somewhat artificial and schematic and reflect collective modes of thinking. This characteristic is so prominent in the literature of 1948 that many literary critics in Israel commented on it immediately.

The literature of the 1948 generation is similar, in this sense, to the institutional journalistic writing that preceded the "new journalism." Reality is generally described not from a cold and intellectual or bemused distance, but as the report of a committed journalist who identifies emotionally and ideologically with the event he is describing and with the participants in it.

The protagonists in many of the stories (especially the war stories) are stereotypical Sabra fighters—upright, with limitless devotion to their people and their comrades, serious in their views, but facile in their colloquialism. The tragedy in their characters is an "institutionalized" tragedy—that of people forced to sacrifice their lives in the struggle for independence and to proudly pay the price of the national revival. It is not a tragedy that comes out of the evil in man, out of alienation, or out of internal conflict. Their suffering generally reflects collective, not personal and intimate, suffering. They are not all charismatic commanders like Uri, the protagonist of Moshe Shamir's *He Walked in the Fields,* yet even the marginal figures are for the most part "good and dedicated boys" whose heroism and altruism are revealed at the moment of truth in battle and after their preordained deaths, as the genre requires.

The War of Independence itself, which was bloody, is for the most part described from an idealistic perspective rather than a critical or psychological one. The descriptions of the war include neither rejoicing over the defeat and humiliation of the enemy nor victorious exultation and militarism, no songs of glory or praises of the heroes of battle (the same is also true of the soldiers' letters home from the front). On the contrary, the emphasis is on loss and grief. The justice of the war and utter identification with the Jewish collective in its battle struggle are axiomatic. Yet, though the loss and pain that the war produces is the central axis of many of the stories, the writers do not touch on the war's traumatic side—the fears, the sense of helplessness, the uncertainty, the doubts and hesitations that a traumatic event generally wakens.[73]

In their repression of emotions and lack of openness the writers are a faithful mirror of their generation. The same repression is evident in the letters the Sabra fighters sent home from the front (this includes unpublished letters and letters written by Sabra volunteers in the British army who witnessed horrifying human suffering). They wrote little—and generally did not write at all—about the experience of the war, even though between the lines it is frequently clear that their hearts were churning from what they had seen.

Whereas in the stories the ideological dimension is mostly implicit, the works of the Sabra poets and songwriters (most prominently, Chaim Guri, Zerubavel Gilad, O. Hillel, Shlomo Tanai, Didi Manosi, and Chaim Cheffer) display ideology overtly and explicitly. Moreover, while a majority of the stories are based on the personal experiences of the young writers, the poems and songs deal largely with ideas—mostly Jewish and Zionist ones. Critic and scholar Shalom Kramer wrote of the typical Sabra poet that he "is happy in the revelation of nature in the homeland, in the building of the settlement, and especially in the conquests of the Hebrew village in general and of the kibbutz in particular, and beyond this he joins himself in his body and soul to these achievements." Especially to the point are Kramer's words on the primary message in Sabra poems: "the feeling that you live not as an individual alone but as a nation and that your strength increases along with its strength."[74]

The stylistic similarity among the poets is even greater than that among the prose writers, the central reason being the decisive influence of the Hebrew poets, whose poetry was studied and recited in the schools (Bialik, Chernikovsky, Zalman Schneur, S. Shalom, Yitzchak Lamdan, Yonatan Ratosh, Leah Goldberg, Avraham Shlonsky, and others) and especially the influence of Natan Alterman, who was much admired by the younger generation.[75] "Most of the generation's poets were decisively influenced by Alterman," commented Ziva Shamir, a scholar of Hebrew literature and poetry, "and there was almost no young poet who was not 'accused' of dragging Altermanian norms into his poetry."[76]

This "mobilized realism" in both poetry and prose is founded on the Sabra writers' emotional identification with the object of their writing (the Zionist organizations) and on their actual participation in the Zionist culture they wrote about. But it also derived from the overt and covert expectations that were, in a sense, hung around the neck of the young writer of the 1948 generation by the directing hand of ideology.

The complaint that the Sabra writers and poets suffered from a "castration of fancy" can be explained by the fact that during a revolutionary period reality casts a shadow over imagination and to a certain extent paralyzes it. This has a sociological reason. In a revolutionary period, when the individual is called on to lend a hand to the national effort and to make an impact on reality, imagination is interpreted as escape and selfish detachment, or as preoccupation with the unimportant and neglect of the important. The community implicitly forbids the individual to travel off into his inner being and encourages him to suppress his spiritual side, his imagination, and his distress, out of fear that he will detach himself from the general cause and perhaps even sweep others away with him. The individual is required to internalize the external world and to become one with it.

Such aversion to and fear of the world of the imagination and the inner world of the individual recall the fears that traditional religions have of psychological probing. Religion, including national religion, seeks to trace out an internally coherent world, not a world of contradictions and doubts. (This is almost certainly the reason that what is called the post-Zionist era is characterized by a tendency to psychologism.) Moreover, even though religion is built on mystical foundations, it fears the forces of metaphysics—or at least a different metaphysics from the one it proposes—because fancy, imagination, and individualistic thinking are liable to present the ideal in a distorted mirror or to confront it with other ideals, and so to fracture conventions and even lead, God forbid, to apostasy. For this reason, traditional Judaism treats kabbalistic mysticism with great caution. According to tradition, entry into the "forbidden grove" is permitted only to elders of strong faith. Young people are warned against dealing with the supernatural, lest they become "others."

Apparently, then, at the foundation of the young writers' and poets' aversion to critical writing was not only the threatening shadow of the fathers and the institutional supervision of the literary doorkeepers—the editors of the literary periodicals—but also the fear that critical writing would weaken their society, which was caught up in a struggle for its very existence.

THE SONG OF SONGS OF DANI AND URI

The Sabras frequently wrote personal testimonies of events of importance to the nation. The writing is almost always warm, enthusiastic, and sensitive to the pulse of life in the country. Expressions of patriotism appear in intimate letters to lovers, siblings, and parents, and in personal diaries. This shows that these patriotic expressions were spontaneous and sincere, for in these private communications there was no need for pretense. The nationalist sentiment they contain is no weaker than in the public and official organs, and perhaps is even stronger. One Sabra wrote in a letter to his mother from the outpost where he was stationed: "As for the vision—after all, a genuine and good Zionist is founded on 'inner fervor,' 'a Jewish heart,' and so on. May we all be blessed with these."[77]

The force of the Sabra's national feeling is also reflected in the high frequency with which the word "homeland" is used in Sabra texts, and especially in the warmth and fervor of its use: "There is no man too good to die for the homeland. However, many do not have the privilege of such a death. Whatever the case—if the Land of Israel is in danger, I want to defend it with my life!"[78] This outburst of patriotism, quoted from a Sabra's private diary, is not exceptional. Similar ones abound. Also numerous are declarations of loyalty to the beloved native land, like: "To you have we sworn we shall defend / All within you fully / O homeland, we shall defend / So long as blood flows through our veins."[79]

Personification of the homeland also stands out in Sabra texts. The homeland is likened to a mother or a lover—imageries whose source is European and which characterized the works of the Second and Third Aliyot poets. One Sabra wrote: "Please stretch out your hand / O Motherland / Hold us close / Strongly / And we, your builders, your sons / To whom suffering is known / Those who hate you we know / To repel."[80] Or, in the passionate lyrics of a lover: "My love, my homeland / I admire all in you / Of homelands the smallest / For you my arms have strained / My blood and my vigor are my gifts for you."[81]

Comparing such compositions with the Bible's Song of Songs is unavoidable. It should be recalled that the Song of Songs was interpreted by the sages—even if their interpretation was forced—as a love song between the Jewish people and their God. Certainly, the erotic metaphors of the writings point to the Sabra's deep emotional attachment to his country.

The Sabras' written language is full of pioneer words and slogans. "Privilege," "homeland," "we shall be worthy," "the greatness of the hour," "it has fallen as the fate of our generation," "the people Israel," and other such expressions are common—especially in the pieces written for the newsletters of the kibbutz youth societies and youth movement chapter houses. Yet they also appear in letters and in birthday cards.

This idealistic and patriotic vocabulary, full of explicit and implicit exclamation points, is most notable in the many poems published by Sabras in literary periodicals and youth movement newsletters, or found in drawers and knapsacks after the deaths of the authors and then published in private memorial booklets and in *Scrolls of Fire*. In fact, the very inclination of the Sabras to write poetry testifies to the idealistic fire that burned in their chests. Pioneer coinages are indeed common in many Sabra poems, and the Sabras seem not to have declaimed such expressions merely by rote, but rather to have used them in outbursts of sentiment, as from believers' hearts overflowing with waters from the spring of faith. Clearly, not only the high language of these ideological messages but also their emotional content was instilled in the Sabras and, it may be said, became part of the language of the Sabra soul.

Spurring readers to action for the nation is also common in Sabra texts, especially those written by counselors and commanders. Sometimes these have the character of revivalist calls patched together from the usual Zionist slogans. They contain the guidance and direction of those who have seen the light of the (Zionist) faith and wish to pass it on to others, or of those who feel obligated to impel others to follow in their footsteps. A soldier wrote in a letter to his friend: "I hope that you, too, will join those who will make up the ranks of the fighters. Remember always, that there is no heroism—there is only the national duty. Goodbye!"[82]

Reproof and chastisement are directed at those whose ideological faith has become a bit weak (these are not, of course, cases of apostasy but only signs of indifference, or "low spirits"—such as anxiety and melancholy). Such words appear in some of the letters to the newsletters and periodicals and also in more personal letters. For example, a Sabra rebuked his girlfriend, apparently for having expressed sadness at his absence, because weakness did not befit the hour:

> It is not right at all that you are feeling bad. You need to know how to control yourself. I must tell you that even I have felt bad, but now, since the matters with the Arabs began, that is, since the Hebrew state came into being, there is no place for feeling bad. I know and understand that my place now is not at home, but in the place they determine for me, and I must not make special requests or complain. It seems to me that you should also feel as I do. It is necessary, necessary that I not be at home, even if it is hard, even if it is very hard.[83]

The letters also reveal the authors' feeling that theirs is a momentous era and that it is their great privilege to live in such times. "Sons are we to a savage storm / A stage on which a land will form / In days of dread and winds that rage / We are born—this is the age,"[84] says one writer, and another reflects: "When I think of the years that have gone by, of the years that are to come, and of the present era that I live in, pride flashes within me for being privileged to live in this time."[85]

One of the linguistic codes that testifies to the sense of intoxication and the idealistic enthusiasm and commitment that characterized the

Sabras is the different forms of the word *hagshama,* as both a noun and a verb, that appear again and again in Sabra writings. Translated from the German word for a concept adopted from German culture, *hagshama*[86] carried a much larger set of connotations than its simple dictionary definition—"realization" or "consummation"—would imply. It functioned as a common code expressing idealistic commitment and the emotional satisfaction of fulfilling a mission. It combined the realization of a dream or ideal, that is, the actualization of a utopian idea, with self-realization or self-actualization—a melding of the individual and public domains. For the Sabras, *hagshama* was transformed from an abstract noun to a concrete noun referring to specific actions, as if the action itself (joining an agricultural settlement) and the content of that action *(hagshama)* had become one. This unification of action and meaning was so routine that no one gave it any thought. The Sabra would say, "I am going to *hagshama,*" just as he might say, "I am going to Haifa."

STRIVING TO SURPASS
THE PIONEERS' EXPECTATIONS

Many Sabra fighters, especially those from kibbutzim and moshavim, express in their letters a strong identification with the world of their parents, teachers, and leaders, and an admiration for the generation of the founders. This is especially notable in the letters of the sons and students of pioneer leaders.

Most of the letters to parents that were published in memorial anthologies and preserved in archives were written with great seriousness and high pathos. This style derives, very likely, from the distance between parents and children that was the norm at that time. But there seems to be something else as well—a desire not to disappoint the parents, to meet their high expectations in everything connected to what was dearest to them—*hagshama*. A characteristic example is a letter written by Chaim Ben Dor, then fourteen years old—a city child who had been sent to school at Kibbutz Yagur:

Dear Parents!

I am proud that I am already an adult. I am fully alive, happy and joyous, sad and depressed from different things. I feel happy that the yoke of the general good has been laid on me, or more precisely, that I have placed the yoke of the general good on my own back and bear it. And I scorn, as it were, or pity my friends who are older than me and do not sense how much young people need energy and desire to bear the yoke. For me, happiness is concern, not unconcern. Perhaps in the course of time the concern will be difficult, but now . . . I desire, as they say, to put myself at the service of my people and land and the world and the workers and everything, so that I can fix and renew things.[87]

Many of the Sabras express in their writings the sense that the previous generation is putting them to a great test. They aspire with all their souls and might not only to avoid disappointing their parents and to meet the test, but also to exceed their expectations. The explanation for this lies again in the similarity between total ideology and religion. In the ideological system, as in the religious system, the son turning away from his parents' values is not interpreted as excessive independence or tolerable rebelliousness, but as a serious emotional wound to the parents—as if spitting into the well from which they have given him water to drink each day. Every parent has great hopes that his child will aspire to and realize his expectations; but in the framework of a religion—and what we have here, it should be remembered, is a secular religion—founded on a rigid and conservative system of values, the expectations may well be stronger and so may be passed on to the child in a more assertive way. Religious parents want their child to follow in their footsteps and thus implicitly validate and confirm their own path in life. The Sabra children responded to this expectation with all their heart.

THE SABRA'S SENSE
OF NATIONAL RESPONSIBILITY

A profound sense of responsibility pervades the letters of Sabra soldiers. They neither expressed the weariness of the draftee nor complained about the length of their service or the conditions they endured. Nor did they write much of personal matters. These soldiers did not feel like simple enlisted men who have nothing in the world but their trench and the next furlough. (While there were cases of desertion and evasion of service in the Palmach, they were marginal and were severely condemned.)[88] The tone of the disgruntled soldier can be found only here and there in the letters of recruits in the British army during World War II, who sometimes expressed alienation and severe disappointment at the missions they had been assigned and at their distance from events in Palestine. The letters depict, for the most part, soldiers with a sense of moral obligation and mission, willing and anxious to serve above and beyond the call of duty. This profound sense of national responsibility is expressed in the letter of Elad Peled (then a squad commander in the

Palmach) to his parents. He wrote in response to a letter from them on the occasion of his nineteenth birthday, in which they had implored him to begin thinking about some "purpose" to his life:

> I have done a kind of personal inventory on my birthday . . . if I am today in my [proper] place and am fulfilling what a Hebrew boy in this country must do then I have a great deal to thank you for. . . . Very likely if it were not for you I would be somewhere else and doing something else. . . . I am asking myself: Is this a purpose? Do I not regret it? And I respond with certainty: No with a capital N. . . . And when we are fathers and our sons ask us: "Father, what did you do then in those terrible days?" then we will have to give an answer. . . . And it will be good for the father who will tell his son that his place then was in the front line and he stood bodily everywhere [needed]. . . . I have no regrets about any of my actions. I think that I am doing what I must do. If you could only see the enthusiasm and dedication and comradeship that prevails among us who are in action.[89]

It seems reasonable to assume that the sense of personal responsibility expressed in many of the Sabra letters that I examined, most of which were written by soldiers who fell in battle, is partly due to the relatively large proportion of officers and junior officers among those who fell. It is evident, however, that this feeling does not derive only from their positions but is deeply rooted within them and grows out of profound concern for the fate of the besieged people and state. One member of the ranks, not a commander, wrote to his girlfriend: "Dear L! [I received your letter.] The picture is more or less clear. It is hard to accept the fact that all these are gone from us. We must be strong despite the great pain. We have no need for concern. We will withstand the test."[90]

The Sabra soldier's sense of personal responsibility also grew out of the objective experience of a fateful engagement. This was an unavoidable war, one in which the Yishuv had its back to the wall. It is clear from the soldiers' letters that they truly felt that they were carrying their nation on their shoulders and that their success or failure in battle would determine whether the nation would live or die.

The indifference of the world's nations to the murder of millions of Jews in Europe drove home to the Jewish Yishuv in Palestine that no one would come to their aid in time of trouble and that they could trust only themselves. This further honed the sense of responsibility of the soldiers on the front line. Also crucial is the fact that the War of Independence was the first war in which the Yishuv fought regular Arab armies. Uncertainty as to the fate of the Yishuv amplified the sense of danger, and the soldier at the front felt like the head or representative of a family sent to defend his home and kin. This feeling was magnified because there were women in the combat units on or near the front line, which constantly reminded the soldiers that this was the fight of an entire nation and that their families were close by. Many engagements were fought near or in settlements in Galilee and the Negev and on the streets of many towns and cities, such as Haifa, Safed, Acre, Jerusalem, and Jaffa. The Sabra was fighting not on a distant front or in unknown terrain but within his familiar landscape, and the reason he was fighting was very clear and concrete.

The awareness among the young commanders that they were fighting a defensive war to save their own homes was no doubt one of the reasons for the great popularity of the book *Panpilov's Men,* which portrays the dogged Russian defense of Leningrad.[91] We may assume that this feeling was also the source of the Israeli army's official name, the "Israel Defense Forces."

VOLUNTEERISM AND SABRA SELF-ESTEEM

In the Zionist religion, volunteerism became one of the fundamental criteria according to which a person was judged not only by society but also by himself. Writings reveal that willingness and ability to sacrifice oneself for the nation, especially in military service, became a personal standard of value, a mirror in which a Sabra compared himself to others. This sense of being constantly tested externally and internally, of struggling between the id of everyday desires and the superego of the ideal is especially notable among kibbutz-bred Sabras. Their observance of the precepts of the secular religion—to which were added the socialist commandments of the communal ideal—was especially strict. Such constant concern over the proper observance of strictures is also characteristic of the pious religious believer.

The cultural mirror in which the typical Sabra examined himself included not only the abstract values of Zionist doctrine but also, and perhaps especially, the judgment and response of his environment to his actions as a soldier and as a member of his commune or movement. Along with the enjoyment that the pious idealist derives from his devotion, one can also read between the lines the gratification that the Sabra felt in terms of the status and honor he received from his service (especially during the early days of the IDF), and the dread of the reproach, disdain, and discomfort that were the lot of those who did not live up to society's expectations.

Many members of the 1948 generation whom I interviewed provided examples of this. Nachman Raz of Kibbutz Geva told me that during the war the leaders of his youth movement pleaded with him to continue to work as a counselor in the Ha-Machanot Ha-Olim movement in Tel Aviv. But being in the rear when so many were fighting, even though he was performing a mission important to his movement and to the nation, caused him great embarrassment and distress, and this only became worse after the war ended. He was especially bothered by the fact that his charges fought and were even killed while he remained in Tel Aviv. "For many years," he related, "I bore in my heart a sense of shame and deprivation and found myself apologizing again and again—even though I had no real reason to do so—to those younger than me." Tzipi Dagan, of the Regavim *hachshara,* related that during the war she worked with members of the group on weapons manufacture. Even though she knew that their work contributed to the war effort, and even though she and her friends worked under extremely harsh conditions and with great dedication, for years after the war ended she dreaded to tell people what she had done and was ashamed to admit that she had not been in one of the units fighting at the front.

As in every society fighting for its very existence, great renumerations were awarded in the coin of personal prestige for actions taken for the general good—especially when they involved sacrifice and risk, while condemnation of and contempt for those who avoided national service reached high levels. The natural inclination to seek prestige and social recognition was channeled in altruistic directions—particularly toward taking part and excelling in battle. Military volunteerism thus rose not only out of idealism but also out of the aspiration to enter the social trajectory that would bring the highest reward. This aspiration became much more intense after the founding of the state and of the IDF.

The combination of the sense of duty to excel in public service (primarily in the military) and the desire to win the recognition of the community is characteristic of charismatic Sabra figures of the memorial anthologies, such as Jimmy the Palmachnik and the early paratroopers Yermi Bardenov and Gulliver. The wish to take part in every combat action, not to miss any excitement, and to receive the most dangerous and challenging combat assignment was common to the biographies of many Sabra fighters, especially the commanders, even in later generations. Many are described as battle-hungry, huddling in their coats next to the unit headquarters waiting for an assignment. This is especially notable in the early 1950s, with the beginning of the retaliation operations commanded by Ariel Sharon. So badly did they want to participate in the "male experience" that brought them prestige that sometimes they took turns: "If you were on one operation, then you had to give up your place in the next operation to your comrade."[92]

THE MEANING OF DEATH
FOR THE SABRA SOLDIER

The idealism of the Sabra reached its height during the War of Independence. By 25 June 1948 a total of 1,432 Jewish soldiers had fallen in the war. Of these, 451, or 31.5 percent, were from the Palmach, yet the Palmach's manpower in that period comprised no more than 20 percent of the total forces of the Haganah and the IDF.[93] In the end, one out of every four fighters who fell during the war were from the Palmach, and 3,000 Palmachniks were wounded. Among the IDF commanders, most of whom matched the Sabra profile, the proportion of casualties was even higher. The high number of casualties gave a dark cast to the letters sent home from the front by Sabra fighters. The sense that death was lurking everywhere also appears in their diaries and even in the poems found among their papers. One of them secretly wrote:

> It is so clear that I will see the end:
> The dawn will smile (it always smiles, each day),
> But what of that, if I now imagine
> It telling me hello a final time?
> The dawn is smiling and it seems to me,
> Is it so very horrible to die?[94]

In not a few letters—especially among those written before the first cease-fire, which began on 11 June 1948—the writer seems to actually "know" that he is next in line, because of the high losses in his unit. So, for example, one Palmachnik wrote:

> We're so many in the platoon, the company, the battalion. A given amount of time has gone by since the first one fell. It follows that a certain number fall during a certain amount of time. The logical and clear conclusion is this: after a given time, which can be estimated in advance, we will join those who have gone.[95]

Even though the soldiers knew they had every chance of dying, fear of losing their lives did not affect their willingness to continue to bear the yoke, as is evidenced by a letter from a soldier to his girlfriend:

> Today—our role in life demands of us complete willingness to give up our lives. . . . Your letter took me out of my mood of accepting the necessity of

dying. I will try to overcome the yearning for life that your letters awaken in me. But today the thought of life and the fear of death are, in my opinion, luxuries that we cannot afford.

The letter concludes with a chilling resignation to fate:

> We need the clear recognition that we must be the vanguard, that there is no doubt as to our future; the question is only when and where. And any desire to flee this fate is only an insult to the right of those who are already on the other side of that boundary.[96]

The very appearance of this letter in the Palmach newsletter during the war testifies that it reflects that generation's attitude toward death. A certain resignation to death is evident not only in what is included in the Sabra letters but also in what is absent from them. Nowhere in the internal publications, the diaries, or the letters—even the most personal ones, which were not published in the memorial anthologies—did I find any challenge by the Sabras to the horrible personal price they had to pay, nor any reservations about the meaning of life in a "land that devours its young people."[97] On the contrary, when the cost in blood is mentioned, it is described not as meaningless, the result of blind fate, but as the price to be paid for a higher purpose.

Even when death struck mercilessly at family, acquaintances, and friends, the firm Zionist faith of the fighting Sabra was not shaken. A letter written by a member of an agricultural training group to her parents about the death of her boyfriend in battle does not remonstrate at her bitter fate, but rather bolsters the spirits of her parents and comforts them. This phenomenon of comforting and encouraging parents appears again and again in the letters:

> Is all well with you? It is hard for me to write because the pain has not left my heart, and my soul still bewails the catastrophe that has befallen us. Have you heard? Our Yehudele has fallen. . . . I still do not know all the details. But one thing is clear to me: Yehuda died a hero's death and knew why he went and to what he devoted all his strength and energy. . . . My dear parents, the loss is difficult for all of us, but for me doubly—and I have one request of you: be strong and do not cry much. He was one of many and the role he filled requires us to continue to follow in his footsteps. Be strong and of good courage! See, this is the request of your daughter, whose boyfriend it was who fell.[98]

Clearly, for the Sabra, martyrdom for the homeland was parallel, in many ways, to martyrdom for God. The demand to make a sacrifice, even of one's life, for saving the nation was considered a legitimate demand, and combat service was considered not only a duty but a great privilege. "I think that all who were with us that night on Mt. Canaan will never forget us," said Elad Peled of the conquest of Safed:

> That Friday night, the fifteenth of April 1948, when the entire company stood for inspection under the spotlights in the large cinema auditorium, I walked along and selected the thirty-five men who would set out with me a short time later to besieged Safed. All of us knew, even though we did not say it out loud, that there was a chance that we would never return. Nevertheless, I will never forget the gazes of the company's soldiers as I walked past them to decide "he will go" or "he will not go." I am sure that many of those whom I did not choose have never forgiven me. The initiative, the volunteerism, even at the price of death, was an unquestioned rule of behavior.[99]

The scribbled wills that many fallen soldiers left in envelopes addressed to their parents, girlfriends, or wives, inscribed "to be opened if I do not return," tell the story of the young fighters' complete willingness to pay the highest price and to go toward their deaths with complete resignation and without protest. One of the wills reads: "My going was necessary and inevitable; I did not go at the behest of outsiders but consciously, myself. After all, it was you who educated me to this. . . . To suffer? No matter. To die? No matter."[100]

These wills very likely created a social dynamic of their own and encouraged other Sabras to leave such notes in the same spirit to their loved ones. The most famous will of this type was found among the papers of Noam Grossman. He wrote: ". . . my salary and the compensation my family receives—for the establishment of a fund to buy rifles for the organization. . . . Do not eulogize me—I did my duty!"[101] The simple words, expressing devotion and humility, were quoted several times by eulogizers in memorial anthologies, and by Zionist leaders, including Ben-Gurion. Grossman's words were perceived as a continuation of Trumpeldor's renowned "It is good to die for our country." They became a symbol of the Sabra generation's unreserved loyalty and represented the passing of the torch of heroism from the first to the second generation. The death of friends reinforced the Zionist ideal by making it a matter of conscience for those remaining to continue to bear the yoke—to preserve the values for which blood was let and young lives cut off.

Zionist idealism and patriotism were not hurt by the deaths of the fighters, but actually became stronger and more determined. This dialectic of loss exists in many religions, including Judaism. In the Kaddish memorial prayer recited over the open grave, the mourners do not lash out at God but rather praise him—"May his great name be magnified and sanctified." In this way, the Jewish religion turns a purposeless and meaningless death (and every death, when it comes down to it, is meaningless) into something meaningful, something that brings psychological healing to the family of the dead person. Similarly, the idealism of the Zionist religion served as a mechanism of comfort, mostly via the culture of memorialization. Faith in the Zionist destiny granted meaning to random and cruel death in battle. The soldiers died in the name of Zionist ideals, and at the same time the ideal endowed death with moral value.

CHAPTER 2

The Elect Son of the Chosen People

The Myth of the Chosen People

Most if not all religions implant within the devotee the belief that he is
"chosen"—one of God's elect on earth. His faith makes him worthy of
being counted among the "children" of the "great father," and in the
case of a national religion, among the members of a holy nation with a
universal mission. Whereas elitism is one of the elements of most religious systems, in Judaism it is perhaps the central one. The verse "For
thou art a holy people to the Lord thy God, and the Lord has chosen
thee to be a special possession to himself, out of all the nations that are
upon the earth" (Deut. 14:2) is one of many in the Jewish canon that illustrate this conception. The belief that the Jewish people, as a nation,
have been chosen by God and given a destiny and a mission is fundamental to Judaism and is inherent in concepts such as "the chosen
people." Psychologically, for Jews, the term "Jew" denotes a member of
the nation that has been chosen from among the other nations.[1]

Zionism's founding fathers, most of whom were at least partly educated in the values of traditional Judaism, considered themselves chosen
not because of their Jewish identity, but instead, because Zionism was a
unique movement with a universal mission. From Zionism's inception
many Zionist ideologues dreamed of the establishment of not only a national home for the Jews but also an exemplary society that would be a
light to other nations. "Zionism will never cease being a vision, even when

we gain the Land of Israel, our homeland," Theodor Herzl wrote, "since Zionism, as I conceive it, is not only the aspiration for a free and safe refuge for our poor nation, but also includes the aspiration for moral and spiritual perfection."[2] Many leaders of the Zionist movement concurred. "Our enterprise is not solely a national enterprise," Nachman Syrkin wrote, for example. "We wish to revive the Jewish people and establish, in the Holy Land, a high place for the entire human race."[3]

Among the pioneers of the Second and Third Aliyot, who adhered to the vision of a socialist utopia, the ideal of an exemplary Jewish society had a concrete meaning—the creation of a just society based on the Marxist principles of equality and brotherhood. Both openly and by implication, their writings express the feeling that they were a small band of the elect who had been granted enlightenment and who had taken it upon themselves to lead a historic social revolution. "From our very beginnings the awareness throbbed within us that we were the emissaries of a poor nation. . . ," wrote Berl Katznelson. "We believed that the labor movement was created for great things; we felt the wind of greatness and learned to extend lines that linked the smallest of our actions to the greatest ones in the distance."[4] The term "pioneer" itself, perhaps more than other terms, expressed the elitist identity of the Zionist settlers.

This sense of social superiority particularly permeated the kibbutz movement, which considered itself the leading cultural force in the Yishuv and a form of society that, while not great in numbers, was superior to every other society known to mankind. The kibbutz practice of documenting every last detail of the community's life, the intensive preoccupation with community history, the glorification of the achievements of the founders and their children, the common use of the first-person plural ("our farm," "our children"), all testified to the movement's sense of purpose and perception of its own uniqueness.

The belief that the Jews were a chosen people and that this status had enabled them to survive the tribulations of their history was inculcated into the Sabra's education. From preschool through grade school, in the youth movements, and during military service, the Sabra was taught the myth of chosenness. Through textbooks, stories, and songs he learned to see himself as the scion of an ancient, exceptional nation whose story was etched in the pages of human history. The author of one textbook, *Figures and Events in Our History,* wrote in the first chapter, "The Eternal People":

> The existence of the Hebrew nation throughout the generations is one of the wonders of human history. We are members of the eternal people. Egypt, As-

syria, and Babylonia, the Canaanites, Tyre and Sidon, Persia and Media, Greece and Rome—all the ancient peoples of great repute who gloried in their power are lost and gone, but our nation endured seven circles of agony in the shadow of three powers and remains young. . . . The history of our people shines with deeds and creativity that give it a place of honor in the community of nations. The Hebrew nation was more wondrous in ancient days than all the nations that encompassed it.[5]

The effects of this education were soon felt. The idea that the Jewish people were a chosen people, destined to be a light to all nations, penetrated deeply into the hearts of the young and took up residence there, as can be seen in their compositions and letters. For example, a student at the Herzliya Gymnasium wrote:

For this is the nation that has produced great heroes, zealous for freedom, and from whom rose prophets who prophesied the rule of justice and honesty in the world—because this nation is a heroic and noble nation and only the bitter and harsh life of Exile debased it, and this nation is still destined to be a light unto the nations. As the prophet said: "For out of Zion will go forth Torah, and the word of the Lord from Jerusalem."[6]

The socialist Zionism of the labor parties, in whose doctrine the children of the agricultural settlements and the socialist youth movements were educated, taught the younger generation to see itself as an elite. The labor Zionist ideal was presented as a new model of Jewish excellence and as a social utopia that should serve as a prototype for others. The children of the settlements learned to perceive their lives as the realization of a sublime ideal of equality and concern for their fellow men, and to see themselves as members of a priestly caste meant to set an example for the Yishuv and for the entire world. This education produced a class snobbery that will be discussed later.

The Jewish struggle against the Arabs, especially in the War of Independence and the Sinai Campaign, reinforced the myth of the chosen people in the Israeli public consciousness and in particular among the Sabras—just as it reinforced the myth of redemption. The victories over an enemy superior in arms and in numbers (or at least so it was perceived) confirmed the moral and qualitative preeminence of the Jewish people and as much as declared that "we are indeed foremost."

The links between religion and holy war, militarism and messianism, and victory and the tribal cult are ancient ones. Victory in war has always been considered a concrete expression of the superiority of the victor's faith and community. The triumph of the conquerors was proof of the power of their patron saint. So too, Israel's victories also received a mystical, messianic interpretation in Israeli culture—even if only by implication—and this confirmed the Sabra's elitist self-image.

The Rejection of the Diaspora

THE SABRA AS A "GENTILE JEW"

Zionism may have been founded primarily to solve the problem of anti-Semitism, but it also grew out of the envy of the gentiles that developed among European Jews during the Enlightenment era, when contacts between Jews and non-Jews became more extensive. The gentile seemed to live an uncomplicated, unsophisticated life that held great appeal for the Jew.[7]

A corollary of this envy was the rejection of the figure of the Diaspora Jew,[8] a rejection sometimes so strong that, paradoxically, it resembled anti-Semitic characterizations of Jews. Traditional religions often create and then vilify a stereotype of values they reject. The religion's sense of superiority is based in part on the condemnation of the "other"—the other generally being heretics or the strongest rival religion. National religions are no different. In the South African national religion, for example, the "other" was black, whereas in the Japanese national religion it was the white race and in the American civil religion it was the Communist.[9] So also, the repudiation of the Diaspora and the Diaspora way of life, and especially the stereotyping of the Diaspora Jew, indirectly sharpened the boundaries of the Zionist national religion and stressed its superiority over traditional Jewish religion.

The forceful rejection of Diaspora culture in order to underscore the superiority of pioneer-Zionist culture is a phenomenon that recalls, in its sociological characteristics, the process that took place between ancient Judaism and Christianity, which grew out of and rejected Judaism. Indeed, as the institutional and spiritual roots of the Zionist religion in Palestine reached deeper, the negation of the Diaspora became more intense. This peaked in the 1930s and 1940s. The common use of the term "Diaspora" (which implied that all the world's Jews were a single entity, without any differences from country to country) in the Yishuv period was the most obvious sign of the conceptual distinction between Zionist Jews living in Palestine and the reprehensible Jews who preferred to live in other countries.

At the center of the anti-Diaspora ethos (which has been widely described and analyzed in the research literature in recent years) was a moral distinction between the Diaspora Jew and the new Jew—the Israeli Jew. This distinction found symbolic linguistic expression in the Yishuv period in the term "Hebrew" (which was really a synonym for "Zionist") and, after the state was founded, in the term "Israeli."[10]

The view that a new and improved breed of Jew had been born in Palestine was also a tool of Zionist propaganda and was deployed by the Yishuv in the Zionist organizations in the Diaspora, especially in Eastern Europe. When Nachman Raz, a young Sabra and one of the leaders of Ha-Noar Ha-Oved, was sent by his movement to an international conference of socialist youth movements held in Poland in 1948, his Jewish hosts there were in awe. Everyone was dazzled at the appearance of this representative of the new breed—a Palestinian Jew. In his journal he wrote:

> Our appearance here was for them a surprise and elicited great interest, especially after they learned that we are not just "regular" people from the Yishuv but "native-born." . . . They looked at us as if we were people not from this world. By the way, we ran into this everywhere among the Jews of Poland. When we were asked how many years we had been in Palestine and our answer was, of course, "we were born there," mouths would gape and people would stare at us in wonder.[11]

ANTI-DIASPORA EDUCATION

Because the anti-Diaspora ethos was central to the Zionist religion, it was promoted in Zionist "houses of study" and soaked up by the Sabra consciousness from a young age. It was taught in school and through textbooks, especially books on Jewish history written in the years 1930 to 1948.[12] The Diaspora Jew was described as the diametric opposite of the pioneer of the Land of Israel and was portrayed along the lines (and to a large extent under the inspiration) of anti-Semitic stereotypes. One textbook, for example, explained: "[The Jews of the Diaspora] became accustomed to fear a driven leaf, began to be unmindful of their dress and their gait; their aesthetic sense degenerated, and they lost all sense of respectable appearance."[13]

Young people were taught the history of European Jewry, both indirectly and directly, as the history of Zionism. Emphasis was placed on the pogroms of modern times, which demonstrated that Jewish life in foreign lands was pointless and that the Jews were blind to the dangers lurking there. Jewish history books provided long descriptions of the physical agonies of the Jewish people, while explicitly and implicitly condemning the Jews as passive victims. One scholar of these textbooks notes that they are remarkable "in the tone of open contempt of the descriptions of the pogroms, to the point that it seems as if the writers identify with the aggressor more than with the victim."[14] "The chapters describing the pogroms," she adds, "create the impression that the writers believed that the Jews of the Diaspora were punished justly for their refusal to acknowledge the truth of Zionism, and they reverberate with the Yishuv's disappointment over the lack of response from Diaspora Jewry to Zionism's call to settle in Palestine."[15]

Contempt for the "Jewboys of the Diaspora," who were described as simple-minded villagers, was steadily fed into Sabra consciousness. The Sabra was educated to see himself as the opposite of the stereotypical Diaspora Jew—as belonging to a better breed of Jews, as a prince of the new Israeli kingdom. He was imbued with the sense that history had assigned him a decisive role in the realization of utopia: the creation of the genius of the new Jew. Admired from all sides, the Sabra assimilated this mythological image of a "more successful Jew," and this reinforced his self-confidence and especially the superior and patronizing attitude he developed toward the Diaspora Jews and toward the new immigrant who had just come from the Diaspora and so still stood for the old Jew.

THE SABRA AS THE HANDSOME YOUNG DAVID

The Zionists greatly admired the physical beauty of the native, the "Jewish gentile" who had been anointed king of the new Israel, and they contrasted him with the ostensible ugliness of the Diaspora Jew. This adulation was evident even during the First Aliya period. Writers of that era—Ze'ev Yavetz, Hemdat Ben-Yehuda, Yehoshua Barzilai Eisenstat—described the native as a robust youth with "gentile" characteristics, a kind of Jewish *muzhik,* or Russian peasant—strapping, self-confident, and strong-spirited, as opposed to the stereotypical Diaspora Jew, who was pale, soft, servile, and cowardly.

Especially prominent in descriptions of the native are his masculine vitality and health and his alienation from Judaism. The criteria are European-Christian ones, which have their source in ancient Greece and Rome: a body that is slender, lithe, sturdy, suntanned, and tall, with a long neck, a head crowned with hair, high cheekbones, a turned-up nose (in contrast to what the anti-Semites called a "Jewish nose"), and a clean-shaven face with Slavic contours (the beard being a Jewish trademark). As early as 1899, Shaul Chernikovsky used the terms of Hellenistic masculine beauty to express this Hebrew ideal in his poem "In the Presence of the Statue of Apollo." [16] The poems of Uri Zvi Greenberg, Alexander Pen, and S. Shalom also portrayed the new Hebrew in the vocabulary of "gentile" male virility and as "the prime human product" of Zionism.

The male beauty attributed to the hero of the mythical culture of the Land of Israel was also characteristic of the heroes of other national religions, such as the German, the Italian, the Soviet, the Japanese, and the American. This standard of beauty is especially notable in the visual arts. In posters and notices put out by the national institutions in Palestine in the 1930s, and in the work of graphic artists, painters, and photographers of the Fifth Aliya, which brought many artists to Palestine, the Sabras are generally sturdy, handsome, and erect men. The image was first modeled after Soviet propaganda posters, which portrayed a stereotypical muscular Soviet laborer; later inspiration was also drawn from Hollywood's leading men, such as Gary Cooper, John Wayne, and Johnny Weismuller. [17]

Envy of the gentiles, the desire to look like them, and the aspiration to produce a new breed of Jew in Palestine were the basis for the great amount of attention the founding generation gave to the physical appearance of the Sabra. So, for example, writes Ya'akov Cohen:

> Many of the elements of our aspiration of seeing a new kind of Jew in our land have been realized in part by [the Sabra]. Your first glance when you meet a young native-born man will reveal a flourishing, muscular, tall body. The hunched back and the bent gait that many scholars have identified as almost racial trademarks seem to have vanished, and the anxiety and fear of the "gentiles" and the feeling of inadequacy and inferiority that were the lot of the young Jew in the Diaspora seem to have been pulled out by the roots. [18]

For the pioneers, the difference between the physical appearance, accent, conversational style, and mode of dress of the first and the second generations was proof of the successful Jewish metamorphosis that had occurred in Palestine. It was a source of great pleasure to them. "I would watch him from the side and think: That's it! Something both new and ancient is emerging, a pure Hebrew type of primeval days," a pioneer wrote in a memorial book for a young man born at Kibbutz Ein Harod. "There was not a trace of the Diaspora in his character. He was like a clod of the homeland's earth in which the fertile forces of abundance are inherent. What perfection and individuality!" [19]

The photographs of the fighters—male and female—that appeared in the memorial literature, the daily press, the periodicals, and the albums were generally of the most handsome and best-built Sabras. These along with verbal depictions made beauty (largely male beauty) into a principal motif in the mythological image of the Sabra for the generations that followed as well.

This is the place to clarify a fundamental point regarding the Sabra's physical image. Of course this adulation of the younger generation was partially idealization. The influence of anti-Diaspora stereotypes and the fantasies of the founding generation are evident. But there was also some truth in the distinction between the typical young man of the Yishuv and the typical young Jew of Eastern Europe. Many Sabras, especially those from kibbutzim and moshavim, were raised in a rural environment and in an open educational system that allowed and even encouraged outdoor activity and sports. Their physiques were built up through these activities and through the hard labor of farming, in which they participated from a young age, as well as by the military training that many underwent. Their active lifestyle and physical uninhibitedness (expressed in the way they dressed—undershirts and bare feet) were fundamentally different from the passivity and physical introversion that characterized the Eastern European yeshiva student. The nutrition received by young natives was also different from Eastern European food—there was less meat and an abundance of fruits, vegetables, and dairy products. All this had a physical effect and in fact created, to a large extent, a new "breed" of young and sturdy youths.

Intuition suggests—and photographs seem to confirm—that while the image of the rugged pioneer was inspired by socialist realism, the image of the Sabra was based in part on the actual appearance of the new generation. Well-known Sabra figures, such as Yigal Allon, Yitzchak Rabin, Avraham Eden, David Elazar, and Chaim Bar-Lev—all of them later generals in the Israeli army—indeed fit the often-repeated but difficult-to-translate line in "The Song of Friendship": they were *yifei ha-blorit ve-ha-to'ar*—"of handsome forelocks and countenance." They, too, had Slavic features, but with the unique shadings of the Land of Israel.

The differences between the Sabra and the young Eastern European Jew were indeed natural and universal, the result of different conditions, even if the pioneers gave them mythic dimensions.

"SING, YOUTH, THE SONG OF OUR FUTURE"

The emphasis on the youth of the Sabra in counterpoint to the image of the old, bent-over, and helpless Jew of Europe, "Grandfather Israel," should be considered against the backdrop of the cult of youth that characterized the Yishuv and early state periods. This cult was inspired by European nationalism, which flourished at the end of the nineteenth and the beginning of the twentieth centuries and reached its height with the rise of Fascism. The rebellion against the feudal, aristocratic, and monarchic past in Europe was indirectly a rebellion against an autocratic establishment associated with images of dynasties and degenerate elders. Nationalism gave a figurative kick to this world of the "elders" and emphasized the future. The young person symbolized the new blood that was being infused into the social system—the freshness of modernity; the optimism, effervescence, and dynamism of the technological-industrial world; and especially, the quickened pulse of the renewed nation. The mythical cultural heroes of the new world were rejuvenated; the Herculeses and Apollos shunted the Platos off the stage.

The influence of the European cult of youth was conspicuous from the very beginning of Zionist settlement in Palestine, and with the birth of the second generation it gained force. Youthful figures were emphasized in art and in literature, and great attention was given to the education of the younger generation (for example, the establishment of youth movements and other organizations for young people). Adulatory expressions were used to describe the young people—the "youth of the dream" and the "wonder youth." There were public discussions, articles, seminars, and conferences on the "youth of the future" and the "state of youth," "youth values," and "the education of youth." The word "youth," in all its Hebrew variations, was omnipresent.

The cult of youth was influenced not only by European nationalist culture but also by Communism's spirit of social revolution. Soviet youth represented the blank social page that had been opened by the revolution and the liberated "new man" who was born of the revolution. Much the same was true in Zionism. As Herzl wrote in 1901, "Join together, young men. We need you. You must be strong and upstanding. We need your strength and your knowledge. 'Jewish boys' was until now an insult. Turn that around. Make it into a name of honor."[20] For this same reason, many Zionist organizations and publications in Palestine and elsewhere added the adjective "young" *(tza'ir)* to their names: *The Young Person's Newspaper (Iton Ha-Tza'ir)*, the Young Guard (Ha-Shomer Ha-Tza'ir), the Young Maccabees (Makabi Ha-Tza'ir), the Young Workers (Ha-Po'el Ha-Tza'ir), the Youth of Zion (Tze'iri Tzion), the Young Citizen (Ha-Ezrach Ha-Tza'ir).

The admiration for youth was also inspired by the cult of fallen war heroes that sprouted in Europe out of the compost of the vast killing fields of World War I. The lithe, muscular young person, full of fighting spirit, symbolized perfect humanity. "Dripping with the dew of Hebrew youth,"[21] wrote Natan Alterman of the young Hebrew men and women who presented the nation its independence "on a silver tray."

Notably, the Sabras themselves fostered the image of the vibrant youth, identifying with their role as Zionism's "favorite sons" and wanting to create a clear distinction between themselves and the older political leadership. This was expressed, for example, in the epithet "the old man"—first applied to Yitzchak Sadeh (who was only in his fifties at the time) and then to Ben-Gurion.

The protagonists of *Pack of Lies*—Fat Chaim, Abed, Little Samuch and Big Samuch, Jory, Benny, Ofer, Pishke, Sad Nissan, Abu-Lish's brother—as well as the protagonists of Puchu's popular book *A Gang Like This*, published in the 1950s, were all wild young people—children dressed up as soldiers and soldiers dressed as children. The works of Sabra writers made frequent use of words that emphasize youth, as in Shmuel Bas's song, popular in the youth movements: "Sing, Youth, the Song of Our Future."

The Sabra and the Holocaust

THE MYTHS OF THE PARTISANS
AND THE ILLEGAL IMMIGRATION OPERATION

The Holocaust played an extremely important role in establishing the anti-Diaspora ethos and thus reinforcing the Sabra's sense of superiority. The murder of millions of Europe's Jews shocked the Yishuv, but feelings of compassion and empathy for the survivors were accompanied by an "I told you so" attitude. It was as if the Yishuv were reprimanding the survivors for remaining in the Diaspora and not answering the call of Zionism, which, they maintained, had offered a national solution as early as the end of the nineteenth century. "These times have once more [shown], in a terrible light, the fundamental truth of Zionism, which is: the Jewish person cannot exist in the Diaspora," said Yitzchak Tabenkin, one of the leaders of the kibbutz movement, at a meeting of the Ha-Kibbutz Ha-Me'uchad council in July 1943.[22] The anti-Diaspora concept was so deeply rooted that it led to a certain insensitivity—at least until the middle of the 1950s—about the Holocaust. An example can be found in a letter by a kibbutz woman who had enlisted in the British army, written from her base in Egypt. Even though she already knew something of the dimensions of the catastrophe, she wrote:

> Every time I think about the murder of the Jews a horrible trembling runs through my entire body, and I frequently think of it. But it does not pursue me every day, perhaps because I don't actually know anyone there. But there are so many of our people in the [Jewish] Brigade, and people that I know, and I write to many of them and just think of them all the time. Aside from that, Chaim, how many of those Jews who were murdered could have come to Palestine and did not because they wanted a more comfortable life? Who knows, maybe it is their punishment. When it comes down to it, Chaim, whoever wants to come to Palestine, nothing stands in his way, and I don't think I need to tell you that, right?[23]

This insensitivity, which has its base in the anti-Diaspora ethos, was expressed in the letters of Yishuv volunteers in the British army who encountered Holocaust survivors. The general impression given by the letters is that despite a sense of a common fate with the survivors and real pain at the horrible suffering of European Jewry, there was no deep psychological trauma, as the dimensions of the catastrophe demanded. Instead, there was fairly restrained pity and empathy, sometimes accompanied by a pinch of embarrassment, suspicion, arrogance, or the condescension of the proud soldier toward the "displaced persons," "refugees," or "lost souls," as they were called by the Yishuv. The letter writers devote few words to the atrocities—perhaps in part because they were accustomed to keeping their feelings inside, and perhaps because of difficulties in communicating with the survivors. They evince little interest in the personalities of the Jewish refugees they met or in the hellish agonies suffered in the death camps.

In the newsletters put out by the Jewish soldiers in the British army (*Ha-Chayyal Ha-Ivri* and *Ba-Ma'avak*) one finds but a weak echo of the Jewish tragedy, the emphasis being instead on the actions of the Yishuv fighters. The very fact that the Jewish Brigade's encounter with the survivors had only minor reverberations in the Yishuv and none in the Sabra writings published after World War II testifies to how cool the encounter was.

For the veteran members of the Yishuv, the catastrophe in Europe made all the more stark the differences between the Diaspora Jew, who was ostensibly led "like a lamb to the slaughter," and the new Jew, the pioneer and Sabra, a proud and self-respecting Jew who heroically withstood the nation's enemies and even defeated them.[24] The view that if the Jews of the Diaspora had done as their brothers in Palestine did they would have not been slaughtered, or would have at least "died with honor" as the ghetto rebels did, was expressed by many Yishuv leaders.[25] "Had the entire Diaspora been taught to stand up in this way, perhaps they would have changed something, saved something, at least their honor and self-worth," said Yitzchak Tabenkin at a youth convention in 1943.[26] The subject of "loss of honor" was of great importance to the Sabras. The Jews in the Diaspora had not acted honorably, and the subliminal message given to the young people of the Yishuv was: "We expect you to act differently." In his speech at a Ha-Noar Ha-Oved convention in July 1943 in Tel Aviv, Tabenkin told his attentive audience: "And I want to say to the convention of Ha-Noar Ha-Oved, to which young people have come from the city and the moshava and from the farm, from kibbutzim and moshavim: Do you hear? They have called on you to stand up till the end for the honor of the remnant of the Jews. . . . What is Jewish honor? War for the land."[27] This expectation that the Sabras should reinstate the Jewish honor that had been sullied by the Holocaust was of great importance in motivating the fighting Sabra in the War of Independence.

The distinction between the heroic and honorable death of the Hebrew and the shameful death of the Diaspora Jew was expressed in veiled terms. Those killed in the Holocaust were said to have "perished," while Jews who died fighting in Palestine had "fallen."

A prominent vehicle for pointing out the differences between Diaspora and new Jews was the myth of the Jewish partisans, which became an important part of school Holocaust Day ceremonies. (Teachers and pupils alike were especially fond of "The Song of the Partisans" and "The Song of the Rebellion.") This myth was born after several of the ghetto rebel leaders came to Palestine—Abba Kovner in 1945, Tzivia Lubetkin in 1946, and Yitzchak "Antek" Zuckerman in 1947. Their speeches at conferences of Ha-Kibbutz Ha-Me'uchad were emotional affairs. They brought out the distinction between Holocaust and heroism and sharpened the ignominious image of the "Jew who dug his own grave," "who did not rise up with the shovel that was in his hands to strike at the German's head."[28]

Ostensibly, the myth of the partisans was meant to laud the heroism of the Jews who had rebelled against the Nazis, and thus contradict the charge of Diaspora spinelessness. But a close look at the elements of the myth shows that it in fact reinforced the distinction between the deaths of Jews in Europe and the deaths of Jews in Palestine and, indirectly, the distinction between "Diaspora" and "Hebrew" personalities. This distinction was made in three ways.

First, the partisans and the Warsaw ghetto fighters were presented—especially in textbooks—as exceptions that proved the rule and compensated for the actions of the majority.[29] The myth of the partisans bore the subliminal message that it was possible to act differently. The active rebellion of the minority underscored the passivity of the majority of Jews. "The victory in the ghetto, the victory of the Jewish person, was to die with honor, weapon in hand, and not as sheep led to the slaughter," said the order of the day issued to the Palmach's soldiers on the fifth anniversary of the Warsaw ghetto uprising.[30]

Second, the partisans and ghetto fighters were depicted as having acted differently from the typical Diaspora Jew because they had adopted the Zionist ethos and Zionist values of active defense. They were compared to Trumpeldor, Dani Mas, and other Yishuv heroes. (This was made easier by the fact that most of the ghetto rebels were in fact members of youth movements.) Palmach corporal Elad Peled wrote toward the end of 1945:

> I see before my eyes the beaten Jewish child, the tortured woman, and the cowardly man of the Diaspora at the time of the pogroms, and in contrast Rozka and her friends in the ghettoes (you must have read "Flames in the Ashes"). And she, Rozka, and Tzivia and Yitzchak Zuckerman and Mordecai Anielewicz and our nameless comrades, who do their deeds without acclaim, they are the blazers of the trail, theirs and mine.[31]

The distinction between the humiliating death of the Jew in the death camps and the heroic death of the partisan, who acted in the new Hebrew combat spirit, was also expressed in the name of the national day of remembrance for the Holocaust dead—a memorial day that became a holy national "holiday" and a rite with its own fixed ceremonial elements. A siren sounds in the morning, during which the entire nation stands at attention; the official memorial Yizkor prayer is chanted at the official ceremony at the Yad Vashem Holocaust memorial; the radio stations play mournful songs, and schools and youth movements conduct public recitations of relevant texts. Notably, it is not called Holocaust Day, but Holocaust and Heroism Day. The strained conjunction of the murder of the six million with the heroism of a small group of Jewish underground fighters who carried the banner of the Zionist ethos—much written about in recent years—was meant to create an association between the catastrophe of the Holocaust and the Zionist solution. That link has made this national memorial day into the holiday of the Zionist object lesson.

Third, emphasis was put on the connection between the partisans and the handful of Haganah fighters, most notably Enzo Sireni, Chaviva Reik, and Hannah Szenes, who parachuted into Europe to aid them. The deaths of these three paratroopers made them into martyrs, and they came to symbolize the fraternal alliance of the "new race of Jewish heroes"—the partisans on one side and the Sabras on the other.[32] This was, of course, reinforced by the fact that most of the organized ghetto fighters were members of local branches of the same socialist-Zionist youth movements that the Sabras themselves belonged to. This fraternity is evident in an issue of *Alon Ha-Palmach* from 1944: "We felt the brotherhood—the brotherhood in arms of the Jew fighting for his country, his honor, his people, wherever he fights. In the heroism of the fighters in the Diaspora we felt the single root, ours and theirs, the Maccabean root that lies so deep in our history in this land."[33]

Another aspect of the Holocaust that contributed to the value distinction between the Diaspora Jew and the Sabra was the heroic enterprise of getting the Holocaust survivors out of Europe and to Palestine. In contrast with the myth of the partisans, into which the Sabras were inserted in a somewhat superficial way, in this case Sabras—the members of the Haganah's marine branch—did indeed play a critical role. The illegal immigration story as it is told in Zionist literature underlined, even if indirectly, the contrast between the active Sabra and the passive Diaspora immigrant Jew. It glorified the ship captains who evaded the British navy and the mighty marine Palmachnik who bore women and children on his back into the Promised Land (numerous photographs of this type appear in the official albums).[34] Until the appearance of Leon Uris's novel *Exodus*—written, not coincidentally, by a non-Israeli—the vicissitudes and heroism of the illegal immigrants themselves were minimized, and the Palmach marines were made the heroes of the epic.

MENDING BODY AND MIND:
THE SABRA AND THE HOLOCAUST SURVIVOR

The rejection of the Diaspora also affected the Sabra's attitude toward the Holocaust survivors in Israel—a subject that has aroused great scholarly interest in recent years. A number of labels emerged confirming the Holocaust survivors' moral and social "inferiority" to the Sabras. One of these (which in the 1990s would be the subject of sharp criticism) was the label "human dust." This expression, connoting people without spine, without personality, who were blown hither and thither by the wind, was coined by writer David Frishman in the 193os and later applied by Yishuv leaders to the Holocaust survivors. "A mixed multitude of human dust without a language, without education, without roots, and without any roots in the nation's tradition and vision," Ben-Gurion said of them. "Turning these people of dust into a cultured, independent nation with a vision will be no easy task."[35] Other labels applied to the Holocaust survivors were *agadim,* from the Hebrew initials for "people of the mournful Diaspora" and much used by members of youth movements; *sabonim,* or soap bars, applied to the refugee immigrants because of their white skin and softness, or with black humor, because of the soap that the Nazis manufactured, so rumor had it, from the bodies of murdered Jews. The term "surviving remnants" appeared in textbooks and in youth movement guidebooks. Two other reasons for the perception of the Holocaust survivors as inferior should be noted. First, some Yishuv's leaders regarded the Holocaust as a process of reverse natural selection—it was the worst Jews who had survived. Second, many of the survivors preferred an urban, capitalistic (and in many cases traditional or religious) lifestyle to the collective, secular "life of consummation" practiced in the kibbutzim and moshavim.[36]

As noted earlier, the image of the Diaspora Jew as weak in body and mind in contrast to the strong and healthy Hebrew was rooted deep in the pioneer ethos even before World War II. The poor physical condition of the Holocaust survivors, many of whom suffered from disease and malnutrition, served to reinforce the old stereotype. These immigrants were perceived not only as strangers (like every immigrant arriving in a new land) but also as physically and mentally ill.[37]

The view of the Diaspora as a disease is reflected in the youth movement newspapers and can be found in many pieces written by Sabras.[38] "There is no need to go on at length about the negative aspects of the Diaspora," one of them said:

> "In the Diaspora they will go into captivity"—this was always one of the most severe punishments, in concrete terms. In the word "Diaspora" the Jew sees riots, murder, and blood. For us in Palestine, who have not had the taste of the Diaspora, just looking at those degenerate figures fleeing here each day from the conflagration of the Diaspora is enough. But it is not the body only that degenerates in the Diaspora; the Diaspora attenuates the people's spirit. Since the people are not close to and working the land, they wander; and it is in this image of the beaten wanderer that we always see the "eternal Jew."[39]

Many of the Holocaust survivors arrived with damaged bodies and scarred minds, but the anti-Diaspora ethos encouraged the Sabras to view these injuries as products of the Diaspora itself, rather than of the Holocaust. Such a view can be seen in the statement of a Ha-Machanot Ha-Olim counselor in 1937, before the Holocaust, regarding twenty young German Jews who had been taken into her movement: "There is a kind of self-hatred in them, against the Diaspora within them. . . . The child educated in the German Diaspora has the character of that Diaspora imprinted in him."[40] In response, educators and counselors considered the absorption and education of the young immigrants in the labor-movement melting pot as a process of not only medical, psychological, and social rehabilitation but also cultural rehabilitation—a resocialization. (It is important to emphasize that Israeli caretakers still had no psychological understanding of trauma survival and thus remained unenlightened about the emotional state of the children under their care.)

The immigrants themselves were greatly influenced by those who took them in. They saw themselves as needing physical and psychological rectification, and not just because of the horrors of the Holocaust. One immigrant wrote:

> Even though we underwent a period of training overseas, we are still "green" and have much to learn. In particular, having lived through the dark period in Europe and witnessed the great atrocities on our own flesh, we must detach ourselves from all that. Each of us needs to forget the past, to begin a new future, to heal our souls from the foundation—quite simply, to be born again.[41]

Encounters between Sabras and young Holocaust survivors took place mostly within two frameworks: the kibbutzim and the army. The kibbutzim were the major destination of young people who had been absorbed into the Youth Aliya program, a Zionist project that brought young Jews to Palestine, generally without their parents. The army became a theater for such encounters because of its need for reinforcements during the War of Independence.

The attitude of the kibbutz movement toward the Holocaust survivors—in fact the attitude of the entire veteran Zionist elite—was ambivalent. On the one hand, the ethos of ingathering the Jewish people led to sincere effort and the investment of large resources in facilitating the absorption and rehabilitation of the refugees. On the other hand, there was apprehension that the cultural fabric of the kibbutz, in particular its intimate, communal way of life, would be affected; this fear, along with the influence of the anti-Diaspora ethos and its associated stereotypes, produced paternalism, arrogance, and sometimes even rejection of the immigrants.

However, it was not only ethnocentrism and anti-Diaspora sentiment that made assimilation difficult for the refugees. The factors that hinder the absorption of strangers into any society, especially a small one, were also at work. The fact that, in general, the kibbutzim did not create common social frameworks for the kibbutz children and the immigrant youth increased the isolation of the immigrants and the alienation between the two groups. Furthermore, since adolescents by nature tend to form groups and identify with them—and in kibbutzim this inclination was reinforced by the communal and independent life lived by the children—strangers have more trouble being absorbed into adolescent society than into adult society. The process generally involves a painful period of degradation and condemnation. Jeers and insults were common in the encounter between immigrants and kibbutz Sabras, and sometimes reached a level of cruelty and savagery—something that characterizes young people the world over.

Holocaust survivors who successfully endured the trauma of the initial encounter with kibbutz society were completely assimilated and themselves became Sabras in every respect. There were four reasons for this: (1) the kibbutz, by nature a total society, worked on the human psyche twenty-four hours a day; (2) a large portion of the Youth Aliya children arrived without relatives (about 49 percent came without parents), and some of these children were taken in and made full members of kibbutz families; (3) kibbutz children lived apart from their parents in special children's houses, which served to narrow the gap between veteran and immigrant young people; and (4) working on the kibbutz enabled the young immigrant to quickly attain a Zionist status symbol—working the land.

The same ambivalent attitude toward the immigrants was prevalent in the army. The survivors who joined the Palmach brigades (often shortly after arriving in Palestine) got a chilly, often contemptuous, reception. "We were repelled by them and kept our distance from them," a native-born Palmachnik related. "The girls turned their backs on them almost completely and the boys had a superior attitude—of Sabras against foreigners, us and them. . . . There was no contact at all between us and them in their first months in the company, and they were severely offended and insulted."[42]

The immigrant members of the Palmach were referred to as *gachal*, the Hebrew acronym for "overseas enlistment." As historian Hannah Yablonka has noted, this "was a kind of classification that freed the natives from having to establish personal relations and confront the shallowness of their generalizations."[43] The term testified to the Sabra elite's patronizing attitude toward the newly arrived immigrants.

The Sabras were also angry that the immigrants seemed to have un-justifiably received the prestigious status of Palmachniks. Many of the veteran members of the Palmach considered the new enlistees like stepchildren who have just joined a closely knit family or regarded them as a threat to the internal harmony of Sabra society. The newsletter of the Yiftach Brigade stated: "We miss the good old days, when our camp was pure, when we could be friends and comrades of every single person, and sit together around the campfire to sing and tell tales and have fun. Today, what can we do with them?"[44]

Avraham Adan, a company commander in the Negev Brigade and later an IDF general, told the following story about his first encounter with the new soldiers from the Diaspora who manned his unit:

> It was my first encounter with [such] soldiers. They spoke in Yiddish. . . . At first they praised me—they had been in the country for two weeks and I was the first one who had gathered them together for a talk. . . . Up until then they had not been given a chance to express themselves, and no one had asked how they felt, what they thought about the training, and how they were being treated. Afterwards they got to their grievances, which were many: they said they were being treated in a humiliating way by the NCOs who were training them. The young NCOs raised their voices at them and even threw stones at them. Some remarked sharply that the way the commanders were treating them reminded them of the way the Germans had treated them.[45]

As in the kibbutzim, the alienation between the Sabras and the immigrants in the army was the product of the cultural and linguistic gap between the two groups. In the end, however, the military framework proved to be the more efficient one for assimilating the immigrants. The longer the newcomers stayed, the stronger their acquaintance with the Sabras became. Fighting together in the War of Independence in particular was a unifying experience through which many immigrants became Sabras in every sense of the word, even to the point of eventually reaching high ranks in the IDF.

The Israeli Melting Pot: Sabraism as a Cultural Seal of Approval

IMMIGRATION TO PALESTINE AS RELIGIOUS CONVERSION

The rejection of the Diaspora meant that Israel was seen as something like a factory for the production of the new Jew, the "standard model" Israeli. This idea was captured in the expression "melting pot," which came into use during the mass immigration of the 1950s and reveals the resemblance of the Zionist political hierarchy to a church hierarchy. The Zionist national religion, like other traditional religions, sought to create cultural as well as ideological homogeneity. (The transition from the multitude of Diaspora cultures to a uniform Israeli culture is also evident in the phrase "the ingathering of the exiles," which became a common idiom during the mass immigration.) A cultural melting pot ostensibly means smelting the material of the incoming cultures and casting them into a new mold, which results in a blending of cultures; in practice, the immigrant cultures were cast in the favored Hebrew—that is, Sabra—mold.

The melting pot concept is characteristic of all immigration societies, including the United States in the mid-nineteenth century. In Israel, however, it took on the additional ideological meaning of erasing the Diaspora past. The immigrant understood that in order to be accepted into Hebrew culture he had to abandon or keep in low profile his previous Diaspora culture and faith, and had to fit himself into the Hebrew mold. This indirectly signaled the advantage of the Sabra native, since the Israeli mold had been made in his image.

It is hard to avoid a comparison between the cultural steamroller used to imbed the immigrants in the Sabra community and the "personality transformation" that new adherents to religions and cults undergo. The cult or religion accepting a proselyte into its ranks demands that he reject his previous beliefs and be "born again." The emphasis on the immigrant's inferior character, not just his cultural inferiority, was meant to mark the chasm between the "authentic adherent" (the Sabra) and the "convert" (the immigrant). The immigrant was expected to change not only his habits but also the very structure of his personality.

HEBREW NAMES AND DIASPORA NAMES

The practice of giving native-born Israelis Hebrew names (first from the Bible, later, names related to the land itself) and of Hebraicizing family names began during the First Aliya. The new Hebrew names became a Zionist symbol that distinguished between Jews from the Diaspora and Jews from the Land of Israel. As Yudke says in Chaim Hazaz's "The Sermon," one of the best-known Sabra texts and one that was taught in the schools: "A man of the Yishuv is ashamed to be called by a common and regular Jewish name and is proud to be called, say, Eretzyisraeli or Avnieli. Chaimovitch, you will agree yourselves, is a Jewish name—too Jewish;

while Avnieli—that's something else, the devil knows what. It has a strange ring to it. Not Jewish! Proud! So we have a lot of Gideons, Ehuds, Yigals, Tirtzas."[46] At first "new-old" private names from the Biblical and Mishnaic periods were given, especially names of Biblical heroes. The most popular were short names, like Gad and Dan, and names of heroes, like Yiftach, Gideon, and Yoav. At the end of the 1950s national names were added, such as Yechiyam ("long live the nation") and Amikam ("my people have risen"), as well as the names of kinds of rocks and local plants, animals, and locations, such as Alon (oak), Oren (pine), Erez (cedar), Dafna (laurel), Tzur (rock), Eyal (ram), Yarden (Jordan), and Kineret (the Sea of Galilee).[47]

The most popular names, and those most associated with the Sabras (especially Sabra commanders and counselors) were Dani, Uzi, and Uri. These were common in children's stories and poems that appeared in the children's press in the 1930s and 1940s. *Davar Le-Yeladim,* written by Leah Goldberg and illustrated by Arieh Navon, portrayed the adventures of Uri Kaduri. Uri Kesari, coiner of the term "Sabra," adopted "Uri" to replace his Diaspora given name, Shmuel. The name became even more popular after the publication of Rachel's poem "The Barren Woman" ("Had I a son / His name would be Uri"). Uri is also the name of the Palmach-generation Sabra in Moshe Shamir's mythological novel, *He Walked in the Fields.*

Dani was a classic Sabra name in the 1930s. It appeared in stories and poems about the Sabras, such as "Dani, Eat Your Banana." Dani also appears in its alternate form Dan, together with the typical girl's name Tamar, on the first page of the book *My Friend,* a first-grade reader ("Dan stood. Good morning, Dan."). The name was chosen not only because it is simple to read but also because it was a stereotypical Sabra name. It makes another appearance in Miriam Yellen-Shtaklis's popular children's poem "Dani the Hero,"[48] published in *Davar Le-Yeladim* in 1941, and in *The Dani Book,* published in 1943; it also starred as the name of one of the protagonists in the language column, "Those Sabras," published in *Davar Ha-Shavu'a* in the years 1949–1950.

Uzi was another typical Sabra name, and it was no coincidence that when Natan Alterman wrote in his popular weekly newspaper feature, "The Seventh Column," about the Palmachniks who were deported by the British to Cyprus together with illegal immigrants on the ship the *Shabbetai Lozhinsky,* he called them "Red-Headed Uzi from Mescha, and Dani Jamus, and Efrimke Kruvi."[49] Nor was it a coincidence that Amos Keinan's column in *Ha'aretz* at the beginning of the 1950s was called

"Uzi and Co." Uzi was the witty Sabra prankster, while Yerachmieli (which means "may God have mercy" and thus has traditional Jewish associations) was the ridiculous character, representing the anachronism of the labor movement and the bureaucratic calcification of the regime of the 1950s, in Keinan's view. The name Zalman was identified with the sloppily dressed Diaspora Jew.

The names Uzi and Dani, denoting Sabra buddy types, are also common in articles published during and after the War of Independence in the newsletters of battalions and brigades and in the army periodicals (*Ba-Machaneh, Ba-Machaneh Gadna, Ba-Machaneh Nachal, Iton Ha-Magen*). They also appeared frequently in the skits of the army entertainment troupes.

The symbolic role of the name as a Hebrew marker, creating a distinction between the Sabra (largely those born in the agricultural settlements) and the immigrant, and even between the Sabra and his pioneer father, is notable in the literature of the 1948 generation. Many of the Sabra heroes of S. Yizhar, Natan Shacham, Chanoch Bartov, Yigal Mosinzon, Moshe Shamir, Chaim Cheffer, Didi Manosi, and other writers and poets of their generation were given typical Sabra names, such as Uri, Gadi, Dani, Tzvingi, or Avner. Others were given traditional names with a diminutive suffix added to denote fondness—this serving to "convert" the name into a Sabra one and expressing love of the Sabras. Such were Rutke (from Ruth), Mishke (from Moshe, or Moses), Sheike (from Yeshayahu, or Isaiah), Bentzi (from Ben-Zion), Rubik (from Reuven, or Reuben), Tzvike (from Tzvi), Motke (from Mordechai), Yosefele (from Yosef, or Joseph), Chaimke (from Chaim), Dudu (from David), and Avrasha (from Avraham, or Abraham). Some of these names were invented by the Sabras, and some were taken from Yiddish and Russian. The immigrants appearing in the stories, on the other hand, were given traditional names, almost always without diminutives, and were often not given names at all.

Many of the immigrants' names were classic Jewish names in their countries of origin or were in languages other than Hebrew (such as Yiddish, Russian, Polish, Moroccan), so they symbolized Diaspora Jewish culture for the natives. Thus, Hebraicization of the new immigrant's name was an important mechanism in the process of acculturation.[50] It meant one was closing the door to the Diaspora past and rectifying one's old "Jewish personality." It was part of the "conversion" of the proselyte into the Zionist national religion, a ceremony that required (as in most religions) giving up one's previous identity and adopting a new one.

The practice of changing an immigrant's name characterizes most (perhaps all) immigrant societies. But in Yishuv and Israeli society, unlike other immigrant societies, this process was imbued with ideological content and was accomplished with the open intervention of the agents of socialization, which testifies to its importance. In schools and immigrant transit camps, teachers and social counselors urged pupils and their parents to Hebraicize both names, but especially family names. The army also mobilized itself enthusiastically for this mission and even appointed a names committee. The committee issued a booklet of Hebrew names with an introduction explaining the importance of the Hebraicization of foreign names, and thousands of copies of it were distributed to all army units. This cultural campaign was not coercive, but the suggestion to change one's name was nevertheless made aggressively and was supported by ideological and nationalist arguments.

In fact, there was almost no need for propaganda to promote the Hebraicization of family names, since the negative badge of the Diaspora motivated many immigrants (especially those absorbed into Sabra organizations) to do so voluntarily at the time of their immigration or soon afterward. Like immigrants everywhere, they wanted to assimilate into the local culture, and especially sought to help their children acclimatize in the new country and become Sabras. Immigrant families at first reluctant to change their family names for emotional and traditional reasons in the end agreed to do so because of pressure from their children. This was especially so in the agricultural settlements. The children wanted to rid themselves of all signs of foreignness that opened them to ridicule by their Sabra fellows.

Still, there were many young immigrants who were integrated into Sabra organizations and who themselves became Sabras in every respect while preserving their original first and family names. Changing these names was thus not a necessary condition of being absorbed into Sabra culture, but only one of the elements. Furthermore, most of the native-born Sabras in fact had traditional Jewish names, such as Nachum, Chaim, Moshe, or Yitzchak—though rarely foreign names like Franz or Sasha. Often they had been named after a relative who had passed away. Their parents in many cases also remained loyal to their traditional, foreign family name. Nevertheless, children who were given a Hebrew family name—mostly the children of veteran families, especially those living in moshavim and kibbutzim—or better, a Hebrew first name, won a Sabra status symbol that gave them a cultural advantage and sharpened the distinction between them and the immigrants.

The story of Dahn Ben-Amotz, who would later become an Israeli culture hero, is a fine example. Ben-Amotz came to Israel with the name Moshe Tehilimzeiger. He changed this to Moshe Sha'oni and then to Dahn Ben-Amotz. By his own account, he came to feel that in order to be considered a Sabra by those around him and by himself, he had to change not only his family name but his first name as well to something as typically Sabra as possible. The name, for him, was a symbolic entry ticket into Sabra society.[51]

The importance of a Hebrew first name and, more important, a Hebrew family name was especially marked in the distinction between the Sabras—the great majority of whom were of European origin—and the young immigrants who came from the Islamic world or who were born in Palestine of parents who had come from those countries. Out of a profound sense of communal unity and adherence to Jewish tradition, these Oriental immigrants remained faithful to their traditional Jewish first names and to the family names that designated their clans in their country of origin (Wazana, Bokobza, Der'i, Ohana). In remaining so, they unintentionally doomed their children to a culturally inferior position, preserving their foreignness in a society whose social elite was largely Ashkenazi. It is hardly coincidental, then, that one of the marks of class mobility for these Oriental immigrants in the early 1980s was the process of changing family names and giving new Israeli names to their children.

THE HEBREW ACCENT
AND THE DIASPORA ACCENT

One of the first markers of Hebrewness created by the pioneers was the use of Hebrew as a spoken language. As elsewhere, the revival of the language symbolized the revival of the nation. The national and ideological importance of the language produced "language sentries," such as the Only Hebrew Association and the Battalion of Defenders of the Hebrew Language—organizations that worked to repress the public use of foreign languages and instituted an unofficial boycott of Yiddish.[52]

The pioneers imposed on themselves the severe and unbending rule of speaking only Hebrew, but made no great effort to get rid of their Ashkenazi accents. They associated the Ashkenazi accent with the Diaspora, while considering the Sepharadi accent more authentically "Hebrew." However, changing their accents was beyond their power. In the end, the real revolution in accent was accomplished by the native-born

Sabras, who created an Israeli accent that is an amalgam of East and West. The symbolic link between the revival of the language and the national revival granted the Sabra—identified as "the first natural speaker of Hebrew in the last two thousand years"—a special social status. The Sabra who grew up speaking the Hebrew language created the Israeli accent, and thus his accent became a status symbol and a social resource. The Sabra idiom became the new Israeli idiom.

Unlike names, which the immigrants could change immediately and so provide themselves with a marker of Sabraism, they could change their accents only with difficulty, if at all. This was detrimental in particular to the immigrants from the Islamic world, who had trouble ridding themselves of their Oriental accent and adjusting themselves to the native, Sabra accent. Biographies, as well as journalistic interviews with immigrants who came to Israel at a young age and were absorbed into Sabra organizations, indicate that young immigrants felt that they had been truly absorbed and had rid themselves of their "Diaspora hunchback" only when they managed to adjust themselves to Sabra language, including its accent, pronunciation, syntax, idioms, and word stresses.[53]

The Sabra as the
Ashkenazi Elite's Favorite Son

When the State of Israel was established, Ashkenazim comprised 85 percent of the Jewish population in Palestine. This demographic preeminence reduced but did not eliminate the Ashkenazi elite's need, and urge, to defend its political and cultural hegemony with ethnic status symbols. The need intensified, however, with the mass immigration of Jews from the Muslim world after the establishment of the state, for within just a few years the Ashkenazim were only 60 percent of the population.[54]

The Oriental immigrants, like all other immigrants, were perceived by the Israeli establishment as in need of a cure for the Diaspora disease from which they suffered, a cure that would turn them into Sabras. But in the case of the Oriental immigrants, the usual differences between the natives and the immigrants were supplemented by the cultural differences between East and West. The Yishuv leadership, and the Sabras after them, treated the Oriental immigrants with a mixture of affection, compassion, condescension, and arrogance—the products of the combined ethoses of ingathering the exiles and rejecting the Diaspora. The common wisdom regarding the acclimatizing of Oriental Jewish youth to their new country was that they should discard the Oriental culture, which the establishment considered backward, and ascend to a higher cultural level by adopting the characteristics of the Sabra and the more advanced Western culture.

Since the young state had little money and was faced with an influx of immigrants that doubled its population during its first five years, many of the newcomers were housed in tents. The Orientals, who were less likely to have family and connections in the veteran population, made up the bulk of the population of these transit camps. Unemployment, poverty, and the breakdown of family and community structures led to a high incidence of crime and delinquency, and this, of course, confirmed the Ashkenazi establishment's prejudices about the inferiority of Oriental Jewish culture. The establishment saw little hope of changing the adults, but Oriental children and adolescents were considered candidates for Sabraization. The kibbutz movement enlisted itself in this project by sending its own young people to serve as counselors in the transit camps and by bringing Oriental youngsters to live in kibbutzim within the framework of what were called Youth Societies. But the enterprise was paternalistic by nature and as a result, generally created more alienation than closeness between the absorbing society and the newcomers. Both sides sensed that the cultural chasm was deep and wide, and the Sabras' sense of superiority was reinforced.

The youth movements also did their part, at least formally, to absorb the immigrants. The most active movement was the one sponsored by the Histadrut's Ha-Noar Ha-Oved Ve-Ha-Lomed—the Working and Learning Youth—which opened branches in poor areas and took in young people who had to work for a living by helping them learn a trade. Yet the movement's branches remained homogeneous and no real mixing took place between the working youth, most of whom were Oriental, and the learning youth, who were largely Ashkenazi. The Histadrut's attempt to enlist Orientals to work as youth counselors was not a success.[55]

The youth movement newsletters of the period contain occasional calls for closer relations with the Oriental immigrants,[56] but the general impression is that these were just lip service and not representative of actual deeds. If there had been actual activity it would have created more reverberations in channels of Sabra expression. During the 1950s, Ha-Noar Ha-Oved, Ha-Shomer Ha-Tza'ir, and the Scouts all established special departments to handle the transit camps, but these actually contributed to the polarization between the two ethnic groups. The Sabra counselors, most of whom were Ashkenazim, considered it their job not only to assist the immigrants, who had been set down in the middle of a strange culture with no means of their own, but also to serve as Zionist missionaries and preach the Zionist gospel to young people who had grown up in a backward and primitive culture.

The arrogant attitude toward the Oriental immigrants was a response not only to their Diaspora origins and their foreignness, but also to the fact that so many of them could not read and write. Moreover, most of the Orientals were religious in both belief and lifestyle. Most of them continued to observe their traditions and refused to accept secular Israeli culture, despite the efforts of the secular establishment to wean them away from their religion during the period of the mass immigration.[57] The young people were reluctant to adopt a secular lifestyle because it would mean painful conflicts with their parents and relatives, and the Oriental family structure was particularly patriarchal and traditional. Moreover, these young people were deeply bonded to their religious traditions and maintained emotional links to a family tradition that included food, music, and special customs. One reason for these stronger ties to family and tradition is purely demographic. While 46 percent of the Youth Aliya immigrants who came from Poland and Eastern Europe were orphans, less than 1 percent of the Youth Aliya children who came from Morocco and Iraq lacked both parents.

These cultural differences explain why only a few of the Oriental immigrants were absorbed by the kibbutzim and became Sabras in the full sense.[58] Even when they were welcomed with all good intention, the cultural differences were very deep and the sense of foreignness remained.

It is important to emphasize that none of the Sabra organizations were exclusively Ashkenazi and all of them included, to a greater or lesser extent, young people of Oriental origins. The Palmach, the most important Sabra melting pot, had some soldiers from Islamic countries, and because of their knowledge of the Arabic language and culture as well as their "Oriental" appearance, some of them took an active part in Palmach intelligence operations. Nevertheless, their cultural influence was minimal (it was evident largely in songs and the culture of the campfire); most of them adopted the dominant Western-Ashkenazi-secular culture.

The shunting aside of Oriental culture within the Palmach also derived from the Ashkenazi profile of the great majority of its officers and NCOs. This majority was also the reason that the military units that carried on the Palmach tradition—Unit 101 and the Paratroopers—were also largely Ashkenazi in character, despite the fact that many if not most of the Paratroopers in the 1950s were Oriental.

The superiority that the Ashkenazi Sabra felt toward the immigrants from the Islamic world and the Oriental youth's sense of inferiority were also connected to the sociological dynamic of social stratification and power hegemony of earlier and veteran populations, which characterizes young immigrant societies. The Ashkenazim had carried out the Zionist revolution and established the new Yishuv, so by the very nature of their precedence they held the key leadership positions and were the guardians of the dominant, Ashkenazi culture. The issue of the ethnic gap has been discussed at length in the sociological literature and this is not the place to discuss it in detail. But since being Ashkenazi was one of the characteristics of the typical Sabra—one of the elements of his image— I will touch here on three of the points having to do with the Sabra's elitist consciousness and education.

First, when the pioneers, who were Ashkenazi, dreamed of creating a "new Jew," though some of them—especially at the very beginning of the Zionist immigration to Palestine—dressed this new Jew in the romantic garb of the noble Arab sheikh, their model was more the Russian Cossack and the American cowboy. While they sought to eliminate the Diaspora past, they did not want to cut themselves off from European culture. Their goal was to create a modern secular society in Palestine, and the new Jew was meant to be secular, educated, and modern. The Oriental Jew was the opposite. He was religious, an observer of tradition, and uneducated (by European standards). Moreover, his external appearance and culture resembled that of the Arab, who was considered by the Zionist leadership to be backward and, even worse, the enemy of Zionism. The term "Sabra" thus became a synonym for "Ashkenazi Sabra," at least as regards the social images attached to it, even though there was an Oriental minority among the Sabras. The meaning of the term "Sabra" at that time, it should be recalled, was "young people from good (that is, Ashkenazi) families."

Second, a number of factors in Israeli culture reinforced the Sepharadi's sense of inferiority. The mass immigration from the Arab world, especially from North Africa, occurred after the establishment of the state. The young Oriental immigrants were not part of the Israeli "Mayflower nobility," and their sons were not "native sons" like the Sabras of the same age, nor did they benefit from the prestige of having pioneer fathers. The parents of the Oriental youth came to Palestine with him or were buried somewhere in a lost homeland. The Oriental youth felt that "they"—the people of the agricultural settlements and their children— had established the country, while "we" had come to something already prepared in advance. This led to a sense of inferiority. This sentiment was expressed in writing only a generation later, in the books of authors such as Amnon Shamosh, Sami Michael, and Eli Amir, who had come to Israel from Arab countries as children. In his autobiographical work, *Scapegoat,* Eli Amir tells the story of a group of young people from Iraq and Morocco who were educated at a kibbutz in the early 1950s while their parents remained in transit camps. He recounts: "I couldn't help comparing Dolek to my father. Even though I loved my father very much, I had a kind of hidden resentment of him. I could never brag about him as the Sabras did: 'My father began all this, he was among the first ones.'"[59]

The Orientals' sense of inferiority was magnified by the educational system, which stressed the accomplishments of the pioneers and linked this to their European past. At the same time, it ignored the heroic past of Oriental Jewry, which had preserved its faith in a sometimes hostile environment. It also ignored the Zionist accomplishments of Oriental Jews, for example, the Yemenites who worked in the moshavot during the time of the First Aliya and the underground Zionist movements in North Africa and Iraq. Jewish history textbooks published from the beginning of the century to the present day told the history of the Jewish people in the modern age as largely the history of the Ashkenazi community in Europe. The non-Ashkenazi communities were mentioned only briefly, or not at all.[60] The young person came to perceive the success of the Zionist movement exclusively as the achievement of pioneers who had come from Europe. The message received by the Oriental Jews was that they had played no real part in the Zionist epic.

Furthermore, the educational establishment (teachers, principals, writers, and researchers) was composed almost entirely of Ashkenazim, and some of them had a stereotyped view of Oriental Jewry. This was largely the product of ignorance and a sense of cultural superiority that grew out of the large educational and technological gap between European and Asian-African culture (it should be remembered that the fields of sociology and psychology were still in their infancy in Israel).

In addition, the Oriental Jews arrived in Israel after an authentic Israeli secular culture, based on European culture, was already in place. Oriental folklore was considered foreign and thus un-Israeli and was placed out of bounds. Sabra-Palmach folklore, in contrast, was based on the pioneer model and was thus accepted enthusiastically by the founding generation. The kibbutz and moshav natives, the members of youth movements, and the Palmach soldiers who sang nostalgic songs about Europe to the accompaniment of a harmonica or accordion were participating in a kind of tribal memory based on a fabric of associations and ambience of a manifestly European character. It is no coincidence that these songs eventually became part of the folklore of Israeli society as a whole.

The third point is related to the paths of class mobility for the Sabra and the young Oriental Jew. One sociologist has used the term "sponsored mobility" to describe a social mechanism in which members of the elite or their agents choose, through a formal or informal selection process, the candidates for advancement in the social hierarchy.[61] The most conspicuous characteristic of sponsored mobility is that the winnowing out and selection of candidates for the elite is accomplished early in the process—in contrast with normal, open mobility in which it is done in the final stages. Early selection obviously reduces the chances of those who have not grown up within the elite and who have not followed the normal path of advancement to be absorbed into the elite and to obtain key positions in society.

In many ways, a pattern of protected Sabra mobility developed in Israel, in accord with the theoretical lines described above. The youth movements sought their members from within the upper and upper-middle class—that is, in the municipal academic high schools and the kibbutz schools. The Palmach also, at least in its early stages, enlisted its volunteers from the youth movements, the moshavim, and the kibbutzim. The criteria for making the first cut, before the ranks were opened just before the War of Independence, included an ethnic component. Yitzchak Tabenkin, for example, stated explicitly: "In the initial period there should not be a large percentage of Sephardi material, which is of dubious [quality], so that it will not introduce a bad influence in the initial period."[62]

The military leadership was selected from among the men of the Haganah, the Palmach, and the veterans of the Jewish Brigade, most of whom belonged to a single social milieu. The political leadership would also later grow out of the military organizations.

The Sabra thus had a closed path of advancement—from youth movement counselor and leader to *hachshara*, to NCO or an officers' course, to command of a small force and participation in battles, leading to advancement in the military command and eventually, entry into the military and civilian leadership. The intimacy of the Yishuv and early Israeli society and the organizational and ideological links between the different arms of the agricultural settlements (the youth movements, the Palmach, the kibbutzim, the labor parties) made the Sabra circle even more closed.

The pioneer youth movements, more than any other framework, played a decisive role as the first stage in the Sabra's path of sponsored mobility since they prepared the Sabras for their future roles. As movement members, the young Sabras practiced personal responsibility for others, team work, and democratic procedures such as meetings, debates, and elections. They were equipped with the social resources necessary for social advancement—Sabra slang, folklore, cultural knowledge, and personal connections. The last was enshrined in a new Hebrew word, *protektzia*, which denoted the connections that one needed to get ahead, or in fact to get anything done. The youth movements thus filled the same role as the English "public" school—they created a common infrastructure of culture and values for the members of the middle class and served as training schools for leadership, producing the new Israeli elites and "nobility."[63]

The youth movements were almost completely closed to new young Oriental immigrants, however, with the exception of Ha-Noar Ha-Oved, which sought out working youth who were not in school. This largely blocked the integration of Oriental youth into the elite. There were further reasons for the low participation of Orientals in the youth movements. First, most of the Oriental youth arrived in the 1950s, some twenty years after the youth movements were established and after the establishment of their Ashkenazi-secular character, and this discouraged many Oriental youngsters from joining them. Second, most youth movement chapter houses were in affluent neighborhoods, close to the academic high schools, and were thus more accessible to the middle class—meaning largely veteran Ashkenazi families—than to Oriental youth, who lived in poorer neighborhoods, in small towns in outlying regions (the development towns), in moshavim established for immigrants, and during the mass immigration, in transit camps. Third, the youth movements were by their very nature designed for young people attending school who had free time after school and whose families needed no additional income. Many Oriental youth worked to supplement their family's income and thus could not participate in youth movement activities.

The cultural chasm between the young Ashkenazi native and the young Oriental immigrant and the hegemony of the Europeans in the agricultural settlements, the leadership of the Yishuv, and the early state sharpened the Sabra's sense of superiority in his own eyes and in the eyes of both the Ashkenazi and Oriental communities. The latter felt that their children could not be included as Sabras, as "all-Israeli boys." In *Scapegoat* Eli Amir wrote:

> We feared [the students from the regional school in the valley]. It was "them and us." They would pass us like we were empty air. We would move out of their way so that they would not notice our existence. . . . One evening we found ourselves striding up the small hill to their castle. From below we had always seen it facing us and we had not gone there, and here we were at its gates. Embarrassed, awkward, dumb, like villagers who found themselves in a luxuriant capital. . . . Really, we regarded them as the sons of gods. And why was that so surprising? They were the masters of the house. Here they had breathed their first breath, here they had imbibed the Hebrew language, they had set down roots in this land, they had skipped over these rocks and wandered these open spaces. It was all theirs.[64]

Blocking paths of mobility to young Oriental Jews reinforced their class inferiority in Israeli society and bolstered the status of the Sabras—in their own view and in the public view—as a social elite. It is thus no coincidence that years later, when interethnic tensions erupted, they were depicted by Oriental leaders as a conflict between the Oriental development towns and the Ashkenazi-Sabra kibbutzim.

The Bren and the Brightest

THE ELECT

A tradition of closed revolutionary coteries that carefully chose their members developed in the Yishuv at the very beginning of the Zionist period. The first agricultural communes, the kibbutzim, the moshavim, the Labor Battalion, and the pioneer youth movements chose their members and developed their images as selective groups.

The elitist consciousness was developed and made more sophisticated largely in the military groups, most of which functioned in the underground. Nili, Ha-Shomer, Orde Wingate's Night Squads, and the Haganah's Special and Field Units all shared the aura of small, closed, and intimate bands of fighters whose very existence was a rumor whispered from one ear to another. Yitzchak Sadeh, one of the leaders of the Haganah, developed the Special Forces (first in the Haganah, later in the Palmach) and endowed them with the romanticism of young, elite units at the vanguard of military missions.[65]

The Palmach, more than any other organization, presented itself from its very inception as ʋ ʋmall, extra-establishment body whose purpose was special missions demanding boldness and ingenuity. The process of selecting candidates was strict, particularly during the first stages of the organization's establishment.[66] Y. Libtrovsky, commander of one of the first Palmach companies, testified that he chose his unit's sixty soldiers from among five hundred candidates.[67]

The image created by the selection process was no less important than its military value. The connection between the Palmach's small size and elitist self-image attested to by the resistance and disappointment, especially among the veteran members, prompted by the opening of its ranks to new immigrants and youth from "the [bad] neighborhoods" with the approach of the War of Independence. The old-timers feared that the Palmach would lose its uniqueness, and thus indirectly its prestige as a selective and homogeneous unit.

Exclusivity—both military and social—was also the reason for the Sabra's attraction to elite units such as the Palmach, Commando Unit 101, and later also the Paratroopers, the Marine Commandos, and the Air Force. Being a member of a small and intimate unit allowed the new recruit to feel like someone who was destined to raid rather than to fight, to attack rather than to defend, to be a fighter rather than just a soldier, to be one of the guys rather than a cog in the military machine, to have fun rather than just do a routine job.

Unit 101, which was set up in 1953 by Ariel Sharon to counter the infiltrations of Arab terrorists, contributed perhaps more than any other IDF unit to the institutionalization and sophistication of the army selection processes that first arose in the Palmach period—and this despite the very short period of about six months that the unit was active. The unending sifting of the candidates, both at the time of acceptance and during the course of their service, strengthened the sense of being an elect among the veterans who "held out," and made them see their service as both a dream come true and a challenge.

In Unit 101 the screening was linked to an informal selection ceremony— a kind of facetious hazing ritual in which the old-timers thought up arbitrary tests of courage. These ceremonies, which had their source in the Palmach, the agricultural schools, and the youth movements, later became very popular in elite units of the IDF (especially for basic training and "hell week"). Such rituals were possible because of the informal character of the units (which began with the Palmach), the sense of superiority of the experienced soldiers, and the candidate's fierce desire to be taken into the unit—for which reason he was willing to cooperate with those who were putting him to the test. This practice created an intimate family atmosphere among the soldiers and distinguished them from the general rank of IDF soldiers.[68] The distinction was sharpened by status symbols of unkemptness—allowing these soldiers to go around with their shirts unbuttoned and not tucked in, without berets, or even in civilian clothes.

The rumor of difficult entry tests, strict selection processes, and humorous ceremonies reinforced the romantic and secretive image of the first IDF combat units and motivated many Sabras, fired up with personal ambition and adventurousness, to line up at their gates. Gradually—and especially after the Sinai Campaign—the elite units became paths that granted a kind of "diploma" of personal excellence that was relevant not only in the army but also in the civilian sphere. A young man who was accepted into one of these "high *yeshivot*" saw himself not only as fervently fulfilling the precepts of pioneerism and devotedly serving his country, but also—perhaps especially—as a kind of prodigy and "superman." (The change that took place in image of the military profession in the 1950s is discussed in more detail later.)

With the establishment of the IDF, and particularly with the establishment of the officers' school in 1949, the selection process began to be institutionalized and more sophisticated. The degree of selectivity gradually became the principal criterion for ranking the army's units, and indirectly the criterion by which the status of their soldiers was determined. The process by which candidates for the Paratroopers, the Marine Commandos, and the Air Force were chosen became the male rites of passage and their myths.

In the 1950s the army began to use psychotechnical tests (IQ tests, Rorschach tests, psychometric examinations) to rank and assign enlistees.[69] These tests, which were then considered scientific (today we know that their validity is open to question), served as scientific seals of approval as to the high and rare quality of those who passed them and so added to those enlistees' elitist image.

Whereas the Palmach selected its men largely on an ideological basis and sometimes needed to persuade and induce young men to enlist, in the Marine Commandos and the flight school the selection process had the aura of an achievement test determining the personal level of the candidate and the extent to which he was appropriate for the elite unit. Air Force ads in the newspapers were addressed, for example: "To Israeli youth with education, courage, and superior health."[70] The motivation to serve the homeland was no longer sufficient for Sabras of the post-1948 period; now they had to meet physical and psychological criteria of achievement, such as high levels of physical fitness, stamina, aptitude in navigation, and marksmanship.

Because of their stringent selection processes, the elite units and the combat officers corps became Sabra incubators, as it were, with an almost homogeneous population (one fifth of all pilots were kibbutzniks and the decided majority of them were Ashkenazi graduates of academic high schools). Also contributing to this homogeneity were the "tribal-clannish" practices that grew up alongside the formal selection process— one soldier bringing his friend in and another recommending a member of his kibbutz or moshav. The ranks of these units were filled with young people from the educated, economically comfortable stratum who had been permeated with Zionist education. As a result the public saw an almost complete identity between the Sabra and the elite Israeli fighter. Songs of praise for these soldiers were thus indirectly songs of praise for the Sabra. The propaganda slogans "The finest to the Air Force" and "Follow me to the Paratroopers," coined in that period, included a generous dose of Sabra elitism. After all, if "the finest" were Sabras, then, by implication, the Sabras were the finest. The insignia of the army's units became marks of belonging not just to elite military organizations but also to a restricted stratum of young people—"the best of the youth."

Those who won a place in one of the elite units were admired by their friends and indirectly brought renown to the institutions in which they had grown up and been educated (the youth organization, the kibbutz, the boarding school, etc.). In this way a military aristocracy of young people with a manifestly Sabra cast continuously developed, and in time it became a political aristocracy.

The congruent cultural background of the members of the elite units also contributed to the internal social dynamic of the group. The intensive contact among the members of a homogeneous group of young people functioning as a total institution turned these units into socialization workshops that heightened the typical Sabra trademarks of language and dress among their members. This furthered the identification of the figure of the Sabra with the figure of the fighter in the elite army units.

BEING IN THE KNOW

Rules and norms of preserving secrecy are of utmost operational importance in an underground organization. But secrecy has another purpose as well. It gives the organization an air of mystery, and those who are in on the secret share a collective status symbol. This, apparently, is one of the reasons that a culture of secrecy characterized several of the military

organizations in the Yishuv and in Israel. The Bar Giora organization
(later Ha-Shomer), for example, functioned according to conspiratorial
rules. Its members were initiated in a mystery-shrouded nighttime ceremony and were sworn to secrecy and absolute loyalty to the organization.[71] An aura of secrecy also surrounded the Haganah, the Palmach,
and Unit 101. The appearance of the Palmach word *zaks* (or its Yiddish
form, *zeks*), meaning secret or a secret operation, in many nostalgic expressions of the period indicates the centrality of secrecy in Palmach folklore. *Zaks* would in later years be replaced by the term *shushu*.[72]

The mark of secrecy made being party to the secret a special entitle-
ment and raised the value of membership in the group that knew the secret: "To spend days and nights in the same company with such an important person, in a job that is secret from secretland—top, top secret!
Nothing could be more secret. There was a great deal of allure in that,"
related Netiva Ben-Yehuda.[73]

> In the period of the War of Independence and the establishment of the state
> everyone in the country had a huge desire to be in the know, and your im-
> portance was measured by how close you were to knowing. But I knew [things]
> that no one else would ever know, I really, really felt myself in the know . . .
> it was really doing something for the homeland. That I understood. That was
> really being a member of the underground.[74]

The elitist function of the culture of secrecy could explain why there
were secrets in the youth movements also, even though they generally
served no practical purpose. This was especially the case in the group
from which the Ha-Machanot Ha-Olim movement grew. This circle of
graduates of the Herzliya Gymnasium was organized at the end of the
1920s and was later called "the old circle." It surrounded itself with the
secrecy and intimacy of a monastic order. Covert swearing-in ceremonies
in caves and interring scrolls in secret locations also added an element
of contrived surreptitiousness to many ceremonies of the Scouts and Ha-
Shomer Ha-Tza'ir. There was a folklore of secrecy at the agricultural
schools as well. At the Kadoorie School, for example, the students would
conceal a secret book containing their writings in a location known only
to the seniors. This fondness for the clandestine was also the result of
exposure in childhood to a genre of mystery fiction that was popular at
the time[75]—in particular *The Detective* series by the journalist Shlomo
Ben-Yisrael (Gelper) and his colleagues,[76] in which the protagonist, David
Tidhar, was a kind of Sherlock Holmes of the Yishuv.

Secrecy glamorized the halo surrounding the secret units in which the

Sabra served. Restricting information and creating (sometimes artificially) differentials of information roused the imagination, produced stories of heroism and *chizbatim,* and contributed to the mystification of the Sabra group. The aura surrounding Unit 101 in the 1950s is one example. Scraps of information spread by word of mouth created a "Thousand and One Nights" saga that sprang out of the fertile imagination of the Israeli public.

The secrecy surrounding the Palmach, Unit 101, and the Paratroopers associated them with other famous secret groups, such as the World War II partisans, the underground organizations, army intelligence units, and the secret services, all of which were foci of the military mythology of the two world wars. The genre of suspense and war stories, which flourished in literature and cinema worldwide after World War II, also affected the IDF elite units' self-image and led them to imitate the images produced in books and on the screen. The huge popularity of Yigal Mosinzon's *Hasamba* books in the 1950s derived to a large extent from their motif of secrecy, which was an important element of the nostalgia for the War of Independence and of the culture of militarism that began to develop in its wake. The young people—the second generation of Sabras—were captivated by the secrecy and the clandestine adventures of this group of young fighters, a kind of kids' Palmach, fighting undercover against the British and the Arabs.

ESTABLISHMENT-APPROVED MISCHIEF

Sabra elitism was also expressed in the tradition of practical jokes and collective misbehavior and the practice of recounting these pranks to each other. This lighthearted "gang" folklore developed in the Palmach's mobilized *hachsharot* and was passed on to other youth groups, such as the youth movements and agricultural schools, reaching its peak in Unit 101 and in the Paratrooper Brigade established in the 1950s. It included pilfering products from the kibbutz food stores and moshav warehouses; stealing chickens from the kibbutz chicken coop for roasting at campfires; sneaking into cinemas; stealing signs off city streets and army bases to decorate the headquarters of one's own Palmach unit; raiding orchards and watermelon fields; outwitting sentries for the fun or the challenge of it; conducting hazing rituals for basic trainees and new members of the youth movements; fooling teachers, commanders, military policemen, and new members of the youth movements; breaking into bases and offices to steal equipment needed by the unit; and misbehavior by soldiers while off duty (trespassing, throwing smoke bombs, doing target practice on various civilian items).[77] All these were fundamental experiences that a "real" Sabra had to have and, even more so, had to tell.

The prominence of mischief-making in Sabra culture is attested to by six "cultural words" (words, generally slang, unique to a given culture and difficult to translate into another language) that are all contextually related:

shatara	From the Arabic for "cunning" or "sharp"; meaning an act of daring, but usually used sarcastically to refer to a not particularly dangerous prank. It was first used by the adolescents at Nahalal to refer to small, "harmless" thefts.
sechiva	Thievery as a prank, or a theft that is permissible and will be passed over. ("It wasn't really stealing. It was *sechiva*.")
siluk	Taking something without permission. ("He took [*silek*] ten eggs from the chicken coop and made us an omelette.")
fil'uach	Stealing as a prank. ("He stole [*file'ach*] a hen and three eggs from the coop.")
hitfalchut	Sneaking in, infiltrating, entering a movie or show or football game without a ticket. ("He used to sneak [*hitfale'ach*] into the cinema every day.")
meticha	A falsehood told maliciously so that someone will think it true, as a way of making the hearer look foolish. ("Don't give me that story [*meticha*]; go tell it to your grandmother.")[78]

These pranks and jokes were natural outbursts of energy and youthful playfulness—a part of the youth culture—and they characterize unified groups of young people everywhere who spend most of their time together (and who are often, as with the Palmach *hachsharot*, cut off from their external environment). In the Palmach, such actions kept up morale through days of fatiguing routine, especially the waiting period during World War II, when the Palmach was not active militarily.

The petty thefts and other pranks worked to break the boredom of the inactive periods, to tighten the bonds of the adolescent band (a shared delinquency creates a kind of common secret that unites the group), and to sharpen the adventure in national service. But they played an additional social role. Like the selection ceremonies and the secrecy, they demarcated the class separation between the elect Sabra organizations, with their special style, and non-Sabra or noncombat groups, which were perceived as inferior. As with the jokes about immigrants, here too the unstated purpose was to build up the elitist Sabra image by caricaturing other groups, such as soldiers in service roles. The military police (who represented the conventional discipline of the institutionalized army) and the guards at the gates of army bases symbolized to the Sabras the inferior noncombat soldier, later called "jobnik."[79] During the evening get-togethers, when the Sabras told their tales of how playing tricks on these other soldiers—setting "ambushes" for them, evading them, and so on—their victims were described as simpletons and idiots who could be toyed with by the cunning, conniving Sabra fighter and ever so easily be made into the butt of a good joke.

Unit 101 and the Paratroopers played an important part in fostering and institutionalizing Palmach-style mischievousness within the IDF. These units also played pranks and tricks as a way of expressing the superiority of the combat soldier to the jobnik, and thus indirectly of the Sabras to other groups in Israeli society. "Because of our feelings of superiority, which we overstated to no little degree, we sometimes permitted ourselves to say things that are better left unsaid today,"[80] related Meir Har-Tzion about his period of service in Unit 101.

These escapades and "petty" offenses were characteristic of an elite that felt it was permitted things forbidden to others because it was sacrificing more than others. Walking the thin rope between the permitted and the forbidden was also a way of putting the establishment to the test, a constant reclaiming of the special rights that the Sabra group deserved as an elite serving its country. The pranks expressed the anti-institutionalism of an intimate and exclusive guerrilla unit—its right to act autonomously within the larger organization as an elect group with special rights.

The stories and *chizbatim* about these pranks took root in Sabra culture and became part of the culture of discourse. They created an immediate, somewhat artificial nostalgia, and a romantic group image. The night raids for food and the tricks played on the sentries and military police were meant to assert the self-confidence, intrepidness, and adventurous spirit of the young fighters—these "hoodlums and outlaws," to employ the terms that labor movement leader Levi Eshkol used fondly for IDF Chief of Staff Moshe Dayan.

This piratical adventurousness was influenced by heroes of war and adventure literature as well as the protagonist of Hemingway's *For Whom the Bell Tolls* (a very popular book among Israeli youth) and the stars of Westerns, action films, and war movies—the noble savages, irresistible to women, who populated the postwar Hollywood films. The Sabra wanted to be a bit like the fun-loving and crafty heroes of these stories, whose fundamental morality and noble purposes allowed them, on occasion, to violate the dry letter of the law.[81] In the works of the "mouth-pieces of the generation" as well—the songs, *chizbatim,* stories, and poems of Sabra writers—the Sabra prank was a primary expression of a rowdy and winning youth culture, one of the facets of the "Huckleberry Finn-ish" Sabra bad boy.

It was not just the Sabras who viewed their pranks as the legitimate privilege of an elite—most of the adult representatives of the establishment and the moral norm-setters (teachers, commanders, political leaders) did so too. As far as they were concerned, these were venial sins—even positive character attributes—that expressed the lovable, playful, cunning, rough-hewn, anti-establishment character of the native, his youthful charm and grinning sociability. This is evidenced in the slang terms listed earlier, which denote a forgiving attitude toward communal transgressions of thieving and lying, and which were absorbed into the Hebrew language and warmly received by political leaders, educators, and literary critics.

Officially, the Palmach command frowned on pranks, especially the thefts from the kibbutzim that hosted the *hachsharot*—most likely out of fear that the kibbutzim would not want to host the Palmach groups any more. "It is best to know that the people on the farms take a dim view of [these pranks]. . . . Where is the line? . . . The line is to not begin,"[82] states an article in one issue of *Alon Ha-Palmach*. But this was largely lip service, because in practice everyone in the Palmach was delighted with the folklore of these youthful pranks, and the practical jokes and petty crimes were viewed like the scratches given by a cute little puppy.[83] The older generation called the youngsters "clowns" and scolded them for being "naughty"—words that conveyed a kind of smiling reprimand by fathers against their bold and impertinent offspring and thus indicated the Sabras' special status in the eyes of the establishment and the high social credit given to them.

Sabra misbehavior was also forgiven because it expressed, for the older generation, the instinct for freedom and independence attributed to the "new Jew," the natural joy of life of the mythological Sabra, and perhaps also the raw, dross-like roughness of the "untrained" native who grew up, so the myth said, in nature. "A girl like most of our Sabra girls. . . .

She was proud and solid of character. The girl was independent and rebellious—like a symbol of that native generation of the homeland,"[84] wrote Anda Pinkerfeld-Amir about a Palmach girl. This vitality, spontaneity, and warm-bloodedness had been part of the mythological profile of the new Jew as far back as the time of Ha-Shomer, whose members were influenced by romantic images of Russian *muzhiks* and Cossacks.

A further reason for absolution was that the pranks were a kind of escape valve for the pressures felt by young people who bore the burden of their community's defense. The establishment sanctioned Sabra practical jokes as part of an unspoken contract—this elite was granted special rights in exchange for accepting the role of the new Jew and the yoke of defense (perhaps this also explains the later leniency toward the antiquities thefts of one of the senior Sabras, Moshe Dayan). In fact, the normative distance between *sechiva* and theft and between a *meticha* and a lie was the distance between the way in which society forgave the transgressions of Palmach or IDF soldiers and the way it condemned the same kind of actions performed by young people from the marginal culture (for example, from the transit camps).[85] The Sabra had a license to be outspoken and to misbehave, but it was a very constrained kind of misbehavior.

STATUS SYMBOLS: STOCKING CAP,
KAFIYYEH, MACHINE GUN, AND JEEP

The elitist image of the Sabra group (and in particular the military organizations) was also marketed via visual status symbols. The male Sabra's appearance included almost deliberately haphazard dress; a work shirt or youth movement shirt; khaki pants or work shorts with large pockets sticking out of them; a stocking cap, Australian hat, or red paratrooper's beret; a bedouin *kafiyyeh* (headdress) tied around the neck like a cowboy's bandanna; a dusty army coat, tattered from constant use; "Biblical" sandals, worn even in the winter, generally without socks. Also de rigueur was short, unkempt hair with forelocks either falling over the forehead, peeking out from under the hat, or pulled back; an unshaven beard; tanned skin; and a dust-encrusted face. Finally, the typical Sabra, as he appears in photographs, would sport Sabra fashion accessories: a Sten submachine gun, a Bren rifle or, in the 1950s, a made-in-Israel Uzi submachine gun (the eponymous Uzi became an inseparable part of Sabra folklore); a rucksack worn over the shoulder and resting on the hip; and for those who were lucky or who had rank, a jeep.

The jeep and the pickup truck were of special symbolic importance and figure in any number of popular nostalgic songs written by Chaim Guri and Chaim Cheffer.[86] Like many other popular heroes, the mythical Sabra had a (motorized) war horse. The jeep symbolized the class privilege of the modern cavalry[87] and reinforced the romantic image of the fighting Sabra. The open vehicle, with its horsepower and maneuverability in the field, also expressed the freedom, machismo, and power of the fighting Sabra—the cowboy of the Israeli wilderness.

Linguistic Expressions of Elitism and Narcissism

DAVKA, KACHA, BETACH, AND SMOCH

The elitist tone of colloquial Sabra speech lies in its stresses, its syntax, and especially in its typical mode of response. The response is impertinent, cocksure, and arrogant, and often expresses contempt for the questioner and disregard for the question. It is expressed in common words that are difficult, if not impossible, to translate into another language. While some of these were adopted from other languages (largely Yiddish, Arabic, and Russian) rather than invented by the Sabras, in Sabra parlance they received special connotations. The most common of them follow:

Davka	This word of emphasis carries the connotation of doing something unexpected or undesirable, whether your interlocutor likes it or not. ("I told you not to make any stops along the way, but you *davka* had to go visit your girlfriend at the kibbutz.") The word comes from Yiddish, which in turn took it from Talmudic Aramaic (where, however, it does not bear the same contrary connotation) and was assimilated so completely into the Sabra culture of discourse that in time it turned into a noun and an adverb ("*davka* behavior"; "he did it to him *davka*"). However, it is often used simply for emphasis ("As a matter of fact, that's really *[davka]* where I wanted to go in the first place"; "Why are you standing

precisely *[davka]* here [and not somewhere else]?"). As far as I have been able to determine, there is no precise parallel for this word in other languages, so it can be taken to reflect a mood or a norm characteristic of the group that uses it. It expresses the Sabra's *chutzpah,* another word from the Yiddish that has entered English as well as Hebrew and is also a description of Sabra behavior. The *davka* spirit is one of defiance, disobedience, standing one's ground, doing things out of spite and stubbornness—all founded on an awareness of one's own worth.

Kacha   This response, roughly equivalent to an American child's "just because," is used to avoid giving a more specific example. (Uri: But why won't you do it? Uzi: *Kacha.*) This laconic reply also indirectly denotes contempt for the questioner: "I don't want to answer just now or provide the motives for my action," "It's none of your business," or "I'm going to do whatever I damn well please."

Betach   This means "of course," but with a Sabra inflection it expresses absolute certainty. It is a positive response given with perfect confidence and without hesitation: "*Betach* I'm right, what do you think?" It also carries a sense of having no regard for what has just been said. When Uri answers *Betach!* to Uzi's question, he is not only giving an answer in which he has absolutely perfect confidence, but is also, as it were, censuring Uzi for having even imagined that such a question could arise. (Uzi: Do you think we can take that hill with just one platoon? Uri: *Betach!* What a question!)

Me'ah achuz	Literally, "one hundred percent." The connotation is "great," or "without a doubt, of course." ("*Me'ah achuz* you won't pass the test.") In some contexts it is synonymous with *betach,* expressing the same self-confidence and disregard for the interlocutor's query.
Eifo!	This is the interrogatory "where?" but the Sabra used it with an exclamatory inflection to mean "that can't be," "no way," "absolutely not." It also conveys self-confident disregard.
Ma pitom!	Literally something like "what, all of a sudden." It connotes "no," "wrong," "it's not that way at all." (Uri: The Palmach assassinated Lord Moyne. Uzi: *Ma pitom!* Next thing you'll say is that the Palmach liquidated Count Bernadotte!) Its elitist tone is similar to that of *Eifo.*
Bilbul mo'ach	Used as both an adjective and a verb, this literally means "brain-confounding." It connotes an annoyance, or nonsense. ("What attack? *Eifo* attack! It's just a *bilbul mo'ach.*") It too expresses scorn for the other person and rejection of his opinion.
Eifo? Be-Haifo!	Literally, "Where? In Haifa!" meaning "I don't want to tell you where! Every idiot knows where!"
Lo mithashek li or *lo mithashmek li*	This means: "Right now I don't have the patience or the strength to do it," and expresses independence and contempt.
Be-hayecha and *al tegaleh li et America*	Literally, "on your life" and "don't discover America for me." Used with a disdainful intonation to mean "Don't try to explain to me what I already know."

Azov shtuyot and *al tebalbel li et ha-beitzim*	Literally, "leave off the nonsense" and "don't mix up my balls." The meaning is a contemptuous: "You don't understand a thing about it."
Smoch alai	Literally, "trust me," short for: "Don't worry, you can be absolutely sure that I'll solve your problem very soon and very easily" or "Don't panic, everything will work out in the end." Other similar expressions are *yihiyeh be-seder* ("It'll be okay," but with a large measure of self-confidence); *ala pata* ("I don't care," "I don't give a shit"); *ma'alish* ("it doesn't matter"); *meila* ("so what"); and *dahilak* (*be-hayecha!*, "on your life!").

Smoch was first and foremost a word of reassurance, in many ways a replacement for the traditional expression *be-ezrat Ha-Shem,* "with God's help." It expressed the Sabra's ability and readiness to make do—a myth that became deeply rooted in the consciousness of Sabra youth as well as the public at large, as the victories of the Hebrew fighter over his Arab enemies became more numerous, and the Sabra folklore of the combat units took on flesh. In this sense it was a kind of code word expressing a romantic, uninstitutionalized guerrilla culture. The Sabra who barked out *"smoch!"* was declaring "I don't need precise orders from above. I can act quickly and efficiently and at short notice." In later years, some considered this attitude to be one of the illnesses of Israeli society. *Smoch* expressed the astuteness and craftiness of the fighting Sabra. The man who reassured his comrade with *smoch* was priding himself for his flexibility, cleverness, and ability to quickly adjust to changing circumstances and get himself out of any, even sudden, trouble.

The curt, confident *smoch* also signified a kind of unstated contempt for a person who dared criticize or give advice on military matters to those who considered themselves "the most professional of professionals"—"don't tell me what to do or how to do it." It was the exclamation of the seasoned and impatient fighter shrugging off annoying advice-mongers.

The optimism and cocksureness contained in *smoch* indirectly expressed a sense of invulnerability (a feeling that would be condemned by Yitzchak Rabin later when he was prime minister), and reinforced the willingness of the soldier in an elite unit to take risks and to go to the very limits of his physical ability—to play with fire.

BUDDY HUMOR
AT THE EXPENSE OF NON-SABRAS

Sabra discourse is full of jokes and *chizbatim* that make fun—though usually good-humoredly and even at the Sabras' own expense—of the "others" who did not belong and therefore did not understand. The major targets of wit were the Arabs, the old-timers of the Yishuv and state leadership, the old-timers in the moshavot, Holocaust survivors, and the Oriental immigrants of the 1950s. This jeering spirit was especially characteristic of the *chizbatim* that appeared in the humor column of the army publications and the *Pack of Lies* anthologies of Cheffer and Ben-Amotz.

Among the prominent topics of these jokes and stories are the non-Sabra's—especially the new immigrant's—lack of proficiency in Hebrew and his ignorance of words with inside connotations in Sabra culture, his unfamiliarity with linguistic "errors" that had been made legitimate by the Sabras, and his use of linguistic constructions that had come to mean the precise opposite in Sabra parlance. The older generation (especially that of the Fourth and Fifth Aliyot) was also depicted as inexpert in Sabra language and was frequently satirized in Sabra inside jokes and *chizbatim*.[88]

Unfamiliarity with the native lexicon signaled nonparticipation in the experiences that shaped the younger generation. Making fun of people stumbling over the language, especially over funny slang words, was meant to make the non-Sabras look ridiculous—unable to understand Sabra wisecracks or laugh at the world loudly and without restraints and complexes. In short, the non-Sabras were depicted as people who had not yet disconnected themselves from the Diaspora and adjusted to the Israeli spirit. This seems to be the reason why immigrants from Germany were particular targets of Sabra humor. The Germans, many of whom were middle-class professionals who had fled Hitler, preserved European manners and German "squareness" as well as seriousness, naiveté, and a marked German accent. In other words, they were the polar opposite of the unmannered, insolent, and unbuttoned Sabra. The distance between the German Jew and the Sabra was the distance between the "stranger's" elegant smoking jacket and the unpressed khaki pants and filthy undershirt of the native.

The Sabra's special language became such an exclusive trademark that it was absorbed into the country's young literature as an elitist and stereotypical sign. Many Sabra writers used the spoken language to characterize their Sabra heroes and sometimes even to reinforce the distinction between the fun-loving image of the mythological Sabra fighter and the conventional and hapless figure of the new immigrant.

Wisecracks are found not only in the Sabras' jokes and *chizbatim*, whose tacit role was to establish superiority over outside groups, but also in the derogatory names they attached to the outsiders. *Arabush, arabchuk, araber* referred to Arabs.[89] *Igen migen* was a scornful term referring to the language and accent of an immigrant from Hungary. *Pushtak* or *pusht* was a name for an ignorant, unsophisticated, valueless, and rude person and was used principally to denote young Oriental Jews—"Stop running around with those *pushtakim*." A *zalman* was a soft, hunched-over immigrant from Eastern Europe with knee-length pants. *Yekke potz* referred to new immigrants from Germany and was originally used by Polish Jews, but was warmly adopted by the Sabras.

Attaching ethnic labels to outsiders is a classic phenomenon in immigrant societies. Laughing at the expense of the immigrants serves as a linguistic tool for fixing their outsider status and preserving the cultural hegemony of the veteran native—a kind of antibody against cultural "invaders." Even when the outsider's immigration is valued for ideological reasons (as was the case during the Yishuv and early state period), he and the foreign culture he represents are still a threat to the local culture, which defends itself via a humor that taints the newcomer.

THE NEGEV BEASTS AND THE
SHIMSHON FOXES: ROMANTIC NICKNAMES

An important tool for fostering the Palmach's elitist image was the invention of romantic and humorous nicknames for its members. So, for example, a red-haired soldier would be called by the slang term for that condition, "Gingi," and other physical traits might lead to others being called "Sini" (Chinese) or "Kushi" (black). Company commander Rechavam Ze'evi's dark skin and thin frame prompted the epithet "Gandhi."

Palmach units and IDF units with a Sabra image were called by names with geographic or historical connotations. Examples are the Yiftach Brigade, named after the military leader of the Book of Judges, and the Negev Brigade, named after Israel's southern desert. Other units had romantic titles with a Hollywood flair: the Palmach itself, whose name was an acronym for "strike companies"; the Negev Beasts; the Shimshon Foxes; the Flying Camels; and the One Hundred Percent Commandos.

These names were meant to promote, by association, a heroic image for the elite as a whole. They were part of the separatist language of the Sabra fighters and like the slang, *chizbatim,* and jokes, were based on an internal code of common experiences and on a humor that an outsider would not understand. The romantic aura that surrounded the figure with the nickname (Gandhi, Cheetah) or the unit with the special title (the Negev Beasts) indirectly spread to include the entire generational unit.

The special (and therefore catchy) name of a person or a unit made it easier for that person or unit to make an impression on the collective memory and be turned into a myth. Furthermore the name, being unique, emphasized the uniqueness of the individual fighter or military unit and made him or it a historical entity; it served as a kind of generational or communal brand name, a good marketing tool for the image of the elitist group.

The Myth of the Fighting Sabra and His Symbolic Accessories

THE SABRA'S VICTORY IN THE WAR OF INDEPENDENCE AND THE SINAI CAMPAIGN

Battle sagas appeared among the Yishuv immediately after the first clashes between the pioneers and the Arabs. These war stories were important as milestones in the national biography—mythological kernels from which grew not only military ethoses and myths (such as fighting at any cost and caring for the wounded), but also national ones (love of country, national solidarity). Furthermore, they produced cultural heroes; the fighters who sacrificed their lives and the commanders who led their units to victory were exemplary figures in whose deeds the young generation was educated.

The battles etched into the national memory were largely battles over strategic points or places of national historical importance, and most of them were bloody. The Palmach battalions, which were considered the elite fighting force in the War of Independence, were sent to win the strategic points around which the major portion of the war mythology and nostalgia grew—the Nebi Yosha police station, the road to Jerusalem, Kibbutz Negba, Safed, Be'ersheva, and Eilat. The prominence given to these battles made their commanders (most of whom were Sabras) famous, and also celebrated the role of the fighting Sabra in the campaign. In the same measure this minimized the importance of other units and of non-Sabra soldiers. The role of the fighting Sabra was also emphasized because of the Palmach milieu, which was familiar to the public even before the war, thanks to the poets and writers who served in the force.

In the Sinai Campaign, the army was led by the Paratrooper Corps, which was perceived as the heir of the Palmach. Their landing in the Mitla Pass, at the enemy's rear, became a military myth that to a certain extent upstaged the important role played by the armored corps (whose soldiers were considered less colorful, "squarer," and thus less Sabra). The Air Force deployed jets for the first time and with great success, creating the mythology of the Hebrew pilot that is part of Israeli folklore to this day. The victories in the War of Independence and in the Sinai Campaign were thus viewed largely as victories of the Palmachnik, the paratrooper, and the pilot—and indirectly of the Sabra. The role of other army units and other cultural groups was minimized.

Identification of the fighters with the Sabras was expressed in the memorial at Kibbutz Negba designed by Natan Rappaport, a designer and sculptor of many such memorials. It depicts three fighters of manifestly Sabra appearance (a young farm worker wearing the standard cloth hat that the Sabras called a "dunce cap," a young fighter, and a girl bearing a first-aid kit). Associating the fighters with the Sabras was also the topic of the famous cartoon of 16 April 1948 by Arieh Navon, who drew a Palmach stocking cap on top of Kastel, the hill on the way to Jerusalem that was the site of an important War of Independence victory.

The photograph of the raising of an inked Israeli flag at Um Rash Rash (later Eilat), marking the end of Operation Uvda, became, on publication, part of the mythology of 1948[90] and is probably the most outstanding example of a war symbol instilling in the public an identification between the Sabra and the victorious troops of 1948. The commanders of the Negev Brigade and the Golani Brigade sent a cable to the commander of the southern front: "Announce to the government of Israel. For Haganah Day, 11 Adar, the Negev Brigade [of the Palmach] and the Golani Brigade present the Gulf of Eilat to the State of Israel. Eilat (Um Rash Rash) 9 Adar 1949."[91] After the fact, however, it was not the cooperation between the two brigades that was emphasized, but rather the stunning victory of the Negev Brigade (with its Sabra image) over the Golani Brigade (which was not part of the Palmach) on the prestigious race to conquer Eilat. The victory in battle that ended the War of

Independence was thus also made to symbolize the primacy of the Palmach units and thus, indirectly, the Sabra.

It is important to stress that the war glorified the mythological image of the Sabra not only because of the symbolic way the Israeli elite designed the events, but also because of the heroic deeds of the many Sabras who fought on the front line. War creates myths not only because the nebulousness of war allows the imagination to fill in the gaps in people's knowledge, but also because it fosters individual acts of heroism and dedication. The characters in the mythological narrative emerge from battle larger than life, raised above quotidian drabness—not just artificially but also because there are times when a man's greatness is revealed in emergencies.

War is not part of the regular course of human life. It is a sui generis reality that annuls the soldier's normal sense of time and place. It "cuts him off from all his previous connections, swallows him up, changes his identity, takes over his consciousness."[92] Only a period of turbulence and war, it seems, with its unique circumstances, has what it takes to evoke in a man the complete devotion characteristic of many Sabras and bring him to a once-in-a-lifetime epiphany. Bearing a wounded man under a hail of bullets does not testify to dedication to one's friends in peacetime, nor does leading a charge guarantee that a man will be brave in his civilian life. The fury of battle engenders special powers that are not revealed in normal times.

To a large extent, the war disclosed special traits in an entire generation that found itself thrown into the fray. It removed—almost forced— many young people out of their anonymity and created the soil in which the Sabra heroes grew. "Only wars can turn their heroes into legends and hand them the story of their lives in poetry, as a great gift," poet Yigal Lev would later write.[93]

THE ROLE OF MEMORIALIZATION
IN THE MYTHOLOGY OF THE SABRA

The role played by memorial literature in the creation of a national mythology is not unique to modern times; it is as old as war itself. But modern wars, in which the fighting is done by mobilized civilians rather than professional soldiers for the sake of the homeland (which is itself a modern concept) and in which bloodshed reaches astounding dimensions, has brought the cult of the fallen in battle to its acme.

The memorialization culture of modern Europe, an inseparable part of the new national culture, influenced Israeli memorial culture—even if this influence was indirect and sometimes unconscious. Nevertheless, the two cultures are not identical. Israeli memorial culture has its own codes, derived from the Zionist pioneer values and traditional Judaism. Unique to Israeli culture is the identification of the image of the fallen soldier with the mythological image of the Sabra. Four elements contributed to this identity, which added decisively to the mythologizing of the Sabras in the Israeli public eye.

The first element was the high proportion of Sabras among all the fallen soldiers who were memorialized. Historian Emmanuel Sivan discovered that more than 80 percent of the memorial books were devoted to Sabras and near-Sabras, and this same proportion applies to the *Scrolls of Fire* anthology.[94] Sabras are also overrepresented in other means of memorialization, such as scholarships and sports competitions (four out of every ten), when compared to their proportion among the fallen soldiers (three out of ten). Sivan found that the chances of a person being memorialized in these ways increased with the person's seniority in the country.[95] He also showed that the members of youth movements in the Yishuv were memorialized more than those who had been members of youth movements only overseas, and officers were memorialized two to four times more than their proportion among the fallen.[96] The greater the number of a soldier's elite characteristics (officer rank, high school education, membership in a kibbutz), the greater his chance of being memorialized in an intensive way; the greater his distance from the elite (1948 immigration, less than an elementary education, Oriental heritage), the less his chance of being memorialized at all.[97]

The second element was the Sabras' linguistic fluency and their common practice of writing diaries, desk-drawer poems, and letters. Many of the new immigrants who were sent to the battlefield very soon after their arrival in the country did not speak—and especially did not write—Hebrew well and thus did not leave behind Hebrew manuscripts that could be included in *Scrolls of Fire* and other memorial anthologies.[98]

The third element was the access the families of the Sabras had to the means of memorialization. Many non-Sabras who fell in the war—including many new immigrants, who were taken straight from the boat to the battlefield—reached the country alone, without anyone who might memorialize them afterward. For some, their biographies before their arrival in the country and even their names were unknown. The memorial album genre developed largely in the agricultural settlements and their extensions (the youth movements and elite units) because these organizations had greater access to means of expression that were used for memorialization—from knowledge of the language to access to printing presses and publishing houses and membership in bodies that organized concerts and sports events.[99]

The fourth element was the social profile of the fallen. Most of the commanders who were killed and became myths were Sabras; they were also more likely than others to leave behind papers and other writings worthy of publication.

The high proportion of Sabras among those memorialized contributed to the impression that the Sabra elite, the children of the agricultural settlements, had brought about the victory in the War of Independence and had paid the heaviest price. It was not only the numbers of the Sabras among the memorialized soldiers that created this impression; because of the "Hebrew" ethos, the memorial literature tended to emphasize the Sabra traits of the fallen, even among those who had not been Sabra in character or cultural background.

The mythology of the fighting Sabra was fostered not only by the extent of memorialization, but also, and in fact principally, by its content. Memorialization means profuse praises for the memorialized. The custom of praising martyrs after their deaths is universal.[100] But in the Israeli culture of mourning the praises are especially voluminous and have an extremely emotional character. One reason is that these soldiers fell defending the entire Yishuv, which was in danger of annihilation, and they were memorialized out of a deep sense of gratitude. The Sabra generation was perceived (with a large measure of justice) to have blocked with its own body the enemy's threats to destroy the Jewish Yishuv.

The memorial books expressed the spontaneous gratitude of those who had not fought on the front for those who had fought and paid the price. The superlatives for the fallen were like verbal laurel wreaths placed by the Israeli establishment on the heads of the dead heroes, and indirectly also on the living ones. This bond of indebtedness was expressed in the widespread use, even in the memorial books for single fighters, of general terms such as "our sons," "the children," "the generation," and "the boys."

Gratitude to the Sabras was a major element of the public mood. Besides the memorial anthologies, it was also articulated in literature, especially in the work of Zionist poet Natan Alterman, many of whose poems embellished the memorial books and so became part of the cult of mourning. Alterman had a fierce love for the younger generation. In the 1940s, largely through his weekly column, "The Seventh Column," published in the daily newspaper *Davar,* he served as a kind of barometer of the public mood and became the hymnodist of the Israeli national religion.[101] His extremely popular poems made a decisive contribution to the mythologization of the Sabra. He made frequent use of general nouns like "generation" and "boys," and thanking the young fighters (especially the Palmachniks) was one of the central motifs in his poetry.

His poem "The Silver Tray" became the Israeli memorial culture's most important elegy, a national rhapsody of the Sabra and a kind of requiem for use in national memorial ceremonies:

> So the nation will ask, in awe, overcome and in tears,
> The query: Who is it? And the two of them will quietly say
> In response:
> This is the State of the Jews
> That is given by us, the silver tray![102]

Another reason for the idealization of the fallen Sabra was that by praising and exalting the Sabra generation, the Zionist leaders—the founding fathers of the agricultural settlements in particular—were glorifying themselves and their pioneer enterprise. Their praise for the fallen soldier implied praise for those who had educated and fostered him.

Mythologization of the fallen Sabra in turn mythologized the entire Sabra generation through a motif common in memorial literature— linking the fallen soldier to the rest of his generation through the frequent use of that word, and linking his exemplary figure to the exemplary figures of his living comrades. A fascinating example of this motif can be found in the introduction to the *Scrolls of Fire* anthology written by a mourning father. Its title is "This Generation . . .":

> Since taking on the editing of the papers of the members of this wonderful generation, which gave its life in joy and sanctity so that the entire people could walk tall and proud, I have spent days and nights in the shadow of that glory, diving into the inner recesses of its soul and conversing with its spirit, and sometimes also silently heeding the voice of its blood. . . . Here the generation has risen—and it has taken on vitality and vigor! . . . Here, the self-portraits come together into a single figure and picture, etched with a human quill dipped in the inkwell of truth.[103]

The link between the fallen and their living comrades was made by common use of the general terms "sons," "boys," "young men," "our dead," "our boys," and "our youth" in the eulogies and the dirges for the fallen (largely those by the 1948 poets). Especially common, of course, is the general term "Sabra" or "Sabras" (which became very common, perhaps more so than any of the other terms, after the War of Independence), as in this example: "His figure was that of a typical Sabra, a man of action and reality."[104]

The artists who illustrated some of these anthologies, such as Nachum Gutman and Arieh Navon, also contributed to the identification of the fallen with the rest of their generation. They drew the fallen wearing typical Palmach dress, such as work shoes, a stocking cap, and a rucksack, and so created an associative link between the fallen soldier and the Palmachnik.

The use of generalized terms while emphasizing the link between the individual fallen soldier and his group increased the homogeneity of the collective image of the Sabras. They were perceived as being all made of the same psychological, ethical, and especially ideological material. As a result, the writings of the talented fallen soldiers included in the memorial anthologies became exhibits of the talents of their living relatives and of the soul of the entire generation. As one eulogist wrote: "May this memorial stone of his spirit be yours. The youth will pore over it, turn its pages, walk the paths of his thinking like the paths of their own thinking; for they are indeed of a single cloth, and his words are theirs."[105]

Associating the fallen soldier with the members of his generation also created a connection between his exemplary image and those of his comrades in the youth movement, *hachshara,* and army unit. Idealizing him also idealized his living comrades who had grown up in the same youth groups.

It is worth remarking that, despite the natural tendency of the memorial anthologies to emphasize the positive and beautiful side of the fallen soldiers' characters, and although the published letters were carefully chosen to present only the aesthetic and sublime,[106] the writers and anthology editors did not make things up or glorify the fallen soldiers in an exaggerated way. There were indeed many acts of heroism and sacrifice, and the many Sabras who fell did indeed exhibit the best human traits, such as concern for others, humility, creativity, and a touching youthful innocence.

An additional factor in the mythologization of the Sabra in the memorial literature is connected to the structure of the memorial anthologies and to the cult of revealing the "real character" of the Sabra. These anthologies contained not only glorification of the fallen soldier and stories about him by friends, acquaintances, and family members, but also, and usually principally, songs, compositions, letters, and diaries that he wrote. These revealed to the entire community the hidden talents of the fallen Sabras and their unreserved loyalty to the common good. The publication of private writings became a kind of verbal national ceremony meant to open a window into the inner world of the Sabra sons and daughters. It was meant not only to create a monument to the fallen, but also, and perhaps primarily, to present their pure and noble souls while taking fond pride in "the young generation that has grown up here," signaling a tacit message to the generations that followed: we have these expectations of you as well.

These creative works and intimate letters left behind by the fallen Sabras made a huge impression on the public. "Anyone who reads these pages finds that his heart pounds from the rush of a great spirit, the spirit of a man from Israel, new and original. A sacred spirit emanates from them,"[107] one of the readers wrote. Reading the works of the fallen Sabras created a feeling that young men of great soul and talent, having great promise, had grown up here in Israel and given their lives for their country.[108] This ritual of revelation reinforced the mythological image of the Sabra as rough and thorny on the outside but sweet and delicate on the inside. The ostensibly rugged Sabra turned out to be a secret poet, a sensitive man of the spirit, a devoted family man. "Unseen by strange eyes, perhaps unseen by themselves," David Ben-Gurion wrote of the Sabras, "there were hidden chambers of innocence and beauty in the lion cubs of Israel—of heroism and love, softness and daring—and perhaps only their mothers knew just a bit of them."[109]

It was the *Scrolls of Fire* anthology that in particular painted the picture of the Sabra as a reticent poet and writer and as a potential philosopher or scientist. This entire book was compiled from the works of the fallen. Its very name suggests a newly revealed primeval work or the sacred scrolls of the Torah. The title also evoked the Torah scrolls in which Talmudic martyr Hanina Ben Tardion was wrapped by the Romans when they put him to the stake, described poetically in the traditional Yom Kippur service: "the scrolls that burned as their letters flew skyward."

The ceremony of revealing the sublime character of the fallen Sabra (and indirectly the members of his generation) also symbolized the great modesty of the Sabra hero. "Modest and great" was what poet Yehuda Karni called them in one of his paeans to the Sabras.[110] Many of the eulogists noted this modesty—the Sabra kept his talents hidden and did not publish his writing despite its excellence—and claimed it was the fallen Sabras' most important trait. Since the Sabra papers also revealed an unusually intense love of the homeland, they also represented a kind of ideological modesty—national service performed without expectation of reward.

This reticence reveals a not-coincidental parallel between the images of the Sabra and the saint or righteous person in the traditions of many religions. This is illustrated in a eulogy by Shlomo Lavi of Kibbutz Ein Harod on the thirtieth day after the death of his son:

> My eldest son was a simple man, a faithful worker, honest. He did not speak in the name of ideas, did not proclaim ideas, hated fancy words, but all that was moral and pure was close to his heart without him saying so and without him knowing it himself. Yosef Chaim Brenner would call such people "good dumb Jews" and I call them the honest men, dedicated to action.[111]

THE HEBREW COMMANDER

Most of the Sabra heroes commemorated in the memorial literature and made into national exemplars of virtue were commanders. In fact, the image of the Sabra was not identified in the public consciousness so much with the fighter as with the commander—the new Hebrew warrior. If the Palmachnik and the riflemen in the combat units were perceived as students in "Zionist houses of study," then thanks to the memorial anthologies, the commanders were the prodigies.

Several factors contributed to the prominence of the Sabra commander in the Israeli culture of mourning. First, the Sabras, as Emmanuel Sivan found, were overrepresented at the command level on the front lines (compared to new immigrants, few of whom were commanders).[112] Second, the commanders were better known than the soldiers, and many of them were much admired while alive, making it easier to collect biographical information about them. Third, the commanders were, by nature, the most talented members of their generation and generally had a superior ability to express themselves. As a consequence, they left a larger quantity and higher quality of writings than their soldiers did. Fourth, an anti-Diaspora image was attached to the commander. The emergence of the "Hebrew general" seems to have been the culmination of the Zionist movement's dream. After a hiatus of two thousand years, Jews could finally take pride in their own men of war—Hebrew-speaking Napoleons and Hannibals. It seemed as if the souls of David, Gideon, Joshua, and Bar Kochba had risen up from the earth and that ancient Jewish glory had reappeared (this is apparently the reason why so many of the 1948 commanders had Biblical names like Nachshon, Yoav, Yiftach, and Ben

Nun). The Hebrew commander was the polar opposite of the Diaspora Jew: he was self-confident, proud, and brave, knowing what lay before him; a leader, not a subject. The admiration, over many years, for Yigal Allon and Moshe Dayan, two of the most famous commanders who produced the Zionist revolution, was the veneration of a dream come true. Fifth, the figure of the commander fulfilled the revolutionary society's need for exemplary figures, for normative "lighthouses." The commanders who served as personal examples in their professionalism and their patriotic devotion, who charged at the head of their forces and united their soldiers around them, were models of excellence and were perceived as the nation's emissaries.

The virtues typically attributed to the commander are instructive not only about the character of the mythological Sabra, but also about the Israeli combat culture's system of values and, because of the importance of the commander in a society at battle, also about the Zionist elite as a whole. The following are the major ones.

Charismatic Leader   The "expressive" side of the commander was emphasized over the "instrumental" side. He was presented in texts not as the holder of a position, a bureaucrat in a military organization whose power and status derive from a formal hierarchy, but rather as a charismatic father admired by his soldiers because of his human qualities. The commander was a natural leader whose commission came from his soldiers, so it seemed, and required no formal authorization from above.

Since he was a natural leader, he needed no insignia or marks of rank (many commanders, through the 1950s, in fact deliberately avoided displaying their rank) and behaved with humility, like one of the guys. This kind of commander is characteristic of organizations like the Palmach, a voluntary organization engaged in guerrilla warfare.[113]

This image was influenced in no small way by the well-known novel *Panpilov's Men*, whose protagonist is a Russian battalion commander who transforms his simple soldiers into fierce fighters, fills them with confidence and faith, and leads them through the power of his personality. He does not force his soldiers to carry out orders, but rather plants within them the desire to fulfill his orders by force of his example. The book was extremely popular in the Palmach and in the IDF in its early days, especially among the lower-level officers, and became a kind of behavioral guidebook for them.

Expressive leadership is characteristic of an ideological or religious system, and a military commander in such a system also fills the role of a spiritual shepherd. His nobility indirectly increases the luster of the religious or revolutionary doctrine among his soldiers, whose love for their commander leads them to love the ideology he represents. The commanders' natural leadership indicates that they are indeed the community's elected and beloved leaders—the cream of the crop.

Pursuer of a Mission, Not a Profession   The commander is generally presented as a person who has assumed his role temporarily because of a state of emergency, and not out of a desire to advance up the military ladder. In many memorial anthologies and in combat stories the fallen commander (including members of the IDF's standing army) is a man who has left the barn and the workshop to lend his hand to the war effort. When the war subsides, he will return, according to the myth, to being an anonymous citizen.

The motif of the volunteer fighter was also influenced by the tale of the Maccabees, who according to legend led a popular army (as opposed to the professional Hellenistic army) made up of farmers who had left their plows to defend their homeland.

Military command as a mission, as fulfillment of the call of the movement or one's conscience, was stressed a great deal in Palmach and IDF folklore, since it reinforced the voluntary element in national service (volunteering as a matter of conscience) and demonstrated that the Hebrew fighter was not an avid militarist seeking glory but rather a soldier going to war because there was no other way. It demonstrated even more clearly how Yishuv and Israeli society viewed war and armies. The society saw itself not as militarist and war-mongering, but rather as fighting only when necessary.

In many memorial anthologies and in the war literature the commander is depicted as a man of broad horizons who finds war and army life repugnant and whose mind remains free of military influences. This quality fits well with the classic description of the mythological Sabra—thorny outside and sweet inside. Two fallen soldiers who became cultural models—Jimmy, who secretly played the violin, and Gulliver, who secretly read poetry and philosophy—represented the inner sweetness and delicacy of the humanistic and sensitive soul hiding under the external prickliness of the tough fighter.

Moral Exemplar   The military leader is presented as a person who made himself into a living and personal example of the values he advocated. Furthermore, he demanded more of himself than of his soldiers. "When water was handed out by the spoonful—he was last. And only what was left," related Chaim Cheffer in his poem "The Platoon Commander."[114] The commander was not satisfied with preserving the existing norms and values, but constantly set higher standards.

The figure of the commander leading his troops into battle became rooted in the public consciousness. The commander's cry, "Follow me!" verbalized the intrepidness, determination, responsibility, and leadership of the Hebrew officer—and in fact of the entire defense force. It made him into the very personification of the model revolutionary leader—the vanguard of the vanguard of the Zionist cause.

The commander who charged into battle crying "Follow me!"—thus putting himself in greater danger than he put his soldiers—was also a symbol of the unbounded self-sacrifice of Sabra youth. The "Follow me!" tradition of Palmach commanders later became a moral trademark of combat and command in the Paratrooper Corps and in the IDF as a whole. "Follow me!" stories became central components of IDF combat legends and the IDF's self-image—and thus indirectly, of the self-image of all of Israeli society. "The commander is always the first to surge forward / 'Follow me!' he lets out a cry / Like a pillar of fire rising and shining / Like the pillar of God in Sinai," wrote Dan Almagor, for example, after the Sinai Campaign in a song meant to express the spirit of the IDF's command.[115]

The "Follow me!" ethos served a functional need. It not only was a model of patriotic behavior and sacrifice on the battlefield and an expression of equality between the officer and his soldiers, but also offered the soldiers personal and emotional motivation for self-sacrifice and tenacity. When soldiers revere their commander, they want to do as he wishes, "to follow him through fire and water." Translating this into religious terms, the Zionist religion succeeded in motivating its believers through the charisma of "spiritual shepherds" who were army commanders rather than ecclesiastics.

The Good Parent Parental attentiveness is perhaps the most notable trait in the myth of the commander. Regarding this trait too, *Panipilov's Men,* in which the commander is a father figure, was a great influence. The depiction of the platoon commander as a compassionate and understanding father who treats his soldiers as if they were his children is especially common in the memorial anthologies: "He served as a father to his platoon, and with what devotion he took care of each one, knew each one's private problems, and saw that each one received help from the platoon kitty and from the other men."[116]

The motif of the father protecting his children is connected to the motif of standing in the breach, which is also prominent in the myth of the Sabra commander. In many battle stories the commander encourages and urges his soldiers on in times of trouble. He is the ideological axis that holds the ranks together in difficult times and prevents them from buckling, as Moses held together the Children of Israel in the desert. He bears the national mission on his back even when his soldiers' backs give way because he is imbued more than they with consciousness of the greatness of the hour and the weight of historical-national responsibility.

The myth of the commander-father in its broad application is one of the characteristics of a revolutionary society. Most social revolutions try to reach the individual's heart and save him from his alienation. Their central messages are of human brotherhood and lofty altruism. For this reason, the revolution generally presents leaders in emotional terms—as fathers, mothers, or loving brothers. We love the hero because the hero "loves us" and "looks after us." Here also a social revolution resembles a religion—a religious leader is presented not as a distant and arrogant political leader, but as a paternal figure for his community, like a Catholic priest, who is referred to literally as "father."

Unpretentious Leader   The Sabra commander is depicted as unassuming and humane. He does not become intoxicated with his rank and authority, lording it over his soldiers and taking advantage of them. One expression of this is that officers and soldiers in the Palmach and in the IDF wore the same uniforms.

According to the myth, and in practice as well, the commander lived as his soldiers did: suffered what they suffered and enjoyed what they enjoyed and asked for no special privileges of rank or seniority. In this also the myth of the Sabra commander is similar to that of the religious spiritual shepherd. Many social revolutions (both ideological and religious) have stressed the proximity of the leader to the people, marking the revolution's close contact with and sincere concern for the citizenry. Moreover, many revolutions, because of their collective nature, bear messages of equality and cooperation, and so their leaders are not aristocratic and isolated, but rather are exemplary figures who lead by personal example. Minimizing the hierarchical gap between the officer and the soldier also tacitly validates the demand that the soldier sacrifice himself, because his sacrifice is then made for the general good, not just for a hierarchical leadership.

Scholar of the Military Torah   The role of the leader in a revolutionary period is to spread confidence, because in a state of war and danger, feelings of anxiety and uncertainty naturally proliferate. A leader (especially a military leader) who knows what lies before him, who is sure of himself, who knows his way around, and who radiates calm will dispel anxieties and instill confidence and security—expressed by the Sabra expression *smoch* discussed earlier. This is one of the reasons that military professionalism is an element in the mythological profile of the Sabra commander. "He remembers dozens of things, from maps to shoelaces," is Chaim Cheffer's description in his song "The Platoon Commander." In the memorial anthologies the Sabra commander is presented as a kind of scholar of the Torah of battle. He is expert in all its details, knows what tomorrow will bring, is well versed in the ways of a good soldier and in strategic planning, and his maturity and composure allow him to get to the root of any matter and to distinguish the important from the trivial.

It is important to recall the mutual reinforcement of myth and reality, evident also in the case of the Sabra commander. The elements of the myth were drawn not just from Zionism's abstract ideals and utopian values, but also from the very real figures of the commanders. Conversely, the commanders themselves were educated in the values of the myth and tried to meet those standards—and frequently succeeded. In other words, in practice, myth and reality coincided to a great degree.

The Paratrooper, Pilot, and Marine Commando as Heirs of the Palmachnik

INSTITUTIONALIZATION, MILITARISM, AND MILITARY NOSTALGIA

In the 1950s, Israeli society, the IDF included, commenced a process of institutionalization, one aspect of which was the shift of social prestige to formal positions and titles (military rank, unit, profession, etc.) and away from the person holding the position—to the "occupation symbols" of the formal organization and away from spontaneously created class symbols subject to no formal scrutiny. The military experience gradually became as important as self-sacrifice and professional military expertise as important as national altruism. The fighting Sabra was no longer perceived principally as a willing sacrifice but rather became a professional soldier, a commander for whom war was a profession.

This transformation first took place in the Paratroopers Brigade, which drew its prestige from modeling itself after the British and American airborne divisions of World War II. This association with the "family of the red berets" was perceived to be fundamentally like belonging to the "Palmach family" (even though Ariel Sharon, who was appointed as the brigade commander, had not served in the Palmach). Yet now achievement was no less important, and perhaps was more important, than ideology. The Paratroopers' retaliation strikes in response to the cross-border terrorist attacks of the Palestinian *fedayeen* enhanced the aura surrounding the unit.[117]

Thus, during the time of the consolidation of the Paratroopers Brigade, the myth of the Sabra was gradually displaced, though not reversed. The symbolic center of gravity moved from the cult of binding the son on the altar and gratitude to the fallen fighter to the cult of military experience, in which the emphasis was placed on adventure and on the steeling of the fighter—not, however, on military trappings, killing, and military ceremony. Parachute-jumping became the status symbol of the new Israeli masculinity. Officer rank also gradually came to be coveted by the Sabra, and a military career became prestigious.

This slight shift in the image of the fighting Sabra was clearly evident in the army periodicals *Ba-Machaneh* and *Ba-Machaneh Nachal,* which were in terms of their readership a continuation of *Alon Ha-Palmach,* the Gadna publications, and *Iton Ha-Magen. Ba-Machaneh* described a paratrooper raid: "Sometimes, when you see a war movie in which the main star, playing the ideal commander, makes his plans quietly and serenely, you smile: 'It's that way only in the movies.' But here is the reality—M. is very quiet, very young, very experienced, and very talented. He knows what he's talking about."[118]

Unlike the Palmach and youth movement newsletters of the Yishuv period, which dealt with mourning, pioneer values, and military life, the military organs of the 1950s were largely concerned with the superior combat capabilities and the masculinity of the Sabra fighter (especially prominent is the motif of the paratrooper overcoming his fear of heights).

The increasing importance of the military experience is especially noticeable in the children's stories of the 1950s, especially after the Sinai Campaign. Inspired by the retaliation operations carried out by the Paratroopers and reflecting nostalgia for the Palmach, these stories describe the Sabra fighter, generally a Palmachnik, as a brave and clever soldier who deceives his enemy. Battle is described as an exhilarating experience. During this period children's literature—more and more of which was being written by Palmach and Jewish Brigade veterans—began to develop a genre of "the boy Palmachnik" or "the boy fighter." In these stories, the young heroes joined experienced war horses in their missions, or themselves fought the Arabs, British, or Nazis. The most important of these was Yigal Mosinzon's *Hasamba* series, which he launched in 1950.

The change in the mythological image of the Sabra fighter resulted from three other causes besides the institutionalization of the military profession: (1) the shift in the war with the Arabs from a total war to a duel of retribution and vengeance; (2) an increase in the importance of modern journalistic writing that aspired to colorful depiction of military actions, which roused much interest and inflated the national ego; and (3) the influence of books and movies about World War II, which were very popular at the time.

The military experience was described in the press as the pinnacle of the Israeli experience, and the army was described as a place in which a man reached spiritual heights. The new mythological image of the post-1948 Sabra fighter was personified in the figures of Ariel Sharon (founder of Unit 101) and Meir Har-Tzion (the most prominent of the unit's soldiers).

"IT'S NO LEGEND, MY FRIEND"—
THE MYTHOLOGY OF THE SINAI CAMPAIGN

The process of militarization of Israeli society and glorification of the Sabra fighter was redoubled after the Sinai Campaign. The Israeli soldier, depicted in the press with stereotypical Sabra traits, was perceived in the wake of the clean and quick victory as possessing exceptional human qualities, a human wonder sired by Zionism. The exotic, mythic image of Moshe Dayan, the chief of staff who led the army to victory, symbolized the triumph of the Sabra. Dayan's attributes—fluent and *dugri* speech, boldness of spirit, a playful sparkle in the eye, erect posture, paratrooper's wings on the chest, his youth spent in the agricultural settlements (for good measure, both a kibbutz, Degania, and a moshav, Nahalal), his father a pioneer of the founding generation, himself a Palmach commander with 1948 combat experience, bearing a war wound and the pirate-like eye patch—all these made him into a romantic figure that expressed the new, more military Sabra.

In the wake of the sweeping, swift victory and the small number of casualties, the Israeli public's elation and especially its pride knew no bounds. The press emotionally described the Israeli tanks and armored personnel carriers dashing through the legendary Sinai Desert, with tank commanders directing fire while bravely standing half-exposed above their tanks, shelling the enemy in all directions. The imagery (conscious or unconscious) was that of the cowboy galloping over the prairie in pursuit of Indians. The reserve that had characterized the War of Independence was replaced by national swaggering of the following type:

> Since the time that Hannibal crossed the snowy Alps and Genghis Khan the mountains of Asia, history has recorded few military operations that can compare—in the force of the surprise, in the passage of natural barriers, and in military success—with the heroic march of the Ninth Regiment in the Sinai Campaign.[119]

The superiority of the Israeli army, which defeated the huge Egyptian army, was at times perceived and described in metaphysical terms, and the same language was used to describe the soldiers, especially the young commanders. They were regarded as Biblical conquerors—like Joshua and Judah Maccabee—defending their people, liberating territories under divine sponsorship, and leading a new Jewish march into Canaan. The Sabra fighter was again, as in the War of Independence, magnified as the people's emissary in the performance of the divine will, a warrior guided in all his actions by divine grace. The fact that it was the conquest of Mt. Sinai reinforced the Biblical image of the victory. This was captured in the words of the song written after the war that became the victory's anthem: "It is no legend, my friend, and no passing dream, here facing Mt. Sinai, the bush, the burning bush."

With the Sinai Campaign there was something like a mythological changing of the guard between the Palmachnik of 1948 and the paratrooper and pilot. The heroic battle of Mitla produced the war's chief martyr, who was, not coincidentally, a paratrooper.

The Sinai Campaign was the first Israeli war in which regular armored units fought and in which jets were deployed and the Air Force played a decisive role. The Israeli pilot was a Sabra in the eyes of the public, and the war plane was his war horse. The front cover of the issue of the Gadna magazine, *Ba-Machaneh Gadna,* that appeared after the war displayed a huge drawing of an Israeli pilot, a young man with a nonchalant smile and a cigarette in his mouth, mounted on a jet plane with reins in his hand, like a cavalryman on his horse. Below him an enemy plane plum-

meted in flames while he made a third X next to two others he had previously recorded. Underneath, in large letters, were the words "one less."
Inside the magazine, an article on the Air Force stated:

> The jet. Ancient peoples admired the bow. The Romans feared the mounted
> warrior. We bow before the jet pilot, a term that demands respect, representing
> the twentieth century and its amazing innovations. Admiration for the pow-
> erful machine and for he who controls it. The jet pilot: Taut and in control.
> Split-second response. Top physical condition. Imperturbability. Decisive and
> correct command. These must be the traits of he who climbs into the cock-
> pit of a jet plane, who ignites its rumbling, whistling roar.[120]

The aerial superiority of the Israeli pilot represented to the public the
human superiority of the Sabra, a perception that intensified over time.
The superlatives attached to him were inspired not only by the great victory in the Sinai Campaign, but also by the myth of the "conquest of the
skies" (the "knights of the skies"), which had its origin in World War I
and reached its height in World War II (as attested by the multitude of
American stories and films of that period about the heroism of British
and American war pilots).

"Today is not the day to wear the scarf of modesty," said the commander of the Air Force (a Sabra himself) just before the conclusion of
the Sinai Campaign. "Our unit caused [the enemy] the most damage, carried out the largest number of sorties. Not only did it not suffer any casualties, there are now more combat-ready planes than there were at the
beginning of the combat."[121] This was not just a military declaration; it
was in large measure also a social one. "We are the Palmach" metamorphosed into "We are the pilots and paratroopers."

The negative image of the Arab fighter during the Sinai Campaign also
strengthened the mythological image of the fighting Sabra. The picture
etched in public consciousness was of the shoes that the Arab soldiers
left behind in their hasty retreat. The Egyptian soldier who had cast off
his shoes and ran in panic from the battlefield was treated with contempt
in the Israeli press—especially given the boasts of the Arab dictator before the war. This intensified the "children of Israel's" sense of cultural
and moral superiority over the Arabs.

In the years that followed the Sinai Campaign, the IDF became a major sociocultural institution in Israeli society, and a new media and art
genre, kol ha-kavod le-Tzahal—"congratulations to the IDF"—began to
thrive. It reached its peak after the Six Day War. The foci of attention
were the Israeli paratrooper and pilot, described in the press like Hollywood heroes in an action-suspense picture with a happy ending. Simi-

larly, many of the war stories were constructed as classic adventures, with a noble hero, an evil nemesis, increasing suspense, and a dramatic and happy denouement in the last act. Battle was portrayed as a masculine sport or a duel. This genre reinforced the image of the army as the glory of Israeli society and made the military profession the pinnacle of the ambition of the new generation of Sabras.

CHAPTER 3

Dunce Cap

A *chizbat:*

> With regard to my education and general intelligence, I've never heard of an-
> other Palmachnik who studied as much as I did (three or four years in each
> grade, including several years of advanced preparation in kindergarten . . .).
> The fact that I studied most of the time in a high school (of five or six stories)
> speaks for itself. . . . Once, for example, a delegation of inspectors from the
> education department sneaked into our school in order to check out the stu-
> dents' intelligence, which was, as you know, in steep decline. . . . As soon as
> they stepped into the classroom they saw that I was bright, so they called me
> up to the blackboard and asked me in a low and threatening voice: What does
> it mean to study Torah on one foot, boy? I didn't get flustered and on the spot
> answered that that is the normal state of affairs: the teacher gives the lesson
> and the pupil already has one foot out the door. . . . One of them was so en-
> chanted by my personality that during the first recess he came up to me and
> slapped me a few times on the shoulders. When I asked him what he wanted
> he said emotionally: "You, kid, there's no one else like you!" . . . And a few
> seconds later he added: "Lucky for us."[1]

Training Farmers and Fighters

The Zionist ideologues' ambition to "cure" the Jewish people of their
Diaspora malady led them to negate not only life among the gentiles, but
also the traditional Jewish way of life—the principal part of which was
the study of sacred texts. They sought, as historian Anita Shapira stated,
"to liberate themselves from the bonds of Jewish ethics and to return to

the primal instincts of a natural nation, before spurious norms constrained its passions and instincts."[2] This view was influenced by vitalism, one of the romantic movements popular in Europe at the turn of the century. Mica Joseph Berditchewski, a major exponent of this view in Zionism, maintained that the era of the Diaspora was an era in which "excess spirituality has crushed the stuff of life." Statements in the same vein were made by other thinkers of his time.

The immigrants of the Second and Third Aliyot, who turned their backs on the Diaspora, thus also rejected the Jewish *beit midrash,* the house of study in which they had been raised.[3] In many of their writings, the ideologues and political leaders of the Yishuv fiercely condemned the degenerate spirituality of religion, the passive spiritual culture of the village synagogue that brought so many calamities on the Jews. They advocated instead the simple manual labor of the farmer.[4] It was time, they said, for Jews to roll up their sleeves and change the fate of their people through physical action rather than through prayer and study. The chief consequence of this anti-intellectual ethos was an extreme and ritualistic affirmation of the practical world.

THE IDEALIZATION OF MANUAL LABOR

The ethos of practicality was fundamental to the Yishuv educational system as early as the First Aliya, even before there was a broad generational stratum of Sabras with a distinct cultural profile. In the Zionist movement the consensus was that the goal of Hebrew education, especially education in the moshavot, was to train farmers who would have ties to the land. The education provided for these young people thus had to be directed largely at the practical needs of the new settlements in Palestine.[5] Ze'ev Yavetz, a school principal in one of the moshavot, Zichron Ya'akov, wrote in 1888: "The farmer's great and inclusive capacity is physical strength. Bolstering the strength . . . of the farmer's sons, most of whose senses are stronger than their minds, is best done by giving them something concrete, rather than study of a theoretical sort."[6]

The kibbutz schools, which also served the children of neighboring moshavim, particularly emphasized anti-intellectual values. (In fact, kibbutz education was called "education for productivity.") The core of the kibbutz school curriculum was vocational training in useful trades. "Our schools," wrote David Meltz, one of the formulators of kibbutz education, "want to prepare practical working people who know how to take deliberate action, and who are therefore realistic, rational, and pragmatic.

Practical studies thus justifiably and necessarily take an honored—the most honored—place."[7]

Kibbutz and moshav children received encouragement and social rewards from the older generation largely for their achievements in farm work. This is evident from the kibbutz press, as well as from the memorial literature, in which the eulogizers frequently recall how impressed they were by the practical dexterity of the fallen.

The prestige that the kibbutzim and moshavim awarded for achievement in practical fields was not just to bolster ideology. It was also pragmatic—the young farms needed to train a cadre who could put their hands to the plow, not scientists whose hands held pens and test tubes and who were liable to abandon young settlements whose future was not yet secure. The result was an educational approach that was anti-achievement-oriented, that forgave failure in studies and evasion of the effort that study required. (This does not mean that the level of education was lower, only that standards were not strictly enforced.)

The practical ethos of the laboring settlements also found expression in an unsympathetic view of higher education. The young people in the kibbutzim and moshavim were explicitly expected to do without university studies, since they made no contribution to the communal farm. As a result, the kibbutz schools did nothing to prepare their students for their high school diploma examinations, success in which was the entry ticket to a college education. This attitude was a consequence not only of an agricultural-practical orientation but also of a socialist-egalitarian ethos—that is, fear of creating a separate class of educated people.

The formulators of kibbutz education, led by Shmuel Golan, were influenced not only by the Zionist and socialist ethoses and the functional needs of their movement, but also by the advanced pedagogical philosophies in Europe and the United States, which put the pupil and his experience at the center, rather than the curriculum and student achievement in the form of grades. Psychoanalysis, which demonstrated the shortcomings of overly authoritative education, also influenced kibbutz pedagogy. The kibbutz child was educated in an open framework that emphasized self-discipline, free choice, and amicable relations with teachers.

This educational approach reinforced the adolescent's independence, and its substance and values instilled in him a love of nature, work, homeland, and the movement. At the same time, since it did not emphasize competitiveness and achievement and, in particular, passing high school graduation exams, it prevented most kibbutz and moshav young people from continuing their studies at the two Zionist universities in Palestine, the Hebrew University and the Technion.

Along with directing education toward physical labor, the labor movement also set itself the goal of training the younger generation for battle and heroism, for both ideological and practical reasons. In this it succeeded beyond its own expectations. "Do you know to what our children in the Upper Galilee aspire? To the bow and arrow," wrote one of the educators at Kibbutz Kfar Giladi.[8] The first Ha-Shomer Ha-Tza'ir manual, published in 1917 in Warsaw, stated: "Our intention is—to educate a young Hebrew of solid muscles, strong will, healthy and normal thought without convolutions or sophistry, disciplined, a Jew with all his heart."[9] Health and physical vigor became key values in Zionist education not only because of the practical need to cope with real difficulties and the defense requirements of the Zionist enterprise, but also because they symbolized the pragmatic and brave new Jew who shed the "pale" skin of the Diaspora and rooted himself in Palestine.

Like education for a farmer's life, education for a soldier's life began during the First Aliya. The ethos of combat and physical prowess was instilled in the moshava schools (and later also in city and kibbutz schools) through myths of heroism from the Jewish tradition. Lessons in the Bible and Jewish tradition gave prominence to the figures of military leaders and heroes such as Samson, David, Gideon, Judah Maccabee, Elazar Ben-Yair of Masada, and Bar Kochba, rather than to outstanding spiritual figures such as Rashi, Maimonides, Nachmanides, and the Maharal of Prague.

Plays and pageants presented in the schools—first in the moshavot and afterward in all the Zionist schools—glorified Jewish heroes,[10] and songs for preschoolers made the heroism of the Maccabees, not Jewish wisdom, the central educational value.

Again, education for militarism was motivated not only by ideology but also, and perhaps first and foremost, by the pragmatic needs of a society that had to fight. Training fighters through the educational system was given great impetus when defense needs became more acute in the late 1930s and early 1940s. It was then that premilitary groups were set up in the schools—initially the Chagam, and then the Gadna.

The Chagam—the first incarnation of the Gadna—was founded by

Arthur Biram, principal of the Reali school in Haifa. The concept behind it (influenced, perhaps, by Biram's own German education) was
the training of a coterie of young and disciplined fighters with stamina
and physical strength, rather than a reserve of studious scholars expert
in the Bible and Jewish texts. In February of 1940 the Chagam Committee published its program and goals. The Chagam, the program
stated, would "educate people of discipline, responsibility, courage, and
precision in their movements, decisive in their actions, who prepare
themselves for maximal physical exertion and who can withstand cold,
heat, deprivation, and fatigue; who will be prepared to make every effort and to endure any suffering for the rebirth and liberation of the
nation."[11]

The youth movements and Gadna took high school students to training camps of a few days' length out in the field, in the spirit of the Palmach. These camps were meant not only to "season with romanticism
and add color" to the children's activities, but also to build the young
Sabra's character.[12] The activities were aimed at strengthening the body,
developing stamina and dexterity, and accustoming the Sabra to face danger courageously. Typical exercises included jumping from heights, obstacle courses, nighttime infiltration, and especially, difficult marches, often in dangerous areas.[13]

Just as the anti-intellectual ethos led educators to uphold the manual
laborer and farmer as ideals, so it prompted them to present the fighting man as superior to the thinking man. Social history teaches that a
society generally enhances the prestige of the professions that supply its
current needs, thus making them attractive. The resulting demand to enter these professions in turn creates competition. This social principle becomes particularly operable in a revolutionary era, when a great social
mission is at stake. This is apparently one reason why in the Yishuv and
early state periods, a military command was so prestigious and was preferred by the Sabras (at least during their young adult years) over civilian professions that required a period of study.

A military career did not necessarily mean neglecting one's education,
but that was indeed the case during the early stages of the Israeli military. Higher education was not a prerequisite for promotion in the Palmach, and the IDF commanders were selected on the basis of strict standards of human quality; but objective constraints meant that higher
education—one of the criteria used in modern armies—could not be required by the Palmach and the early IDF.

Minimizing the importance of education in choosing candidates for the prestigious officer rank served as a kind of negative incentive among Sabras for obtaining higher education. Lack of a degree, especially a high school diploma, was not an obstacle to promotion, even in the future. This attenuated the motivation of young people to pursue university studies—at least for the time being. Most Sabras eventually did attend college, and some of them even attained the highest level of academic achievement.

Anti-Intellectualism in Sabra Culture

MANUAL LABOR AND PHYSICAL ACTIVITY

The field, the mountain, and the desert formed the backdrop against which the Sabra in action was portrayed in words and in photographs. A dust-encrusted, sunburned youngster, marching or sitting with his comrades in the open air or engaged in construction, farming, physical training, or the repair of mechanical tools is a figure that appears again and again in the large collections of photographs of the period that lie in archives. Even if some of the photographs are certainly posed, the impression is that the Sabra was a man of the open spaces—someone for whom the field was home and for whom physical activity was a habit and even a joy.

Letters and diaries also demonstrate that manual labor, mechanical expertise, and physical exertion were "ecological" as much as "ideological" for the Sabra (especially for the young person living on a kibbutz or moshav, but also for the urban members of youth movements who spent time at kibbutzim). Many of them wrote from the army to their loved ones about how much they missed the work they had done since childhood in the barn, the field, and the sheep pen.

It was the actual work on the farm, more than the work-oriented education, that tightly bound a practical approach to life and a great love of manual labor to the Sabra's soul. "I was born in a farming village and I live with agriculture. Unceasing daily labor is for me a fact and a necessity—that is, not a matter of choice. I have in any case been educated to desire it and see it as a good life. Without such education it would be very difficult for me," wrote a young man from Nahalal.[14] Farming by nature required complete devotion and hard labor. The kibbutz or moshav youngster thus had to adapt himself to physical work from a young age. The tangible link between "sweat" and "result" fostered a predilection for the field and meadow. The Sabra's love of physical labor was thus not only the ideological love of *hagshama*, but also the love that instinctively binds the farmer to the earth he has cleared and plowed, to the kids he has nursed, and to the machinery he has repaired.

This point reveals one of the fundamental cultural distinctions between the pioneer and the Sabra generations. The pioneer adjusted himself to manual labor out of ideological consciousness, while the Sabra was a born farmer.

TACHLES AND *DUGRI*—ANTI-INTELLECTUALISM IN THE MIRROR OF LANGUAGE

On the linguistic level the mores of pragmatism were expressed by avoiding Biblical idioms, ignoring linguistic fine points, and eschewing the precision of Jewish scholars. The linguistic richness and polemical style of the pioneer generation's speech, influenced by the European Enlightenment culture and the profound spiritual world of Judaism, were replaced by the dry practicality of Sabra slang, summed up in the Sabra cultural word—borrowed, ironically, from Yiddish—*tachles,* meaning "to the point."

The older pioneer generation in Palestine (especially the leadership), which in its younger days had turned its back on religious tradition, nevertheless did not forget the linguistic idioms that it had absorbed in childhood. The pioneers frequently committed the "sin" of interspersing their discourse with verses from the Bible and passages from the commentators. But the younger generation, which grew up largely outside of the home, was locked out of that language by the anti-Diaspora ethos. Hebrew, the language of tradition and sacred literature, was "taken to the street" and turned into a practical, secular language. The freshness of Yiddish, with its vivid expressions saturated with Jewish sorrow and humor and with its folklorish sayings, largely disappeared from Sabra conversation. All that remained of Yiddish were a few sarcastic colloquial expressions that implicitly ridiculed Diaspora life. Yiddish pronunciation, stresses, and lilt, which bore strata of cultural meaning, disappeared. Many words deriving from the intricacies of Talmudic reasoning, including expressions from Aramaic—the Jewish "Latin"—also disappeared from the Sabra vocabulary.

Presumably, being cut off from the languages of their grandfathers and grandmothers—the Yiddish, Russian, Polish, and other vernaculars that had served daily needs for generations—meant a cultural loss for the Sabras. Once the roots of the Diaspora languages were severed, the Sabras were disconnected from the culture contained within the folk language.

An examination of the common words of the period as they appeared in *chizbatim,* in slang dictionaries, and in dialogues in plays and books reveals that Sabra language was emphatically instrumental and was rich in terms that describe everyday experience, as well as in technical and mechanical vocabulary. The source of the Hebrew spoken by the Sabras, according to critic Shalom Kramer, was a "renewed positive approach to the world."[15]

This trait noted by Kramer is perhaps the principal distinction between the "holy tongue" and the new Hebrew of the Sabras—the former was the language of imagination, formal pathos, and story, while the latter was a language of practical and succinct communication about the mundane and the common. The Sabra had to be a linguistic improviser because all he had at his disposal was an ancient language that lacked terms for the modern world. This was apparently one of the reasons for the robust slang in Sabra culture—slang supplied the missing day-to-day words.

The most prominent anti-intellectual linguistic phenomenon in Sabra culture was the development of *dugri* language—an unpolished, utilitarian, simple, and direct idiom. Like many other words, *dugri* itself was borrowed from Arabic, in which it means "straight." It means telling the truth straight to someone's face, without equivocation—the opposite of hypocritical, behind-the-back talk.[16]

Over time, *dugri* acquired broader meaning, until it became a typical Sabra word. It gained the connotation of talk that was simple, not abstruse, not "prettified," outspoken, sometimes impertinent, arrogant, not diplomatic, and not manipulative. *Dugri* also contained an element of pride and irreverence. A person who spoke *dugri* was declaring that he was a Sabra who said what he thought without fear and without the abjectness of the Diaspora Jew speaking to the gentile noble or master. *Dugri* was a sign of honesty, the courage to speak boldly, without embellishment, without prevarication, on a high moral level.

For our purposes, what is important is the practicality of the Sabra's *dugri* language. The long periods spent in military frameworks required rapid speech with an instrumental cast to it. In battle or in a briefing before battle there was no place for intricacy or long "academic" debates. *Dugri* language became speech under fire—concise, pointed, and dry.

The language of the army radio ("roger," "over," "negative," "affirmative") became the language the Sabra used with his friends.

EDUCATION VERSUS *HAGSHAMA*—
CAREER VERSUS CALLING

Among pioneering youth movements in the city also, higher education was placed lower on the scale of values than national service, and the two were sometimes portrayed as contradictory.[17] "Of course we will not force anyone to take up physical labor," wrote one Scout counselor in a declaration to the junior division of his movement:

> On the contrary! We want to create a healthy nation, and a healthy nation needs intellectuals. Those with special talents for science or music will study in those fields. But no one needs to be drawn to studies just because there is some chance that he might someday be a good doctor. Remember: we will always have good doctors, but we don't have enough good farmers![18]

As noted earlier, this set of ethical priorities, in which national—especially military—service was given preference over education, derived not only from ideological priorities but also from the real needs of a society under siege and in danger. The 1940s was a period of what today would be called a "routine of emergency." Under the pressure of events everything took on the character of urgency. The national struggles, especially the War of Independence, changed young people's priorities. Many felt that it was their service, not their thinking, that the system urgently needed. The nation was counting on them, as one Sabra wrote to his girlfriend: "Life today is entirely different from what I believed it would be one day. I do not know what will happen with my studies—whether or not I will be able to fit them into the framework of my service to the nation. But [my studies] take second place in my life today in comparison with other matters on the agenda."[19]

The sense that studies, especially university studies, were a selfish interest and came at the expense of the urgently needed contribution to the collective presented the entire generation of Sabras with a dilemma of conscience. This dilemma would later appear in the memoirs of the Sabras—especially those who reached senior ranks in the IDF—as they described the beginning of their military careers (this may also be a kind of ex post facto apology for not having attended college). When their term of duty was up and they intended to leave the army and complete their studies, their commander would plead with them to put off school and sign on for another term of service in the military. In general, their consciences forced them to follow their calling to the Zionist imperative and remain soldiers. So, for example, Yitzchak Rabin wrote:

> The world war had ended. The possibility of going to study at Berkeley presented itself again. I wanted to go. I spoke with my father. I went to Yigal Allon. "Absolutely impossible," he said unequivocally. "The world war is over, but our war is just beginning." I knew that Yigal was right. A week later I received the command of the Palmach's second battalion.[20]

Sabras gave up formal education not only for ideological reasons but also because of the lure of the great challenges outside of school that the period presented to young people. Attending high school or college at such a critical time seemed like a boring thing to do and meant missing the "real" experience—the exciting national service that awaited the young recruits. Adolescents tasted something of this by pasting up posters, serving as couriers, and so on, and this only encouraged them to enlist.

Young people also preferred the kibbutz, the Palmach, and the army to the university because the more practical frameworks were a compliment to their maturity. Students were perceived as adolescents, while young people in the Palmach or at a kibbutz appeared as independent adults who were bearing great responsibility.

It is important to emphasize that as was the case with the pioneers, there was a certain discontinuity between ideology and reality among the Sabras—especially those from the cities. There was constant tension in particular between the ideologically committed youth movement leaders and the rank-and-file members, just as there was between the army commanders and the rank-and-file soldiers. This lacuna grew wider in the 1950s, when the state of emergency had passed and more options for employment and studies presented themselves. This was expressed as a dichotomy between "career" and "calling" (meaning the dichotomy between individualism and egoism on the one hand and collectivism and altruism on the other), which gradually became part of the discourse.

In practice, most Sabras did not devote their lives to only agricultural labor or military service. The majority did not stop their high school studies, and many—after a preliminary pioneer experience at a kibbutz or in the army—even went on to a university education and a civilian career, becoming part of Israel's urban bourgeoisie.

On the other hand, quite without predesign, the Sabra created one of the most remunerative career paths in Israeli society—the military ca-

reer. For some this provided an optimal match between personal achievement and ideological sacrifice and so resolved the dilemma of career versus calling.

It could be said that from the 1940s, and with redoubled force in the
1950s, there was a tacit agreement between the political establishment
of the labor movement and the Sabra fighters—promotion in the army
and high military status in exchange for giving up high educational status and a professional or political civilian career.[21] This arrangement
strengthened the sense that minimal education would not be a detriment
to a Sabra's future and was almost certainly one of the reasons that many
Palmach veterans put off their university studies.

REBELLION AGAINST TEACHERS

The anti-intellectualism of the Sabras derived not only from imitating
their parents and accepting the role designated for them as the pioneers'
children but also from tacitly defying them. This defiance grew out of
the younger generation's need to find a field in which it could excel. It
first appeared in the 1930s, at the time of the Fifth Aliya, the immigration from Nazi Germany, with the creation of an urban bourgeoisie. The
labor movement bureaucracy became a part of this bourgeoisie—in contradiction, at least as far as lifestyle went, to the pioneer ethos of the
youth movements. The labor bureaucracy's inclination is "to help pupils
find a place in life, whether in officialdom or in commerce or in the free
professions," one Sabra wrote to a labor leader, instead of working for
"the broadening of our horizons and our preparation for understanding
life and choosing the [ideological] way."[22] This culture of defiance was
channeled into student rebellions against teachers, especially at the Herzliya Gymnasium, which was, on the one hand, a bourgeois stronghold
and, on the other, the cradle of the Ha-Machanot Ha-Olim movement.

Early in the summer of 1941 the Agricultural Center issued a call to
urban school students: "Learning youth! To work and to defense!" School
administrations responded to the call for help, and by the end of July
1941, a total of 2,338 students between the ages of sixteen and nineteen
had gone for periods of six to ten weeks to assist ninety-eight settlements
(as opposed to about 400 students in 1939 and about 500 in 1940).[23]
After the success of this aid operation, educators raised the question of
whether to eliminate the twelfth grade. In the end it was decided not to
eliminate it but rather to extend the organized stays in these work camps
to two months. In response, the "pietists" in the youth movements (largely

among the leadership), in their fervor "to take action" for the Yishuv, condemned the school administrators for the decision not to eliminate the twelfth grade, terming this decision "heresy."

One of the more remarkable examples of the attitude of these young people was the "Twelfth-Graders' Letter"—written by a group of teenagers at the Herzliya Gymnasium and published in the Ha-Machanot Ha-Olim newsletter in 1943. The letter called upon twelfth-grade students to abandon their studies, give up their high school diplomas, and enlist in the army in order to serve the national cause.

Other letters appeared in the wake of this one,[24] containing sharp protests against studying "at this critical time." The writers of the letters cannot be suspected of simply seeking an excuse to get out of school, since they also called on their fellows to give up their Pesach vacations for "the general mobilization."

When these demands were not met, some of these young people (largely members of Ha-Machanot Ha-Olim, who were the most vociferous in making this demand, perhaps because they were urban youth living in a bourgeois atmosphere that directed them toward higher education) took matters into their own hands and volunteered for agricultural labor and military service despite the opposition of the educational establishment and the censure of their teachers. Some declared their willingness to forego higher education then and there, and even to interrupt their twelfth-grade studies, which were the most important for earning a high school diploma.[25]

Notably, in this controversy the members of the youth movement showed themselves to be stricter in their adherence to the national cause than their parents and teachers. Apparently, this "miniature rebellion" was a manifestation of a concept found throughout Sabra culture—fighting for a total rather than a qualified realization of Zionist ideals. This sentiment was also behind the establishment of organizations like the Palmach. This may be termed "nonconforming conformity" or a "mini-rebellion within a strict revolutionary framework."

ZIONISM IN QUOTATION MARKS—
ANTI-STYLE AS A TOOL FOR CREATING
GENERATIONAL IDENTITY

The "excess piety" of the Sabras and their tacit defiance of the older generation were also expressed on the symbolic-linguistic level in their opposition to the idealistic language of their leaders. This was a kind of ritual show of anti-style that revealed a hidden competition between the Sabra elite and the pioneer elite. The Sabras' message seemed to be "You leaders only talk while we are doing the work of Zionism," or as one Sabra wrote to his girlfriend: "My friends and I have no free time to talk politics because we are busy working."[26]

Sabra slang contains a fairly large number of expressions that denote repugnance for fancy language and pride in practical action. Some such Sabra retorts are (in rough translation): "Don't talk to me in high language," "Don't confuse my brain," "Don't philosophize," "Don't use pharmacy words with me" (that is, don't use long, complicated foreign terms), "Don't use explosive words" (high-sounding language that means nothing).[27]

The pride of the man of action and his scorn for the man of words was captured in the term "verbal Zionism," or "Zionism in quotation marks" (in writing the expression was literally the word "Zionism" in quotation marks)—"Please forgive me if I've bored you with a little 'Zionism.'"[28] The expression meant pointless verbosity and irritating moralizing in general, not just with regard to ideology. When Sabras wanted to silence a speaker or express displeasure with someone preaching at them, they would say, "He came to shove Zionism into us" or "He came to preach Zionism at us" (the intention being along the lines of "Don't teach a father how to make babies").

These expressions gave voice to the Sabras' sense of superiority over the pioneers and, as men of action in every bone of their bodies, to their vehemence against those who used high-sounding language but did not do enough themselves. But more than anything else they conveyed the Sabras' ire at those for whom preaching and inflated language had become a profession (especially those who pursued a public, party, movement, economic, or political career). The establishment's endless exhortations, including the frequent use of tired and worn slogans, outraged many Sabras, especially those actively involved in *hagshama*. This outrage only grew sharper when the exhortations emanated from a Zionist hack who had come from the city to the countryside to make a pompous, fiery evangelist-style speech to those who were involved body and soul in Zionist action. The barbs aimed by the Sabras expressed cumulative fatigue with the glut of "revolutionary pathos" that gradually took on the nature of a cliché.[29]

The aversion to the establishment's overblown and threadbare slogans grew among the younger generation of the 1950s, when the bureaucracy of Mapai—the ruling Israel Workers Party, later to be the Labor Party—first took on a partisan character. In the mid-1950s, as the country established itself and the state bureaucracy developed, and as urban culture broadened and the peripheral cities grew, the old-time labor movement public began to sense that the country was declining ideologically and becoming fatigued. This derived from the fear of the old-timers and the leadership that they were losing their cultural and political hegemony because of the mass immigration and the increasing shunting of socialist principles to the sidelines. It also grew out of an apprehension that the attraction of the national ethos was waning and the country was undergoing "premature normalization"—a common phenomenon in ideological societies.[30] This fear found expression in newspaper articles condemning the appetite for property and the pursuit of luxury. Wrath (both written and oral) was visited in particular on wayward young people who had ostensibly been infected by moral dystrophy. This preaching by party leaders and officials, which became a kind of periodic verbal ritual, created a sense of disgust among the Sabras, especially the older ones.

Clearly, the Sabras were not sick of Zionist ideology itself; they were only disgusted with ideological, patronizing preaching. There was also very likely a kind of youthful rebellion at work here, reflecting the Sabra's discomfort at being a "good boy." The Sabra condemnation of the establishment concealed a generational struggle—the aspiration of the Sabras to shake themselves free of the paternalism of the older generation and win independence. Their anti-style language, like their military service, thus allowed the sons to engage in the traditional generational rebellion—the "parricide," in Freud's language—through a channel that did not break the backbone of Zionist conformity.

The Sabras' anti-establishment attitude was also linked to other processes of institutionalization and erosion that were underway in Israeli society. For instance, in turbulent periods high language is often used to describe events. The newspapers, books, and poems produced in the 1940s and 1950s were indeed laden with emotional verbiage, and this slowly cheapened the formal idioms in the ears of the Sabras. As the language of pathos was eroded, largely by the leadership, the Sabras found it more and more difficult to describe the emotional events in which they participated and the experiences they had undergone, such as the death of friends. High pathos was ground into fine dust, losing its emotional value, and could no longer encompass an ecstatic and profound situation. The solution to the erosion of words was either silence or simple, economized speech. Small and introspective gestures became a symbolic surrogate, an internal code of authentic pathos, in which an element of Sabra anti-style replaced pioneer style.

The urge to keep speech to a minimum or to speak simply derived also from the need to present the Zionist experience as authentically internal, rather than artificial. Words seemed to cancel out the spontaneity and profundity of primary experience, dividing the emotional whole into little bits and so destroying it. This perception was expressed in the poems of the poet Rachel, a mythological figure of the Yishuv period whose poetry was much admired by the Sabras and was frequently recited at youth movement gatherings:

> Expressions of beauty I know many
> Fine words without end
> That go on so grandly
> Their gaze so proud.
> But my heart goes out to the simple speech of the babe
> Humble as the earth.[31]

Rachel's lyricism and economy matched the Sabra style, and the great love that the Sabras had for her poetry grew largely out of her ability to express "in a few short lines, and with the simplest words . . . the complete identification of a young Jewish woman with her homeland."[32]

This may give the impression that Sabras avoided high language completely. But in practice it turns out that there was a huge gap—a paradoxical one—between the way the Sabra spoke and the way he wrote. This sharp contrast can be seen in youth movement correspondence, especially between counselors and the national leaderships, and in the public calls to action published from time to time on a variety of subjects in the youth movement periodicals. It also appears in letters, and especially in the compositions and poems written for the desk drawer or published in the internal youth movement pamphlets and newsletters.

How can this gap between the spoken and written languages be explained? Beyond the usual stylistic gap between written and spoken language, this seems to be another manifestation of "rebellion within a framework of obedience"—the revolution of the sons against the fathers is not total, but is an expression of the sons' uniqueness within a framework of absolute acceptance of the fathers' values.

The Sabra's Cultural and Spiritual Horizons

CULTURAL AND SPIRITUAL ETHNOCENTRISM

While discussing the intellectual side of the Sabra, one should examine not only the sources of his education and the level and character of his writing but also the subjects that were important to him. An examination of the youth movement guidebooks; the pamphlets put out by the youth movements, the Palmach, and the army; and school newspapers shows that the major topics of interest were intra-movement and intra-Israeli. The theoretical, political, and moral discussions appearing in these forums also revolved around the local culture and its problems. Subjects such as cinema, art, economics, world politics, modern technology, entertainment, fashion, and even youth cultures in other places were almost never discussed, or were referred to only briefly and often from a Zionist point of view and within the local context. Even when an apocalyptic war raged around the world, full of catastrophes and bringing huge changes, the youth press (and for that matter the general press) largely addressed internal issues, such as labor camps, conventions, meetings, and problems within the local chapter of the youth movement.[33]

The humor in the stories, articles, and jokes that fill the youth publications was also local, very much rooted in the experience of the kibbutz, the youth movement chapter house, the army outpost, and the new settlement. Sabra society thus appears as an isolated cultural island entirely involved with itself. This cultural ethnocentrism characterizes both revolutionary societies and societies under siege, and so, it goes without saying, a society that is both revolutionary and under siege. There are, however, some further reasons for this trait in Sabra culture.

Provincial Life in Isolated and Developing Surroundings　The pre-state Yishuv, as well as the country during its first decade, was in many respects a provincial society, compared with Western cultures. While its orientation was Western, it was to a large extent cut off geographically from and not in direct communication with the West. The young country was up to its neck in its own problems of survival and "putting out fires." The urban centers—which are everywhere the intellectual and cultural hothouses—were then in their infancy. In these conditions, the public's, including the youth's, exposure to external ideas and stimuli was minimal.[34]

Furthermore, the Sabras who accepted the pioneer mission were to a certain extent cut off not only from other cultures, but also from the urban cultural centers in Israel itself. (There were connections among the kibbutzim, but in a world with limited communication these were restricted.) The kibbutzim and moshavim, most of which were in outlying regions, and some of which were in distant, isolated, and sometimes even besieged locations in the Negev Desert and Upper Galilee, immersed their residents, including the Palmachniks and youth movement members, in a homogeneous environment centered on itself.

Military service also imposed geographic and spiritual isolation and tied soldiers to a certain routine. Moreover, the soldier was generally living at subsistence level, and his attention was generally focused on obtaining the basic material things that he lacked—sleep, food, and sex.

Security as a Millstone around Freedom of Thought　The tiny demographic dimensions of Israeli society imposed a heavy military burden on the Sabra elite. Those who were called on to devotedly fulfill national missions and direct their physical and spiritual resources toward practical goals were left with no time and energy to devote to broadening their horizons. In other words, a reality laden with emergencies and tensions sank the Sabra into a life of action and denied him the necessary time for taking a more detached view or addressing higher matters.

Roots in the Air　The roots of Sabra provinciality lay not only in his geographic and cultural isolation, but also in the spiritual isolation that was imposed on the Sabras, to a certain extent, by the generation of their fathers. The anti-Diaspora ethos prompted the pioneers to obliterate the traditional culture in which they had grown up, thus cutting the Sabra off from the Jewish cultural legacy.[35] Moreover, the absence of grandparents in most families seriously hampered the transmission of tradition. Everything was intentionally focused on the present in this culture that had just been created, and the culture of the Diaspora past was silenced, as is the practice in many revolutions.

The Sabras were also condemned to cultural isolation because they were the second generation of immigrant families—families that, as sociological research shows, tend to prefer their new culture to the old one they left behind. The pioneers, as well as the immigrants of the Fourth and Fifth Aliyot, displayed the classic immigrant syndrome: they wanted their children to become rooted in the new homeland and to assume a new identity, and at the same time they were pained by their children's disconnection from the cultural roots of the old homeland. The parents' sorrow at their children's lack of roots in the old culture was enhanced because the anti-Diaspora ethos commanded them to efface the past and to leave behind a spiritual world and a rich cultural tradition. As Ezriel Uchmani wrote:

> They [the Sabra generation] never saw their grandmother, much less their
> mother, light Sabbath candles, stretching out her hands and covering her eyes

with them, her heart bathed in tears. Their grandmother was far away and the Sabbath candle was even farther, since we concealed from them—from our children—the reality of grandmother and Sabbath so that it would not arouse in them what we called "religious wistfulness."[36]

THE GENERATION OF MOSES
AND THE GENERATION OF JOSHUA

To understand the Sabra's spiritual horizons and his cultural inclinations it is necessary to take into account the intergenerational dynamic of a revolutionary society. Ideological ferment is generally one of the characteristics of the embryonic stage of social revolutions. Active at this stage are the formulators of the new ideological platform and the spiritual guides—the "lights of the generation." As sociologist Yochanan Peres has pointed out, the revolution's second generation can only rectify, interpret, or update, but cannot innovate.[37] Furthermore, as Anita Shapira wrote, "the experience of countries that have undergone revolutions is that the generation that carries out the revolution leaves such a deep impression on their children that the latter are unable to free themselves from its spiritual domination and take its authority for granted. It is difficult to find an example of a revolution in which the generation that came after carried out another revolution."[38]

The observations made by Peres and Shapira are consistent with Thomas O'Day's theory of the institutionalization of religious revolutions, which is based on Max Weber's model.[39] According to this theory, revolutions aspire, in the process of their institutionalization, to assimilate quickly the change they have wrought and organize it into the fabric of the new life. According to Weber, a revolution needs two types of people—ideologists and practical activists. The latter, the drab soldiers of the revolution, are those who seize the targets marked by the ideologues. In terms of generations, this can be called the Moses and Joshua dynamic. Moses, the charismatic spiritual leader, was the one who carried out the nation's revolution and led it to the margins of Canaan. "We 'came out' from an established order of life, but in many respects we have not 'arrived' at our future order of life,"[40] said Zvi Schatz to the members of his pioneer generation. Joshua, the young, practical leader-warrior-conqueror, was the man who headed the army of conquest and in the end took possession of the promised land.[41]

The Sabra generation was not the creator of the Zionist revolution, nor part of its spiritual leadership, and so did not find itself making the same kind of ideological and emotional pronouncements that the pioneers made. The sons were required to see to the execution of the hopes and dreams of the pioneer generation that preceded them. The fathers were acutely aware of the difficulty they thus created for their sons. The result was a paradox: on the one hand, the pioneer leadership gave its blessing to the natural and naive conformism of the second generation, but on the other hand it feared that the children were accepting the values "mechanically" and so not deeply.

There was another fear as well: making the younger generation dependent on the older generation to the point of paralyzing it (as sometimes happens to the children of great creative artists). In an article in 1937, Baruch Ben-Yehuda, the principal of the Herzliya Gymnasium, labeled this phenomenon the "second-generation complex":

> This is the tragedy of the "second": it is not at peace, it is torn in two. Its heart will not allow it to continue what the "first" began, for it too is "first" in its own eyes. And it cannot be "first." It sets its eyes forward, but the fear of the "first" chases it. Its independence is taken from it. All its life it does not stand on its own, but hangs.[42]

The Sabras themselves were aware of the intellectual "castration" to which the pioneer generation sentenced them. This was expressed and formulated for the most part in the young literature, which functioned like a trumpet for the voice of the Sabra generation. Chaim Glickstein, who along with Moshe Shamir and Shlomo Tenai edited one of the first anthologies of the young generation of writers, *A New Page for Literature, Art, and Criticism,* confessed to this generational weakness and expressed it in his essays and fiction.

The younger generation's sense of intellectual inferiority to the older generation was expressed in later years by Sabras who gazed retrospectively at their younger days.[43] Recognizing this sense of inferiority is important for understanding the Sabras' generational identity, especially their attitude of mixed admiration and bitterness toward the Zionist establishment. As noted by sociologists Yonatan Shapira and Uri Ben-Eliezer, this attitude was also apparent in a certain self-effacement by the young people before the veteran leadership, in an almost complete abstention from political activity in their younger days, and in the fact that they refrained from creating a young opposition.[44]

The younger generation solved, or at least moderated, the second-generation complex in three fundamental ways. First, they emphasized and developed the experience of nativeness (the sense of homeland, knowledge of the land, local slang, etc.)—an area in which they enjoyed cultural superiority over the older generation. Second, rejecting the theoretical (that is, ideological) orientation of the first generation, the Sabras chose through a process of "cultural selection" to define themselves in another field—the military. Here the pioneers could not set foot, and so the Sabras held a professional exclusivity and hegemony. This is also one reason that many of them decided on military careers and filled the senior command staff positions of the IDF for many years. The military profession, in which the sons could outshine the fathers, indeed gave the Sabras a place of honor in the Zionist epic (reaching its climax in the Six Day War) and made it possible for them later to make their way into the political leadership. Third, the Sabras developed a pattern of "super piety." Where they could not change and innovate they tried to prove that their contribution to the Zionist revolution was no less important— in fact was more important—than that of the fathers. Thus, the very same cultural characteristics that expressed the consummation of the ideals of the pioneer fathers also indicated rebellion against them.

REALLY IGNORANT?

All this may give the impression that the Sabra grew up to be a kind of rough-hewn boor. Chaim Guri called the members of his generation "Gavrushes," after the name of the soldier son of Kibbutz Beit Alfa's Dr. Eliahu Rappaport, an artist, thinker, and colleague of Martin Buber. "Among those born here there are also the Gavrushes, the sons of the Rappaports, the friends of the Martin Bubers, who startled the midwives who saw them being born with a monkey wrench and pistol in hand," Chaim Guri wrote.[45]

The idealistic conformity, the culture of *dugri,* and the aptitude for technical and military professions gave the younger generation the image of simple farmers of narrow horizons and a somewhat simplistic perception of reality. But this image is a bit misleading, especially when one takes into account all the facets of education and intellect present among the Sabra (and also because "education" and "intellect" are vague concepts that cannot be measured quantitatively).[46] While the Sabra was an ethnocentrist in his worldview, averse to high language, and chose to present himself as a man of action rather than as a man of thought, he was not uneducated. His formal high school education was of a high level, according to the standards of other Western countries. The Sabras were educated in the select schools of those times, taught by superior teachers, and in this sense it can be said that their education was no worse, and in some ways was even better, than the formal education of their parents.[47]

And what of their nonformal education and their culture of leisure reading and writing? Just as it did among the pioneers, among the Sabras the "anticulture culture" existed largely on the normative level. When one examines their writings (and again, it should be kept in mind that this study deals with the elite youth), the picture that emerges is almost the opposite of their image. These were young people who enjoyed reading serious literature and who in fact produced a large quantity of writing, both to be kept in the desk drawer and not to be kept there. They had a special fondness for poetry, and most of them tried their hand at writing verses and songs in private notebooks. Boys sent poems as gifts to their girlfriends and would learn them by heart in order to recite them to girls they were courting.

In the youth movements, conversations about Hebrew and foreign literature were part of the moral education program. Sometimes literary trials were even held, with a literary character as the defendant, and these were very popular with the young people. The Sabra generation read many translated classics (Hugo, Hamsun, Ibsen, Tolstoy, Roland). Many of the Sabras continued to read journals that were of a very high level (certainly in comparison with modern youth) in terms of both writing and substance. Their letters were also permeated with theory and morals—even if most of it was youthful naiveté and connected in some way with the Zionist and socialist ethos.

The large number of media for expression—pamphlets, newsletters, literary forums, and so on—testifies to a well-developed culture of thought and writing. In fact, it is difficult to find a Sabra organization that did not create some sort of platform for literary and expository expression, and in this, too, the Sabras were very similar to the generation that preceded them. The writings of the fallen soldiers and the youth movement newsletters contain an abundance of creative works (poems, compositions, essays, short stories) written on a high level and testifying to avid intellectual interest. Their achievements are even more impressive given that this was a new society with a new spoken language that required improvisation and innovation. This generation also produced a large quantity of writers, poets, journalists, and in time, scholars who made a lasting impression on Israeli culture.

But above all else, the military world is commonly regarded as a practical arena, by nature opposed to the world of intellectual creativity. In fact, it requires a great deal of intellectual creativity. While the 1948 generation made no ideological innovations in Zionism, it was very innovative in the area of military thinking and strategy, which require in-depth study, analytic ability, and creativity. In fact, this is what produced the IDF, today considered one of the best armies in the world.

CHAPTER 4

The Stamp of
His Country's Landscape

The Return to Nature in Pioneer Culture

The mystification of the Israeli landscape was one of the principal threads from which the pioneer ethos was woven, and as with so many other aspects of the pioneer culture, the source for this was Jewish tradition. The earliest writings about the landscape of the Holy Land, depicting both its beauty and the longing of the exiles to return to it, are in the Bible, and the subject continued to be a staple of the Jewish writer in the midrashic literature, in the composition of prayers, and in religious poetry through the ages.[1] However, unlike Diaspora Jews, the Zionist immigrants' rapture with the landscape and construction of the ideal out of rock (in the words of David Shimoni's poem) was not an expression of yearning for the land of the fathers and its sanctity. Rather, it was a mechanism for marking ownership (in the presence of rival residents) and, more important, a means for creating a new identity of being at home in a land that was foreign to most of them.

This pattern was not unique to the Zionist pioneers. It characterized immigrant-settler cultures in Australia, New Zealand, South Africa, and the United States. In all these cultures the physical conquest of the space was accompanied by a parallel emotional conquest.

The early Jewish settlers established their emotional attachment to the Land of Israel largely through the agency of the writers and poets among them. These composed a myriad of praises for the country's beauty, describing it in primal, legendary terms.[2] Their choice of the Israeli landscape as a central subject in their works was as much an ideological as an artistic choice.[3]

Zionist painters living in Palestine (there were not many) also portrayed the country in a naive, pastoral way.[4] Illustrators of books for both adults and children, as well as those who designed posters for the national institutions, generally portrayed the local landscape as if it were a fairy-tale land or the land of the Bible—a country of olive trees, camels, sand, and stone.

The pioneer's visual and verbal paean to the Israeli landscape—both the natural landscape and the landscape he domesticated—was also a way of saying that he had severed ties with the Diaspora's landscape and thus with its culture and had put down roots in his new homeland. It marked the pioneer's translocation from the "hell" of the Diaspora to the "paradise" of the Land of Israel.

Pioneer pantheism included not only mystification of the Israeli landscape but also mystification of nature itself and, especially, of working the land. This sentiment, which was especially prominent in the teachings of Zionist thinker A. D. Gordon, was influenced by the romantic philosophies that came to the fore in Europe at the end of the eighteenth century (especially in Germany and France), calling for the sensuous unity of man with nature.

Educating the Sabra to Love the Land

"KNOWING THE LAND" AND THE HOMELAND LESSON

Teaching the love of nature and of the country's landscape was central to Zionist education from the turn of the century, but it became more formalized, more extensive, and took a more important place in the curriculum starting in the 1920s. During this period a number of Jewish natural scientists immigrated to Palestine, many of whom became schoolteachers. The Hebrew University was also founded in Jerusalem, and the labor movement consolidated its system of education—the schools in the kibbutzim and moshavim and the labor-oriented schools in the cities. At the same time Zionist writers were churning out songs and stories for children and young people, and most of these were about the link between the Zionist pioneer and the landscape of his homeland.

In the 1920s a number of textbooks and reference books on Palestinian geography and natural history for adults and for young people were published. There was also an abundance of guidebooks for the Hebrew hiker and traveler, most of them put out by the Jewish National Fund and the Histadrut labor federation.[5] The assumption of the authors, as well as of the educators who used the books, was that Jews in Palestine should learn about the land not only for intellectual and practical purposes, but also for ideological reasons. They believed, almost certainly correctly, that there was a connection between knowledge and sentiment—between knowing the land and loving the land—and that instruction in Palestinian geography and natural history was a pedagogical tool for creating identification with the land and a sense of partnership in the pioneer enterprise.[6]

This approach, which integrated science and ideology (and which was employed elsewhere, as in Communist societies), could be seen clearly in "knowledge of the land" books. These works both overtly and covertly linked knowledge with emotion, scientific facts with Jewish and pioneer legends.[7] The very term "knowledge of the land," which was coined during the First Aliya and later institutionalized in popular knowledge-of-the-land quiz contests, indicated the emotional content of these geography books; in Hebrew, "knowing the land" bore a connotation parallel to the Biblical sense of "knowing a woman."

The teaching of natural history and geography in the Yishuv thus served as an ideological tool for instruction in Zionism and especially for attaching emotional meanings to the country's landscape. This was clearly expressed in the name given to elementary school geography lessons: "knowledge of the homeland," later shortened simply to "homeland."[8] The homeland was a major academic subject in the curriculum of the education department of the National Council as early as 1923, and its importance grew at the end of the 1920s and the beginning of the 1930s with the expansion of the teachers' colleges, the growing numbers of publishers, technical improvements in book printing, and the development of geographical research in Palestine. Particularly influential was Nachum Gabrieli's book *Knowledge of the Homeland* (1934), an elementary school textbook, and Tzvi Zohar's *Study in the Spirit of the Homeland* (1937), which included topics and lesson plans in geography.

Ostensibly, these "knowledge of the homeland" books were intended for geography instruction in the lower grades, but in fact they contained a mixture of subjects—natural history, agriculture, geography, Jewish history, and Hebrew literature. Thus they served as propaganda material for the pioneer enterprise and were meant to imbue the pupils with the basic ideological messages of Zionist nationalism. These books described with nationalistic fervor the country's sites and landscape largely in their historical-ideological context. Along with geographical facts, such as the height of Mt. Tabor and the boundaries of the Upper Galilee, the Yishuv pupil learned "ideological facts," such as the story of how the moshava Metulla was founded. He learned what crops could be raised on the coastal plain and in the climate of the Negev Desert, but also about "the draining of the swamps," "illegal immigration," "the joyous drawing of water," and "fields newly adorned with lush green trees" in the Land of Israel.

Some of the ideological messages in the homeland books are explicit and intentional, whereas others are implicit, conveyed in key words and phrases such as *aliya,* "illegal immigration," "pioneer," "making the desert bloom," and in questions that implied social expectations, such as: "You want to be a settler when you grow up, correct? Which would you prefer: tree crops, field crops, or a mixed farm? Answer briefly in your geography notebook."[9] These books are also remarkable for the emotional way in which they describe the physical environment, which accustomed the Sabra to view the landscape with a "Jewish heart," not with a "scientific head."

The youth movements also perceived the landscape through ideological lenses. Unlike the more universal pantheism of the British scout movement founded by Baden-Powell, which influenced the form taken by the Yishuv's youth movements, the pantheism of the pioneer youth movements was manifestly nationalistic, close in style to the German *Wandervogel* movement.

The ideological importance of "knowledge of the land" instruction meant that it was taught in military as well as civilian organizations, first in the Haganah and then in the IDF. In the 1950s the subject was an important part of the training of both soldiers and officers. The IDF published many books and instruction booklets on the subject, trained professional instructors (NCOs, women soldier-teachers, and officers) in the knowledge of the land, and established field schools—institutions unique to the Israeli army that served as bases for the study and teaching of the knowledge of the land. The instructors were largely Sabras in terms of their social characteristics, and this fact contributed to the public image of the Sabra as an expert in the knowledge of the land. The field schools became Sabra institutions in their own right and were similar in their human composition and their way of life to youth movement chapter houses and kibbutzim.

Taking schoolchildren on nature hikes was already common practice in the "modern" Jewish schools established in Palestine (for the most part in Jerusalem) in the mid-nineteenth century,[10] but it became integral to the pedagogical philosophy of most teachers during the period of the First Aliya. The purpose of these trips was to teach in an enjoyable and entertaining way and relieve the monotony of classroom study, while allowing students to stretch their limbs, and also strengthening the ties between teachers and pupils. In addition the trips fostered a link between the students and their surroundings, provided access to examples of the theoretical material being studied in school (largely in natural history and geography), allowed students to "discover" natural phenomena for themselves, and improved their Hebrew language skills (by identifying objects found around them).

The children took a jar or basket on such trips for collecting the things they found (beetles, butterflies, turtles, hedgehogs, wildflowers) and journals and observations sheets for recording their impressions along the way. The items they found on their trips were displayed in the school's natural history corner.[11] Dr. Yehuda Leib Matmon Cohen, one of the founders of the Herzliya Gymnasium and for many years a natural history teacher, coined the motto "school in the heart of nature," meaning direct contact between the pupil and the natural environment;[12] Sh. Ch. Wilkomitz, principal of the village school in the moshava Rosh Pina, coined the term "the natural learning method," according to which "the student learns not only with the aid of his mind and memory but also through his five senses."[13] The natural learning method, especially in the form of nature walks, was institutionalized and disseminated gradually through the teacher training colleges.[14]

In the 1920s, when Mapai became the leading Zionist movement, environmental education, including field trips, became a fundamental element of Zionist education. The nuances of labor Zionist values were added to the field trips—Hebrew labor, communal farming, and anti-Diaspora sentiments. "The Israeli student is not always imprisoned, like the student in the traditional Jewish school was, within the bounds of his school and schoolyard," wrote writer and educator Mordechai Michaeli. "School field trips broaden his mind and the range of his gaze and enhance his motivation and activity."[15]

In the cities, regular and preschool teachers would have their pupils perform agricultural work in the school garden and would take them on trips to nearby fields and open spaces. Kibbutz and moshav children went on study trips to become acquainted with their surroundings at least once a week. Special attention was given to learning about the domesticated flora on the farm; viewing the fields when they were plowed and sown, when the crops sprouted, and when the grain was harvested and winnowed; and observing the vineyards and orchards through their seasons—grafting, leafing, flowering, and picking. On these trips the students also absorbed information, unmediated, about local topography, wild and domestic animals and plants, and the local insects and birds. In particular, they could feel the living pulse of the farm.

Another way of strengthening the youngsters' link with the land and with nature was having them participate in the farm work. Kibbutz and moshav teachers would go with their pupils to pick fruit, olives, and grapes, especially in the hot season. This custom grew first and foremost out of the kibbutz approach to education, which emphasized learning in the framework of life itself.

Involving children and teenagers in agricultural work was also meant to imbue them with a sense of belonging to the rural community and to the local landscape. Even though hard work on the farm sometimes came at the expense of vacation time, kibbutz children loved it, both because it flattered their maturity and because of the enjoyable closeness to nature. Of course kibbutz and moshav children did not just work for educational reasons. There were economic reasons as well—working hands were needed, and the children had to be trained in agricultural tasks so they could join the farm's workforce as soon as they were old enough.[16]

For city children, farm chores were replaced by tending the school garden (in the context of lessons in agriculture, to which two hours a week were devoted, beginning in 1942),[17] as well as participating in work camps on kibbutzim, usually held during vacations and organized by the schools or by youth movements. Even though city parents had no desire for their children to become kibbutzniks, they welcomed the work camps for ideological reasons. Among the bourgeoisie, who intended for their children to remain in the city and pursue white-collar professions, the common wisdom was that their children would not be harmed and would in fact only benefit from a short period of pioneer work, and that it was certainly good for them to make a personal contribution to the national cause by helping in outlying settlements. In this way the urban Sabra was also connected to nature and to the country's landscape and could actively participate in the pioneer ritual.

Volunteer work on farms with other teenagers was a fun experience of free and independent living for city children. Since they grew up in urban families, this freedom was much more meaningful than it was for kibbutz children, who grew up in children's houses. Manual labor in the fields and orchards was not felt to be a chore, but rather was an enjoyable youthful experience. It was also nice to leave the city for a natural setting and for what was perceived as a healthy way of life.

Time spent at a kibbutz working shoulder to shoulder with children from the working settlements linked the urban Sabras to the rural culture and the kibbutz movement and made them feel at home there. For those who chose kibbutz life, it was also preparation for becoming settlers themselves. These periods of farm work produced abundant memories and common symbols and were the source of many songs that echoed the experience of labor and its moral significance.

As a member of youth organizations, the Sabras also gained familiarity with nature on overnight camps in the woods, conducted several times a year in the tradition of the German *Wandervogel* and the British scouts. Camp activities included hikes and outdoorsmanship, campcraft, and scouting. Like the work camps on the kibbutzim, these camps also had about them elements of romanticism and independence; they were breaks in the routine that provided an outlet for youthful energy. Furthermore, they created an opportunity for an experience shared by both sexes and were therefore very popular with young people.

The love of nature, as well as how to survive in it, was taught in military and paramilitary organizations (the *hachsharot* and the Gadna) as part of combat training.[18] In the Palmach, the Gadna, and IDF combat units military training camps were set up, generally in a wooded area, with the intention of teaching the trainee how to live outdoors. Campers erected their own tents and slept in them, learned to cook outdoors, to camouflage themselves, and to build improvised facilities from materials found in the woods and the field. Hikes and navigation exercises were also part of the didactic menu, complementing the field knowledge learned in the youth movements.

THE ANNUAL FIELD TRIP

The tradition of the annual field trip (a longer field trip than the ones just described, lasting several days in the older grades) had its inception in the "trips to the moshavot" that were instituted in the moshavot schools of the First Aliya. These trips were made by the children of one moshava to other moshavot, both nearby and distant, and lasted several days, sometimes several weeks, at the end of the school year. The children's arrival at another moshava was a day of celebration, including a joyful, formal, and public welcoming ceremony.[19] The trips symbolized the link between the moshavot and the Yishuv schools and served as a kind of coming-of-age and independence ceremony for the children of the moshavot.

What began early in the century as a local initiative of a few Zionist teachers became in the 1920s an educational tradition and a focal point of Sabra education in the schools and youth movements. The annual trips were of special importance in the high schools and youth movement chapters of the cities, where their physical distance from the mythological rural space created a certain dissonance between idea and practice. The trip was a holiday and a kind of Zionist sanctification ceremony, in which pupils and their teachers left the secular urban space for the sacred Zionist rural space. The many kinds of transitions—from "education" to "action," from an intellectual to an emotional experience, from passivity (sitting) to activity (walking), from a multilingual and multicultural world to an unadulterated and isolated Zionist world, from the familiar and routine medium of the classroom to an unexpected social medium in which the distance between the teachers and the pupils grew smaller— all made the trip a unique and exciting experience. Along with its aspect as coming-of-age and Zionist sanctification ceremony, the annual trip served several other social functions:

- Annual trips were one of the few means in that period of acquainting young people with the more distant parts of their environment, whether region, district, or country. Such conversance was important in a society in which there were few means of transportation, especially for residents of outlying settlements, who grew up geographically isolated and without mechanical means of mobility.

- Visits to Jewish settlements (especially on youth movement trips) were meant to induce young people to identify with the model of the working settlement and make them want to join one. Many trips did, in fact, produce this result. A Herzliya Gymnasium trip to the Dead Sea led to the establishment of a group that founded Kibbutz Ein Gedi, and the trips to the Jezreel Valley made by members of the group that later became Ha-Machanot Ha-Olim led to the establishment of Kibbutz Beit Ha-Shita.[20]

- The annual youth movement trips created ties between different chapters and youth movement groups and strengthened the social connection between the Sabras and the settlements.

· The sites visited on these trips (settlements and institutions that were generally well known at the time) brought home to the young person the geographic and social boundaries of the settlement and labor enterprises (which did not include the Arabs, the British camps, and the old Yishuv—the Jewish religious communities that had existed in Palestine prior to Zionism), as well as their huge achievements.

· More than anything else, these trips were a means of inflating the sails of the youthful soul with the national spirit. Their organizers viewed them first and foremost as annual revival campaigns, meant to strengthen the connection between the Sabra and his homeland.[21]

The routes of these trips generally included sites of Jewish historical importance—some of them ancient ruins—and viewing them shaped the ideological prism through which the Sabra saw the landscape. "How we rambled and roamed among the ruins," one Sabra wrote in a letter, "and everything around full of faint hints and fragments of echoes of distant and early days that have passed over this wonderful land of ours."[22]

Many educators used the Bible as a guidebook and described the landscape to their pupils in the context of Biblical stories. The landscape was mythologized and turned into a stage for a national historical pageant before the eyes of enchanted pupils, bringing home to them the richness of the nation's past that endowed some of its spirit on the present.

"LIKE A WILD PLANT"

In order to understand the "pantheist" side of the Sabra character it is also necessary to consider the ecology—the natural environment and climate itself—in which he grew up; for the Sabra's environment affected his connection to the landscape no less than did cultural norms. The Sabras of the moshavim, moshavot, and kibbutzim grew up close to nature in sparsely populated agricultural areas. Many farming settlements were established close to a source of water (a spring, a creek, or the sea), a natural forest, or (in the south) majestic desert cliffs—pastoral natural treasures to which boys and girls were attracted as if by magic.

The settlements themselves were awash with greenery that surrounded the buildings in every direction. In the early kibbutzim before 1920 there was no architectural planning, and landscape design was a spontaneous improvisation. Neither were there professional Jewish gardeners, except for a small number in the moshavot. The first trees, shrubs, and flowers in the sun-scorched plains of the Jordan Valley were planted "as an immediate response of the settlers to the harshness of the climate and the bare landscape with which they had to cope. By planting, the pioneers tried to improve their living conditions a bit and create a more comfortable and pleasant environment for the members of the kibbutz, most of whom had come from the richly green landscapes of Europe."[23] The formal design of the kibbutz's external appearance was conceived by the German Jewish architect and urban planner Richard Kaufmann, who was invited in 1920 by Arthur Ruppin, the Zionist official responsible for settlement activity, to plan the settlements set up by the Palestine Office of the Zionist Organization. Kaufmann was a product of the German school and had planned cities and garden suburbs in Germany and Norway. He planned most of the agricultural settlements in Palestine in the 1920s and 1930s, and it was he who designed the kibbutz and moshav as green settlements. In the third decade after the founding of the kibbutz and moshav there was an influx of Jewish gardening and landscape professionals who had studied overseas, and they worked to enhance the kibbutz gardens and lawns. During this period most of the kibbutzim planted the large grassy areas that in time became characteristic of their appearance. After the 1950s, when most kibbutzim were linked to the national water supply system, gardens and lawns spread over the entire residential area of the kibbutz, in some places covering fifty to seventy-five acres. From that period to the present day a kibbutz may be easily identified by its characteristic landscape—a rural settlement full of green and surrounded by a broad belt of fields and orchards, resembling a botanical garden or nature reserve.[24]

The kibbutz landscaping also played a symbolic-ideological role. The development of plant life symbolized the development of the kibbutz community and its taking root in its land. The common, fenceless garden symbolized the common home and the lack of distinction between the individual and the community. The arrangement of the plants, which was in the naturalistic style of an English garden, rather than in the decorative, geometrical forms characteristic of the French garden, indicated the spontaneity, simplicity, modesty, and informality of the kibbutz culture; the vivid green of the kibbutz also indirectly hinted at leaving behind the depressing dimness and dankness of the Jewish house of study in Eastern Europe.

The Sabra who was born on a kibbutz or moshav or spent time on one as a participant in youth movement camps, Palmach *hachsharot,* and so on thus lived in close and daily contact with nature. He was planted along channels of water and his growing environment was, as Zerubavel Gilad, a native of Ein Harod, described, "a childhood oasis."

Childhood in the heart of nature, as for rural children everywhere, steeped the Sabra in sensuous memories of flora and fauna—the aroma of the earth after the first rain, the perfume of the citrus blossoms, the sharp stench of the cowshed, the glitter of morning dew, the first wildflowers along the road, the cycle of the agricultural year, around which the cycle of community life revolved.

The Sabras' "pantheistic soul" was also nourished by the freedom they were given to ramble through the nearby countryside. In the protected community life of the kibbutz, moshav, and moshava there was no need to fence in the children in order to protect them; in small settlements there was no danger of them getting lost or of being hit by a car, so their wandering space in and around the settlement was not restricted. On the kibbutzim children enjoyed particularly great freedom and independence because of the autonomy of the children's houses, in which there was minimal oversight of the children's movements. Kibbutzniks grew up as "wild children," for whom nature was home. Children went around freely in laughing, vocal bands, barefoot or in rough leather sandals, in tattered undershirts or bare-chested—untamed children, "Huckleberry Finns," their skin freckled and their hair bleached, salty with sweat. Freedom, independence, and life in a nonurban environment were the basis for small nature adventures. Hide-and-seek in the granary, secret hiding places, secret night hikes in the surrounding mountains, campfires in the woods or on the beach, moonlight bathing in a nearby spring, in the reservoir, in the sea or in a river, collecting wildflowers or insects were all matters of routine for them. Nature was the Sabra's playroom.

The city Sabra also enjoyed relative freedom. The low buildings and minimal industry in the new cities moderated their urban character and gave life in their neighborhoods the character of a community. In all urban centers, even the largest, there were many nature spots with plants, earth, and sand. Even in the developing metropolitan center of greater Tel Aviv, boys and girls walked barefoot, dressed in undershirts. Sabra author Dan Omer called them "sand children."

The climate also contributed. In the Mediterranean climate it is possible to live outside. Nine sunny months a year allowed young people to spend their time in the open spaces instead of being confined to their homes. The "scintillating land," as it would later be called by S. Yizhar, produced children of the sun. With their tanned skin and their minimal clothing, they resembled children in other countries with similar climates, such as Greece, Australia, and the western United States.

In the Palmach or the army the Sabra would continue to live close to nature in an environment that was fundamentally nonurban. "We lived in small pup tents scattered through the gullies, like gypsies, with dust in everyone's mouth and the sun beating down on us," Zerubavel Gilad wrote.[25] In the Palmach, outdoor life was routine mostly because, as an underground organization, it could not maintain permanent bases. It had to make do with temporary training camps and mustering grounds. Life in the field was important in combat as well. This made the Palmachnik into a man of the field, for whom the mountain and valley were home.

The Myth of the Sabra Scout

Whereas among the immigrant pioneers acquiring expertise in the landscape of Palestine was a means of creating native identity, for the Sabra it was a status symbol meant to express the superiority of the natives over both the older generation and the new immigrants.

The Sabra's erudition in topography, history, archaeology, and Palestinian flora and fauna, which he acquired in his childhood ramblings,[26] on youth movement field trips, and in military organizations, is evident in many Sabra texts. Topographical terms were common in letters (especially those written to members of the older generation), in diaries, and in literature.

It was not only native status that made the identification and definition of places, plants, and animals an accepted practice in Sabra organizations. It was also, and principally, a matter of ideological, patriotic status. Knowing a place meant loving it and owning it. Rattling off the names of local plants and places was a way of declaring one's devotion to the Zionist idea, just like the religious scholar's expertise in the holy books expressed religious tradition and devotion. So also, fallen Sabras were often praised in the memorial literature for their knowledge of the land, not as the result of scientific interest or military necessity, but as a manifestation of their love of the land.

The ideological meaning of expertise in the landscape's secrets produced a kind of unspoken competition among the Sabras, recalling in terms of symbols and value goals, the tacit competition between Jewish religious scholars over fluency in the sacred literature. It produced "great scholars in the Torah of the Land of Israel," such as Tuvia Kushnir, Yitzchak Zamir, and Meir Har-Tzion, who were known for their phenomenal familiarity with the country's paths, plants, and animals. They walked the length and breadth of the country and learned to identify by name the shiyest of the plants and animals and the most desolate and distant of the mountains and crevices. Their expertise in the landscape and their ardent love for the physical space of the country were one reason they became admired figures and were considered great patriots.

The Palmach also contributed decisively to the tradition of expertise and familiarity with the country's landscape and to turning this talent into an Israeli status symbol, especially through the development of reconnoitering as a fundamental subject in combat training.[27] Reconnoitering was part of taking Yishuv defense activities beyond the boundaries of the settlements themselves, as practiced by the Haganah's Mobile Forces, the Field Troops, the Jewish auxiliary guards sponsored by the British, and Orde Wingate's Night Squads.[28] Though the first reconnoitering operations were done without professional training, this changed with the establishment of the Palmach.

Fear that the German army in North Africa would reach Palestine prompted the Yishuv to make preparations for a guerrilla war against the invaders, and this required thorough study and military analysis of paths, hideouts, commanding and observation points, and natural obstacles. It called for expertise in the collection of intelligence (topographic data), topographic analysis, and navigation with map and compass. The first Palmach soldiers were assigned this work by British officers in the context of their cooperation in the war against the Nazis. The British made an important contribution to the reconnoitering profession in the Palmach not only by passing on the results of their vast experience but also by preparing the first topographic maps of Palestine and so revealing the lay of the land in depth.

When the danger of a German invasion passed and the military ties to the British were severed, the profession of reconnoitering and knowledge of the terrain continued as part of the Haganah's war against the Arabs. Collection of topographical data and enemy intelligence became a routine job for the Palmach, which saw itself as a mobile offensive force. Palmach fighters regularly went out on reconnoitering missions to collect military information on the Arab villages and their environs, including access routes, water sources, and hiding places.[29]

Most of the reconnoitering work was done by platoons and squads of scouts (both male and female) that were an integral part of the Palmach's companies, as well as by a central reconnoitering platoon.[30] These platoons and squads, led by the Palmach's most senior commanders, turned reconnoitering into a profession of the highest standards and laid the professional foundations for the IDF's intelligence work. In the War of Independence, the Givati Brigade's mobile reconnoitering company, known as the Shimshon Foxes, became famous, and in the 1950s Unit 101 and the IDF's reconnoitering special forces became known for their superior navigational abilities. The fact that the label "reconnoitering unit" was attached to the IDF's most elite forces, whose missions were not limited to navigation, indicates the importance of reconnoitering as a military status symbol.

The scout's job was not limited to gathering intelligence. It also included leading forces into maneuvers and battle, tracking (to locate enemy infiltrators), planning marches, finding places of concealment along operations approaches and return routes, and locating sources of water. The critical nature of these activities made reconnoitering a prestigious profession among the Sabras and marked the reconnoitering units as illustrious status groups and as Palmach and IDF myths. But this prestige derived not only from their professionalism and military importance but also from the fact that they indirectly marked the rootedness of the new Jew—self-confidence in hostile territory (whether enemy territory or the desert itself), the physical aptitude and courage to move through the darkness like a wild animal (the opposite of the stereotyped cowardly Jew), and nativeness (the native knows the country's mountains and crevices). "In all places the scout's job is to discover the enemy's country and help conquer it. With us, his job is to discover the homeland and help conquer it," said Benny Maharshek, the Palmach's political officer, in a statement that itself became part of the 1948 mythology. The scout heading the force may well have embodied the Zionist movement's image of itself as a vanguard, a movement leading the Jewish camp, blazing a trail for it.

The symbolic importance of reconnoitering made it a key military achievement and one of the most important identity symbols of the Palmach veterans. Stories, skits, poems, *chizbatim*, and nostalgic songs were embroidered around the image of the scout. The Palmach's "shapers of the past," with some exaggeration, depicted all Palmachniks as trained scouts, and in doing so contributed to the mythologization of the organization and its members.

The March

FROM HIKE TO MARCH

In the 1920s, the Histadrut's Cultural Committee organized popular hikes to places famous in the country's and the Jewish people's history, led by special guides under the direction of Ze'ev Vilnai. The routes of these hikes went outside the areas of settlement into distant places uninhabited by Jews, and some of them lasted several days and were extremely difficult.[31] This launched a new tradition in the history of the Zionist hike—the march.

The march differed from the hike in seven ways (this is not a dichotomous distinction, since the boundaries between the march and the hike were somewhat fuzzy, and the word "hike" was sometimes used to describe a march and vice versa): (1) The march involved a long stay in the field (three days or more). (2) The march required physical exertion (because of the length of the route, heavy equipment, climactic conditions, and limited water) and demanded physical and psychological stamina. A hike was meant primarily for enjoyment and education, while the march was meant to be excruciating, to fortify the participant, and to test him. (3) The march required complex navigation with the help of a topographical map. (4) The destination of the march was more important than the journey, and therefore all or part of the way was covered at night. (5) The march included an element of discovery and "conquest" of a place (a spring, a peak, ruins). (6) Most marches were conducted in the country's desert regions, so the participants were more isolated than participants in hikes. (7) The march included manifestly militaristic elements (walking in columns, military dress, water rationing), as well as an element of danger. In military groups the march had tactical importance, and therefore included specifically military elements such as camouflage, a swift pace, and reconnoitering.

The marching culture gained momentum and became a fundamental element in the national folklore in the 1940s. There were four reasons for this: the "discovery" by the youth movements of Masada, which turned into a major site for marches; the resistance to the restrictions on movement imposed by the British; the establishment of the Gadna in the cities and its parallel incarnation on the kibbutzim, the Kibbutz Brigade; and the founding of the Palmach.

Trips to the Dead Sea, including the ascent of Masada, began in the 1920s, first within the framework of the upper classes of the Herzliya Gymnasium (headed by Dr. Bograshov, who had a special love for geography),[32] and continued in the 1930s, within the framework of the Ha-Machanot Ha-Olim movement. Then, in 1942, a study seminar was held on the peak of Masada for forty-seven counselors from Ha-Noar Ha-Oved, Ha-Shomer Ha-Tza'ir, and Ha-Machanot Ha-Olim, at the initiative and under the direction of Shmaryahu Gutman of Ha-Noar Ha-

Oved.[33] In its wake, youth movement members discovered the mythological potential of the march to Masada and began to ascend the desert
escarpment in large numbers. Carrying canteens on their belts and jerricans on their backs; sporting heavy packs loaded with canned food (generally sardines), a few loaves of dry bread, halvah, chocolate, a pistol, a
pocketknife, and rope; toting sleeping bags on their shoulders; dressed
in work clothes cut from rough fabric, high boots with gaiters, and a
"dunce cap"; bearing maps, Bibles, musical instruments (generally har-
monicas and recorders), and high spirits, caravans of young people would
make their way through the parched desert. The march would generally
last three to six days and include stops for meals, nighttime gatherings
around the campfire, and spending the night in sleeping bags under the
stars—all of which made the march into a social event of the first order.

In August 1939 the British authorities declared large areas of the Negev
Desert and Judean Desert closed to hikers. The official reason was to keep
an eye on the smuggling activity in these regions, but the Yishuv saw it
as the White Paper policy edict—an attempt to deny the Jews access to
large portions of the country.[34] The youth movement marches to the
Judean Desert, the ends of the Dead Sea, the Tzin Canyon, the Large
Crater, Ein Gedi, and other distant points, while ignoring the British restrictions, granted the marches a national and heroic stature, a kind of
proud national defiance—"we are here nevertheless"—and also an element of danger, making the marches almost military.

During that same period, Zionist schools (especially the Herzliya Gymnasium, the Reali School, and the kibbutz schools) began making their
annual class trips longer, both in days and in kilometers, and these became exhausting marches that required great determination. They were
held under the direction of the Gadna and the kibbutz youth regiment,
which saw them as a tool for training the future fighter. For several years,
the Gadna conducted five-day marches from Tel Aviv to Tel Chai in com-
memoration of Tel Chai Day. For the Gadna, like the youth movements,
Masada became a youth fortress, a temple of Israeli patriotism and, to
a large extent, also of militarism.

With the establishment of the state the Gadna marches became exhi-
bitions of national strength and vitality. In the spring of 1950 the Gadna
organized a highly visible mass march by a thousand Gadna recruits to
the peak of Masada—the number of participants being the number of
Jews who had been besieged at Masada in ancient times. It was called
the March of the Thousand; a film crew recorded it and it was the talk
of the country.

A year later the March of the Two Thousand to Masada was held, and from then on a mass Gadna march—not only to Masada but also to Jerusalem and other places—became an annual tradition.[35]

In the 1950s, during Moshe Dayan's term as chief of staff, the march became an important element in the swearing-in of army basic trainees. Hundreds of infantrymen, after a difficult march, would ascend the winding trail to the Masada peak in a long column to be sworn in at night in a torchlight ceremony.

THE MILITARY MARCH

The Palmach, more than any other body, was the organization that in the 1940s raised the march to the level of a principal educational enterprise. The Palmach also encouraged its associated youth movements to conduct marches in distant areas and would send its own scouts to guide the hikers and its own men to protect them in the desolate areas of the Negev and Judean Deserts. Aside from the march to Masada, the Palmach conducted traditional marches to Modi'in (the home of the Maccabees), to Tel Chai, from Jerusalem to Ein Gedi, around the Dead Sea to the Arnon Canyon, as well as climbs up Mounts Tabor, Muchraka, and Meron. The march was central to the Palmach experience because it filled several complementary roles:

· The march was used for security purposes: to create an armed Jewish presence in various regions of the country, tantamount to a declaration of ownership; to create a deterrent; and to gather information and intelligence (the participants in the marches helped in the preparation of reconnaissance dossiers).

· Marches through sparsely populated territories, far from the eyes of British and Arab intelligence, were used for live fire exercises. They were also an innocent cover for the soldiers, since youth movements also went on marches and weapons could be concealed in jerricans and knapsacks.

· As in other armies, for the Yishuv soldiers the march was a partial simulation of the battlefield and a way of training the soldiers to function under pressure and danger and to perform missions at any price. Setting out at night, moving silently among Arab villages, sometimes in dangerous areas, was meant to sharpen the fighters' senses and develop their combat skills.

· For Palmach *hachsharot,* the march served as an efficient means of preserving military fitness during periods when the soldiers were engaged in civilian labor on the kibbutzim.

· The march was meant to provide a common experience that tightened the bonds between the fighters and was vital for forging the solidarity of the unit and building mutual dependability among the soldiers.

· During World War II the marches were meant to preserve high morale. The nonintervention policy imposed on the Palmach by the Yishuv leadership frustrated the Palmach fighters. The hikes were a tool for creating drama and a sense of adventure, danger, suspense, and romanticism—adrenaline-producers for young people who were otherwise sitting around doing nothing. This was the reason for the exaggeration of the dangers of the marches and the development of an entire folklore of suspenseful and mysterious stories about clashes with Bedouins in the Judean wilderness and the stashing of weapons.

· Palmach marches had as much didactic ideological value as they had military value. "The marches and hikes are an intrinsic element in our training," wrote one of the soldiers in *Alon Ha-Palmach* after a march to Mt. Hermon. "Through them we learn to love the homeland, to protect it, and to be at home in it. . . . In my heart I carry a deep experience of contact with the country's landscape, an experience that will not pass."[36] Walking the land and sleeping in the open symbolized the unmediated contact with the soil of the Land of Israel and a direct connection with its landscape. Concluding the tough marches at sites of historical importance (Masada, Beit She'arim, etc.), and the swearing-in and certification ceremonies that were held at the end of many marches made them into something like mass pilgrimages to Zionist "sanctuaries."

· The common suffering represented the Zionist sacrifice. The march was a ritual that embodied a common declaration of love for the homeland. This also created solidarity—what anthropologists call "pilgrim's communitas." "We worship the land as a man worships his God," one of the Sabras wrote. "The commandment to know it (with our feet and by the sweat of our brows) is a holy precept for us. . . . A stranger cannot understand it."[37] The marcher struggling with the slopes and the steep ascents was like the pioneer struggling with the boulders on his land. Sufferings imprinted the landscape on the body of the pioneer and his heir, the Sabra, and symbolized his willingness to make a sacrifice. The Land of Israel is "acquired through suffering," and the Sabra acquired it through the suffering of the hike.

· More than anything else, the experience of the march was meant to put the marcher to the test, to be a kind of litmus test of the quality of the individual and his company. This was also the reason for the special emphasis that the Palmach (and, under its influence, the youth movements) placed on physical difficulty. "Our attention was always given, even in marches during times of peace, to distance, swiftness, stamina, water rationing," wrote Palmachnik Matti Megged.[38] The marches often caused back pains, ankle fractures, rashes, blisters, heat stroke, and thirst to the point of loss of consciousness. The physical difficulty was the source of march slang. A person who hopped from one leg to another because of blisters had the "frogs" and one who walked with his legs spread apart because of a rash had the "wolves."[39]

THE MARCH AS A TEST OF SOCIAL POTENTIAL

An analysis of the descriptions of the marches in Sabra writings, including marches by youth movements and army marches after the founding of the state, reveals three complementary elements of the test to which participants in marches were put:

Mental Fortitude Their physical and psychological difficulty gave the marches the character of tests of willpower, stamina, self-control, and determination. Physical weakness, fatigue (which one could not admit to), and wounds were not considered sufficient reasons to desist from the march; on the contrary, they were often considered good reasons to go on, because torturing oneself was a real test of the one's endurance and self-control. It was not the power of one's muscles that was being tested, but rather the mental power to overcome weakness, to withstand pain, to keep cool, and to overcome natural urges. Therefore, fainting or physically collapsing, especially on Paratrooper marches in the 1950s, was not considered failure but was in many cases seen as a sign of success. It testified that one had gone to the limit of one's physical endurance—real evidence of determination and devotion. A man who forced the march to halt or complained of difficulties or pain would be labeled a wimp.

The emphasis on willpower and the ability to withstand suffering was meant not only to test a person's quality, but also to make it possible for him to reach a state of spiritual euphoria at the end of the difficult march—just like the euphoria awaiting the believer at the end of a day of fasting he has imposed on himself. The struggle on the march was not a struggle with competitors, as in an athletic competition, nor a struggle for a quantifiable achievement. It was a man's struggle with himself—with his passions, his pains, and his weaknesses. In fact, many described the hike's moment of completion—generally after an exhausting climb up a mountain—as a moment of euphoria, satisfaction, and a sense of victory. This sense was reinforced when a swearing-in ceremony was held at the end of the march. Moreover, the emphasis on the struggle against the body's weaknesses (coping with the urge to drop out of the hike because of fatigue, thirst, and so on) created a kind of collective euphoria, since it allowed all the participants in the march to "win."

The march was also regarded as a test of character in the Gadna and youth movements, not just in the army, since the members of these groups were future soldiers. The restrained behavior of a youth movement member during a march was an important way of ranking his human qualities—and for choosing counselors.

The physical and psychological challenge presented by the hikes made them in a way into rites of passage. Every stage of maturity had its level of difficulty. Moving from each stage to the next higher one in the youth movement, the Gadna, and army courses was marked by ever more difficult, more daring, and longer marches, preparing the member or soldier for a higher level of personal ability and maturity.

The perception of the marches as tests of character, as measures of human quality, made them important entries on the Sabra résumé. A person who had been through a large number of difficult marches was considered a person "with a record." The prestige accruing to the participant in a march was expressed in the Sabra culture of discourse in expressions of self-glorification such as "Have you climbed up there yet?" "Were you ever in that place?" "Don't ask what hell we went through there." As with every test, its difficulty depended on the severity of the march, and this was one of the reasons that march organizers would add further, gratuitous challenges to the already difficult walk, such as a miserly water ration, a heavy load on the back, a minimum of stops, and a quick pace (in the army these difficulties were added in order to harden the soldiers). The tough hikes in the Palmach and in the IDF's elite units became famous—the greater the torture, the greater the prestige of the unit.

The March as a Sociometric Exam   According to the common wisdom that a person is tested in times of trouble, the march was also a test of altruism and mutual responsibility. The participant in the hike was under the watchful eye of the group and its leaders (teachers, counselors, and commanders) and was measured by the extent to which he took care of his friends, provided support for the stumblers, and put the good of his comrades before his own good at times of crisis.

The physical difficulty of the march created extreme situations of having to choose between one's own benefit and that of one's comrades who were also suffering—just as under fire in battle. From the perspective of social psychology, the march can be seen in terms of its group dynamics as something of a common pressure cooker that removed the person's daily guise and revealed his real character.

The character of the march as a test of "Thou shalt love thy neighbor as thyself (if not more)" was emphasized by presenting it as a common task and achievement, rather than an individual one—just like conquering an enemy outpost, which required the cooperation of the entire unit. Presenting the achievement in collective terms loaded additional expectations on the individual—aside from the expectations of his personal success, his duty and contribution to the group's success. The common preparations; joint navigation; sharing the burden of carrying the jerricans of water, the equipment, the food, and the weapons; sleeping together out in the open; collective campfires at the interim stations; mutual aid during tough ascents; covert and overt competition between platoons and companies—all these turned the march into a ritual of group solidarity that produced a "diploma" in comradeship. The motto was "we are walking," not "I am walking."

The March as a Test of Patriotism   The march was not only an expression of the covenant or marriage between the Sabra and his homeland but also a test of loyalty. Overcoming physical difficulty was a mark of the fighting pioneer spirit. According to the myth, only the chosen ones, those who overcame the mental and physical obstacles along the way and reached the finish point, were worthy of being numbered among the pioneer guard. "Indeed, only the best of us reached the peak. The rest of the weak and tired with the fractured and broken limbs trudged [back] to Merchavia [in the valley]," wrote a member of Ha-Shomer Ha-Tza'ir about a march in the Jezreel Valley ending with a steep climb.

The symbolic meaning of the marches as national awakening calls, as demonstrations and tests of collective willpower and determination, and as a kind of mass asceticism declaring loyalty to the Sabra framework and thus indirectly to the nation and the state, is what inspired the popular variation on the march—the treks, which began in the 1950s.[40] The treks, especially the mass trek to Jerusalem, were a national ritual of showing the flag throughout the country, of national solidarity and love of the homeland, and above all a demonstration of collective overcoming of difficulties: "If you will it, it is no dream." "It was an experience, that trek. It was a pilgrimage that was all song, that was all cheering and demonstration of power and enthusiasm," related one of the trekkers to a reporter from *Ba-Machaneh Gadna* in an article headlined "The Entire Country Left-Right." "We felt, if I may be allowed to say it, the courageous pulse of this nation beating at a uniform rate."[41]

MEIR HAR-TZION AND INDIVIDUAL MARCHES

Alongside the tradition of youth movement marches and popular treks, there began in the 1940s—increasing considerably in the 1950s—an informal tradition of marches done individually or in small groups of young people. These marches, in which two to four close friends participated, were meant to satisfy the Sabra's passion for wide-open spaces that was not fulfilled by the institutional hikes and marches. A sense of adventure, the desire to prove one's independence, rebelliousness against friends and adults, as well as youthful one-upmanship (gathering unique experiences and displaying one's courage), were also at the foundation of the attraction these marches held.[42] Unlike school trips, which were aimed at observation, and Palmach and Gadna marches, which were demonstrations of nationalism or military exercises, the individual marches were principally challenges. Many of them were adventurous and dangerous, involving scaling cliffs and crossing the border (after 1948). Because of the danger, most of them were surreptitious; the young people set out on them without the permission of their parents and counselors. Sometimes these escapades ended in British prisons or even in death (because of dehydration or encounters with hostile Bedouin tribes on the other side of the border). Because of their secrecy, risk, the sense of independence they required, and the small-scale rebelliousness they involved, these marches became, over time, an important element in the tradition of Sabra adventurousness.

Among the developers and disseminators of the Sabra tradition of "forbidden marches" the most famous is Meir Har-Tzion, a Sabra who reached adulthood during the period when the state was established. The forbidden marches he and his imitators went on to Petra in the mountains of Jordan, the Ein Gedi cliffs, the Arnon canyon in Jordan, the escarpments of the Judean Desert, Mt. Lebanon, and Sinai were a kind of 1950s folkloristic variation of the individual marches that some kibbutz and moshav youngsters (such as Tuvia Kushnir and Yitzchak Zamir) went on in the 1940s. Their motivation was a search for thrills in the drab days of the early state that came after the stormy 1940s, and the aspiration of the Sabras who had not participated in the War of Independence to best the Palmach Sabras, or at least to produce for themselves a new social status symbol. The new border created in 1948, beyond which lurked (at least according to the public image) an enemy dripping with hatred and desire for revenge—the "infiltrator" and the "terrorist"—affected the flavor of the individual marches of the 1950s.

Like many members of his generation, Har-Tzion was born and grew up on a kibbutz (Ein Harod), and followed the classic Sabra path. He had all the Sabra traits in their pure form and in the special configuration of his era—the end of the War of Independence; the broadening of the Jewish country's borders, which opened up new landscapes; the beginnings of the regular army; the consolidation of the myths of 1948; and the escalation of attacks by the Arab *fedayeen*. His diary—published twenty years later as a book—is thus in many respects no less a generational than a personal journal.

Har-Zion seemed to embody—consciously or unconsciously—the epitome of the Sabra's anti-Diaspora ethos and the folklore of nativeness and combat. He was described by his friends—and appears in his diary—as independent, wild, and defiant, a sturdy young man of exceptional courage, fun-loving, at home in his homeland, with a strong sense of nativeness. Like other Sabra heroes, he was a classic product of Sabra culture on the one hand and, on the other, a social bellwether who created new molds and widened the borders of the culture. In fact, it is possible to say that Har-Tzion's marches both expressed and heralded the egocentrization and militarization of the new Sabra of the 1950s.

Har-Tzion exemplified the ideological extremism possible in all religions, including the Zionist religion of the 1950s. Every religion produces its fanatics—those individualistic individuals (such as the Ba'al Shem Tov, the founder of Hasidism) who take the primary symbols and expressions of faith to an extreme in a process of intensifying piety and ideology and making a show of religious symbols. The march, as noted, was one of the expressions of Zionist faith, and it was only natural that believers would arise who would make their imprint on its overt and covert ritual aspects.

As a Zionist devotee Har-Tzion did indeed take to extremes the ritual aspects of the youth movement and Palmach group march. One of them was facing and overcoming danger. He chose destinations for his marches that were distant and risky, both geographically (for example, he loved scaling the steep and dangerous face of Masada) and in terms of hostile populations (for example, traveling across the border). This made them, and similar marches by others, operations of macho daring. Har-Tzion wrote, "I would get up early, at four in the morning, and stride in the dark to the mountain, sometimes also at night and in the afternoon. Simply, it is nicer, more attractive, and more interesting to go early in the morning. It is dangerous and therefore also interesting at night because there are infiltrators."[43] The jewels in the crown among these marches were the ones to Petra in Jordan. These became a kind of Sabra sport, a covert competition for breaking records of difficulty and danger.

Freedom and independence were also taken to extremes in the forbidden marches of Har-Tzion and his imitators. Leaving without advance notification (sometimes actually fleeing in the middle of the night), rambling through distant locations, and sneering at danger expressed the disposition of a Hebrew Buffalo Bill. Har-Tzion was (though not consciously) a pure incarnation of the "new Jew," recognizable from his potent sense of freedom and independence, and this was one of the reasons that he became a mythological figure.

On these marches, Har-Tzion and his companions underwent sensuous experiences of being at one with nature. His journal is full of descriptions of encountering the primal land, of absorption into nature and of osmosis with the desert cliffs and crevices—walking in water with his shoes on, walking naked in the wadis under a fierce sun, picking wild fruit, spending nights in a sleeping bag under a full moon, climbing precipices. In fact, there is a similarity between the pantheistic feelings of Har-Tzion and those of S. Yizhar, the Palmach writer—Har-Tzion flirts with the Land of Israel landscape with his feet, while Yizhar does so with his pen.

The physical torment of the regular marches metamorphosed, in the forbidden marches, into a sensuous experience. It lost some of its ideological meaning and turned into individual satisfaction of natural urges. Har-Tzion's journal describes how he exulted in harsh conditions and made them into ecstatic experiences of the physical tension between severe denial (of sleep, water, comfort, food) and its satisfaction—drinking cool water from a spring hidden among the boulders after a parched day, baking Bedouin bread on an improvised open-fire oven, opening a can of food after a long fast, drinking coffee while relaxing one's aching muscles after climbing a peak. The experience of the march resembled, in this sense, the intoxicating experience of the long-distance runner—self-denial ending in catharsis and elation.

The sociological importance of the Har-Tzion-style marches was that they turned the "communal holy worship" of the youth movement, army, and popular marches into the "intimate holy worship" of the individual. The mechanism of the march shifted from a ritual and public obsession that served collective needs into an instrument of individual exaltation and euphoria in a way that, to a certain extent, recalls the Bratislaver Hasidic practice of lone contemplation in a forest. In a march undertaken by an army company or unit, the achievement is shared by many participants; in an individual march, the achievement is individual. This is a private, and therefore more satisfying, ecstasy.

This phenomenon of a collective ritual that undergoes a process of individualization, adding a creative element but also eroding its original character, was typical of the process of institutionalization of the Zionist religion. It was also evident in other fields, such as song, dance, humor, and language.

Sabra men and women soldiers

*Festival of the First Fruits—the pioneer version of the traditional
Shavu'ot holiday—at Kibbutz Beit Kama*

The commander —
Sheike Gavish, Palmach
commander and, like
a number of his comrades,
later a general in the IDF

The kumzitz *— the Sabras' favorite leisure activity*

A kibbutz agriculture lesson

Gavrush (Gabriel Rappaport), born at Kibbutz Beit Alfa—an early Palmach soldier and one of the colorful figures in Sabra mythology

Palmach hachshara *group having fun*

Sabra fighters as part of the 1948 mythology—a photograph that appeared on the cover of Ha-Olam Ha-Zeh *in 1949, after the war*

Bedouin headdress as a native Israeli status symbol

Hillel Lavi of Kibbutz Ein Charod—one of two brothers who fell in battle and in death became exemplary mythological figures

Palmach soldiers resting during training, March, 1943

"The stamp of his country's landscape"

The jeep as an elitist status symbol—
soldiers of the Harel Brigade

CHAPTER 5

Uri of Arabia

Conflicting Images of the Arab

The first Zionist settlers' perceptions of the Arabs were conflicting and fluid. These images had a number of sources: wishful thinking, political interests, ignorance, and naiveté, as well as contact and commerce with these neighbors, the profound cultural and economic chasm between East and West, and the bloody territorial conflict, which worsened as the years went by.

The Arab as Hebrew   The pioneers of the Second and Third Aliyot believed that Bedouin culture resembled ancient Israelite culture, so they drew on the Orient as a source of symbols for the ancient Hebrew nation.[1] This perception was actually a mixture of two approaches: romantic and scientific (or pseudo-scientific).

The romantic approach was based on the primal nature of Bedouin culture. The Bedouin way of life seemed to the pioneers to resemble the ancient ways of life described in the Bible and in the Rabbinic literature. Like the ancient Israelites, the Bedouin herded sheep, used beasts of burden to plow and winnow, pressed olives for oil, ground wheat with millstones, baked bread over a fire, lived in tents sewn from goatskins, wore robes, practiced hospitality, and belonged to a tribal community that lived near sources of water. This perception was reinforced by the mythological Semitic blood tie—according to both Jewish and Arab legend, the

Arabs were descended from Abraham's son Ishmael, while the Jews were descended from his other son, Isaac. In the 1930s and 1940s, scholars at the Hebrew University, following in the footsteps of their European colleagues, provided anthropological and archaeological confirmation of the kinship between the Arab way of life and that of the ancient Israelites. "The peoples of the East as a group preserve their customs and thus it is possible to learn even from the customs practiced among them now about ancient Israelite practices," wrote Dr. Yehuda Bergman in a 1945 article in which he set out practices, proverbs, and superstitions that were similar among Bedouin and Jews.[2]

There were scholars who went even further and argued that the Bedouin living in Palestine were lost Hebrews, descendants of the ancient Hebrew tribes or descendants of Jews who had abandoned their religion because of persecution.[3] Those who held this view, among them lexicographer Eliezer Ben-Yehuda, based their conclusion on the findings of linguists, geographers, and folklorists around the world, and especially on the strong link between literary Arabic and Hebrew, which was for them proof of the close ethnic relation between the Arab and the Biblical Jew.

Another link between the Arab and the Hebrew was the old Sepharadi communities concentrated in the country's holy cities. They were believed to be the direct descendants of the ancient Jews because of the similarity of the Sepharadi way of life to Oriental culture; the same view was held of the Yemenite Jews who immigrated to Palestine at the beginning of the century.[4] According to a legend elaborated by some Zionists, the Yemenite Jews were in fact the mysterious Jews of Cheivar, nomadic heroes destined at the time of redemption to lead the Jewish people in the liberation of their homeland.[5] The young people and writers of the Second Aliya told themselves that if a distant tribe like the Yemenites had reached Palestine, maybe there were still Jewish Bedouin tribes to be found,[6] and some of them went to search for the Jewish tribes in Transjordan.[7]

It is important to note that the portrayal of the Bedouin as the descendants of the Israelites, or at least as preservers of Israelite culture, served a political purpose as well—it helped the Zionists anchor the right of the Jews to Palestine and reinforced their feeling that they were the lords of the land. However, both views—the Arabs as preservers of Hebrew culture and as descendants of the Hebrews—were adopted by only a few and for but a brief time.

The Arab as the "Noble Savage"   At the foundation of the Orient's allure for the pioneer was a romantic attraction to "natural primitivism" and to the "mysterious Orient" that had its origins in the beginning of the nineteenth century. Rationalism and the alienation of industrial culture produced a reaction in Western Europe, a longing for a primal, pre-monotheistic society perceived as pastoral, pure, and harmonious.[8] A few of the Jewish immigrants who came to Palestine at the beginning of the century were influenced by this romanticism and viewed the country's Arabs, and the Bedouin in particular, as pure, primal people, free of capitalist complexes and hypocrisy. The hot-headed Bedouin, simple in his ways, resourceful, hospitable, and brave, was for them a noble savage. Of course this view of the East was founded in great naiveté and a shallow familiarity with Arab culture, and like the image of the Bedouin as a descendant of the Israelites, was the provenance of a very small number of pioneers. It lasted for only a short time in Zionist culture, but as we shall see, it had a certain influence on Sabra culture.

The Arab as a Model for the New Jew   Oriental symbols were also adopted in the construction of an anti-Diaspora identity. According to the mythological stereotype, the Arab was a reverse image of the "abject" Diaspora Jew. "We are a withered and weak people with little blood. A nation like ours needs savage men and women. We need to renew and refresh our blood. . . . We must have Jewish Bedouin. Without them we will not move, we will get nowhere, we will not get out into open space. Without them the redemption will not come," said Romek Amashi, the protagonist of Ya'akov Rabinowitz's novel *The Wanderings of Amashi the Guard,* who dresses like a Bedouin and lives "a life of freedom in the heart of nature in the Choran Mountains."[9]

For some pioneers the Bedouin was a man of the earth, free of the spiritual complexities that engulfed the scholar of the Jewish town. He was a "bold fighter," a "man of the desert," and a "man of honor," who lived simply and in harmony with his physical surroundings. So, when educator Yisrael Rivkai described the tempestuous character of his Sabra students, he was impressed by "the huge leap in the psychology of the people, a leap over thousands of years." "One must come to Palestine," he wrote,

> to be in the company of native-born youth in order to realize that such a huge leap is really possible. Among the hundreds of students in the educational institution from all over the Diaspora, there are a few dozen natives—second

and third and fourth generation to those who immigrated from the Diaspora.
A bit critically and a bit as a sign of affection, they call many of those native-
born students "Arabs"—This student is a Jewish Bedouin! That student is an
Arab Jew in all details![10]

The notion of the Arab as an exemplar of the non-Diaspora prototype character was expressed, even if in an artificial and romantic way,
in the Oriental attitudes that the men and women of the Ha-Shomer guard
force—and before them the young people of the moshavot—adopted.
These, in turn, were important reference groups for the Sabras. The fer-
vent desire to be Jews of a new, better breed led to the self-conscious imitation of Arab dress, language, and folklore. "He wanted to become an
Arab, to be in his total Hebrewness like them, for the Hebrew in him to
be like the Arab in them." So wrote Rabbi Benjamin (Yehoshua Radler-
Feldman) in his eulogy for Berele Schweiger of Ha-Shomer, who had been
murdered by Arabs.[11] This phenomenon, which sociology calls "the ex-
travagance of status symbols,"[12] to a certain extent also characterized
the Palmach's Mistarabim unit, whose soldiers disguised themselves in
Arab garb. The Mistarabim model of behavior served multiple purposes,
mixing folklore, image, and security. The adoption of Bedouin customs
and attitudes was not only an important tool for becoming familiar with
the enemy and making the Jewish settlers more respectable in his eyes,
but also as a way of stating that the Sabra had shed the skin of the Diaspora and developed a native Land of Israel mentality. Such practices
were indeed welcomed by the Yishuv. The Mistarabim had many imitators, and many, especially the romantically minded, were fascinated by
them, for here seemed to be additional proof that the dream of the new
Jew had been realized.

The Arab as a Member of a Primitive Culture   The notion of the Arab as a
member of a primitive culture—less romantic and more patronizing than
the other views—was, however, the dominant one. The Arab was considered technologically and economically backward, and due to inter-
marriage, bad hygiene, and poor sanitation, unhealthy. Arab villages and
Arab neighborhoods in the cities were full of garbage and filth, and their
homes stank from fires fueled by goat droppings. The Arabs suffered from
bitter poverty, illiteracy, and the peculiarities of their culture—the patriarchal and exploitative structure of the tribe and clan, the Bedouin tradition of the blood feud and spoils, and the unending battle for the honor
of the man and the community. For the Jewish immigrants, these were
manifestations of a primitive culture far distant from progressive Euro-

pean culture. Therefore, they perceived their work in Palestine not only as redeeming the land of their fathers for the Jewish people, but also as bringing modern civilization to this backward and primitive region. "Believe: our race's sister, the Arab, is here / . . . we will come to instruct him, great in wisdom and experience," wrote poet Uri Zvi Greenberg.[13] Reverberations of this perception can be found in articles and in literary works for adults and young people. So, for example, Tzvi Lieberman's *Oded the Wanderer,* later made into the first full-length Israeli feature film, depicts the pioneer as the apostle of civilization to this barren and forgotten region who saves the Arab "natives" from their ignorance and illiteracy.[14] "You are the learned, educated Jews who know everything, and we are savages," a Bedouin says to Oded, the book's stereotypical Sabra protagonist.[15]

This perception grew stronger as the Yishuv developed economically, culturally, and technologically and the gap in living standards between neighboring Jewish and Arab settlements grew wider.

The Arab as the Descendant of Ishmael   The patronizing attitude toward the Arab also derived (though less consciously) from the myth of the rejected and humiliated brother, Ishmael, described in the book of Genesis as "a wild man; his hand will be against every man, and every man's hand against him." In Jewish tradition, the Arabs are the descendants of Ishmael, the scorned and inferior son of their common father. He and his mother, Hagar the maidservant, were banished to the desert in favor of Isaac, Abraham's better-loved "Jewish" son, born of his Hebrew wife, Sarah. The Arabs, according to Jewish tradition, were also the descendants of Esau, the Edomite, the hirsute savage, bitter son of Isaac who lost the blessing of the first-born.[16] He sold his birthright to Jacob, the "Jew," who had exploited his weakness to trick him.

The Arab as Amalek, the Bloodthirsty and Cruel Enemy   Contradictory perceptions of the Arabs coexisted, but under the pressure of events the negative slant came to predominate. The Arab was regarded as not only a member of an inferior culture but also a bloodthirsty and vengeful nemesis. The view of the Arab as a dangerous and deceitful enemy was already present in the Yishuv during the First Aliya, following clashes between the settlers in the moshavot and Bedouin and Arab peasants. Not until the 1920s, however—after the attack on Tel Chai; the bloody riots in Jerusalem in April 1920 and in Jaffa, Petach Tikva, Rechovot, and Hadera in May 1921; and the massacres in Safed and Hebron in 1929—

did the perception of the Arab as a virulent and cruel enemy become dominant. In these incidents enraged Arab mobs attacked Jewish settlers. The Jews "saw themselves as helpless 'victims' of the aggression of an ignorant majority incited by the clergy," Anita Shapira wrote.[17] The fact that the hardest-hit Jewish communities were those in Hebron and Safed, two cities in which Jews and Arabs had lived together for generations, was taken as proof of the Arabs' murderous and treacherous nature, and many in the Zionist camp called for separation between Jews and Arabs. During this period the Jewish press in Palestine frequently used the words "pogrom," "massacre," and "slaughter" to describe the Arab attacks, and this reinforced the image of the Arab as a new version of the Biblical Amalek, the prototypical anti-Semite. Notably, the consolidation of this view was also part of the process of delineating the identity of the Zionist Yishuv, since defining the foreign and different is part of identifying the self.

The rising national ferment among the Jews in the wake of the Balfour Declaration; the strengthening of the settlement enterprise throughout the country; the demographic growth of the Jewish Yishuv in Palestine during the waves of immigration of the 1930s and 1940s; and the intensification of Palestinian national consciousness, which reached its peak in the Arab Rebellion of 1936 to 1939—all these amplified the enmity between the Arab and Jewish populations and reinforced the negative image of the Arab in the eyes of the Jews. In the light of Arab atrocities—the murder of old people, women, and children—the Jews came to regard Arab combat culture as repulsive, and the abyss of suspicion and animosity between the two peoples deepened. From the 1940s onward, the view of Arab society was largely political, and there was less and less interest in Arab culture. The Arab was described, especially in the press, as a cruel and bloodthirsty enemy with a moral code hinging on vengeance and honor—as different from the moral codes of the Judeo-Christian "guilt" as east is from west. The most common image of the Arabs was that of an inflamed and rabid mob pouncing like a bird of prey on Jews.

Attitudes toward Arabs in Sabra Education

THE ARAB IN TEXTBOOKS

The contradictory images of the Arab detailed above may be found in textbooks and in the literature for children and adolescents with which the Sabra grew up. They shaped his dichotomous attitude toward Arab culture. The folkloristic-exotic description of Arab life, especially the life of the Bedouin (the weddings, the preparation of coffee, the meal in the tent, the Arab *fantasia* dance, and Arab horsemanship) was something that writers for children and adolescents were especially fond of, and their audience lapped it up.[18] In a few of the geography books for Hebrew schools that came out in the Yishuv period, the Arab was described very colorfully. He "loves life, his surroundings are loud and full of happiness, especially in the marketplaces."[19] There were also romantic stories about the Ha-Shomer guards, reminiscent of Karl May, the German author of Westerns, in which heroes adopted the combat practices of the natives. The Hebrew Ha-Shomer guard, in Arab dress, galloping on an Arab mare over the mountains of the Galilee, sitting cross-legged and erect in the Arab's tent and speaking his language, was for Yishuv youth parallel to the white American galloping on his wild horse over the prairies of Arizona and Texas, conversing with the Indians in their own language (another character along the same lines was Lawrence of Arabia, with whom Yishuv youth were also familiar).

Two stereotypical characters generally stood out in stories about Arabs for young people—the Bedouin shepherd and man of nature, and the fighting sheikh. The fighter is described in many stories as a figure of exotic glory, shrouded in mystery. He wears an Arab headdress and rides a noble Arab mare fitted with a colorful bridle and a saddle of twisted wool. A rifle is slung over his back, and an inlaid pistol or dagger is at his waist; rounds of bullets are crossed on his chest. His face is sunburned and creased, his mustache is twisted upward, and his obedient and faithful servant is at his side.

Resonances of this romantic outlook may be found—although not with great frequency—in children's compositions. A boy wrote in a composition on a field trip:

O Bedouin! How I love you, and how my soul longs to be like you! How dear you are to me! They are the symbol of nature, lovers of freedom and liberty! I look down on their small black tents that spread out on both sides. I envy you. If I could only be with you a single day, a single hour, a single moment. How happy I would be then.[20]

Alongside this romantic view was a patronizing and arrogant view of the Arab. Arabs were depicted in many textbooks and other books for children as ignorant members of a sluggish and backward feudal society. Moreover, they were frequently presented as ingrates for not properly appreciating the progress that Zionism had brought them. The message was: if the Arabs would learn from the Jews and reach their cultural level, tension would end.

The blend of humanism and paternalism that characterized the Hebrew school system's attitude toward the Arabs during the Yishuv period was a mixture of romanticism and realism, a desire to approach and an instinct to avoid. More than anything else, it betrayed ignorance about everything to do with the culture of the Arab inhabitants of Palestine. This is clearly reflected in Sabra compositions. For instance, a twelve-year-old girl, a member of Ha-Shomer Ha-Tza'ir, wrote:

> We see the Arab village there—black tents, black children, black clothes, black cows and goats—and I ask: Are they in mourning there, and what lament is this? No! There is no mourning there and it is no lament—this is the costume of good people who have not received an education. It is the song of the Oriental man—of a lower level, true, yes, but still the Arab is a son of nature and understands beautiful nature; he does not leave it for even a moment. . . . These savage customs . . . when I think of them a lot, I reach the conclusion: While there are customs that are not nice, among them there are also beautiful ones connected to nature, and if the Bedouin detaches his tent from the mountain rocks, only then will he be severed from his nice and not-nice customs. . . . The peak where Elijah built his altar stands blue in the distance, and I recall: Our forefathers, too, were like this. The Arabs are a nation that has become retarded in its culture. Cultured people think it is shameful to converse with a Bedouin man. Don't let your hearts rise. In many things the Arab nation is superior to European nations, and we who are close to the Bedouin must try to make peace with them rather than fight with them.[21]

At the end of the 1940s, as the conflict with the Arabs intensified and spread throughout the country and took on the character of a violent conflict between two peoples, sweeping negative characterizations of the Arabs began to dominate Zionist textbooks. The geography books of the 1920s and 1930s taught the Sabra that the Bedouin "seeks war, booty, and spoils and is a primitive artifact in the modern world."[22] History books of the same period taught that "the Arabs are robbers, vandals, primitive, easily incited. . . ."[23] Negative stereotypes became stronger in children's literature as well.

Arabs were generally portrayed disparagingly in textbook discussions of Jewish-Arab relations. Especially prominent is the depiction of them as traditional "Jew haters" (Amalekites). The words "pogrom," "slaughter," and "massacre" in descriptions of Arab attacks on Jewish settlements were meant to create a moral and historical continuum between the acts of anti-Semites in the Diaspora and the acts of the Arabs in Palestine. Also

common were descriptions of the Arabs as one of the natural obstacles
that the early settlers had to deal with. One of the pamphlets in the series
To Youth: The Israeli Library tells the story of the settlement of Rishon
Le-Tzion. The author does not mention the neighborly relations that many
of the moshava's first settlers had with the local Bedouin or the great contribution made by Arab workers to the development of the moshava.
Rather, when discussing "the hardships that young Rishon faced," he describes at length the "thieves and robbers who sought prey on the Jaffa-
Gaza road"[24] and the Zionist settlers' struggle against them.

The shock of the Holocaust reinforced the perception of the Arab as
a modern anti-Semite aspiring to destroy the Jewish people. The battle
against the Arabs thus became a battle against the anti-Semites. This notion was bolstered by the cooperation between the Palestinian Arab leader
Haj Amin al-Husseini and Hitler, and by the Arab leadership's adamant
demand that Britain block Jewish immigration to Palestine after the war,
despite the horrible catastrophe that had befallen the Jewish people. Both
during and after the war the Arabs were described in the press and in
textbooks as "agents of hatred" whose hostility was "racial" and whose
actions were contemptible, in the tradition of all enemies of the Jewish
people.

In geography, "homeland," and history textbooks published after
1948, the noble savage had completely disappeared. His place was taken
by an ignorant, wild, incensed mob, and notably by the cowardly Palestinian attacker who fled in panic and abandoned his property and home.
The ungratefulness of the Arab was also stressed—the Zionists had
brought him material advancement but he had responded with destruction and ruin.[25] A similar image was developed in Israeli cinema, then
in its infancy, and in literature for children and adolescents.

Textbook descriptions of Arabs were one-sided, shallow, and generalized and ignored many aspects of Arab culture, the Arab's human complexity, and his legitimate aspiration for nationhood. It is hard to say,
however, that the portrayal was entirely false or racist. The Bedouin and
the Arab peasant, and to a large extent the urban Arab as well, were in
fact generally backward in their economy and education, and their culture was not democratic.

REPRESSION OF THE ARAB PRESENCE

The contradictory images of the Arab just described certainly influenced
the Sabra's view of the Arab and his culture. But an examination of the

texts dealing with Arabs shows that the Sabra was influenced less by what was said of the Arab and his culture than by what was not said. The Arab was not described positively or negatively so much as he was shunted aside, sometimes virtually obliterated from consciousness. This phenomenon is so central to the Jewish outlook that even as enemies in war, Arabs get very little factual attention, and the attention they do get is the same sort given to natural impediments. Especially obvious is the "banishment" of the Arabs from descriptions of the landscape in textbooks. The few descriptions of Arab settlements generally present them as marking the site of an ancient Jewish settlement, or treat them like inanimate natural features, such as rocks and fields.

One reason for reducing and blurring the Arab presence on the cognitive map of the Sabra—indeed, of the entire Zionist population—was political. Discussion of a phenomenon grants it existential validity and increases people's awareness of it. Speaking little about the Arabs obscured their presence as an established fact and therefore a problem demanding a political solution. A second reason was ideological and cultural. The Zionist immigrants were so caught up in their own social world that they viewed reality through filters that emphasized their own presence and blurred that of others. A third reason was the Jewish immigrants' belief that the Arabs were no more than a marginal problem in the achievement of their dream; the Arabs were in the category of guests in the Jewish national home.

Journalist and novelist Arthur Koestler, who reported on the Zionist enterprise and had prescient insights, took note of this. He wrote sarcastically in his diary that the Zionists treated the Arabs as "a mere accident, like the presence of some forgotten pieces of furniture in a house which has been temporarily let to strangers."[26]

Bedouin culture received more in-depth treatment in the textbooks, but this too was to a certain extent in terms of stereotypes, emphasizing the Bedouin's exotic customs (in particular their hospitality), as well as, implicitly, their nativeness.

The interest in the Bedouin and the inattention to urban and village Arab culture—which in fact was dominant in that period, at least in Palestine west of the Jordan River—may have been prompted not only by the romantic charm of the Bedouin, but also by their nomadism. They were gypsies of a sort,[27] only temporarily tied to a specific location, with all the consequent political implications.

Arab culture in general and Palestinian culture in particular were also given little attention by Zionist pedagogues. The school system had no textbooks on the Islamic tradition and the differences between Arab sub-cultures. The curriculum also dismissed or else omitted the Arab national claim and the Arabs' strong and historical link to their land. The pan-Arab movement was not even mentioned. Neither was their history in Palestine given any real attention. The Arabs were generally described as one of the waves of foreign and transient occupiers that the Land of Is-rael had known (along with the Assyrians, Babylonians, Greeks, Romans, Byzantines, and Crusaders), or as nomadic desert tribes who had settled in Palestine, where they lived miserably: "Their homes are little boxes of clay and cow dung that are dotted here and there like molehills on a fur-rowed field."[28] The authors of history textbooks also kept to a minimum descriptions of those eras in which the greater part of the Jewish people were in the Diaspora and other nations ruled Palestine. Neither was the question of the expulsion of the Arabs from their villages and cities in the War of Independence put on the school agenda in the 1950s.

The educational system also devoted few resources to teaching Ara-bic, and the language was not part of the education of the native-born child of the Yishuv, nor was it part of the education system later, under the State of Israel. True, the question of the study of Arabic did concern the school system in its early stages,[29] and annotated Arabic readers for schoolchildren were issued in 1931. But the language in these readers was literary rather than spoken Arabic, and the large difference between the two meant that this study was of no help in enabling young Jews to communicate with the country's Arabic-speaking inhabitants.

There were years in which a more concerted effort was made to bring young Jews into contact with Arabic culture. At the beginning of the 1940s the school system of the labor movement devoted a not in-significant number of high school class hours to the study of Arabic (two to three hours a week out of a total of forty in the ninth and tenth grades). Even then, however, Arabic was considered of secondary importance to English—it was only an option, and students could take French or some other subject instead. Furthermore, it was available only in some schools and not in all grades.

In 1947 the leaders of the labor movement appointed a committee to formulate proposals for the study of Arabic "in our educational institu-tions." The committee did not deal simply with Arabic language in-struction; it also proposed "providing our children with knowledge of the Arab people and allowing them contact with the neighboring nation." Because of the War of Independence, however, the recommendations were forgotten.[30]

The youth movements were no different from the schools in their attitude toward Arab culture. In the 1930s, *Ba-Ma'aleh,* the organ of Ha-Noar Ha-Oved, made an attempt of sorts to acquaint its readers with Arab culture via a feature teaching basic words in Arabic, but this was the exception that proves the rule.

The Sabra was cut off from Arab culture not only spiritually and intellectually but also physically. The Arabs lived in separate neighborhoods and settlements and had but a modest school system, separate from the Jewish one, and this forestalled any daily contact between young people. The proposal made by Britain's Peel Commission to establish common schools for Jewish and Arab children was not at all acceptable to the Yishuv leadership. This resistance was not only because of the cultural gap and the mutual distrust that had grown over the years, but also because schools were considered tools for Zionist-national socialization, not just institutions of education. Nor were school and youth movement field trips and marches used to provide an acquaintance with the Arab world, even though most of them passed close by Arab settlements and so established at least eye contact with the Arabs in the region.

The Sabra was also isolated from Arab culture because of religious taboos. The definition of the Arab as a *goy,* or non-Jew, ruled out in advance any possibility of cultural integration. Even when Arabs were portrayed favorably in textbooks, in the press, and in literature, they were still foreigners—outside the pale of the Jewish-Israeli national definition. The possibilities of living together in a common community or a common home, of studying in a common school, and certainly of intermarried families were never even hinted at.

EDUCATION TO REDUCE HATRED

In a discussion of Sabra education about relations with the Arabs, one extremely important point should not be ignored: the absence of verbal and other expressions of hatred, malice, and vengefulness against the Arabs as a people and as individuals. One notable characteristic of Sabra education was that it imparted a creed of reserve and restraint. Even after harsh clashes with the Arabs, in which the Arabs were aggressors and many Jews were killed, the Sabra was not exposed, at least not formally, to expressions of loathing, racism, and incitement.

Contemporary Hebrew literature and poetry that directly or indirectly addressed the political murder of Jews by Arabs attest to the restraint of hatred as the norm. Antipathy, invective, and execration of the murderer are rare. Threats and calls for revenge are also not common. What one finds is largely a feeling of pain and loss, sadness and helplessness.

The ethos of self-restraint in the face of the Arab enemy's malevolence in part grew out of the moral codes of the modern world that had been imprinted on the founding fathers. However, it was also the product of a desire to emphasize and instill a sense of Jewish moral and cultural superiority in contrast with the "barbaric" and "hot-headed" Arab.[31] This self-restraint was a marker of an elitist culture that perceived itself as capable of rising above primitive instincts of revenge. The mythological concept of "purity of arms," which would become one of the most important symbols of Israeli military culture, was especially meant to symbolize the humanitarian "pureness of heart" of the Hebrew fighter. Significantly, the ethos of self-restraint and reserve does not mean Christian passivity or pacifism. These are at odds with the anti-Diaspora ethos of the new Jew, who was supposed to stand up to his enemies. What it meant was an aggressive but considered and controlled response to Arab assault.

The Sabra was taught to have pity (but a pity mixed with contempt) for the Arab fighter, but not to hate him. The Arab fighter was seen as primitive, ignorant, and unfortunate, misled by the false promises of his leaders. An interesting illustration of this is an exchange of letters between the children of Kibbutz Negba, who were evacuated from their home during the War of Independence, and the parents and teachers who remained to defend the kibbutz against the Egyptian army. Even when the kibbutz was in danger of destruction and its members in danger of losing their lives, there were no expressions of hatred or vengefulness in the letters of the adults. One of them described the Egyptian attack in a letter to "the dear children who have left their homes and who will quickly return":

> The cruel Egyptians are fighting against us. They are fighting against the trees, too, as if someone were not letting them plant trees in Egypt, and they come to uproot, cut down, and break apart the fig tree, the tall silver-leafed plane trees, the fruit trees, the loquat, and the almonds—what fools! . . . They threw bombs on the barn. How cruel they are! As if someone did not let them raise cows and milk them. Who didn't let them? The English gave them tanks; they would have done better sending them tractors so they could plow and raise clover and alfalfa and plant mangel-wurzel and raise cows. Instead the English sent them tanks. . . . Too bad. There are many good people in the world who suffer because of a small clique of bad-hearted, cruel people. Oh! If only everyone would join hands and finish off those cruel people, wars would end in this world.[32]

Arabism as a Palmach Status Symbol

The imitation of the Arab and the adoption of Oriental symbols as a kind of local fashion characterized the Sabras even before the Palmach generation—the young people born on the moshavot and the graduates of the first few classes of the gymnasiums.[33] But the Palmach, which was very much influenced by the combat culture of Ha-Shomer, was the Sabra organization that most prominently fostered these symbols in Sabra culture as part of Israeli identity.[34] The use of elements from Oriental culture in the Palmach was meant to build up the militia image of the new unit and to instill it with a native Land of Israel identity.

Especially notable was the phenomenon of the Palmach's Arab platoon (the Shachar unit), an elite organization around which legends were woven. Known as the Mistarabim, or "Arabizers," commanded by Yerucham Cohen, the unit members adopted status symbols similar to those of Ha-Shomer. In their group photograph they look amazingly like Ha-Shomer—in Arab dress, with weapons in hand. Their expertise in the Arab way of life and in Arabic idioms was the envy of their peers.

This flaunting of Orientalism in Sabra culture was evident in the adoption of Arab apparel (in particular the *kafiyyeh*, or Arab headdress, wrapped around the neck), in the folklore of the campfire, which included Bedouin customs such as sitting cross-legged in a circle, cooking bitter Arab coffee in a special pot over the fire, brewing boiling-hot tea spiced with mint or sage, and communal singing accompanied by an Arab drum, a shepherd's pipe, and rhythmic hand-clapping. It could also be found in the composition of songs in the Oriental style, and in the singing of Arab melodies with Oriental cadences. There were also Arab dances, Arab greetings and nicknames, Arabic exclamations that entered Sabra speech, and a general Arabization of the spoken language.

The most salient Oriental influence on Sabra culture was in language, and this could be found in jokes, curses, names, *chizbatim*, as well as in fiction writing. Some 10 percent of the words in the slang dictionary written by Sabras Netiva Ben-Yehuda and Dahn Ben-Amotz are Arabic borrowings, mostly via the Sabra generation. Some of these words kept their Arabic pronunciation and meaning, some retained their pronunciation but their meanings changed, and some were either deliberately or inadvertently mutilated and became new words. Words such as *ahsan* (okay), *inshalla* (God willing), *abadai* (strong man), *dahilak* (on your life), *jam'a* (gang), *mabsut* (happy), and *ma'alesh* (no matter) were not only widely used but became part of the Sabra vocabulary.[35] Arabic words were especially common when it came to cursing. About 30 percent of the Arabic words adopted into Sabra slang were curses.

Sabras may have borrowed words from Arabic first and foremost because there was an immediate need for terms and Arabic was available. Hebrew lacked any number of necessary everyday words, and Arabic was a good source for the missing ones, not only because of its phonetic affinity to Hebrew but also because it contained many expressions pertaining to the Palestinian context. For instance, Arabic provided words for elements of the local climate (hence *hamsin*, the hot south wind of the spring); for features of the landscape (*hirba*, ruin); for local vegetation (*hubeza*, a native legume with an edible seed); and for popular games (*julim*, marbles; *tiara*, kite).

But adopting Arabic words was more than a matter of practical communication; there was also a desire to develop communal status symbols. The Arabisms were most of all symbols of nativism, like the elements of Arab style adopted by Ha-Shomer. They were meant to mark the Sabra's expertise in the codes of the land—its flora, fauna, and topography, and also its language, character, and mood. The Arabisms also reflected and marked the Sabra's culture of togetherness and *dugri*-ness. Family relationships, friendship, and hospitality were expressed in Arabic words, such as *ahui* (my brother, but used by the Sabra as a term of address for a close friend); *sahbi* (my friend); *keif halak* (how are you?); *saha* (health, as in "wear it in good health" or "gesundheit"); *tefadal* (please); *sahtein* (the dual form of *saha*, used in particular as a term of dismissal—"if that's what he wants, so be it"); *ya habibi* and *habub* (my friend—a term of address). These all expressed direct connections and Sabra friendship. The Arabic word that expresses Sabra culture more than any other is the greeting *ahlan*, which means not only hello, but also welcome and please. This word became a kind of Sabra code for closeness, a slogan of friendship, and in time became the accepted informal greeting throughout Israel.

The use of Oriental symbols, especially in the area of language, was also meant to create a common codex of Sabra experiences, customs, and mentalities and so enhance Sabra uniqueness (and thus, indirectly, its superiority). This finds expression in words that denote Sabra life, food, and games, such as *falha* (field crops); *nagla* (load or trip, as in "it took three trips to get the wheat into the silo"); *sabres* (the sabra fruit); *fistuk* (pistachios); *mishmish* (apricot; this is the Arabic pronunciation, which has become so prevalent that few Israelis today probably know that the original Hebrew pronunciation was *mishmesh*); *felafel* (a sandwich made with pita bread filled with salad and balls of fried chickpea paste); *tehina* (sesame seed paste); *humus* (also a paste made of ground chickpeas); *kafiyyeh* (the Arab headdress); *finjan* (the pot used to make Arab coffee). There were also adapted terms describing different types of people: *jada* (strong man), *abu ali* (a violent person), *mukhtar* (leader), *fisfus* (the act of missing something), *razaleh* (a beautiful woman). And there were words of evaluation, such as *achbar* and *al ha-kefak* (great!), *bugeras* (headache, in both the literal and figurative senses), *zift* (horrible), *batich* (nothing, worthless), *salamto* and *salamtak* (good guy, worthy of credit).

However, one should not err in taking these words as evidence that the Sabra had developed a close relationship with Oriental culture. On the contrary, they are evidence of the distance between the two. The improper use of words such as *finjan*—which in Arabic means the cup coffee was drunk from, not, as the Palmachniks used it, the pot in which coffee was made—demonstrates the trivial way in which they drew on Oriental symbols. There was also a clear sense of humor and ridicule in the use of Arabisms, and this testifies to the cultural distance from and even contempt for the Arab and especially the Arab mentality.

A word can take on a humorous tinge if the character who generally uses it is considered funny or grotesque. This was the way Sabras used Arabic words. Since there was a consensus about the caricatured image of the Arab (a consensus that gained much strength in the wake of the war), the use of his language was a joke on him. The Sabra who used Arabic words was, as it were, dressing up as an Arab. The cultural snob dresses up, in a kind of deliberate reversal, as the primitive, but this is a self-conscious primitiveness. When the Arab says *razaleh*, which literally means "doe," he means a young girl, and when he says, "*Be-hayat Rabak,*" he means simply "Upon God's life!" The Sabra uses the same words when he is being lighthearted or facetious.

The facetious use of Arabic words was meant to create an internal vocabulary linking the speakers of the language. A good example of this is the Sabra use of the word *abu,* which literally means "father of," and in Arabic is a title of respect. The Palmachnik used it with a bit of jest. So, for example, the prototypical oaf in Sabra *chizbatim* is called Abu Lish. The same principle is at work in the *janantini* ("you fooled me"), the Oriental coffee songs that were so popular in the Palmach. Their Arab origins gave them a hint of jocularity, making them into "in" jokes.[36]

This, by the way, is the reason that Palmach slang also included many

Yiddish words. According to the anti-Diaspora ethos, the Sabra should, on the face of it, have refrained from borrowing words from Yiddish. But the repugnance for Yiddish, which symbolized Diaspora culture, made Yiddish words into inside jokes: *nudnik* (nag); *bluffer* (bluffer); *broch* (complication, tangle); *zeks* (secret), *hap-lap* (something done in a hurry); *yotzmach* (a nothing, a worthless person); *yahneh* (a person who looks worse off than he really is, who dresses or holds himself badly).

The military struggle with the Arabs shattered what remained of the Sabras' naive romanticism regarding the Arabs. In fact, the romantic image had already worn away during their childhood. Many Sabras, especially those who had grown up on kibbutzim and moshavim, were the neighbors of Arab peasants and Bedouin. Some had been in fights with Arab youths or had witnessed thefts and other hostile acts by Arabs against their Jewish neighbors. Some of the senior and veteran Palmach commanders (those called "Yitzchak Sadeh's boys") had even participated, as members of the Field Companies and Special Companies that had preceded the Palmach, in military operations against Arab villages as part of the Stockade and Tower campaign and the Yishuv's battle against the Arab Rebellion. These experiences turned the Arab into an anathema in Sabra consciousness, or alternatively, into a primitive and grotesque enemy whose stupidity made him lose again and again in his fight against the Jews.

Combat Culture and the Attitude toward the Enemy

In recent years there has been a heated academic debate over the moral behavior of the Zionist combatants of 1948—especially the Palmach's fighters—in battle and after battle. Testimonies presented by scholars have indicated a complex reality, one certainly less heroic and moral than that described in the "establishment" historical literature of the State of Israel's first decades. Nevertheless, even today, after new evidence has been gathered and the ground has been prepared for research that is less ideologically driven, the picture is still blurred and multifaceted.

Since this subject is complex and charged, it justifies a separate study, especially after the opening of the relevant files in the IDF and Haganah archives. I can only present briefly and thus somewhat superficially the attitude of the Sabra fighter toward his Arab enemy during and after combat. The following is how it seems to me after reading the published scholarly work and after studying the fighters' diaries and letters, as well as army publications, documents produced by Palmach headquarters, orders of the day issued in "battle sheets," the instructions by senior and junior commanders distributed to the soldiers, and the files of the Palmach's military prosecutor. Talks with a number of veterans also helped me complete the picture.

In orders of the day, battle sheets, and company newsletters no material was found on "polishing one's swords," nor was there evidence of fiery tirades against the Arab population or Arab fighters,[37] or of incitement to slaughter and take revenge on those who surrender. The writers make frequent use of general concepts, free of normative and ethnic connotations, such as "enemy" and "invader." Here is an example from a leaflet distributed to the soldiers of the Negev Brigade on the eve of the Chorev operation:

> Soldiers! We will fight heroically and wrathfully against the enemy, but let us not stain our war with inhuman behavior toward civilians and surrendering soldiers. The brigade commander wishes all of you, privates and commanders, a peaceful Sabbath! We have no peace today, but rather war; we are fighting for peace. There is no peace without freedom, and there is no freedom without vanquishing the enemy.[38]

The instructions, directives, and orders of the day given to soldiers before battle and the battle sheets and leaflets distributed to the general population during the campaign and after the conquest of Arab settlements testify to a very high moral sensitivity on the part of the commanders, the great majority of whom were Sabras in their social background. The soldiers, most of whom were new immigrants who had been educated in a different code of warfare, were strictly forbidden, on penalty of court-martial and severe punishment, to confiscate property of any type. They were instructed before combat to treat prisoners with honor and to avoid desecrating holy sites, which they were neither to loiter in nor use as cover in battle. They were warned against looting, abuse, robbery, and rape. The moral sensitivity of the command level, which set the norm for the soldiers, was evident not only in these prohibitions themselves, but also in the large amount of space devoted to these warnings, even in texts meant to fire up the soldiers before battle or to commend them for their success after victory. Especially interesting and indicative is the restrained tone of the leaflets distributed after conquests, after many soldiers had fallen. Here, for example, is a leaflet from the

military governor of Safed, distributed after the city was taken by the
Yiftach Brigade:

> The first stage in our lives commands us to control our tempers, to find a so-
> lution to impose order and discipline in keeping with our military and civil-
> ian needs. . . . As for our Arab neighbors, Jewish Safed was reminded by the
> previous disturbances and those of today what our Arab neighbors have done
> to us. I believe that the blow with which Arab Safed was taken by our sol-
> diers will open the Arabs' blinded eyes and they will understand that the way
> they have treated their Jewish neighbors is unacceptable. They must accus-
> tom themselves, if they wish, to new conditions and to a new order, and they
> must tear the urge to conquer from their hearts.[39]

The assertive language with which the warnings were written also
testifies to this attitude of restraint. "Conquer yourself"; "do not be
tempted"; "preserve your honor"; "do not disgrace yourself"; "no Jew
will raise his hand"; "our lives will be pure"; "preserve the army's honor";
"no man should dare touch their property"; "do not break the bounds
and bring theft into our camp"; "the sword of our soldiers will not touch
a man who requests our protection"; "may our camp be pure"; "they
should be treated with respect"; "our war is just and pure and no man
should sully it with forbidden deeds"; "may we never harm the deep religious sentiments of the Arab people"—such expressions, which appear
in the documents of the IDF brigades that took part in the war,[40] testify
to the importance given to moral purity and the commanders' sincerity
and commitment to the moral norm.

Though the orders and instructions did in fact warn against these acts,
they did not succeed in entirely preventing violations. The prohibition
against looting, for example, was violated on a large scale. "At first,"
historian Alon Kadish has written, "the looting was a search for sou-
venirs—'I want to take something to remember the victory: a ring, a
kafiyyeh, a dagger.' The commanders did not attribute any importance
to the phenomenon and at least some of them did not see anything wrong
with it. The same was true of taking food for immediate needs, including a chicken or sheep."[41] This breach in the dike gradually grew into
informal permission to seize property for the basic needs of the army of
occupation and items such as radios and sewing machines for the combat units and the mobilized *hachsharot.* Some of the money that was
taken was set aside for a fund for the support of the families of the fallen
and for their memorialization, and this served to "launder" the looting.
The sanction for taking spoils for the unit prepared the ground for taking spoils for private purposes. The extent of this phenomenon is not

clear—at least among the Sabras. The problem of private spoils worsened with the conquest of the cities of Lod, Ramle, and Be'ersheva, where well-off Arab families lived.

The looters were censured, though, both by the political leadership and by the high army command, which was Sabra in its background. The military periodicals (not only those of the Palmach) also contained condemnations of looting.

But to a large extent the attitude toward the looters was forgiving. There were several reasons for this: (1) heavy equipment or large sums were generally not taken; (2) many of the looters were new immigrants, Holocaust survivors, who were pitied by the commanders; (3) it was difficult to punish a man who had fought and risked his life just a few days before;[42] (4) there was great anger against the Arabs for starting the war, and looting was perceived, if not formally, as a kind of punishment; (5) it was clear to everyone that since the owners had fled the country, this property would never be returned to them; (6) there was a tradition of lenience toward *sechivot*—those playful thefts described previously;[43] and (7) there was a tendency to prevent these deeds from being publicized, so as not to damage the image of the Israeli soldier and arouse a sharp international reaction. In fact, only a few soldiers were tried and punished.

Another moral issue was the demolition of houses and the expulsion of the Arab inhabitants.[44] It seems that the Sabra soldier did not seethe with boundless hatred or seek revenge. But he was indeed insensitive to the fate of the masses of deportees and somewhat heartless when it came to their suffering. This callousness is especially ironic and tragic, given that these Sabra soldiers were the heirs to a nation that had suffered deportation, for whom exile was wound up in the national identity. Sabra commanders and soldiers generally saw no evil in expelling Arabs and blowing up their homes, and at the senior officer level there were those who urged the Yishuv leadership to exploit the military success by enlarging the country's borders and ridding it of Palestinians. There were several reasons for this view.

Expulsion of Arabs and demolition of their homes had military purposes. They kept the abandoned houses from serving as bases for hostile activity. They were also meant to punish and deter terrorists and other collaborators with the Arab armies, to prevent the return of Arabs to strategic locations, and to prevent the development of a fifth column in the occupied areas.[45]

Another reason is that the State of Israel's first, provisional government had no clear policy on the fate of the Arabs in the occupied territories. The dramatic developments on the battlefield and in the international theater and the supreme effort expended to hold off the invading armies pushed aside many other matters, including this one.[46] Furthermore, the extent of the Arab flight and the ease with which they could be forced to leave surprised the leadership. They vacillated between the desire to enlarge the small country's borders and get rid of a large part of its Arab population on the one hand, and the serious moral implications of the expulsion on the other. By the time a decision had been made, it was too late. In the absence of a clear policy, the point was decided by the soldiers and commanders in the field. The army considered the flight and expulsion of the Arabs as part of the battle—a simple expression of the surrender of the enemy. The Israeli commanders also viewed the demolition of homes from a military, not a psychosociological or political, point of view. To the commanders the Arab settlements were armed camps from which the enemy had fought, and blowing up the homes was perceived as part of the destruction of the enemy infrastructure and a completion of the act of conquest.

The demolition of homes and the expulsion of the Arabs were also perceived by the Sabra soldiers as a fitting punishment for the "gangs" and "rioters" (as they called them) who had for years sniped at Jewish convoys and murdered Jewish civilians with great cruelty. And the soldiers took the Arabs to be responsible for the death of many of their comrades-in-arms.

Other reasons are due to the education of the Sabras. Because of the Sabras' lack of connection to Arab culture, the Arab turned from a subject into an object, which reduced the soldiers' sensitivity to the injustice being inflicted on the individual Arab and his family. The Arab's human image was also blurred by the great focus placed on the Jewish collective identity and on the Arab as the evil Amalek. Many Sabras did not concern themselves with the question of who the Arab was and what had happened to him because, in keeping with their education, they viewed him as a metaphysical, abstract evil, an invariable datum in the Jewish reality.

One of the important mirrors for this objectification of the enemy was the literature published by veterans of the Palmach soon after the end of the war. These stories, based on battlefield experiences, are notable for the extent to which they ignore the Arabs and suppress their problems as individuals and as a nation. In the few works in which Arabs appear, their faces as characters are almost always hazy.

While most of the young writers evince pity for the defeated and humiliated Arab, they make no attempt to understand his soul and his suffering in any profound way. They tend to describe the Arab characters without complexity or personality, in contrast with the Jewish characters, who have clear identities and desires. They are "the enemy" beyond the mountains of darkness; the murdering, burning hand; the booming cannon; the voice of incitement; or the ignorant, submissive, groveling prisoner. They are also the amorphous, defeated mob; the panicked peasants abandoning their villages, their houses of clay, their filthy yards. They, their women, their old people, and their children disappear beyond the border into nowhere. The exception is S. Yizhar, who in his 1949 stories *Hirbat Hiz'a* and *The Prisoner* portrayed the imperiousness of the Jewish soldiers and the contempt with which many of them treated the conquered people.

The clay houses in the Arab villages, the odor and the filth, the ants, the fleas, and the lice that swarmed in the houses and yards—all these cheapened the Arab's loss of home and village in the eyes of the Jewish soldiers. "This tattered humanity . . . the poverty and imbecility of miserable villages. Suddenly their hem is lifted—their homes, yards, their outsides and insides. Suddenly their garment is lifted up to their faces, the shame of their nakedness is exposed, and here they are destitute, parched, and stinking"—thus S. Yizhar describes the Sabra soldiers' impressions in the conquered village in *The Prisoner,* a book that because of its sincerity has become controversial in Israel. The conquerors felt they were obliterating a miserable, impermanent settlement and that the deportees, like gypsies, could quickly build themselves something new elsewhere. The hasty flight of quite a few Arabs, who did not defend their homes to the death and stay on their land to the bitter end as the Zionist ethos demanded, reinforced the (mistaken) impression that the Arab had only a tenuous connection to his home and fields.

The Arab peasant's perceived primitive way of life (eating with his hands, living alongside his livestock, the use of ancient methods of agriculture, the high birthrate, the harsh rule of the men over their women and children, and the autocracy of the *mukhtar* over the clan and the landowner over the tribe); his fatalistic worldview; his strange appearance to Western eyes (headdress, wide pants, and robe); his practice (detestable to the Jews) of pleading and groveling before the conqueror—all these lessened his human image and the ability of the Sabra soldier to identify with him and develop empathy and compassion for him as one of his own kind.

Presumably, the Sabra soldiers' attitude toward the Arab refugees was also affected, even if indirectly, by the anti-Diaspora ethos in which the Sabras were educated. The tendency to look down on the "bowed heads" and "bent backs" of Holocaust refugees to a certain extent dulled the sensitivity to the suffering of the Palestinian refugee, who was forced to wander the roads and beg for the compassion of his Arab brothers. The teaching that the Jews were the country's legal owners and the Arabs were "resident aliens" also limited the conquering Sabra's sensitivity to the horrible suffering and sometimes injustice inflicted on the deportees.

And what of deeds by Israeli soldiers that are considered war crimes by enlightened countries—the murder of prisoners and unarmed civilians, rapes, beatings, mass slaughter, and putting prisoners before firing squads? Most of the documentary material in the IDF and Haganah archives regarding such cases in 1948 has not yet been made available to scholars. Studies based on documents from Palmach headquarters and the United Nations indicate that there were indeed such cases, even if they were not common, and that they were concealed from the public for political and other reasons. But these studies do not clearly show the extent of the phenomenon; nor do they lead to the conclusion that war crimes were an accepted norm, certainly not among the Sabras, who were the commanders and counselors. Again, it is important to remember the severity with which the soldiers were warned in operational orders and battle sheets against harming the Arab population. So, for example, a Yiftach Brigade order of the day reads, in huge letters: "In every case of robbery and murder the violator will be punished with the full force of military law . . . may our weapons remain pure and brave in battle!"[47] This tone testifies to a rigid code of self-restraint and to the commanders' alertness to the possibility that such restraints might be loosened. It is difficult to believe that there was a huge gap between the norm and the reality—although the high frequency of such orders also indicates that deviance existed to some extent.

Moreover, the letters of fallen soldiers—which were not published and therefore did not undergo a process of editing and censorship—contain no echo of war crimes. Since these were educated and sensitive young people who lived in a society in which there was a fairly large measure of freedom of expression (at least in the area of morals), it seems reasonable to assume that war crimes were not a common phenomenon that underwent collective censorship. In the letters of members of the Yishuv who enlisted in the British army there are, in fact, pointed comments on the behavior of their comrades who engaged in looting and rape against occupied populations and Nazi prisoners, but again these acts, which are not set out in detail in the letters, do not indicate that this was a mass phenomenon. The fact that these actions were criticized shows that they broke a moral code and were not routine and accepted.

There were those who viewed the deportations, demolitions, and other Palmach acts of cruelty as proof that the mythological image of the sensitive and moral Sabra was untruthful and hypocritical. True, the Sabra soldier was not saintly and his weapons were certainly not always pure. But in my evaluation, in comparison with soldiers of other armies, the Sabra was a "restrained fighter"; the picture (with its missing pieces) of his behavior in battle is consistent with the human failings and the positive qualities that characterize him in other areas.

In a discussion of the combat culture of the Sabra it is also worth noting the moderate way in which the victory over the Arabs was celebrated. The Sabra soldiers—and, in fact, the entire IDF—were not intoxicated with victory. They did not celebrate with drumbeats and bugle calls in front of an exulting and cheering crowd in city streets and squares. The combat units conducted local victory ceremonies at the sites that were conquered and in army bases, but these were largely modest (sometimes on a family level), and they lacked military elements like goose-stepping and gun salutes.[48] The IDF gave out only a few decorations to battle heroes, and officers' uniforms were not covered with war badges or medals. None of the fallen commanders was commemorated with a special memorial statue, and the modest monuments to the fallen listed the names of the dead soldiers one beside the other, without regard to rank. In fact, the rank was generally not even noted. The exultation of victory is also muted in Hebrew prose and poetry about the War of Independence. The writers generally address the unfortunate results of the war—death and loss—and not the joy of the sterling victory over the enemy.[49]

CHAPTER 6

Monks in Khaki

One of the things that stands out in old photographs of kibbutz teenagers, members of the pioneer youth movements, and Palmach soldiers is their simple and uniform dress. They all wore dark work pants or faded khaki shorts with plain, heavy dark or gray shirts hanging carelessly over the pants; as often as not, the boys would be bare-chested or in a loose undershirt. On their heads they wore stocking caps, Australian hats, or cloth "dunce caps" made of rough cloth and of a simple design (the pioneers had worn Diaspora-style caps with brims), their hair flowing out from underneath. Their feet were bare or in heavy work shoes, army boots, or sandals. All these visual details clearly marked the Sabra. Especially notable is how uniformly and simply the girls dressed. Their hair was done up in a ponytail or in braids, and they wore wide khaki shorts held to their thighs with elastic bands, white and black Russian shirts (with or without embroidery), and Eastern European jumpers, their necks and wrists unadorned and their faces free of makeup.

This is how these young people looked not only on military duty, at work, and on hikes, where simple and functional clothing was required, but also at celebrations and in places in which it is customary (at least in the Western world) to dress carefully and even to dress up—at lectures given by leaders and counselors, in school, and at formal occasions such as gatherings and memorial ceremonies.

The uniform look of the Sabras in the different youth organizations, the proletarian dress even on formal occasions, the emphasis and even flaunting of simplicity all indicate that this way of dressing was part of a cultural style and served as a group status symbol. Like other characteristics of the Sabra, the style was the outward manifestation of a value system—an ascetic code.

Austerity in Pioneer and Sabra Culture

The Yishuv ethic of making do with little had its source in objective economic scarcity.[1] The immigrants of the Second and Third Aliyot came to Palestine without property. They wandered with a few belongings from one place to another in search of work that even when they found it, barely supported them. Alternatively, they engaged in hard manual labor at new settlements established almost without capital in places with few natural resources—in arid areas or malarial swamps. The climate was harsh, and harassment and theft by Arabs were chronic problems, making life even harder.[2] The pioneer in an outlying settlement generally had to make do with a few items of clothing from the communal store, battered work shoes, a wooden platform in flimsy barracks for a bed, a common open-air shower without hot water, and plain, sparse food. Nor did the inhabitants of the cities in this period have an easy life. Many of them lived in highly crowded conditions with deficient sanitation, earning barely enough to pay the rent.

In the 1930s and 1940s the economic situation in Palestine improved slightly; the immigrants of the Fourth and Fifth Aliyot brought private capital with them and created a petit-bourgeois class. This was especially the case in the three large cities, where a culture of leisure and fashion (coffee houses, dance clubs, hairdressers) developed. The kibbutzim and moshavim also stabilized economically over time. Nevertheless, the Sabras who grew up on the moshavim and kibbutzim, as well as the bourgeois urban youth, hardly had a life of plenty. They did not starve, but they lived modestly with few luxuries. They grew up in an atmosphere of economy both because of the living conditions in a frontier society and because modest living became an ideal in and of itself.

Asceticism was not only an economic necessity but also a value choice, or at least a normative interpretation of reality. Values, symbols, and folklore were dressed, after the fact, in a prosaic reality of scarcity and modest living, as were many other ethoses, myths, symbols, and communal styles. The values of asceticism had their source, first and foremost, in socialist theory. Ascetic practices, especially among members of the working settlements, expressed scorn for property and for capitalist fetishism.

Private property, especially luxuries, even if rightfully purchased, symbolized in Marxist doctrine the old exploitative civilization that had made its money at the expense of the deprived.

Austerity communicated both the individual's willingness to subordinate his personal needs and desires to the success of the common enterprise and the unceasing effort demanded of the individual for the achievement of the common Zionist goal. The pioneer who gloried in austerity and abjured luxury stated through his monasticism the superior moral position of society over the individual. The daily frugalities for the sake of the achievement of the Zionist program became ritual acts.

The practice of collective frugality also stood for the primal state, the "nothingness" from which, in the future, the great "something" would grow. Austerity meant voluntarily facing a test, and it was thus an act of heroism. It also expressed altruism. It showed the willingness of the pioneer to do without for his fellows and thus demonstrated his solidarity with his community.

Asceticism also marks greatness of spirit through the juxtaposition of external dearth and internal richness. The pioneer living in leaky barracks, wearing a rough and patched undershirt or frock, and pursuing manual labor was like the Franciscan monk in his simple robe occupied with his holy work. Material poverty seemed to magnify spiritual wealth.

Here is the place to note that in this aspect of Sabra culture, as in others surveyed in this book, there was a gap, even a tension, between ethos and actual behavior. However, even if in practice people found it difficult to be orthodox ascetics, the force of the ethos held back public displays of consumerism and ostentation and affected dress, housing, eating habits, and leisure practices.

Asceticism as a Style:
Dress, Language, and Customs

"A BLUE SHIRT
IS GREATER THAN ANY JEWEL"

The ascetic value in pioneer culture was evident largely in dress, and in outward appearance in general. The pioneer's dress had a Tolstoyan quality to it. Poor and worn-out, sometimes demonstratively so, clothing implicitly denoted the removal of social masks, the purity of one's values, and spirituality.

The Sabra's drab and uniform appearance indicated not only prole-tarianism but also the seriousness that characterizes a society of naive and mobilized believers, in which the individual's will is given over to public endeavors. Simple dress was thus a symbol of status and of class, and the pioneers adhered to it to the point of reverse fashionability, even when there was no practical need for it.[3]

As a disseminator of ascetic symbols, the Sabra was a loyal follower of the pioneer tradition, and this despite the fact that in his era, with the broadening of the consumer culture in the large cities, there were more temptations to violate this code. Simple khaki dress became a trademark of the Scouts and the Gadna not just because of military and British influence, while the socialist youth movements (Ha-Shomer Ha-Tza'ir, Ha-Noar Ha-Oved, and Ha-Machanot Ha-Olim) sported faded blue shirts—workers' shirts, "greater than any jewel," in the words of the Ha-Noar Ha-Oved anthem. These were a symbol of the proletariat.[4]

Khaki and blue shirts were contrasted with the flowered and colored shirts tailored in accordance with Western fashion. A flower-print shirt was a symbol of ostentation, while the khaki and blue shirts (worn de rigueur outside the pants) were made of rough cloth of a uniform and austere shade and expressed simplicity, modesty, and idealism.

However, the Sabras, like the pioneers, made the anti-ostentation of simple dress into an ostentation in its own right, with definite and strict rules of fashion, a kind of "modest flashiness" or "ostentation of sloppiness"[5]—an anti-style that turned into a style.

Austerity and uniformity of color characterized not only the dress of the period, but also the homes, the memorials to fallen soldiers, and the national flag—exceptional among the majority of national flags for its cool colors.[6] Uniformity of color also symbolized the unity of the labor movement. The khaki of the pioneers, the youth movement, and the Pal-mach was a kind of national uniform marking the common identity and faith of those who wore it, making it hard to distinguish among them—as in a Hasidic community.

BARE FEET, SANDALS, AND *BLORIT*

The encounter between the ascetic ethos and the anti-Diaspora ethos pro-duced three Sabra status symbols of appearance: bare feet, simple leather sandals, and tousled forelocks—the *blorit* of Sabra song and legend. These quickly became part of the stereotypical and mythological image of the Sabra in literature, poetry, painting, caricatures, posters, and film.[7]

And as with other Sabra traits, there was mutual influence between myth and reality—the mythological image and the internal system of values nourished each other and created, in the end, a characteristic Sabra style.

Bare Feet Walking barefoot and, for men, bare-chested was common, especially in the kibbutzim and moshavim. It began in the pioneer cultures, particularly among the members of Ha-Shomer. The heroes populating the stories of the writers of the First and Second Aliyot are described as being barefoot like the Bedouin. Ya'akov Rabinowitz described Ha-Shomer member Berele Schweiger, who was for him the incarnation of the new Jew: "Barefoot Jew! And like a savage soul." Removal of clothes was for him and his generation a symbol of abandoning the traditional orthodox Jewish dress for a healthy culture.

Bare feet also meant unmediated contact with the land (thus the significance of dancing the hora barefoot). Israeli barefootedness, absorbing the spirit of the Land of Israel through the soles of the feet, appears also in the 1948 stories whose heroes are urban Sabras who walk barefoot through the sands of "Little Tel Aviv."

Sandals The practice of wearing sandals began among the pioneer generation during the Second Aliya, but these were shepherds' sandals handmade by individual pioneers for their own use. Among the Sabra generation, wearing sandals began in the youth movements and gradually became an institutionalized collective practice. The simple "Biblical sandals"—two parallel brown leather straps on a thin leather sole, generally worn without socks—were created fortuitously when two members of the Ha-Machanot Ha-Olim movement at Kibbutz Beit Ha-Shita set up a low table and with some primitive tools began to repair shoes and produce new sandals. The sandals made a huge impression on the movement and quickly became a hit and the fashion for the entire country.[8]

These sandals carried Biblical symbolism, as the name given to them in the 1950s implies. They were recognized as giving the Sabra the appearance of a Biblical shepherd or Maccabean soldier, as depicted in European art.

The Blorit Tousled hair was one of the most prominent trademarks of the Sabra, yet its beginnings, like those of sandals and barefootedness, lie in pioneer culture. In Jewish National Fund leaflets and pictures from the 1920s and 1930s, the pioneer is depicted with a mane of hair catching the wind and long forelocks flowing out from under his Russian beret. The *blorit* was a declaration of independence and also an imitation of the simple non-Jew, the farmer and Cossack, in Eastern Europe. As Rivka Ma'oz, a folklorist and literary scholar, has noted, the tousled hair was a kind of "rebellion against the religious stricture of covering the head and against the explicit prohibition that viewed the forelocks as a mark of the non-Jew, an Emorite practice, as is written: 'These are the ways of the Emorite, he who cuts his hair like the non-Jews and who makes forelocks' (Tosefeta Shabbat 6:1)." As Ma'oz explains, "In letting his forelocks' go wild," there was also "a kind of anarchistic uprising against the establishment and a rejection and negation of refined Western culture."[9] The link between long forelocks and the pioneers was set in Israeli consciousness to no small degree because of the famous wild forelocks of labor movement leader Berl Katznelson, who was much admired by young people. Ben-Gurion's unkempt hair also contributed to this association.

The imagery of the wild *blorit* also drew upon Russian revolutionary fashion, and intentionally or unintentionally, it also seems to have had Biblical significance, expressing identification with Hebrew heroes such as Samson and David. Like bare feet and chests, tangled forelocks expressed the youthful, gypsy-like vitality and liberty of the new Jew, who was open to the world and to naked and sensuous nature.

For the Sabra, the uncombed *blorit* became a visual and mythological status symbol. It appeared in drawings, caricatures, poetry, war literature, and especially in memorial literature. Wavy forelocks granted the stereotypical image of the Sabra youthful energy and innocence— and so magnified the pain and loss of the fallen soldier and emphasized his Sabra character. This is the reason why the tousled *blorit* is part of the description of the fallen soldier in three much-loved laments that have become Israeli classics and standard elements of memorial ceremonies.

Hagshama Youth versus Salon Youth

The ethos of asceticism and the idealization of farm life encouraged a disparaging attitude toward the cities. The people of the kibbutzim and moshavim considered urban leisure practices (cinema, clubs, coffee houses)—in fact city life in general—not only contemptible bourgeois activities but also expressions of vapid addiction to the capitalist vanity fair and sacrifices to the bourgeois Moloch. "City life is not so pure, . . . so full of value for the individual, for the Jewish people, and for the country, as our life is!" a kibbutz native wrote in his diary. "We do not need to ask ourselves: why do we live just this way? We have a purpose, a role, an aspiration, and motivation, which will not give way before any force in the world."[10]

Those most angry with the urban populace were kibbutz- and moshav-bred young people who volunteered to be youth movement counselors in the city. For them, the accelerated process of urbanization and the expansion of the bourgeoisie in the 1930s and 1940s created a very harsh dissonance between ideals and reality. They realized that the leaders of the labor parties lived lives that were bourgeois in every way, in contradiction to the official stance of the labor movement, and occupied themselves with political intrigue and advancing their personal interests.

The anti-city sentiment permeated Sabra consciousness so deeply that it was not only the kibbutznikim who found the city and everything connected with it repugnant: the members of the socialist youth movements did too. The young people from the Herzliya Gymnasium who founded the Ha-Machanot Ha-Olim movement explicitly distanced themselves from the streets of the city and declared the leisure culture that had begun to flourish in Tel Aviv and Haifa in the 1940s "idol worship." "And when the way becomes clear it leads to a profound inner rejection of urban life," wrote one of the movement's members, in a statement typical of the period.[11] The newsletters of the pioneer youth movements and of the chapter houses dismissed urban culture not only by condemning it but also by devoting little space to consumerism, leisure, fashion, and style.

Spending time in a coffee house and, even more so, in the cinema was for the youth movements—especially at the beginning of the 1950s—a sign of going bad and of abandoning one's values.[12] It was associated with egocentric hedonism (the opposite of self-sacrifice and *hagshama*), anti-asceticism, courtship culture, capitalist economy, and submitting to foreign culture (which contradicted the ethos of supporting local production).

The Palmachniks, including those who came from the cities but were educated in the socialist youth movements or were assimilated into kibbutz life through the *hachsharot*, also considered the city, its symbols, and its patterns of leisure to be far removed from the national values. During the war other reasons, in addition to socialist and Zionist ones, arose in support of this view. The nation needed to mobilize all hands. Thus there was anger toward the city youth who did not join or contribute to the war effort. Moreover, in most wars the city is the calm rear, far from the tumultuous front. The soldier who comes to the city on leave sees civilians caught up in their daily routines and their private preoccupations. They seem to be living on another planet, and this arouses a sense of alienation in the soldier. Such feelings are reflected in Palmach and battalion pamphlets, and also in the generation's postwar literature.

The value distinction between urban and rural lifestyles was prominent in the literature and theater of the late 1940s and 1950s. The city and its residents were depicted as filthy and corrupted, and city life was associated with the process of abandoning one's ideals. This can be seen, for example, in Aharon Megged's books and plays, *Chedva and I, Hannah Szenes,* and *Far Off in the Arava* (dramatized under the name *On the Way to Eilat*).

The contradiction in values between urban leisure (or leisure that was considered urban) and Zionist *hagshama* was captured in the epithet "golden youth." This term was used for urban young people who sinned by enjoying themselves too much and giving themselves over to pleasures such as smoking and drinking.[13] Coined with reference to the Golden Calf of the Pentateuch, "golden youth" was commonly used in the 1940s and 1950s by political leaders and educators, most of whom themselves lived in the city. It generally appeared in discussions about the decline in ideological and national fervor and the possibility of premature normalization, which were liable to weaken national endurance.

The rejection of the city and its culture was also expressed in the adjective "salon": In "salon society" couples did "salon dances"—the jazz or slow, romantic dances considered bourgeois. This general derogatory term was applied by the Zionist "gatekeepers"—by both the establishment and the Sabras of the Palmach and youth movements—to the fashion of dance clubs and dance parties (the fox trot was especially popular) that swept through Europe and the United States in the 1930s and, little by little, penetrated Yishuv society. There was diametric opposition "between adherence to the ideological movement centered on the country's open spaces, fields, and developing areas, and the clique shutting itself up between the four walls of its salon," as sociologist Yochanan Peres has written.[14] This opposition created constant tension between imported "salon dances" and Israeli folk dances, which competed for the heart of the younger generation. A kibbutz girl wrote in her school newspaper:

> The dance evenings [of waltzes and polkas] instituted in our society just now in my opinion lead society as a whole in an improper and disagreeable direction. The sixth and seventh grades must cease dancing these dances and

dance only folk dances. It is enough to dance a polka once or twice in a dance evening, but the rest of the time they should dance folk dances.[15]

The rejection of "salonism" was connected to the socialist ethos as well. Salon dancing, as its name implies, was perceived as an activity that took place in ballrooms and so was a bourgeois and antisocialist activity.

Avoiding Etiquette

Asceticism applied not only to the way a person dressed but also to the way he treated others. Simplicity of dress was complemented by simplicity of manners and lack of etiquette. One reason for the minimal rules of politeness was that this was a new frontier society, small and rural, which like other frontier societies was notable for a primary, noninstitutionalized system of relations. However, there were also ideological justifications. Like dressing up, proper manners were an expression of decadent bourgeois society, and doing without them was a statement of proletarianism. So, like simplicity of dress, abstaining from the rules of etiquette became a goal in and of itself, a sort of ostentatious vulgarity.

The pioneer practice of keeping etiquette to a minimum was also influenced by the Tolstoyan view of bourgeois life as false. For the pioneers, and for the Sabras after them, etiquette was a hypocritical system of relations, whereas simple ways simplify the relations between human beings and cure them of the ills of decadence.

It may well be that the pioneer repugnance for etiquette contributed something to the Sabra's playfulness, prankishness, roughness, and desire for independence, which over the years became some of the most prominent trademarks of "Sabra chutzpah," and even notable status symbols. These qualities were evident in brash, direct speech and in the rejection of verbal niceties. Sabras looked down on people who said "please," and they made fun of the manners of German Jews. This intentional and deliberate indelicacy led to the use of physical gestures to replace greetings. One example is the strong slap on the shoulder used by one Sabra meeting another, which has become a typical Israeli gesture.

The Sabras went much further with their impoliteness than the older generation did, which created a certain generation gap. Immigrants who arrived in the Fourth Aliya and afterward were particularly shocked by what they termed "uncivilized" Sabra behavior, and some even wrote angry letters and articles in the party, movement, and national press.

For the Sabra, simple ways also conveyed being an equal among equals and fit with the family-community character of the Sabra generation. This simplicity was a way of life that expressed a common religious view, as does the lifestyle of ascetic sects such as the Amish and Baptists.

Asceticism and Military Culture

The ascetic ethos of the Palmach did not derive only from its objective financial plight; it was nurtured also by the cultural link between the Palmach and the kibbutz, and by the pioneer education of many of its commanders, who grew up in the laboring settlements.

Asceticism was evidenced in the Palmach in the absence of hierarchical status symbols of decorations and rank, in the equal salaries of officers and soldiers, in the common mess halls for officers and soldiers, in the minimization of such "military nonsense" as ceremonies and parades, and in the simple uniforms.[16] In fact, many Palmachniks wore no military uniform at all. With the establishment of the IDF, however, rank, hierarchy, and uniforms became more acceptable.

Even in the IDF, though, some of the Palmach's ascetic spirit survived. Moderated military exhibitionism became an IDF trademark. This was an army that minimized ceremony, formal symbols, and military ostentation, and there was a definite antibureaucratic milieu. During the first years after its establishment, many officers, including those of high rank, dressed haphazardly and often went without their insignia as a kind of reverse status symbol. Historian Shabetai Teveth relates that Moshe Dayan, who more than any other IDF commander made the IDF into a cultural extension of the laboring settlements, "walked to his general's office without a hat or insignia and in sandals and gave friendly slaps on the shoulder to those who came to see him there."[17]

Sloppy dress was one of the most prominent status symbols of the Sabra soldiers in Unit 101 and the Paratroopers and later in the IDF elite units. There was a tacit agreement that an infantryman (and even more so the soldier in an elite unit) was permitted not to dress according to the rules or not to devote too much attention to order and cleanliness. Grunginess served as an informal class identity tag and an important macho symbol (washing, according to the macho stereotype, is a fundamentally feminine activity). The man who dressed sloppily was a tough guy who was never spoiled and was not afraid of discomfort. He was a man of the field in his soul (here was an intersection between pantheism and asceticism) and thus a good soldier, one for whom the conditions in the field were natural.

The simple, sloppy appearance of the Palmach soldier and the early IDF infantryman was meant to reinforce the image of the army as a popular militia, even once it became a regular army. It was also a symbol of an outer roughness that hid an inner complexity, and of the purity and modesty of the soldier who performed his heroic work quietly.

Sexual Puritanism

Another aspect of the pioneer and Sabra culture of restraining needs and urges, different in nature from the traits noted thus far, was sexual puritanism. This was evident in the restrained courtship culture and in the confinement of sexual relations, in general, to marriage (although not necessarily formal religious marriage). "In general a couple would just talk and talk. We almost never had relations until there was a permanent connection," one pioneer women recalled.[18] Talking about sex was also taboo, and outward manifestations of love, even the simplest such as walking hand in hand, were kept for places where no one saw them.

There were several factors at the foundation of the pioneer's puritanism. The first was the spirit of the times: romanticism, sexuality, and pornography had still not swept the Western world in a tidal wave of films, books, and advertisements, and sexuality had still not been separated from marriage and become a legitimate pleasure in its own right. The norm of modern secular society in that period was discreet courting and sexual relations after marriage.

The second factor was the traditional Jewish homes from which most of the pioneers had come. "There were lots of inhibitions in the relations between boys and girls. In practice, they still had the small-town mentality," one pioneer woman related. "Subconsciously they wanted to be like everybody else in the world, and everyone looked for a boy to marry, even if they didn't have a real wedding."[19] True, traditional arranged marriages were not the practice in pioneer society, but the transition to open courtship in the Western style was too radical for young people who had been raised and educated in a traditional home.

The third factor was the living conditions. In a small, closed society suffering from crowded living conditions, the possibilities for private courtship, much less sexual relations outside of marriage, were very limited.

How did the "romances" begin? Today you say "they're going out together." Then you said "they're already reading together." We lived in the girls' room, four girlfriends. When one of the girls' boyfriends would come in "to read together," the others would leave. That's how Yitzchak would come in and

I would read Achad Ha'am with him. The romance lasted a long time. But when it came down to it, until when would that be? There were no rooms.[20]

The fourth factor was the socialist worldview, according to which courtship was an aristocratic or bourgeois custom that had no place in a revolutionary society.

The fifth factor had to do with the connection between love and sex on the one hand and individualism on the other. Love was something personal and private, and sex even more so; in a society oriented toward a national mission they had to be kept in check. Open physical attraction to the opposite sex connoted a kind of hedonism, a kind of devotion to the private pleasures of the body in a period in which the individual was expected to devote his whole being to the fulfillment of national and Zionist goals.

The sixth factor was connected to the family character of the Sabra group and to the cooperative ethos of socialist Zionism. Public displays of affection were considered a violation of the purity of interpersonal relations in an intimate society founded on the principle of cooperation, and an undesirable emphasis within the family-style unit. The typical romantic view of small revolutionary groups of cooperative-communal orientation is of a well-knit family of brothers and sisters. Relations between its members are based for the most part on feelings of brotherhood, responsibility, and communal interest, not on physical desire and private interests.

These factors were at the foundation of Sabra sex education. It was a problematic area, full of contradictions and awkwardness, as the ascetic ethos, the traditional Jewish ethos, European moralism, and the socialist ethos of equality clashed with the spirit of modern psychologism that began to spread during that period.

The socialist youth movements addressed the subject of sexual relations only infrequently, and then cautiously and with a deterrent approach. The goal of sex education was, on the one hand, "to do away with preconceptions and vapid thoughts" and, on the other, to provide "a critical approach to the problem of the family and sex in a capitalist regime, and to create proper attitudes and approaches to the question of the woman and her liberation." Youth movement counselors were expected to avoid the question of sex and to focus on teaching values regarding a life of love and establishment of a family "that have been distorted in bourgeois society through marriage based on economic considerations and because of the pressures of the capitalist city—double standards, prostitution, and venereal diseases."[21]

It should be remembered that the counselors were themselves young and sexually inexperienced, so they were embarrassed to talk about sex. It is also important to emphasize that in this period there was a great deal of ignorance about sexual matters, and sexual information was generally conveyed behind closed doors, and even then not explicitly.

The kibbutzim took a pedagogical approach of restraint with regard to sex not only because of socialist taboos but also because of the method of communal education. Psychologist Bruno Bettelheim noted two restraining factors regarding sex in the culture of the kibbutz Sabra. The first was the restricted contact with parents and especially with mothers, which limited the physical contact and warmth that, according to Freudian theory, are necessary for physical openness with the opposite sex and the desire for physical contact. The second was the communal life of boys and girls in the children's room at the age when sexual tension emerges and the mechanism of shame develops. "You don't fall in love with or marry someone who sat on the potty with you when you were a kid," the young people explained to Bettelheim. The boys and girls who grew up together in a single room and showered in a single shower had to suppress their feelings for each other. Sexual attraction among them created guilt feelings and shame and was repressed as a means of survival in the closed group. An important point arises in this context: in contrast to kibbutz peer groups, in which almost no couples formed, in Palmach *hachsharot* there was no implicit or explicit taboo against romantic attachments within the group, and many couples—and even marriages—formed. While sexuality was restricted, it was not for the psychological reasons that Bettelheim observed.

In the kibbutz schools and in the urban gymnasium high schools, sex was a pedagogical taboo, and the subject would generally be addressed only in a few discreet talks by an enterprising doctor or teacher. Lectures on sex were given only rarely in the context of classes in biology, health, and hygiene, as may be learned from the book by Yehuda-Leib Matmon-Cohen, principal of the Hebrew Gymnasium in Jaffa, *Textbook on the Fundamentals of the Theory of Man and the Preservation of Health for High Schools*.[22]

During the time the Sabras were growing up, Palestine, and in fact the entire Western world, was in a process of metamorphosis with regard to the publication of sexual guidance and reference material. Such material was becoming more available due to developments in medical science and the growth of the behavioral sciences, led by psychology. Little by little, beginning in the 1930s, books on sex began to appear in Palestine.

These were mostly Hebrew translations of works written by European doctors, psychologists, and psychiatrists,[23] supplemented by books written by Jewish doctors and educators in Palestine and elsewhere.[24] The emphasis was on the biological aspect of sexual phenomena, and especially on sexual dysfunction. Very little space, if any, was devoted to sexual technique and to the emotional significance of sexual relations. These books focused on restraint, on the dangers (biological, psychological, and social) of sexual activity, and on what was perceived as sexual deviance (prostitution, "concubinage," masturbation, homosexuality). They exhibited ignorance, stereotyping, and various prejudices.[25]

Nevertheless, the very fact that sex was now being written about, that there was explicit and public discussion of human sexuality, patterns of relations, prostitution, and other such matters, was a social innovation (certainly for the traditional Jewish world) and reflected a new spirit of pluralism that had arrived from the West. It affected the world of adolescents as well. These books were the first manifestations of a sincere and courageous attempt, under the inspiration of psychology, to shake off preconceptions.

In the area of sexual literature there is another matter worthy of attention: despite the conservative character of the kibbutz movement (especially Ha-Shomer Ha-Tza'ir and its associated kibbutz movement, Ha-Kibbutz Ha-Artzi),[26] the kibbutz presses published most of the printed matter on sex during this period. Kibbutz movement periodicals occasionally included articles on sex education (such as the above-mentioned series in Ha-Shomer Ha-Tza'ir), and the very fact that they appeared is a cultural milestone.

The relative openness of the kibbutz movement on sex education results from several factors. First, Freudian theory was hugely influential on the labor movement, which included the teachers of the younger generation. Second, the revolutionary way of raising children developed at the kibbutz—separated from their families and in children's houses, in which boys and girls of a given age grew up together in the same building and even the same room—raised questions about relations between the sexes. Third, the kibbutz attributed great importance to an atmosphere of openness—"an atmosphere of truth,"[27] as it was called—in society in general and in education in particular. Fourth, there was the socialist ethos, one of whose principles was the equality of women.

What of the sexual behavior of the Sabras in practice? The most prominent characteristics in the Sabra culture of love and male-female relations were self-control, shyness, and embarrassment. This was so for several reasons: the ethos of emotional restraint, the conservatism of the parents (the perception of sex as a sin), the socialist ethos (the perception of love and intimacy as manifestations of individualism and separation from the group), and close supervision. As with the pioneers, public displays of love between boys and girls in the youth movements were restrained and modest.

Courtship between a Sabra boy and girl before they became a couple was restrained, hesitant, and bashful, an exchange of hints and glances. It was not acceptable to frequently change boyfriends or girlfriends, and after a romantic connection was established it generally lasted a long time. Many married their first love.

Talking about sex was considered among most Sabras in all contexts to be a violation of privacy and would be met with discomfiture and blushes. Even close male or female friends did not generally talk or ask advice of each other about sexual matters, and letters between boyfriend and girlfriend (at least those that I have examined or have been told about) generally contain no erotic language. Their style is very emotional but it is restrained, often hesitant, and very literary, as if taken from the Russian novels of the period. For example, a girl at Kibbutz Geva wrote to her boyfriend at the front:

> My Barzak, may much peace be with you! Tonight there was a party for all the young people at Geva, but when you are not here it has no attraction for me. Don't laugh, that is really the case. In general I have been so sad these past few days since I returned from vacation, I simply need you by me to feel good again. . . . Your Aunt Liza slept here this evening. It's really too bad that she can't see you, my precious. She took an interest in me. To see couples walking, emerging from the party into the night with its shining, hinting moon—it simply pains the heart, and then the feeling of loneliness, of sadness, and love grows stronger. Shaul, come soon, I am dying. I have heard that matters are a bit difficult, fighting and so on. Be strong and healthy, my precious. Good night, my love, and good-bye. Yours, Penina. (It is already very late and if I wrote things that are a little funny I'm sure you'll understand.)[28]

In the Palmach, sexual relations were a taboo. Netiva Ben-Yehuda wrote about this in her autobiography:

> This phenomenon, the attitude toward sex, really astounded me when I first came to the Palmach. It didn't fit in with all the legends we'd heard about the Palmach beforehand. All the famous swagger of the Palmach veterans was sexless. . . . Always, when people ask me if there really was purity of arms in the Palmach, I answer: "Purity of arms I can't say. But sexual purity there

certainly was." . . . Sex was disgusting not only in the Second Aliya, but with us, too. . . . There weren't even any dirty jokes.[29]

Only a few—and not youth movement members younger than enlistment age, but members of the mobilized Palmach *hachsharot*—engaged in full sexual relations, even in the face of some disapproval from the group. In any case this came only after a long romantic friendship and as an additional stage in the couple's emotional relations. Casual sex was almost unheard of. This is one reason that many members of the mobilized *hachsharot* and the Palmach married at a relatively young age, between twenty and twenty-three (another factor in early marriage was the sense of loneliness and anxiety produced by the war). An additional reason premarital sexual relations were not accepted was the crowded conditions and the lack of privacy in the living quarters of the *hachsharot*.

In general, sexual relations were not the dominant element in romantic relations—at least not to the extent that they are today. Friendship was the main thing. The common expression for proposing a romance to a member of the opposite sex was "to offer friendship." In Sabra culture one's boyfriend or girlfriend was not perceived as a sexual object, and his or her physical beauty, while having some weight in the choice that was made, was not the central consideration. For this reason, neither men nor women gave much attention to their physical appearance. Makeup was considered almost whorish among the women, and even jewelry was frowned upon. The moral and social character of one's partner was much more important. The most sought-after character traits were social popularity, national and movement altruism, the ability to express oneself well in writing, leadership, seriousness, and sometimes also a sense of humor (in the buddy-humor style).

The attitude toward sexual relations was thus bifaceted. On the one hand, sex was considered an expression of deep connection between a man and woman; on the other hand, it was a sin and a weakness. There was also, of course, great fear of unplanned pregnancy, since during this period means of contraception were not easily available.

The tendency to refrain from overt displays of love was a product not only of shyness but also of the fact that the couple was part of a group that lived as a family, often in a common tent or barracks (as in the agricultural communes of the pioneers). For this reason, for example, couples would often enter the kibbutz dining hall separately. The connection with one's partner was interwoven with the life of the group, not separate from it.

The long conversation held by two lovers (first ostensibly by chance, then intentionally) was the most common courtship ritual. However, the intimacy and the distancing from the group were momentary, for regular conclaves by the group were the top priority, and intimate conversations were not to come at their expense. The subject of these group meetings was also the group itself—the activity of the smaller or larger Sabra organization and its members. Letters between lovers often addressed national issues. Boyfriends and girlfriends spent a lot of time telling each other about public affairs, describing in detail national and movement achievements in the army and on the farm, touching on the love between them only at the margins.

Still, it is important to emphasize that the Sabra culture of love was somewhat more open than that of the pioneers. This difference was reflected in their clothes. The khaki shorts of the woman of the Palmach or kibbutz were shorter and more casual than those of the pioneer, and the shorts worn by youth movement girls, held tight against their thighs with elastic, resembling gym shorts, were shorter and more revealing than the pleated skirts worn by the pioneer women of the 1920s. There was also a notable difference in dances. One common youth movement dance, "Boy Takes Girl," for example, was a kind of unconscious combination of the hora and a salon dance and was foreign to pioneer culture. Moreover, while the pioneers saw dance as largely an ecstatic expression of ideology, for the Sabras it was also an attractive encounter, charged with a certain energy, between boys and girls and was an important part of the process of courtship.

Unlike the pioneers, for whom puritanism was an assumption, romantic and sexual restraint created contradictory feelings and even tension for the Sabras. This tension was apparently stronger in the Ha-Noar Ha-Oved and Ha-Shomer Ha-Tza'ir movements, which had more connections to pioneer culture.[30]

CHAPTER 7

Our Gang

The Kibbutz Community

THE FIRST AGRICULTURAL COMMUNES
AS HASIDIC SECTS

The pioneers of the Second and Third Aliyot were not just Zionists seeking to establish a Jewish polity; they were revolutionaries who wanted to create an entirely new and specifically Jewish society. As socialists, they took as their goal the creation of a commonwealth in which relations between people would be based on true equality, mutual assistance, and mutual respect. The economic forces that, so they believed, controlled the structure of human relations in a capitalist society would no longer determine the fate of men and women.

When the pioneers came to Palestine, they left behind their parents, siblings, and hometowns. They were alone in Palestine, without a family to anchor them. This situation together with the socialist ideal encouraged cohesive pioneer fellowships that were very much like families. The members of communes shared similar backgrounds, including the experience of having come to a new land and adopted a new language, and this enhanced their cohesiveness. Although the early communes were small and few in number, they created a standard of socialist living and Zionist idealism that became a model for the entire Zionist labor movement, and indeed for Yishuv and Israeli society as a whole.

The close personal relations between the members of the early communes and the ideological fervor that they shared gave these groups the character of a Hasidic sect; for Hasidim also emphasize fellowship and devotion to a shared way of life. In fact, the analogy between the pioneer commune and the Hasidic sect is no mere metaphor. Hasidism was a very real influence on the pioneers, and many of them refer to it explicitly in their memoirs. "Hasidism is the spring from which we drew our song and from which we nourished our souls in those first days,"[1] related Yehuda Ya'ari. Indeed, the very word *kibbutz* is of Hasidic origin. It is the word that Bratislaver Hasidim used to label their gatherings on the Rosh Ha-Shana holiday, when they met at the grave of their founder in the Ukrainian town of Oman to pray and to study his writings.[2]

There is an important difference between the pioneer and the Hasid, however. In Hasidism the fellowship is a by-product of shared devotion to God and reverence for a holy man. For the pioneer the commune was a goal in and of itself. As the socialist ethos dictated, social relations were at the very center of the commune and were the subject of endless discussions, inquiries, conversations, and meetings. Records of many of these have been preserved in kibbutz journals and in the archives of the kibbutz movement.

THE KIBBUTZ AS AN EXTENDED FAMILY

The population of the kibbutzim grew by accretion and natural increase in the pre-state period, turning them from tiny agricultural settlements into rural communities in which two or more biological generations lived together. Despite this growth, the kibbutz continued to consider itself an extended family. This was not only a matter of socialist ideology. The extended kibbutz family was meant to replace the traditional Jewish nuclear family and incorporate ties to the nation, the movement, and in the case of the Sabra, to the peer group as well.

This was perhaps not as revolutionary as the kibbutznikim thought. Traditionally, ties to and solidarity with the local community were an important part of Jewish life in the Diaspora. In fact, there is a paradox here, for the pioneers who fled the East European Jewish villages to found a new kind of community in Palestine in many ways modeled the kibbutz on the Jewish villages they had grown up in. As in those villages, in kibbutzim there were close relations between neighbors, an insular community with a shared identity, community institutions, and strong pressure to conform to the community's norms.

In the kibbutz, however, the authority of the family patriarch was replaced with the authority of the extended family. Thus meals were not family meals with the father at the head of the table but communal meals held in a dining hall. Holidays were observed not within the family but communally. Observances such as lighting the candles at the beginning of the Sabbath were generally performed in the dining hall rather than at home. "The strong impression made by the kibbutz Hanukkah party has still not left me," wrote one kibbutznik. "[The candle flames] forge us into a single body and we sense how close we are to each other, feeling like brothers."[3]

If the kibbutz was one extended family, then the children were not the children of individual families but rather of the community as a whole. Indeed, in kibbutzim children were regarded as products of the commune. They were created and tended by and belonged to the community as a whole. In the kibbutz version of the traditional Shavu'ot holiday, the Festival of the First Fruits, the master of ceremonies would read the names of the babies born during the previous year just as he read the statistics on the wheat harvest or the number of calves born in the barn. When the kibbutz had a school graduation ceremony, the entire membership attended, not just the parents of the graduating children.

The writings produced by the kibbutznikim served to reinforce and internalize the community's cohesion. Kibbutz members produced an abundance of articles, pamphlets, and newsletters that expressed and extolled the community's solidarity and the sense of belonging.

FROLICKING ON THE KIBBUTZ LAWN

The kibbutz communal family structure, which celebrated and fostered togetherness and the values of cooperation, made the kibbutz-born Sabra into a "social personality"—a consumer of the togetherness that the social environment provided. Common property and common labor on the communal farm accustomed the Sabra to think in collective terms and blurred in his consciousness the distinction between his identity as an individual and his identity as a part of the group. This is evidenced in the letters written to their kibbutzim by young kibbutzniks who were serving in the Palmach and in the Jewish Brigade. They frequently addressed the kibbutz as a whole (often placing their greetings to the kibbutz before their greetings to their parents), pleaded to be sent up-to-date information and internal newsletters, and expressed their longing for kibbutz life and people. The letters make it clear that these young people considered all the members of the kibbutz to be family.

Yet an even greater influence on the Sabra's social personality was the "children's house" (for preschoolers), the "children's society" (the kibbutz's communal education for adolescents), and the kibbutz educational institution that was unique to the Ha-Shomer Ha-Tza'ir movement—a boarding high school where the children of several kibbutzim studied together, something like a communal adolescent kingdom itself run as a kibbutz. These unique institutions, which created an almost autonomous society of children, provided the three primary psychological influences on kibbutz children—a powerful emotional attachment to their fellows, conformism, and dependence on the group.[4]

The common daily routine in the children's houses, preschools, and schools and the shared clothes and toys put the communal imprint on the kibbutz child from a very young age. Kibbutzim, especially those of Ha-Shomer Ha-Tza'ir, forbade parents to buy personal clothes and toys for their children, and even prohibited parents from hanging a personal picture in the child's room next to his bed, to ensure that there were no special privileges. As a result, the children were absorbed into a single, homogeneous group of uniform appearance, and the possibilities of individual expression were limited.

Psychologist Bruno Bettelheim argued in his famous *Children of the Dream* that because of the long period of time that the kibbutz child spent with his peers, he feared not the disapproval of his parents, but rather that of his peer group. The young person, Bettelheim wrote, is part of the "we" that insistently demands that he does one thing and not another. A person can hide from his parents and even from God, even if their voices awaken in him greater fear than that of any other human agent. But he cannot hide from a system of social supervision that he himself is consciously a part of.[5] The kibbutz child was indeed almost always in the company of his peers, and for this reason he was almost always under their inquisitive, judgmental, and categorizing gaze. In such conditions it was difficult to change and to be different.

It is important to emphasize that communal pressure exerted on the individual is a universal phenomenon and is not unique to kibbutz life. But because of the intensity of kibbutz life and the disconnection from the parental home, this pressure operated under optimal conditions in the children's house. The kibbutz way of life significantly amplified the centripetal force that the peer group exerted on the child.

The separation from the parental home and the mutual activity with members of the group throughout the day and night drastically reduced the possibility of being alone and also created mutual psychological dependence among the children.[6] This implanted in the kibbutz child the habit of solving problems communally ("to think as a group") and reduced his ability to take a distant and critical view of himself and his comrades.

The mutual dependence was magnified as the peer group moved, over the years, from one children's house to another and from one caretaker to another. Bettelheim argued that in this situation, where one's bed, toys, and caretaker (who to some extent took the place of the biological mother) changed, the peer group became the most stable element in the young person's life.[7]

The kibbutz adolescent's need to seek companionship with other youths derived not only from the nature of life in the kibbutz but also from psychological factors typical of adolescence. At this age friendship is vital in shaping the young person's internal world and is generally found in same-sex friendships, which may endure throughout the adolescent years.[8]

The kibbutz-born Sabra's identity and dependence on the group was strengthened in school. One of the philosophical principles of kibbutz schools was education for a common social life. "Our school stands on three things," a kibbutz educator wrote, echoing a well-known maxim of the sages: "ideology, labor, and the child's social life."[9] The frequent celebrations, field games, and field trips conducted by the schools promoted a school spirit and made learning fun. School was a childhood paradise, about which the children of the period wax sentimental to this day.

The intensive emotional link between the kibbutz Sabras and their "gang" is echoed in their letters: "I feel excellent and the only thing I lack is company and friends,"[10] wrote a kibbutz child who had to leave the group for his studies. Another wrote to his friends: "Am I really doomed to live far from the group forever? Can it really be that you will go [off together] and I will be elsewhere . . . just not with you? No! That never entered my thoughts and I don't want it to!"[11]

A verbal indication of the profound connection between the kibbutz child and his peers was the frequent greetings that young people sent to each other through friends and in letters. Many of these greetings were addressed to the group as a whole and not to a single close friend.

The common life of the young people at kibbutzim was indeed full of enchantment and gave them a sense of security, but in order to paint a complete picture it is important to state that it also caused a sense of suffocation, especially among the vulnerable, the sensitive, and the individualistic. The difficulty of finding privacy and the constant close quarters with others produced anxiety, frustration, and sometimes anger, and even then, prompted quite a few young people to leave their kibbutzim and seek their futures in the cities.

Testimonies to this oppressive atmosphere appear in newspaper interviews with members of the generation many years later and in the testimonies of kibbutz educators. It is difficult to find evidence of such feelings in the Sabras' own writings, perhaps because criticizing the group, which was like one's family, was considered taboo. But it emerges between the lines here and there.

THE KIBBUTZ SPIRIT IN THE YOUTH
MOVEMENTS, THE PALMACH, AND THE ARMY

The cultural influence of the kibbutz Sabras on the Sabra population in general was much broader than their demographic weight might indicate. This influence was effected at three points of contact: (1) the strong connection between the Palmach *hachsharot* (in the 1940s) and the Nachal groups (in the 1950s) and the kibbutzim that hosted them; (2) the contact between members of the youth movements and the kibbutzim in which many of their work camps and other activities were held; (3) the kibbutz members who were sent to serve as youth movement counselors in the cities. These influences encouraged a culture of cooperation and brotherhood in the kibbutz spirit within these Sabra frameworks. The fact that the command levels of the Palmach and the Paratroopers included a high proportion of kibbutz members also contributed to the creation of a kibbutz atmosphere and kibbutz culture in these organizations.

The youth movements in the cities had many of the characteristics of kibbutz society. Especially akin to the kibbutz was the intensive association of young people with their peers. While the urban youth movement members lived with their families, they studied in the same school, sometimes in the same class, with their fellow chapter members and spent much of their free time in the same neighborhood and in the youth movement chapter house. They also spent time together at work and Scout camps, during visits to kibbutzim, and on field trips and hikes during vacations.

Many describe the atmosphere in the youth movement chapter house as familial, and the impression is that from a psychosociological point of view, the interpersonal relationships were similar to those between members of a commune or cult: "You have the passion to divide your heart up into pieces and to serve it to every friend. You get the desire to kiss and embrace every friend. . . . The club is the place where I found myself and where I created myself. Who knows if in my life I will ever again have such a pure place!"[12]

Chapter house newsletters and diaries devoted a great deal of space to discussions of events in "our group," "our chapter," "our brigade," and "our movement." They seem to have been introverted groups preoccupied almost entirely with themselves.

Youth movement groups in particular resembled kibbutz groups in the "common brain" that thought as one and the "common heart" that felt as one—created through the close mutual relations and constant social pressure. Everyone discussed everything together, and everyone decided everything together.

The "social talks" and "inquiries" that were part of the routine of kibbutz educational institutions and youth movement chapter houses (especially in Ha-Shomer Ha-Tza'ir), as well as the composition of a "book of life" (something like a collective journal, like those kept by the pioneer communes), both expressed and shaped the "common heart" of the group. These talks and inquiries promoted unmediated and sincere relations between the members of the group and a sense of "completeness" and harmony among them. These talks had a confessional character, the individual baring himself to his fellows (though not in the total way common in modern psychological group dynamics), and working out his social difficulties with the rest of the group.

It should be noted that the dependence that the children of bourgeois immigrants had on their peers was all the stronger because of the chasm between the immigrant parents, who found it difficult to sever their ties with the culture of their countries of origin, and their children, whose adjustment to the new life was easier and, even more so, vital to their survival.

There was great similarity between the kibbutzim and the agricultural youth villages of Ben Shemen, Mikveh Yisrael, and Kadoorie. Many of the students at these schools had arrived in Palestine as orphans, and for them the peer group was a replacement for the family that had been murdered in the Holocaust. The same was true of the orphans who lived on kibbutzim within the framework of Youth Societies.

The Palmach in the 1940s (as well as the Nachal in the 1950s) was also similar to the kibbutz in its norms and in the relations between its members. The soldiers of one unit "lived together in a closed storeroom, ate at a single table, enjoying common pleasures and training and working shoulder to shoulder."[13] This intensive life together in all-encom-passing frameworks—"total institutions," in sociological terms—with a common system of values and a similar social background forged the Palmach soldiers into a single social body and created a sense of family.

The Sabra organizations also resembled the kibbutz in the all-inclu-siveness they exhibit when they are considered together. The structural and cultural links between them set out a continuous life path, fully pre-determined, along which the Sabra passed from one framework to an-other in accordance with his age and circumstances. As with the kibbutz child, his entire group went through these stages together. The Sabra's whole life was spent in community and, more critically, in the company of his peer group. He was made to function consistently as a member of a group rather than as an individual, and for this reason he had to de-velop "survival power" within the group.

The familial, communal culture of the kibbutz affected not only the Sabra organizations but also society as a whole—including urban soci-ety, which was a minority. Jewish identity with its historical baggage, the cultural and economic isolation in a hostile environment, the common traumas, and the mourning rituals that united the entire nation all rein-forced the intimate character of life in the country and granted the Yishuv and the young state the nature, sociologically, of one large kibbutz.

The Culture of the Circle

FROM HASIDIC DANCE TO THE HORA

Sociological and anthropological literature is full of descriptions of tribes that create a sense of unity through ecstatic rituals, especially through communal song and dance. The familiar words and sounds sung in uni-son by the members of the tribe and the uniform movements and clap-ping make the individual feel he has become one with the group, part of a tribal whole that is greater than the sum of its human parts. The com-mon emotional expression and the physical closeness between the dancers intensify the thrill and create a kind of contagious fervor that French so-ciologist Gustave Le Bon has called the "collective brain."[14]

The hora dance was one of the most notable manifestations of the pi-oneer community ritual and its religious fire. In their memoirs many pi-oneers write about the infectious enthusiasm and intoxication of the dance, of the sweeping and mesmerizing elation they experienced while dancing the hora.

The hora was thus amazingly like Hasidic dance (with the important difference that the hora mixed the sexes) and in fact served a similar social and psychological purpose—the assimilation of the individual into the collective to the point of shedding his material self. The pioneer imitated the Hasidic dancer almost completely: He closed his eyes, bobbed his head, stamped his feet to an accelerating tempo, sang loudly— sometimes accompanied by a harmonica or accordion—to the point of hoarseness or voicelessness, waving a handkerchief over his head to intensify his fervor. Furthermore, many of his dances were to traditional melodies, some of which were in fact Hasidic in origin.[15]

The pioneers' dancing made a huge impression on the Sabras (especially those born and bred in kibbutzim) and infected them with its ardor. The youth movements and Palmach inherited the pioneer hora, and its communal ecstasy warranted it a central place in their culture.

It was not just ecstasy that gave the hora prominence. The dance exemplified several complementary ideological messages that created a single normative picture. It expressed the need to strengthen each other and be strengthened together in the face of difficulties. It symbolized the centripetal attraction of the individual into the communal circle and his assimilation into a unified Hasidic-like community. It is no coincidence that one of the earliest pioneer dances was called "Rise Up, Brother." The closed circle and joined hands were also symbolic of socialist values. As Gurit Kadman, a prominent choreographer, stated, they represented "equal rights, the absence of class; there are no differences of sex or quality in the performance of the dance."[16] Furthermore, the joined hands symbolized the inseparable chain of the Jewish generations, made explicit in the lyrics of the hora song, "the chain still continues." (The lyrics were by Ya'akov Orland, who together with composer Mordecai Zein wrote many of the most popular new Zionist "gospel" songs.)[17]

The dances—usually done barefoot—also expressed the potent connection of the pioneer to the land. For this reason, among others, the establishment of a new settlement would be marked by the dancing of a wild hora.

Like other patterns of pioneer folklore, the hora, which began as a spontaneous outpouring of "the joy of the poor," was gradually institutionalized and improved in Yishuv and Israeli culture until it metamorphosed into the Israeli folk dance. Composers, costume designers, and choreographers from the labor settlements developed it into one of the symbols of those settlements, and especially of the pioneer youth movements.

At the dance festivals at Kibbutz Dalia, a tradition that began in 1944, dance became one of the ritual tools of the Zionist national religion. The frenzied horas of the dance troupes, made up of Sabras from kibbutzim, moshavim, and the youth movements, were celebrations of unity, youthful joy, and the vitality of the new nation. After the first such festival, folk dance clubs multiplied at the kibbutzim and in the cities, and there was an increasing demand for new dances and songs. At the second festival, in 1947, only locally created Israeli dances were presented, and by the third festival the number of troupes and dance lovers had increased enormously. By the fourth festival, in 1958, folk dancing had become a broad popular movement of troupes and clubs throughout the country and a kind of national folklore and sport.[18]

Expressive of the symbolic importance of folk dancing in Israeli culture and of its importance as a means of idealistic exaltation were the dance circles that filled the streets of Israel when the United Nations vote on the establishment of the Jewish state was announced. The declaration of independence and the hora dances were from then on linked in the collective consciousness, and in time these circles of dancers became part of the tradition of Independence Day and so a symbol of national identity. Supported by national institutions, dance companies began being sent overseas as Israeli artistic ambassadors, and they marketed, with great success, the image of the new Jew—the Sabra.

Another expression of the importance of folk dancing as an Israeli symbol was the attempt to make the dances part of the cultural life of army units. At the beginning of 1949, the IDF opened its first course for folk dance instructors, and attempts were made to get army units to dance to music on the radio. These were not successful in the end, but the IDF contributed to the development and establishment of the hora as a folk dance in another way—through the army's entertainment troupes, which frequently included such dances in their programs.

ZIONIST GOSPEL MUSIC

One product of the Zionist national revival in the Land of Israel was the composition of a large inventory of popular songs. The songs were written to answer a demand—sing-alongs were a major form of entertainment. Experts in the field agree that both the size of the repertoire and its quality are exceptional given the small size of the Yishuv in the pre-state period. While no thorough scholarly study of these songs has yet been made, it seems reasonable to assume that such a study will conclude that these popular songs match the prose of the period in their importance, originality, and worth.

The musical tradition of the early Zionist settlement period was drawn from a variety of sources: Yiddish songs (some of the melodies were sung in Yiddish); Slavic, Moldavian, and Russian folk songs; Hasidic songs and Jewish prayers; socialist protest songs; and the popular Oriental songs that the pioneers picked up in Palestine.

At first the immigrants sang "imported" songs, but gradually a group of talented composers emerged, creating original melodies to the words of the poets of the national revival in Palestine and in the Diaspora. From the end of the 1920s, at kibbutz and moshav celebrations, in the schools, and in the cabaret shows and theaters of Tel Aviv, a musical style evolved that was influenced by spoken Hebrew and by musical developments in the West. This determined the basic forms of popular Israeli songs, including those of the Sabras.

Most of the Hebrew songs were about nature and work, the world of children, the holidays, the country's landscape, and after the War of Independence, the experience of war, loss, and memory. Melodies were also written for verses from the Bible and verses of the great Hebrew poets.

What needs, then, did Hebrew song and the tradition of public singing answer? The pioneer settlers frequently sang together because of the immediate need for entertainment in a small society with few resources, and because of the need for an outlet for feelings of loneliness and existential stress felt by people living in cultural isolation. However, like the hora, the song was also an element in the community's ecstatic ritual. It wakened and united, as did the singing of a choir in a synagogue. In fact, the Hebrew term for the sing-along translates literally as "public singing," a term that consciously parallels the religious term "public prayer." And certainly the sing-along was as much ritual as entertainment.

For the pioneers, public song was a remnant of the synagogue culture, a means of shoring up people's spirits, and part of the formation of the new Israeli culture. But for the youth movements it was a central and defining element of the youth culture. Song was an unquestioned, integral part of every activity; learning new songs was considered vital to the communal life of the youth movement chapter. The boy or girl who knew all the lyrics to favorite songs was admired and envied by the others.[19] When the chapter gathered on Friday evenings or engaged in any other routine activity, the meeting would always be opened and closed with a song. The Sabras sang even more on field trips, where songs were a means of expressing their elation and releasing tension. Furthermore, travel by bus or truck in those days was lengthy and exhausting because of bad roads and slow vehicles, and singing was a good way of passing the time.

In each chapter house, at each camp, on each hike, there were leaders who swept the rest along with their enthusiasm and served as conductors of the chorus.[20] Organizing public singing was considered one of the duties of the counselor, and counselors learned new songs at counseling seminars. Most of the guidebooks for youth movement counselors instructed their readers to lead a lot of sing-alongs.

Youth movement members sang together with great enthusiasm, with tremendous earnestness, and sometimes with real soulful devotion. Their singing, especially of melancholy songs, was in this sense like prayer, and it gave the chapter house the character of a small Hasidic synagogue.

Public singing was a way of practicing social unity, not only because the many voices combined into a single voice, but also because of the ritual that accompanied it. This was described by Netiva Ben-Yehuda:

> On the grass every single evening, everyone would expect from all kinds of soloists that each would contribute his selection—his famous one. In general, the songs were sung in a certain order, as in a suite: There were songs that were always sung together, in packets, fixed, and always after finishing a given song you knew which song came after it. The order depended of course on the local song leader, who ran the entire business as he saw fit—literally a kind of director who was permitted to decide on his own but was open to suggestions. Every time there was a gathering, the best "song starter" in the field would, as you might say, be "elected" to the job by general consensus, and at certain moments he would assign the role of soloist—or two "soloists" in harmony—to someone for what everyone knew was "his" song.[21]

The sing-alongs were so loved by the members of the youth movements and so important to the atmosphere of the chapter house that many, especially the counselors, kept a song notebook (in Ha-Machanot Ha-Olim it was called the "song satchel") in which they laboriously collected the words of the songs they loved as if they were stamps or postcards or autographs in a yearbook. The songs were collected from various sources—parents, older counselors, teachers from kindergarten through high school, neighborhood pals, and later, the radio and the few recordings that were available. The movement songbooks, both printed and improvised, indeed contained a mixture of Hasidic songs, socialist youth movement songs, songs of the partisan fighters in Nazi-occupied Europe, songs of the land and of shepherds of the early Zionist settlers, and Russian folk songs, alongside new songs written and composed in Palestine.

There were even modern folk songs and dance songs from the United States, France, and elsewhere—translated or with their words revised to fit the local culture. Only a few songs were unique to a specific movement; most were sung by all of them, having been passed on by word of mouth in joint camps and seminars.

The socialist movements, until the 1930s, tended to sing a lot of "proletarian" songs and labor songs with socialist content brought by the founding generation from overseas. (The younger generation considered most of these alien and ridiculous and generally sang them in a farcical tone.)[22] But gradually, especially in the 1940s, their place was taken by songs with a general national message—songs of struggle, freedom, heroism, loss, settlement, and illegal immigration.[23] There were happy, light songs, but the best-loved were the lyrical, melancholy ones, most of which were written to Russian melodies and sometimes even had words translated from the Russian.[24] These were songs of yearning for past days and of hope for future ones, playing on the Sabra's patriotic sentiments.

The Russian songs, translated into Hebrew, were popular with young people not only because many of them had heard these melodies in their homes (in some cases as lullabies), but also because they were an informal expression of patriotic and heroic identification with socialist "Mother Russia," with the partisans who were heroically fighting the Nazis, and with the mythological Russia as depicted in the great literary works of Tolstoy, Dostoyevsky, and other great Russian writers.[25]

In the Sabra milieu, as in pioneer culture, songs were an important means of reinforcing the individual's association with the group. This is how a Ha-Shomer Ha-Tza'ir girl described her movement's song nights:

> Singing in unison, deep from the heart. . . . You feel the people's pounding hearts penetrating the world of the musical sounds, and with the wonderful harmony of classical music you feel that these are your brothers, they are yours. . . . So heartwarming is the feeling that these many people are linked one to the other and that no great force can deter them from the trail they have blazed and are walking on.[26]

Public singing was also a mechanism for assimilating the individual into the group and promoting a sense of belonging. The unity of the voices imbued the singers with a unity of thought, and joining in musical harmony meant becoming a part of the group's social harmony. Sing-alongs also enforced a common musical taste and common musical conditioning and so strengthened the young person's connection to the group.

Another role played by public singing was that of rooting in the Sabra the values of Zionism and love of the homeland. It supplemented the messages he was given in his education and reflected and reinforced them through an emotional musical experience. Many of the songs had ideological content, as can be seen by their names: "We Will Go Up to the Hula Valley," "To the Top of the Mountain," "We Sing to You, Homeland and Mother," "We Will Be the First," and so on. Through words packaged in pleasing melodies the Sabra repeated by rote the values of love of the homeland while feeling a painful sweetness. The integration of beautiful melodies with patriotic Hebrew poetry spoke to the Sabra heart and became part of his internal code.

Every program or event to mark a national holiday included public singing, and special songs were even designated as appropriate for each occasion. So, for example, a Ha-Machanot Ha-Olim guidebook recommended that counselors conclude the program titled "Fear and Heroism" by singing "We Will Be Strengthened Here" and "The Galileans Rejoiced," and end the program on Joseph Trumpeldor by singing "From the Valley to the Hill," "In the Upper Galilee," "Go Up to the Hill," "Who Will Save Me from Hunger?" and "In the Galilee and at Tel Chai." The program on "The Defense of Metullah" was to be concluded with the songs "Here in the Land That Our Fathers Yearned For," "O, Homeland," "If You Will It, It Is No Dream," "We Sing to You, Homeland and Mother," and "Come Up, Come Up, to the Land of the Fathers."[27] There were also guidebooks for parties containing precise instructions on what to sing and when, determined by each song's educational and moral value.[28]

National songs were also an important tool in Sabra education because they allowed the Sabra, in keeping with the anti-intellectual ethos, to express pathos without sounding pretentious. Music seemed to mitigate the verbal cliché and allowed emotionally charged words to be pronounced matter-of-factly.

The youth movement song culture blossomed and even developed in the Palmach, especially in the mobilized *hachsharot*. The young fighters frequently sang together—accompanied by harmonica, accordion, mandolin, balalaika, recorder, or Arab drum—in labor camps on farms, at evening gatherings, in training camps, and while traveling by truck. And the Palmach especially loved singing around a campfire and on marches. Every platoon and company had a "cantor" who led the band from one song to another, who animated and conducted its singing, as did the song leader in the youth movements.

Common experience prompted new melodies that contributed to the

Palmach experience and to group identity. Many songs were written in the wake of an important operation, camp, convention, course, or march, and by singing them the Palmach group would hark back to their common memories. The Chizbatron army performing troupe contributed a great deal to the institutionalization and dissemination of the Sabra-Palmach culture of song.

After the War of Independence, the youth movements adopted the Palmach songs and thus became partners in the war experience, seeing it from the Palmach point of view (since most of the army songs were written by Palmach songwriters). In the introduction to a songbook put out by Ha-Noar Ha-Oved "on the eve of the new year 5709 of our liberty," the editor, Moshe Mosinzon, wrote: "Many, many of our comrades have fallen. The fallen have granted the nation its life. And so for there to be a nation, its youth must be youth, and for it to be youth—it must sing."[29]

The War of Independence led to a great flowering of Hebrew song culture among the entire Israeli elite. The victory and the establishment of the state produced songs of heroism and love of the homeland, and the mass loss generated melancholy songs and laments for the fallen soldiers, which were sung at memorial ceremonies. The institutionalization of civilian life and the disappointment following the Palmach's disbandment led to songs of longing and military and national nostalgia that became an important element in the Israeli culture of nostalgia. All these songs were played on the radio, both on the Voice of Israel and on the IDF radio station. Songs such as "Bab el-Wad," "On the Negev Plains," "Dudu," and "Believe Me, the Day Will Come" became national anthems of a sort and were sung with great enthusiasm at every festive occasion.

In the 1950s many of the popular songs were collected into songbooks for preschools and schools, for youth movements, for cultural institutions, and for kibbutzim. These books contributed to the canonization of the songs and the institutionalization of public singing, making it an important element of the new national tradition. These same years saw the establishment of many singing groups, and countless public song nights were organized.

The words of the songs, expressing love and longing for the land and national hope, as well as their simple melodies, gave these "homeland songs" the character and role of Zionist religious hymns. They were national gospel songs that played on the most delicate strings of the Israeli soul and left the heart with a feeling of sweet wistfulness and the sense of a common fate.

For the veterans of the Palmach, the post-1948 ritual of public singing at gatherings of the "old boys" was important in shaping generational memory, and during this period many songs by Palmach songwriters were added to the repertoire. In singing together the former Palmachniks found some comfort for their common sorrow, a kind of fraternal lament for a lost childhood and for comrades who would not return. "And after the marches, the wars, the loss, the sorrow, and the awful beauty that refuses to end and conceals scars and agonies that will not heal, these songs, which seek with all their power to save the bygone beauty, have returned," wrote Sabra poet Natan Yonatan.[30]

The songs of the 1950s were also part of the national socialization mechanism for the newly arrived immigrants—with the exception of the immigrants from the Islamic world, who remained loyal to Oriental sounds and ancestral melodies. Through the songs the immigrants learned new words, experienced Israeli togetherness, and adopted the national memory. The place of song in Israeli socialization is testified to by the fact that even the IDF instituted public singing on its bases as part of its training program, under the supervision of the cultural officers of the training command. The army magazine *Ba-Machaneh* reported in one of its 1950 issues that "the composer-instructor Dan Aharonovich endeavors in his trips to different bases to foster the educational aspect of instilling folk songs and military marching songs among army people."[31]

The development of Hebrew song also contributed a great deal to the development of the Israeli entertainment culture. The Sabra public singing that evolved in the youth movements and in the Palmach before and immediately after the establishment of the state was polished and disseminated in Israeli culture during the 1950s and 1960s by artists who had served in the IDF performance troupes in 1948. The army entertainment troupes and the civilian equivalents that followed in their wake, as well as kibbutz singing groups, also contributed. This music was received enthusiastically by the public as part of the acceptance of Sabra culture as the dominant Israeli culture. The songwriters of the period contributed dozens of new works to the national repertoire, all of them with a musical redolence similar to that of the songs of the earlier period, consciously and unconsciously creating an Israeli musical style that was popular until the beginning of the 1980s.[32]

THE CAMPFIRE

One manifestation of the Israeli culture of the circle was the gathering of pioneers and members of Ha-Shomer around the campfire for conversation, song, dance, and food. The campfire was a source of vital warmth in the cold nights of the far-flung areas of the Land of Israel, but it also served as a ritual means of unification and contained, as in many other cultures, a store of romantic symbols. These gatherings around the campfire were so loved by the pioneers that they created a tradition of their own, called the *kumzitz*. The source of the word is a Yiddish expression meaning literally "friend, come sit for a while," and figuratively "come celebrate."

Like the hora, the Sabra campfire culture was inherited from the pioneers, but the Sabras molded it to their own needs and made it a key element of their own communal culture. The practice of building a campfire and sitting around it began in the youth movements as a leisure activity in a resource-poor country. The youth movement members would make their fires in vacant lots and in fields adjacent to the new Hebrew cities. But only in the Palmach (beginning with the training camps in the Mishmar Ha-Emek woods in the summer of 1941, and afterward in other camps) did sitting around the campfire become a kind of rite of youth, togetherness, and nostalgia, symbolizing Sabraism. The campfire was the center of the life of the Palmach platoon and company. The company commander would give a talk next to the campfire, and soldiers would read selections from works of literature, nonfiction, and poetry. The "Old Man" (Yitzchak Sadeh) would occasionally appear at one of the campfires and "shoot off cadenced, short sentences, quarried from the rock of the nation's history and experience."[33]

The ritual aspect of the *kumzitz* was evident in its collective, ecstatic, and romantic character and in its unstated ceremonial rules, which included traditional roles: the leader of the public singing, the teller of jokes and *chizbatim,* the expert at building the cooking fire, and most important, the coffee maker,[34] who knew the precise amount of hot liquid to pour into the empty tin cans and who was master of the technique of heating the water (which had to reach the boiling point twice), flavoring the coffee with marjoram and coriander, and manipulating the pot until the coffee developed the requisite head of foam.[35]

The tradition of the *kumzitz,* described with great fondness in Sabra writings, symbolized and reinforced Sabra togetherness through several complementary elements. First, the preparation of the campfire and the *kumzitz* food required cooperation. Second, the fire burning in the dark seemed to detach the celebrating group from the world, creating an atmosphere of intimacy. Third, like dancing the hora, sitting cross-legged on the ground in a circle, shoulder to shoulder, around a common source of warmth and light produced closeness and fraternity. Avidly eating with the hands from a single kettle, sipping coffee from a single pot (the Arab coffeepot became one of the ritual articles of the *kumzitz*) cultivated a romanticism of primal brotherhood.

Alongside its importance as a means of unifying the ranks and creating a way of life, the *kumzitz* was significant in Sabra culture as a rite of nature. Collecting twigs for the fire, sitting around the fire under the open sky far from any urban center, baking potatoes and pita bread on the glowing coals, roasting a chicken on an improvised grill, eating ravenously with the hands, slurping the thick coffee made in the portable pot out of tin cans like the Bedouin—all these elements of the *kumzitz* created the image of a tribe of hunters and gatherers, people of nature meeting in the evening to feast and rejoice in the gains of the day. The *kumzitz* was in this sense a ritual of romantic assimilation with nature, of nativeness and of combat. It reinforced the Palmach image of fighters for whom the wilds were home, like the mythological figures in world folklore (for instance, Robin Hood and Davy Crockett).

The "pantheistic" meaning of the *kumzitz* is also revealed in the tradition of pilfering supplies for it—the *sechiva*. A successful *kumzitz,* according to Sabra tradition, was one in which the food had not been purchased, but rather, was "collected."

In the kibbutz and moshav, the youth movements, the *hachsharot,* and the Palmach platoons, the Sabras learned and perfected the Bedouin techniques and traditions of collection, cooking, and eating in the field. They learned how to identify herbs and how to build ovens from mud and cooking stoves from stones. This also strengthened the generational image of the Sabras as at home in their homeland.

The *kumzitz* was so popular that it became an inseparable part of the mythological image and the folklore of the Palmach and the Sabra. The Sabras themselves contributed to this, since they frequently used the campfire as one of the symbols identifying their generation.[36] It is no coincidence that the campfire song "The Finjan," written by Chaim Cheffer, became one of the best-loved and most popular songs in Sabra culture, and in fact, in all of Israeli society, which adopted the *kumzitz* as part of its national culture. Nor was it a coincidence that Yitzchak Sadeh's regular column in *Al Ha-Mishmar,* later published in book form, was called "Around the Campfire." The symbolic importance of the Palmach campfire can also be found in the organization's emblem—under the stalks of wheat and the sword is the legend "Its campfire will not be extinguished."

In the wake of the rite of the Palmach campfire, the holiday of Lag Be-Omer, whose campfires symbolize those of Bar Kochba and his rebels against the Romans, became the holiday of Sabraism. This was the holiday most loved by the young Israeli natives, the time when everyone sat in circles around the fires, eating with their hands and singing Hebrew songs to the accompaniment of the accordion, recorder, drum, or harmonica. Thus they recalled the rebel leader, the hero of the Jewish people's mythical war, whose descendant the Sabra was.

The Group in Discourse and Language

THE *CHEVREMAN*

Pioneer culture had many words to designate the unified community. The counselor in the He-Halutz Ha-Tza'ir movement was addressed as "comrade" and in Ha-Shomer Ha-Tza'ir he was called "brother." The first cooperative settlements were called *kevutzot,* "groups," before the adoption of the now common form of the same root, *kibbutzim.* Many of the names of Zionist organizations and institutions included the adjective "united." The newsletter of the first commune in Beitania was not coincidentally called *Kehilateinu,* "Our Community." The ubiquitous term *chaver,* which means "member" and "comrade" as well as, literally, "friend," made all members of a movement, party, or kibbutz into comrades and friends as well. While the use of "comrade" or an equivalent is common in many cultures of socialist orientation, it would seem that in pioneer culture the emotional connotation of "friendship" was an important sense of the word, designating the traditional Jewish principle of the mutual responsibility of all Jews for each other. Similar use was made of the word "brother."

Sabra culture also had linguistic markers for solidarity and sociability. Youth movements had special names for their chapter houses that designated the close relation of their members. A chapter of Ha-Machanot Ha-Olim was called a *chug* (circle or club); in Ha-Shomer Ha-Tza'ir it was called a *ken* (nest) or *eda* (community). In Ha-Noar Ha-Oved the chapter was a *kevutza* (group) and in the Scouts it was an *achva* (brotherhood). Sabra language was also rich in cheering hoorays and in intimate nicknames and diminutives.

The Sabras absorbed the pioneer expressions of solidarity and sociability and added more of its own, with an element of youthful "insider" humor. These were variations on *chaver* and its Arabic equivalents:

chevreh, chevres, habub, ya habibi, saheb, sahbi, jam'a. More than any other, however, this sense of Sabra sociability was expressed by the word *chevreman.* This word, which came to the Sabras through Yiddish, was much used by the pioneers.[37] It was adopted by the Sabras and became so common in their speech that it came to symbolize Israeli Sabraism as a whole. While the pioneers used it to mean "a good guy" or "a friendly (or sometimes, idealistic) person," in Sabra discourse it gained a broader meaning—a person who was always ready to take on tasks for the good of the group, a person to be trusted, and above all else, a person who was pivotal to his group, the "life of the party" or the "human dynamo."

The *chevreman,* the "group guy," was the person who exhibited all the Sabra social traits and values: extroversion, activism, friendship, readiness to help everyone (in an effort to be recognized as a good person). He liked to have fun and tried to impress his peers and get attention. He was playful, talked a lot, sparked those around him, kept up morale (for example, by leading public singing). He was the first to volunteer to organize a campfire or get-together and was a joker and noisemaker. These traits made the *chevreman* a well-loved figure in Sabra culture and the instrumental leader of the group—although not the expressive or charismatic leader, a responsibility that required a certain amount of self-restraint, gravity, and distance.

The word *dugri* and the straight talk that it designates indicated, in addition to the code of purposefulness, a code of true friendship in which all barriers are lowered. The Sabra's spoken language stands out in its informality and impoliteness, but especially in its lack of words of authority and respect. It has none of the protocol of class discourse (forms of address, apologies, allusions, terms of respect) and few titles referring to age or rank. *Dugri* talk reflected the family atmosphere and shared fate of the Sabra generation and reinforced the atmosphere of communal cohesion. It found its most notable expression in army language. In the Palmach and the IDF officers were generally addressed in a friendly, informal way by first name and without any of the usual military forms of address such as "sir" or "commander."

It is interesting to note in this context that in some kibbutzim, especially those associated with Ha-Shomer Ha-Tza'ir, children addressed their parents by their first names. This phenomenon may also be a function of the lack of an aristocracy and thus the lack of a tradition of protocol and symbols of class hierarchy. It should also be mentioned that in the years preceding and for several years after the establishment of the state, the weakness, newness, and lack of institutionalization of official frameworks also contributed to the informality that characterized Sabra speech.

HOW'S IT GOING?

One of the cultural expressions of the Sabra buddy spirit was the joyful, loud ritual of encountering friends and acquaintances. This greeting contained three complementary elements expressing sociability. First was the greeting *ahlan,* which served like a code for opening the social interaction. *Ahlan,* like other greetings in other cultures, was not just a greeting but a marker—"one of ours." The second element was the slap on the back, which had two important components—the warmth of the body, expressing warmth of feeling, and the informality inherent in this physical act, conveying the directness of the encounter. The third element was the content of the conversation—fresh gossip about the doings of the other members of the group. The linguistic code for this conversation was the expression *ma nishma*—"what's up," or "how's it going?"

Ma nishma has its equivalents in other languages, but the literal meaning of the phrase is "what is heard?" indicating the pattern of disseminating social information, which was passed by word of mouth among friends. The collection of up-to-date information about "the guys" in dialogue, group conversation, and letters was indeed a basic element of Sabra culture, and says something about the quasi-family connection among the Sabras. The exchange of impressions about one's friends was also a status symbol indicating proximity to the center of events ("I'm in the know") and a broad range of social connections.

Another important element in the encounter between Sabras was the discovery of a common acquaintance from school, from the youth movement, or from the *hachshara.* Discovering a common acquaintance (a frequent occurrence because of the overlap of the Sabra organizations) was an efficient means of creating immediate connection between two Sabras who did not know each other—it was a subject for avid discussion and almost a family tie.

FUNNY GUYS

Slang is produced everywhere there is ongoing use of spoken language, but sociolinguistic research has shown that intensive life within a group is fertile ground for the growth of particularly rich slang. Slang is important to a small group because it sharpens its identity, sustains shared experiences, and creates a code of intimacy. Since slang contains an element of humor, it also provides, as jokes do, a safety valve for the release of tension. This is the reason why in times of war, revolution, and social convulsions slang blossoms (it is known, for example, that British military slang enjoyed a golden period during World War II). Israeli pioneer society—a small group whose members were in constant danger—indeed produced a rich vocabulary of slang, and most of it has been preserved in the internal lexicons put out by the kibbutzim. It is said that the speech of the Labor Battalion was extremely rich in slang, but only a bit of it has been preserved.

Sabra slang was even richer than pioneer slang. This was almost certainly because the Sabra was more fluent in spoken Hebrew than his parents and because the language was a native status symbol. Furthermore, unlike the pioneer, the Sabra lived from birth in a Hebrew-speaking communal framework and took part in war, the classic incubator of slang, where in fact most Sabra slang was created.

Since the Sabras spent much time together as young people, their language was full of the simple youthful humor of comradeship and expressions of playfulness and fun. It was not a humor of pain, understatement, or double entendres. The Sabra humor in *Pack of Lies,* in the humor columns in newsletters and periodicals, and in literature is generally characterized by the "rolling, thundering laugh of the group"—unrefined buddy humor, not the humor of fine points.

The large amount of space that youth movement and army publications devoted to slang testifies to its important place in Sabra culture. Many of the humor columns quoted Sabra slang with its characteristic codes of shared experiences and group solidarity ("We got back at him," "We showed him his place," "We got together and did it").

"TELL US, OH TELL US A *CHIZBAT*"

An important element in the Sabra linguistic tradition was the telling of tall tales, *chizbatim,* generally around the campfire. This tradition of half-true, half-imaginary stories drawn from Sabra, especially Palmach, life included manifest elements of "group work"—a kind of improvised periodic exercise in group dynamics. The *chizbat* teller was something like a tribal medium or oracle who focused the group's attention and elicited common associations, memories, and humor. The group motif was prominent in *chizbatim,* whose popularity was largely due to the Sabra slang and humor that were unique to them. At their center is a cunning gang, fooling all those around them and laughing at themselves. The *chiz-bat*, unlike a fictional tale, had some link to reality, to Sabra life. Its humor was Sabra humor, the characters were familiar characters of the Palmach, and the locations and events were real and historic. The *chizbat* was thus a medium through which the group talked about itself and honed its common identity.

Chizbatim were also one of the first expressions of a common Sabra tradition—nostalgic harking back to the days of the group in its youth, as noted above in the discussion of public singing. Another expression of this sentiment was *The Palmach Book*, published in 1953, which was the common nostalgic creation of the members of the generation, as was the contemporaneous *Pack of Lies*. The longing for the past—which was in fact a very recent past—did not derive only from a yearning for the old thrilling times in the drab days of institutionalization and routine; it was also prompted by a desire to preserve the spontaneous and romantic life of the group. The *chizbatim* and songs that told of the past played on the strings of the soul that all Sabras shared. The past was not just a collection of events that had occurred and ended; it was a collection of common experiences, and remembering them was a central element in the internal culture of discourse.

THE ENTERTAINMENT TROUPE

Sabra buddy humor, *chizbatim,* jokes, skits, and comic songs about the adventures of the Sabra "Hardy boys" were collected and recorded (during the war and in the 1950s), mostly by Chaim Cheffer, Dahn Ben-Amotz, Chaim Levkov, Didi Manosi, Shaul Biber, and Puchu, who were the Palmach's humorists (it was no coincidence that the collection of songs later edited by Guri and Cheffer was called *The Palmach Family*). These writers had sharp anthropologists' eyes and ears that were attentive to events in young Sabra society. They skillfully gathered wildflowers of folklore and arranged them into a humoristic tradition. This tradition became the property of the public as a whole, who saw it as an expression of a deep-rooted, effervescent Hebrew culture.

The Palmach way of life was memorialized by the Chizbatron, the Palmach's "theater" troupe. It was largely the work of this group that made Sabra life into public property.[38] The Chizbatron was established by Chaim Cheffer in February 1948. There were other army entertainment troupes that were influenced by it, and their heirs in the IDF were the Nachal troupe and the troupes of the three major army commands. All of them fulfilled a role that went beyond entertainment. As in many cases in artistic history, a combination of circumstances—the desperate social need for entertainment of the troops and the participation of some exceptionally talented people—meant that the Chizbatron and the other troupes played a decisive part in the creation and institutionalization of the Sabra way of life and in shaping the culture of "a people in uniform"— a people nourished by youthful, soldierly humor and folklore.

The army troupes created a unique entertainment genre that included skits, *chizbatim,* and songs about army life, the Palmach, and youth movement campfires and marches, as well as dances and pantomimes in the spirit of kibbutz celebrations. Their actors played characters and situations from the army, *hachsharot,* and the pioneer youth movements,[39] so their programs were very popular among the Yishuv "nobility"—the Sabras included. "With an army troupe," one critic wrote, "there is no 'show' and no 'play' but rather a 'program.' In the two years of our army's existence they have created a real 'school' in miniature of army troupes. When, somewhere out there, someone says 'tonight the troupe is coming,' everyone knows in advance more or less what the troupe will bring with it."[40]

The manifestly Sabra-buddy nature of the Chizbatron and its heirs derived not only from the program content, but also from the fact that the troupe itself was a Sabra gang—young Ashkenazi men and women in their twenties with native Sabra accents, dressed like Palmachniks, singing songs in youth movement and Palmach style, and dancing the hora to an accordion and harmonica. To the audience, the troupe was a *hachshara,* a youth movement chapter, or a Palmach platoon singing and dancing on the stage. It could be said that the troupes institutionalized Sabra life in the same way that William Cody—Buffalo Bill—and his troupe had institutionalized the American pioneer a century earlier through their Wild West Show.

Sabra Friendship in War

THE BROTHERHOOD OF FIGHTERS

The War of Independence had a decisive effect on Sabra friendship. It produced a brotherhood of fighters of great emotional power that was born out of the unique life-and-death experience of the war. Facing death and a common enemy together created almost a blood bond that was based on fear and collective victory over fear.

One of the manifestations of the sentiment of brotherhood was the altruistic act on the battlefield. The charged psychological situation of engagement in battle produced unique demonstrations of assistance to and concern for one's fellow soldiers. Acts of selflessness under fire are etched in the common memory and become myths in whose light soldiers of all cultures are educated. Battle is described in the national tradition of many nations as a test in which the real, magnanimous character of the individual is revealed—an hour in which masks are lifted.

The importance of altruism as a value is disclosed in the loaded term "cover," common in Israeli war literature. Ostensibly this is a technical military term for providing cover fire for another soldier or unit, but its high frequency in texts and sometimes the literary context in which it appears show that it connotes a code of mutual accountability. It is hardly surprising, then, that the order "Privates retreat—commanders cover," pronounced by Shimon Alfasi during the battle of Kastel, became a motto of the Palmach fighters. These words brought together the myth of the commander and the myth of the comradeship of the soldiers.

One notable manifestation of the brotherhood of fighters was rescuing the wounded. The best-known example is the battle of Nebi Yosha, in which twenty-eight Palmach soldiers were killed on their way to evacuate a wounded comrade. The frequency of rescues in Palmach legend, usually involving great personal danger, contributed to the mythological image of the fighting Sabra as a loyal friend prepared to sacrifice his life for his fellow soldier.

The evacuation of wounded soldiers from the battlefield is a routine matter in all modern armies and is rehearsed during the soldier's training. Still, under the influence of the post–World War II novels and Hollywood movies, it has become a symbolic and ritual expression of national solidarity and lofty altruism. The soldier who risks his life to save his comrade brings battlefield altruism to its acme and becomes a hero.

Under the influence of poetry and prose, combat heritage and memorial literature, the principle of not abandoning a wounded man on the battlefield (or abandoning a prisoner in enemy hands) in time became one of the most sacred mores of the IDF. Rescuing wounded men was not only the highest form of heroism but a supreme obligation. Like other IDF values and myths, its significance extended beyond the military. Like ceremonies conducted for fallen soldiers, it served as a unifying mechanism that broadcast to the nation: "See, we are one united family, in which every Israeli is responsible for every other."

The Palmach fostered comradeship among fighters and made it into a fundamental value of its military culture, inspired by the myth of the "brotherhood of the trenches" in Europe, which achieved almost metaphysical significance in the period between the world wars. The value of comradeship appears in the Palmach anthem and in the Yizkor prayer for the Palmach fallen ("The Palmach will remember the long line of fighters whose names will remain forever as exemplars of supreme sacrifice, faithful devotion, and pure friendship"), in the battalion newsletters, in the orders of the day, as well as in *hachsharot* newsletters, brigade albums, combat heritage and memorial literature, and especially in *Alon Ha-Palmach*. Yitzchak Sadeh's article titled "The Comradeship of Fighters" is a kind of Palmach doxology on this subject, and was therefore reprinted many times.

The value of comradeship is especially prominent in the war songs and poems of Chaim Guri, Chaim Cheffer, and O. Hillel, which are characterized by the words "my brother" and "my friend" and the motif "we two are from the same village," or "from the same tent." Significantly, the dead are also sometimes presented—especially by Chaim Guri—as a united group of friends:

> We will come back, we will meet, returning like scarlet flowers.
> You'll know us at once. It's the silent mountain platoon.
> Then we'll bloom—when in the mountains the shriek of the last bullet
> falls still.[41]

The fallen soldier is part of the "we," "one of us"—Uri and Gadi and Alik and Dudu who "went with us on the tough march / patrolled the border with us."[42] The songs of melancholy and comradeship lamented the loss of the common friend and acknowledged the common pain of the group that had lost some of its members, the common memory, and the sense of guilt of the comrades who had remained alive.

The essence of the Palmach's myth of comradeship appears in Chaim Guri's "The Song of Friendship," which in time became part of the national liturgy, and also in O. Hillel's "The Friendship of the Fighters":

> . . . O Spirit of Friendship!
> Death shall not crush you,
> Nor hordes of foreign besiegers!
> It is stronger than death!
> It is mightier than any army.
> It is greater, too, than our young army. . . . [43]

The ethic of comradeship is also reflected in the memorials to the fallen soldiers of 1948 and 1956. In general, the soldiers' names are listed neither in order of nor with mention of their ranks, and many are designated by intimate nicknames. Many of the memorials bear the Biblical passage: "In their lives and in their death they were not divided."

Wrapped in layers of poems, stories, legends, articles, and speeches, the value of the comradeship of fighters gradually became a national myth, particularly after the War of Independence, and this reinforced its social power even further. Like other Sabra characteristics we have examined, the Sabra fighter influenced the myth of friendship and was also influenced by it. The myth implanted in him recognition of the moral importance of self-sacrifice and altruism, and awareness of the expectations society had of him. They induced him to behave with self-sacrifice and generosity in the wars to come. But this behavior was itself a mythological accelerator—his actions reinforced the myth with new stories, set new standards, and honed the social expectations of the following generations who read the memorial and war literature.

The long and difficult war was a generational birthing that produced brothers in arms. Other elements in this birth process were the chasm that opened between those who had experienced the war and those who had not—including relatives and loved ones who had remained at the rear—and the alienation that followed as a result. Studies of a number of armies have shown that the shared trauma and the painful and exhilarating memories create a sense of common fate among war veterans. "The War of Independence, Israel's longest war and the one with the largest number of casualties, was the most potent experience that we members of the generation experienced as individuals and as the collective," wrote Dan Horowitz in his autobiographical book.[44] His perception has been confirmed by conversations with many other members of his generation. The 1948 generation lost many members during the war (1,050 of the Palmach's 7,000 soldiers). The soldiers bore a common trauma. Some of them had difficulty adjusting to the drab routine days after the war and grasped at bittersweet nostalgia. The experience of the war became an essential part of their personalities, and connections to comrades who had shared in the experience were imprinted on both personal and collective memory. "Here we fought together on cliffs and rocky fields / Here we became a single family," wrote Chaim Guri in his poem "Bab el-Wad."[45]

The familial fellowship of the Sabra fighters was strengthened by mourning for fallen friends and acquaintances. Close ties between the fighters, many of whom had been part of the same group of friends since childhood and had passed through the Sabra organizations together, made the death of comrades as emotionally intense as the loss of close family members: "I am going around like a madman. I cannot accept the death of Musa, Sefi, Dubon, Pilon, and Yisrael. That is when dear and good comrades fall next to me day by day. But when news of a friend of ours reaches me, it is as if a part of my body had been taken from me," wrote one soldier.[46]

In addition to organizational solidarity, the brotherhood of the trenches, and the brotherhood of mourning—which are not unique to the Palmach or to the War of Independence—there are other factors of a unique cultural nature that magnified the sense of family in the Sabra military organizations. The first was the presence of women soldiers in the combat units.[47] Their presence in the outposts, bases, and border strongholds blurred the distinction between the military and civilian worlds and gave the units a sense that they were fighting within their homes. The presence of women also softened the tough, male side of the military organizations, and in particular created an atmosphere similar to those of the youth movements and kibbutzim. Furthermore, the men and women in the Palmach units knew each other from youth movements and *hachsharot*. The sense of family that the presence of women evoked is described in a memorial book for a fallen Palmach soldier:

> Something from the Biblical period was re-created in the relations of the woman to the fighting man. Before each combat action the girls accompany the boys and stand as if frozen, praying in their trembling hearts that the boys will return safely. For a long while after the soldiers leave the camp they still stand caught in their dream and their inner prayer, gazing out into the distance where anger lies. Something similar takes place when the exhausted and weary warriors return from the battlefield. All those verses in the Bible that tell about the dancing of the women at the return of the warriors. . . . Who can find an expression for what they feel in their hearts when they care for the wounded? What artist can commit to paper the feminine movement of the hand touching the button of one of the fighters who has returned from the engagement healthy and whole? Experiences deeper than the sea happen in a camp like this.[48]

The integration of women into male units continued in the IDF (in particular in the Nachal), which became the heir of the Palmach and an important context for the forging of Sabra identity.

FRIENDS TELL ABOUT THE FALLEN

As with most of the myths of the fighting Sabra, the literature of 1948 and the tradition of memorializing the fallen played important and perhaps key roles in the creation of the myth of the Palmach fraternity. The eulogizers went to great lengths in praising the effervescent Sabra brotherhood that the fallen soldier had been part of and described the group as a close family: "And many of them fell as if torn out of the circle of life of that sturdy friendship that all shared," wrote Anda Pinkerfeld-Amir in one memorial book.[49]

The fraternity of the Sabras was also emphasized in the joint memorial booklets issued by Sabra institutions. The subtitles of these booklets— "the words of friends," or "friends tell about the fallen"—were emblems of friendship. Moreover, the publication of a memorial booklet by friends became something like a cult practice, with the same symbolic meaning as the building of a cairn (a common form of memorialization in Israeli culture). The personal contribution of each participant expressed spontaneous solidarity with a comrade and the unity of the group.

The memorialization of the fallen, in which all the soldier's friends and acquaintances participated, symbolized not only Sabra solidarity but also the solidarity of the mourning nation, expressed in phrases such as "the family of mourning" and "memorial to the sons." The large number of memorial booklets, as well as other memorialization projects such as monuments and cairns, gave personal grief a public dimension and created a sense of the nation mourning as one for its sons, as the epigraph of one of the memorial anthologies states: "When a son of parents falls, his memory belongs to the entire nation, which shares the fate of its myriad fighters of the past and of the future."[50]

Epilogue

The Sabras portray themselves in their writings in sets of dichotomies. Fierce Zionist idealism and total conformity to the values of the founding fathers coexist with a penchant for challenging the establishment and developing channels of cultural distinctiveness and independence. The profound seriousness of revolutionaries is superimposed on the mischievous and defiant facetiousness of youth. Lofty pathos in writing accompanies relentless directness in conversation. On one side is the anti-intellectual ethos of the farmer and soldier; on the other a highly developed culture of colloquy and book reading. Their speech is *dugri* and ungrammatical, but they display a well-honed ability to express themselves in writing. They adhere to a communalist ethic, yet they segregate themselves from other groups. They disdain the "exilic" new immigrant, but also identify with his suffering as a Jew and mobilize themselves to bring him to Israel and absorb him. "We are the Palmach," they sing arrogantly, yet their heroes are humble and secret. They create a military culture and appreciate military qualities, but hate war and militarism. Adopting the symbols of Arabism, they disdain and shun the Arab and his culture. The asceticism of khaki goes hand in hand with the swaggering fashion of native and military status symbols.

Some may see this dichotomization as hypocrisy or perhaps as a lacuna between norm and practice. I believe such an explanation to be incorrect, or at least insufficient. As this book shows, these are not necessarily contradictions; they are to a large extent complementary traits or values that characterize a complex culture swinging between the needs of the collective and the needs of the individual, between Jewishness and anti-Jewishness, between utopianism and pragmatism, between innovation and institutionalization, and between war and peace.

These pairs of contradictions that characterized the Sabra culture bring to mind its two best-known figures—Yigal Allon and Moshe Dayan. There is a famous photograph, taken at Hanita, in which the two of them stand on either side of the "old man" (Yitzchak Sadeh, founder of the Palmach), who embraces both as if they were two beloved sons. These two Sabra warriors, native-born Israelis who emerged from the same cultural background, were in fact two entirely different types of men, but the melding of their two personalities is perhaps the essence of the portrait of the Sabra.

From the Zionist point of view, the Sabra is without a doubt a phenomenal success story. The secret of his success probably lies in the socialization that shaped his personality, and especially in four of the many factors examined in this book.

The first factor is the enlistment of most of the best minds—including creative minds in various fields—in the service of Zionist propaganda. This not only created a great chorus that sang out in unison, but also contributed to the aestheticizing of Zionist ideology and granted it spiritual depth. The Sabras were not exposed to shallow propaganda and the rhetoric of the street, but to the idealistic verses of sensitive poets, to the visionary literature of great writers, and to impassioned speakers noted for their broad horizons and social concern. The ideological creations of artists and thinkers of intellectual and moral distinction fortified the emotional mantle of social values and imbued them with glory and sanctity.

The second factor is the tight linkage between the emerging reality in Israel and the utopian vision of Zionism. The reality provided repeated confirmation that the utopian vision was indeed coming true and that the Jewish people were, in an almost mystical way, entering the era of the "Third Temple." The speed with which the Zionist enterprise was building its economic, demographic, and military foundation, climaxing with the establishment of the state and the absorption of mass immigration, confirmed the revolutionary utopianism of the Sabras and reinforced their faith in the Zionist vision. In a brief period of only thirty years the Jewish immigrants had succeeded in reviving their ancient language, creating a social framework based on utopian principles (the kibbutz), setting up an effective defense force and an agricultural and urban system, absorbing waves of immigrants, and establishing an independent state. The word "miracle" gained a very concrete meaning.

The great shock Israeli society experienced a generation later in the Yom Kippur War, despite the victory achieved, testifies to the great importance of the linkage between Zionist ideology and reality for the Israelis. It would seem that while Israeli society was traumatized in 1973 by its heavy losses, it was traumatized even more by the rebuke that this event constituted to its fundamental myths (the Jewish people's fortitude, the inferiority of Amalek, and so on).

The third factor was the great importance attached to educating youth in the values of the Zionist leadership. Everyone taught and everyone directed their gaze to the younger generation, especially to the young people in the agricultural settlements and the students at the gymnasia, and many of the resources of the Yishuv and the young state were allotted to education and guidance.

Teaching school or preschool was a position of prestige not only in the agricultural settlements but in all parts of society, and teachers were regarded as pursuing a national mission of central importance. The political and spiritual leadership took an interest in the younger generation and maintained constant contact with it out of a mixture of paternalism, affection, and admiration. The many conversations that Berl Katznelson and Yitzchak Tabenkin, two of the most important Zionist leaders, had with the members of youth movements and the relationship the prominent poet Avraham Shlonsky developed with the younger generation of Sabra poets demonstrate this. Most important, however, the educational system did not operate as a separate institution detached from other social institutions, as is the practice today. Teachers were not the only people teaching—so were counselors at the kibbutzim and youth movements and commanders in the Palmach and army; entertainers and artists considered it a duty to instill values in the next generation, even without pay.

The efforts of the Zionist "gardeners" to raise Sabras in the image of the Zionist utopia would not have been successful had the Sabras not sprouted in a period of faith in the power of social ideas and ideals and belief in the power of the individual to shape reality. This period, in which human evil plunged to unprecedented depths, was also an era of altruism and, especially, of great innocence. The educators of the Sabra believed with perfect faith in their duty and ability to mold his personality, and for this reason they devoted themselves wholeheartedly to the task.

The fourth factor was the success of the socializers and social frameworks in fulfilling the spiritual needs of the youth. In the kibbutzim, the youth movements, the Palmach, and the army as well, the establishment deftly inculcated young people with Zionist values by creating a sense of fun and a sense of pride. This was done in several ways. First, it created a youth society with great autonomy, which provided a sense of freedom and lack of authority. Second, it encouraged a sense of internal solidarity by minimizing formal rules and organizational hierarchy. Third, it nurtured a sense of exclusivity and chosenness. Fourth, and most important, it created a life of adventure and romantic fascination. The camps in the heart of nature, the mobilizations for working on the kibbutzim, the hikes, the marches—all these were effective means of education precisely because they were very enjoyable for young people.

At the foundation of the Sabra culture was the pioneer culture. Nevertheless, few of the values and cultural symbols of the pioneer were accepted unmodified into Sabra culture. The Sabras elaborated upon the pioneer culture, fortified it, and sometimes gave it a different cast that expressed their generational uniqueness. Critic David Cana'ani wrote of the fictional heroes of S. Yizhar, the greatest of the Sabra writers: "They say amen to the convoy and blaze it a trail; its road is their road and its goal is their goal. Nevertheless, there is in this way of theirs something of the partisan guerrilla—both in the convoy and to its side."[1] These words capture the essence of the complex relationship between the pioneer and Sabra cultures. Perhaps one could say that the founding fathers wrote the score and their children played the music on the instruments of a new orchestra and reworked the melody into a folk tune.

The anti-Diaspora ethos stands, openly and invisibly, at the base of almost every myth, norm, symbol, and ritual that characterizes Sabra culture. The link between Sabraism and the ideal of the new Jew (the opposite of the exilic Jew) is almost taken for granted and is not at all surprising, since Zionism wished to create a new Jew and the younger generation that grew up in Israel was expected and educated to realize the revolutionary utopia. The different meanings contained in the symbols of Sabraism not only reveal the influence of the anti-exile ethos, but also show how and to what depth this ethos seeped—sometimes unconsciously—into different layers of Sabra culture, such as dress, hairstyle, and language. A single custom could simultaneously symbolize several objects of the anti-Diaspora ethos—which gave it a special popularity. The tradition of making difficult hikes through the desert, for example, declared the physical prowess of the Sabra—the opposite of the stereotypical feebleness of the exilic Jew—as well as the Sabra's knowledge of the land, as opposed to the exilic Jew's rootlessness.

The manifold connection between the anti-Diaspora ethos and the entire set of Sabra symbols illustrates the way in which a new culture comes into being in a new society, especially in a revolutionary society. The central ethos is a kind of ideological trunk that sends out new branches and leaves, such as language, dress, and humor.

When the different variables are put together into the formula that shaped Sabra culture, what becomes apparent, alongside the anti-Diaspora ethos, is the enormous contribution of key Sabra figures to the formulation and development of this culture. This confirms sociologist Karl Mannheim's view that the generational unit usually crystallizes around a nucleus composed of the best of the generation, which develops the new self-perceptions and animates the people around it.[2] The nucleus group of the Sabra generation was composed of three types.

The first type were the cultural "copywriters," people of particularly high intelligence, sharp social instincts, and in particular the ability to create art from popular materials. These were the writers, poets, painters, songwriters, singers, and entertainers who grew in the incubators of the agricultural settlements, and especially in the Palmach. Chaim Cheffer, for example, did not invent the tradition of the campfire and the coffeepot, but the song he wrote about the Palmach campfire so well expressed the tastes and sensibilities of the members of his generation that it became a significant part of the tradition of the coffee pot and the singalong, and so contributed to its development. The poems, stories, songs, tall tales, and essays published in the newspapers of the youth movements, the kibbutzim, the Palmach, and the army and performed by the army entertainment troupes made a decisive contribution to the dissemination, perpetuation, and institutionalization of Sabra culture.

The second type were the cultural bellwethers—the charismatic figures with initiative and prominence who internalized and radicalized the cultural characteristics and so pushed the boundaries of the culture. These were generally admired commanders such as Yigal Allon, Moshe Dayan, Yitzchak Rabin, Uri Ben-Ari, Meir Har-Zion, and others who became exemplary figures.

The third type were those who died in battle and possessed manifestly Sabra characters. In their deaths they became myths. The historian George

Mosse has called them "the living fallen." Hannah Szenes, who herself became a cultural lighthouse after her death, described them as follows:

> There are stars whose light reaches the ground
> Only when they themselves are lost and are no more.
> There are people the spark of whose memory lights
> When they themselves are no longer among us.
> These lights glow in the dark of the night—
> It is they who light a person's way. . . . [3]

Among the fallen are those who became "sparks" because of a special act of heroism, but most joined the collective memory through the memorial anthologies published in their honor. Talented youngsters such as Jimmy (Aharon Shemi), Yechiam Weitz, Chaim Ben-Dor, Zohara Levtov, Zurik Dayan, Tuvia Kushiner, Nechemia Shein, and Danny Mas, who left behind many letters and writings—most of them dealing with Sabra life—were greatly admired by the members of their generation because of their noble images, which were burnished and polished in the memorial literature. In their deaths they "bequeathed" to the members of their generation not only life but also the values and cultural style in which they lived. Many young people who read their writings imitated them— they wrote poems for their desk drawers; hid their feelings; adopted a nationalist worldview, a spirit of volunteerism, and a love of the landscape. Jimmy, Yechiam Weitz, and others like them produced many other Jimmies and Yechiams, not only in their generation but also in the generation that came twenty or thirty years after them.

Sociologically and psychologically, the Sabra was indeed a disciple who wished to please his rabbi and even to surpass him. It is important to emphasize, however, that he was not an overzealous disciple and did not always submit to his teacher. His attitude toward the founding generation was a complex one, based, on the one hand, on a sense of inferiority and awe in the face of the spiritual and charismatic image of the founding father, and on the other hand, on the native Sabra's sense of cultural superiority over the immigrant father—the superiority of the "new Hebrew" who had realized the Zionist utopia over those who still possessed "exilic elements." The attitude of the fathers toward the sons was also more complex than people have tried to paint it in recent years. It was an attitude of mastery and paternalism diluted with admiration for their children, the "first fruits." On the one hand they supervised and tracked the behavior of the younger generation (until the youngsters got sick of it), and on the other hand they gave them great leeway. Young people lived on kibbutzim, on training farms, and in youth group centers in independent frameworks, guided other young people, commanded army battalions and even regiments, and established new settlements. The dual nature of the pioneer attitude toward the Sabra derived also from the immigrant syndrome. The immigrant, who has sought a new homeland, aspires to see his child take root in the country of immigration and adopt a new identity, yet at the same time he is pained by the child's disconnection from the cultural roots of the old homeland.

It would seem that the Sabra, who fulfilled the role of the institutionalizer of the Zionist religion, also sowed—paradoxically—the seeds of its secularization, especially via the culture of jest he created. As Umberto Eco showed in *The Name of the Rose*, humor and laughter are the most dangerous of religion's enemies because they challenge the gravity of the pious believer and throw light on the naiveté lying at the foundation of the faith. Even more important, humor is based on viewing reality from a distance, and distance is the first step toward challenging dogma.

A lamina of seriousness coats most of the pioneer writings. Most Sabra texts are notable for their seriousness. However, alongside their earnestness these texts include a great measure of jest and fun, and even a glimmer of social irony. These qualities are found in youth movement songs, newspaper essays, tall tales, local jokes, slang, and even literature. While this is largely buddy humor rather than anti-establishment political humor, the very act of developing a culture of laughter is important as a source of subversion. Alongside their love of melancholy the Sabras liked to laugh wildly at themselves and their surroundings. The Sabra generation was thus the first to bring laughter into the holy Zionist sanctuary— and the first to "defile" and "secularize" it. The laughter of the Palmach led to ever-stronger waves of Israeli humor, including anti-establishment humor, making a larger and larger breach in the defensive wall of solemn Zionist idealism.

The myth of the Sabra was perhaps the most central myth of the Yishuv period. Large numbers of people spoke about the Sabra and discussed the image of the members of agricultural settlements, sometimes critically and with concern, but mostly with contentment and delight. The younger generation itself adopted the term "Sabra" into its speech and so contributed to its dissemination. Even though the base of the preoccupation with the Sabra and the phenomenon of Sabraism was the expectation that the younger generation would realize the vision of the new

Jew, it seems that what lies hidden here is a broader endeavor by the founding generation to create a social identity in a new society. Even though the Sabras were proportionally a small part of society, they were not perceived by the broader public as a marginal sector of singular aspect, but rather as representatives—in their character, style, language, and values—of the new Israeli identity. It was no accident that in the 1980s, when the Israeli value system was shaken by the trauma of the Yom Kippur War, the Sabra and his mythological image were the focus of public attack. Nor was it an accident that the many critics who came to settle accounts with the Zionist system of values first shattered the myth of the Sabra; this myth-shattering reflected the interest in dismantling the existing Israeli identity and creating a new one that was universal in character.

Mythological figures often serve as mirrors of the culture that fostered them. What culture is reflected, then, in the mirror of the Sabra myth? Many scholars and journalists in recent years have described the Sabra myth as nationalist and power-oriented, the product of militaristic propaganda with political foundations. True, it has its nationalist-chauvinist and militaristic foundations (especially that part that developed in the wake of the Sinai Campaign), characteristic of a society that lives by the sword; but to a large extent the mythological profile of the fighting Sabra is composed of manifestly anti-chauvinist and anti-militaristic elements. This is especially notable in the memorial literature, which played a major role in shaping the true Sabra and his mythological image.

Death in battle may have been conceived in metaphysical terms (for the redemption of Israel, etc.) and used to instill patriotic duty—as is common in all wars—but it was not glorified and sanctified in the manner familiar in Third World armies. Fallen Sabras may have been commemorated with saccharine and formulaic praises, but death in battle was not made into an ideal and was not given any transcendental, superhuman significance. Nor did Israeli culture develop a myth of the war experience meant to disguise the terror of war and give it legitimacy, at least not to the degree found in Europe, much less the Third World.[4] When the slogan "it is good to die for our country" was instilled in the Sabra, he was not asked to internalize that it was good to die a hero's death, but rather that death in the Land of Israel had moral significance.

Most of the Sabra memorial books and literary works on the Sabra do not portray him as a great conqueror. Rather, devotion to the homeland and to friends is primary. The Sabra is generally presented as a thinking, sensitive, even fragile character, anti-militaristic, and especially, a man of conscience. This is nowhere as unmistakable as in the widely discussed myth of the commander. The Sabra commander is not an authoritative figure who invokes dread and commands obedience, but rather an unpretentious counselor and a father to his soldiers.

Moreover, even if the fallen Sabra was described in the memorial books using sacred language, it was not a metaphysical sacredness like that of the Muslim *shaheed* or the Christian martyr. The terms "paradise," "rising of the dead," and "eternal life" are almost entirely absent from the memorial literature not only because this is a secular literature but also because death was conceived of in very down-to-earth terms and not as a passageway into a better world. The emphasis is on what the fallen did "for us," and not on the reward they or their families would get in exchange for the sacrifice they made.

Another question that arises in the discussion of the myth of the Sabra is whether the mythological image is much different from the way the Sabra really was. Since the end of the 1970s—the period of the "twilight of the gods" and the slaughter of the sacred cows of the national Zionist religion—there has been a growing tendency to portray the Sabra as a propaganda tool that had no grounding in reality. So commonplace has the connection between the terms "myth" and "Sabra" become that part of the public believes that there never was such a thing, that it was only an allegory, the product of the imagination and wishes of the founding fathers and enlisted writers and artists. "What is the myth of the Sabra?" wrote poet Yehudit Kafri in 1986 in an article typical of the period. "A gaunt reality inflated with so much air that it became a swollen balloon destined to burst; a naked truth dressed up in so many fine garments that falsehood reigns. The myth, like its sister the sacred cow, is thus best shattered."[5]

My findings completely discredit the view that the Sabra is nothing but a mythological figure, or that at most it is a tiny kernel of truth that the establishment manipulatively exaggerated far beyond its true dimensions. Certainly, the Sabras were not cut of a single cloth, and their image underwent idealization and stereotyping by the establishment and by the Sabras themselves. Nevertheless, this study proves that in the period of the Yishuv and the first years of the state there rose a young generation with a unique worldview, folklore, and Israeli style, and that a Sabra character with certain traits came into being, largely in the agricultural settlements. Moreover, analysis of Sabra texts shows that there was a fairly large congruence between the positive mythological image of the Sabra and the fundamental traits that make up the profile of his generation. The Sabras were not, of course, "Sons of the race of David who fell with sword in hand / And simple and lovable as the boy David from the family of shepherds . . ." as Uri Zvi Greenberg described them.[6] But most of the mythological traits in the figure of the Sabra are parallel or similar to the elements of the Sabra culture and of Sabra individuals themselves. For example, the mythological Sabra is rough outside and soft inside. It turns out that there is a basis (even if it is more complex than the image would have it) for this description in the Sabras. The same is true of another conspicuous trait of the mythological Sabra, his being "an oak planted on his land."

The similarity between the myth and reality is not coincidental, since the nucleus of many a myth is reality. Furthermore, as this book has shown, the myth of the Sabra and his real image had a reciprocal effect on each other. The Sabra who read the memorial literature, the battle stories, and the literature that portrayed his mythological image learned to view himself through the mythological looking glass and answered to the covert call of the myth.

When Prime Minister Yitzchak Rabin was assassinated in November 1995, everyone sang for him the song by Natan Yonatan, a member of his generation, "Where are there still men like that man?" For a moment it seemed as if the whole country was once again embracing the myth of the fair-souled Sabra—displayed so purely in the figure of Rabin. He may well have been extraordinary in the path he followed and in his contribution to the Israeli nation, but more than his being extraordinary, Rabin was an unmistakable product of his generation, the Sabra generation, with both its weaknesses and its strengths. In fact, there are many other people like "that man." They grew up as he did in the Hebrew gymnasia, in the agricultural schools, in the pioneering youth movements, the kibbutzim, the moshavim, in the Palmach, and in the first units of the Israeli army.

"The spirit of holiness this hour nests in the thick of events. . . . The divine presence finds its remedy here of all places: on our islands of the quotidian and hard labor in the holy land." So believed the poet Uri Zvi Greenberg, the author of those lines; so believed the Zionist pioneers; and so also believed their heirs, the Sabras. The Sabra indeed became a pious believer in the Zionist national religion, and the Zionist frameworks in which he was educated were like yeshivot, or houses of study, which produced Hebrew Hasidim who devoutly served their homeland. The Sabra accepted the principal doctrines of the pioneer theology as unquestioned dogma; served his rabbis, the fathers of the Labor movement; and sacrificed his life for the sanctity of the homeland. The pioneer Torah, with its myths, symbols, values, rituals, and commandments, stood at the center of the Sabra world, filled its young hearts, and percolated into its deepest spiritual longings.

In the end, as much as the Sabra tried to be a "new Jew" and distance himself from Jewish religion as his pioneer fathers commanded, this distance was only apparent. In fact, his entire being and essence spoke of Jewishness—the gatherings in youth group clubhouses, which were something like Hasidic yeshivot; the tribal solidarity and mutual responsibility; the sing-alongs and mandatory folk dancing; the Jewish myths that nourished his world; his aspiration to be learned in the pioneer doctrine; the sense of chosenness that filled him; and the tribal endogamy that separated him from the Arab *goy*—all these characterized the generation of the new Jews. They were, as their name suggests, new but at base still Jews.

The Sabra soul was fundamentally similar to the Hasidic soul that reached spiritual sublimity. The great majority of Sabra texts are accompanied by the melody of a kind of complex Zionist madrigal built on two themes. The first phrase is the great challenge that life in that period placed before its youth. As one of the Sabras wrote: "This was facing a trial. An idea often presents us with a trial. Have you already grasped it? Have you already committed yourself? Are you already a healthy person?"[7] The second phrase, reverberating no less strongly, is the sense of satisfaction and elation that these young people felt. I find the purest, most concise expression of this sense in a letter from a girl who belonged to Mahanot Ha-Olim, telling a friend of hers about the youth movement. Her words can be applied to all contexts of Sabra life:

> You asked me what the movement gives me. It is difficult for me to answer. You haven't lived in the movement, and things like this must be lived to be understood. Did you ever feel the feeling of satisfaction after reaching the peak after a long and hard climb? Or pure happiness, the happiness of creation by friends after hard and long labor when everything stood against them, fought against them, and despite this they succeeded in building and creating? Or the potent love of a barren tract of land that awakens in you the desire to embrace it all and sacrifice everything? Or the opposite—did you ever feel deep and sincere sorrow for dear friends taken from you before their time and with-

out reason? Have you ever heard a simple and potent poem that expresses joy and also sadness coming from the heart? Have you ever seen a hora of comrades uniting into a single body, dancing with enthusiasm, forgetting the world and all in it and dancing? . . .

Have you ever dreamed a dream so beautiful and so pure as the dream of a new enterprise that you will take part in establishing?

All this is what the movement gives me.[8]

Notes

Introduction

1. See, for example, A. Shapira, "A Generation in the Land" [Hebrew], *Al-pa'yim* 2 (1990): 178–203.

2. On the symbolic importance of the term "Hebrew," see J. Klausner, "Hebrew Man" [Hebrew], *Ha-Shiloach* 14 (July–December 1907): 575–77.

3. On the concept of the Hebrew, the "new Jew," as the polar opposite of the Diaspora Jew, see Y. Luidor, "Yoash," *Ha-Shiloah* 26 (January 1912): 422–25. Judah Leib Magnes called Avshalom Feinberg a "new Jew"—see A. Aharonson, "Three Years since the Death of Avshalom Feinberg" [Hebrew], *Do'ar Ha-Yom* 1 (Shevat 1920). For more on this issue, see Y. Berlovitz, "The 'New Jew' Model in Second Aliya Literature: A Proposal for a Zionist Anthropology" [Hebrew], *Alei Siah* 17–18 (1983): 54–70.

4. D. Almagor, "The Sabra Is Put in Quotation Marks" [Hebrew], *Yediot Aharonot*, 30 December 1977, A1. I would like to thank Dr. Almagor for additional information on the Sabra.

5. U. Kesari, *Memoirs for Tomorrow* [Hebrew] (Tel Aviv, 1975), 133–34.

6. Almagor, "The Sabra Is Put in Quotation Marks." Almagor quoted from *Ketuvim* 21 (16 June 1932).

7. M. Shamir, "With the Members of My Generation" [Hebrew], in *The Yalkut Ha-Re'im Book* (republication on the fiftieth anniversary of the issuing of the first collection, Jerusalem, 1992).

8. On the repugnance the native youth felt for the Diaspora and its symbols, see T. Segev, *The Seventh Million: The Israelis and the Holocaust* (New York: Hill and Wang, 1993).

9. See U. Avneri, "The Floor to the Israeli Generation!" and "Who Are These Sabras?" *Ba-Ma'avak* (September 1946).

10. See U. Avneri, "And the Canaanite Was Then in the Land" [Hebrew], in *The War of the Seventh Day* [Hebrew] (Tel Aviv, 1969); Y. Shavit, *From Hebrew to Canaanite* [Hebrew] (Tel Aviv, 1984).

11. Y. Yatziv, "Sabraism as an Ideology" [Hebrew], *Davar*, 25 September 1946.

12. On the creation of a Hebrew-native culture, see A. Even Zohar, "The Growth and Crystallization of a Local and Native Culture in the Land of Israel" [Hebrew], *Katedra* 16 (1980): 161–216.

13. A. Keinan, "Hebrews and Not Sabras" [Hebrew], *Bamat Elef*, October 1949. Republished in *Proza* in a special issue devoted to "The Literary Failure of 1948" (August–September 1977): 31.

14. On these Sabras, see R. Alboim-Dror, *Hebrew Education in Eretz Israel* [Hebrew], vol. 1 (Jerusalem, 1986), as well as her article: "He Is Approaching, He Is Coming, the New Hebrew: On the Youth Culture of the First Aliyot" [Hebrew], *Alpa'yim* 12 (1996): 104–36; G. Scheffer, "The Appearance of the 'Nobility of Service' in the Yishuv" [Hebrew], *Ha-Tzionut* 8 (1983): 147–80. According to Dan Horowitz, "It is also possible to put in this same group the first members of the Ha-Noar Ha-Oved youth movement—the members of the generation of the founders of Kibbutz Na'an, such as Haganah activists Yisrael Galili and Moshe Zelitzky-Carmel." (*Blue and Thorns: The 1948 Generation, Self-Portrait* [Hebrew] [Jerusalem: Keter, 1993], 77).

15. On the inferior position of the immigrant fighters in relation to the Sabras in the mythos of 1948, see E. Sivan, *The 1948 Generation: Myth, Portrait, and Memory* [Hebrew] (Tel Aviv, 1991).

16. Books of this type especially worthy of mention are *The Sixth Battalion Tells* [Hebrew] (1948); *In the Philistine Fields 1948: Battle Diary* [Hebrew], 4th ed. (Tel Aviv, 1950); *Chapters of the Palmach: From the Mouths of the Fighters* [Hebrew] (1951); *When the Pathbreakers Break Through: From the Diary of a Palmach Soldier* [Hebrew] (1952); *Friends Tell about Jimmy* [Hebrew] (1955); and *On the Path of the Palmach* [Hebrew] (1958).

17. The two official anthologies were Y. Lamdan, ed., *In Memorium: Selections from the Lives and Deaths of the Fallen* [Hebrew] (Jerusalem, 1954); and R. Avinoam, ed., *Scrolls of Fire: A Collection Including a Selection from the Literary and Artistic Material Left by the Young People Who Fell in the War of Independence and Thereafter* [Hebrew] (Jerusalem, 1952).

18. For example, the portraits of Palmach fighters that appeared in the paintings of Aharon Avni, Mordecai Ardon, Mordecai Arieli, Avigdor Aricha, Naftali Bazam, Ludwig Blum, Nachum Gutman, Moshe Bernstein, Shraga Weil, and Moshe Tamir. See G. Ofrat (exhibit curator), *The 1948 Generation in Israeli Art* [Hebrew], exhibition catalogue, Haifa University Gallery, February 1984.

19. Conversation with Yossi Stern, 1983.

20. E. Davidzon, *The Laughter of Our Mouths: A Treasure of Humor and Satire in Hebrew Literature from its Beginnings to Our Days* [Hebrew] (Tel Aviv, 1951), 495.

21. See A. Dankner, *Dahn Ben-Amotz: A Biography* [Hebrew] (Jerusalem, 1992), 144.

22. Z. Gilad and M. Megged, eds., *The Palmach Book* [Hebrew], 2 vols (Tel Aviv: Ha-Kibbutz Ha-Me'uchad, 1953). This was preceded by a partial collection: Z. Gilad, ed., *Chapters of the Palmach: From the Mouths of the Fighters* [Hebrew] (Ein Charod, 1950).

23. For an account of the circumstances under which these books were written, see A. Ofek, *From Tarzan to Hasamba: How Adventure Books Were Written* [Hebrew] (Tel Aviv, 1969), 191–205, 219–33.

24. Quoted in Almagor, "The Sabra Is Put in Quotation Marks."

25. The poems were collected in 1957 in a volume titled *You Call Yourself Youth?* [Hebrew].

26. Dankner, *Ben-Amotz,* 162.

27. Ibid., 161.

28. On the identification of these writers as a young guard see, for example, D. Cana'ani, "In the Convoy and to Its Side: On the Works of S. Yizhar" [Hebrew], in *S. Yizhar: A Selection of Critical Articles on His Works* [Hebrew], ed. H. Naggid (1949; Tel Aviv, 1972), 57–84. Hundreds of books and articles have been written on this young guard. Those I have found to be of special interest are Sh. Kremer, *Changings of the Guard in Our Literature* [Hebrew] (Tel Aviv, 1959); E. Schweid, *Three Watches in Literature* [Hebrew] (Tel Aviv, 1964); A. Luz, *Reality and Man in Israeli Literature* [Hebrew] (Tel Aviv, 1970); G. Shaked, *A New Wave in Hebrew Literature* [Hebrew] (Tel Aviv, 1971); G. Shaked, *There is No Elsewhere* [Hebrew] (Tel Aviv, 1983); G. Shaked, "From the Sea? On the Image of the Hero in Hebrew Fiction in the 1940s and Onward" [Hebrew], *Jerusalem Studies in Hebrew Literature* 9 (1986), 7–22; G. Shaked, *Hebrew Fiction 1880–1980* [Hebrew], vol. 3 (Tel Aviv, 1988); Y. Ben-Baruch, "From the Ties of Shared Experience to the Literature of War: The Literature of the Palmach from 1948 to the Present" [Hebrew], *Iton 77* 100 (May 1980): 164–74.

29. Shaked, *Hebrew Fiction 1880–1980,* vol. 1, 181.

30. On the history of the anthology and its literary and cultural importance, see the articles by Moshe Shamir and Shlomo Tanai in *The Yalkut Ha-Re'im Book.* See also N. Govrin, "*Yalkut Ha-Re'im: A Myth of Continuation and a Myth of Beginning*" [Hebrew], in *The Yisrael Levin Book: A Collection of Studies in Hebrew Literature through Its Generations* [Hebrew], ed. R. Tzur and T. Rosen (Tel Aviv, 1995).

31. Shamir, "With the Members of My Generation."

32. On the popularity of this literature among young people of the middle class and above, see Y. Rimon, "She Walked in the Fields" [Hebrew], *Ba-Machaneh Gadna* 12 (1957): 4.

33. The use of Sabra slang charmed some of the critics and bothered others, but most of them saw it as one of the characteristics of the new literary guard. See, for example, A. B. Yaffeh, "The Young Prose in the War" [Hebrew], *Orlogin* 1 (1950): 188–93.

34. E. Ochmani, "To the Credit of Our Literature" [Hebrew], *Orlogin* 1 (1950): 28–29.

35. IDF Cultural Service, *Spectrum of Writers: An Anthology of Literature by Soldier Writers* [Hebrew] (Tel Aviv, n.d.).

36. See Y. Oren, "Taking Leave of the Sabra Image" [Hebrew], in *Zionism and Sabraism in the Israeli Novel* [Hebrew] (Rishon Le-Tzion, 1990), 81–95; Oz Almog, "The New Pillar of Fire" [Hebrew], *Politika* 42–43 (January 1991): 7–11.

37. Among the most noteworthy of these books in terms of its sharpness and its influence was Amnon Rubinstein's *To Be a Free People* [Hebrew] (Jerusalem: Schocken Books, 1978).

38. Quoted from K. L. Beker, *The Sublime City in Eighteenth-Century Thought* [Hebrew] (Tel Aviv, 1979), 115–16.

39. R. N. Bellah, "Civil Religion in America," *Daedalus* 96 (1967): 1–21.

40. He was preceded by A. de Tocqueville, *Democracy in America* (1835; New York: Harper and Row, 1966); M. Weber, *The Protestant Ethic and the Spirit of Capitalism* (1905; London: Allen and Unwin, 1930); W. L. Werner, *American Life: Dream and Reality* (Chicago: University of Chicago Press, 1964); C. J. Hayes, *Nationalism: A Religion* (New York: Macmillan, 1960).

41. C. Liebman and E. Don Yehiye, *Civil Religion in Israel: Traditional Judaism and Political Culture in the Jewish State* (Berkeley: University of California Press, 1983).

1. Idealistic Euphoria

1. See T. P. O'Day, "Sociological Dilemmas: Five Paradoxes of Institutionalization," in *Sociological Theory, Values and Change,* ed. E. A. Tiryakian (Glencoe, Ill.: Free Press, 1963), 71–89. Also, E. Shils, ed., "Charisma, Order, and Status," *American Sociological Review* 30 (April 1965).

2. From an unsigned letter of April 1948. However, the style indicates that it was written by Meir Talmi in response to a letter sent by Mishmar Ha-Emek's children to their kibbutz after they were evacuated to other kibbutzim in the wake of attacks. Mishmar Ha-Emek archive, file 3.64.

3. A. Cohen, "To Put to Sleep or to Wake Up: Education and Indoctrination through Lullabies" [Hebrew], in *Transformations in Children's Literature* [Hebrew] (Haifa, 1988), 16.

4. For interesting examples, see M. Regev, "'Enlisted' Hebrew Children's Literature" [Hebrew], *Ma'agalei Kri'ah* 7 (1980): 99–166; M. Regev, "Israeli and Zionist Children's Literature" [Hebrew], *Yediot Aharonot,* 8 May 1980, 22; Cohen, *Transformations in Children's Literature*; M. Baruch, *Child Then Child Now* [Hebrew] (Tel Aviv, 1991). On the ideology of the children's periodicals, see M. Regev, *Children's Literature: Reflections* (Tel Aviv, 1992).

5. See Cohen, *Transformations in Children's Literature.*

6. M. Yellen-Shtaklis, "Prayer" [Hebrew], *Davar Le-Yeladim* 10, no. 8 (1940): 9.

7. On the relations between the political establishment and the teachers' unions during the Yishuv period and the political link between the two, see Y. Shapira, *Elite without Successors: Generations of Leaders in Israeli Society* [Hebrew] (Tel Aviv: Sifriat Po'alim, 1984).

8. Z. Zohar, *The Land of Israel in Our Education* [Hebrew], 3d ed. (Jerusalem: Re'uven Mas, 1948), 5.

9. M. Tzur, *Le-Lo Kutonet Pasim* (Without a coat of many colors) (Tel Aviv: Am Oved, 1976), 127. (Hereafter: Tzur, *Without a Coat of Many Colors*).

10. Y. Halperin, "School and Parents" [Hebrew], *Ha-Chinuch* 19, no. 2 (1946): 30.

11. R. Firer, "Consciousness and Knowledge: The Influence of Zionist Values on Textbooks on Jewish History in the Hebrew Language in the Years 1900–1980" [Hebrew] (Ph.D. diss., Hebrew University, Jerusalem, 1980), 20.

12. Council of Israeli Teachers, *To Youth: The Israeli Library* [Hebrew] (1936), 74–75.

13. See also R. Firer, *Agents of Zionist Education* [Hebrew] (Oranim, 1985).

14. Firer, "Consciousness and Knowledge," 70.

15. See A. Koestler, *Promise and Fulfilment: Palestine 1905–1931* (London: Macmillan, 1949), 300. For tables on the arrangement of subjects in the school day, see M. Rosenstein, "The New Jew: The Link to Jewish Tradition in General Zionist Secondary Education in Eretz Israel" [Hebrew] (Ph.D. diss., Hebrew University, Jerusalem, 1985).

16. B. Ben-Yehuda, *Foundations and Ways: Toward Zionist Education in the School* [Hebrew] (Jerusalem, 1952), 23.

17. A. Urinovsky, "For the Rectification of the Study of the Bible" [Hebrew], *Shorashim* 2, no. 1 (1938): 15–16.

18. Koestler, *Promise and Fulfilment*, 283.

19. Ch. A. Zuta and Y. Spibak, *The History of Our People* [Hebrew], 4th ed. (Tel Aviv, 1936), 13.

20. Ben-Yehuda, *Foundations and Ways*, 23.

21. See T. Segev, *The Seventh Million: The Israelis and the Holocaust* (New York: Hill and Wang, 1993).

22. Many examples of this method and the means by which an ideological atmosphere was created in the classroom may be seen in Z. Zohar, *Teaching in the Spirit of the Homeland* [Hebrew] (Jerusalem, 1937); Zohar, *The Land of Israel in Our Education*. See also *Bundle of Letters on the Questions of Communal Education* [Hebrew] 9 (July 1944): 14.

23. *Ba-Moledet*, collection of essays by students in Yishuv schools from the *Lu'ach He-Chaver* contest, 1929 (Jerusalem, 1930).

24. For an especially fascinating collection, demonstrating the idealistic spirit in which the pupils' works were written, see G. Maisel, ed., *The Child in Israel: A Collection of Works of Children from the Age of One and a Half to Thirteen and a Half Orally, in Writing, in Illustration, and in the Playing of Music* [Hebrew] (published by the editor, 1935).

25. Composition dated 24 Iyar 5798 (1938), in Sh. Zuckerman, *A Memorial to His Memory* [Hebrew] (Tel Aviv, 1958), 15–16.

26. Published in *Afikim* 2 (Warsaw, 1933), requoted in Z. Zohar, *The Land of Israel in Our Education*, 159.

27. Zohar, *The Land of Israel in Our Education*, 125.

28. Z. Katarbursky, *On the Paths of the Preschool* [Hebrew] (Tel Aviv, 1952), 23.

29. Ben-Yehuda, *Foundations and Ways*, 27.

30. M. Salomon, diary, 2 November 1941, in *Scrolls of Fire: A Collection Including a Selection from the Literary and Artistic Material Left by the Young People Who Fell in the War of Independence and Thereafter* [Hebrew], ed. R. Avinoam (Jerusalem, 1952), 390.

31. For a semiotic analysis of independence day celebrations, see D. Handelman and E. Katz, "State Ceremonies of Israel: Remembrance Day and Independence Day," in *Models and Mirrors: Towards an Anthropology of Public Events* (Cambridge: Cambridge University Press, 1990), 190–234.

32. M. Pa'il, *From the Haganah to the Defense Force* [Hebrew] (Tel Aviv, 1979), 196–97.

33. Z. Gilad and M. Megged, eds., *The Palmach Book* [Hebrew] (Tel Aviv: Ha-Kibbutz Ha-Me'uchad, 1953), 1: 204.

34. Ibid., 1: 206.

35. Tziona, "From the Mouths of Babes—Echoes of Evil Days—Prophecy," in *Bundle of Letters on the Questions of Communal Education* [Hebrew], vol. 1 (1940), 92.

36. N. Gretz, "Social Myths in Literary and Political Texts in the Period of the Yishuv and the State" [Hebrew], in *Observation Points: Culture and Society in Israel*[Hebrew], ed. N. Gretz (Tel Aviv, 1988), 271. See also N. Gretz, "The Few Facing the Many" [Hebrew], *Siman Kri'ah* 16–17 (April 1983).

37. For a detailed discussion of this myth and its influence, see N. Gretz, *Prisoner in Its Dreams* [Hebrew] (Tel Aviv, 1995); Koestler, *Promise and Fulfilment.*

38. On the ideological manipulation of the Masada myth, see N. Ben Yehuda, *The Masada Myth: Collective Memory and Mythmaking in Israel* (Madison: University of Wisconsin Press, 1995).

39. Y. Ch. Brenner, "Kavim Le-Demuto" (Outline of his character), *Kuntress* 72 (5 Adar Bet 1921). Also published in *Tel Chai—Anthology* [Hebrew] (Tel Aviv, 1932), 141–42.

40. See A. Shapira, *The Sword of the Dove: Zionism and Power, 1881–1948* [Hebrew] (Tel Aviv: Am Oved, Ofakim, 1992), 145.

41. N. Grossman, Ashdot Ya'akov, 1 October 1944, in Avinoam, *Scrolls of Fire,* 533.

42. Mainly in the poetry of Natan Alterman. See I. Tzurit, *The Sacrifice and the Covenant: Studies in the Poetry of Natan Alterman* [Hebrew] (Tel Aviv, 1974).

43. See, for example, the poem "The Tamarisk Tree of Abraham" [Hebrew], in memory of Daniel Reich who fell on the way to the Etzion Block, in *Gadish Poems* [Hebrew] (Tel Aviv, 1952), 428.

44. A. Etzioni, *Kazeh Hayah . . .* (That's how it was), in memory of Avner Ben-Sheffer, published by Ha-Noar Ha-Oved, Herzliya branch, 1949.

45. On the importance of retaining the metaphysical element in the Zionist revolution, see Bialik, "The Hebrew Book" [Hebrew], in *The Collected Works of Ch. N. Bialik* [Hebrew] (Tel Aviv, 1941).

46. B. Ben-Yehuda, *History of Zionism: The Movement for Renaissance and Redemption in Israel* [Hebrew] (Tel Aviv, 1943), 7.

47. N. Zarhi, Netanya, Adar Bet 1948, in Avinoam, *Scrolls of Fire,* 579.

48. Ahuviya, "The Proof of Strength" [Hebrew], in *Like a Plant in the Field: Anthology of Ha-Machanot Ha-Olim in Ha-Tenua Ha-Me'uchedet* (Tel Aviv, 1947), 80.

49. For details on the myth of "our right to the Land of Israel" in secular textbooks, see Firer, *Agents of Zionist Education,* 110.

50. Y. Weingarten and M. Teuber, *Our People in the Past and Present* [Hebrew], vol. 1, pt. 1 (Warsaw, 1935), 57.

51. The term "liberation" indeed appears more frequently than the term "conquest" on Israeli war memorials. See O. Almog, "Memorials to the Fallen in War: A Semiological Analysis," *Megamot* 34, no. 2 (1991): 179–210.

52. Ze'ev, "Palmachnik" [Hebrew], in Gilad and Megged, *The Palmach Book,* 1: 342.

53. For the ideological character of children's games, see N. Lahav, "Games of the Land of Israel" [Hebrew], *Bayit* 4 (1983): 59–61.

54. S. Shalom, "Voices in the Night," from "The Song of the Times," in *The S. Shalom Anthology* (Tel Aviv, 1954), 37. (The poem itself was written in 1938.)

55. Quoted in Ch. Cheffer, ed., *Calendar: The Calendar of the Palmach* (Tel Aviv, 1991), 20.

56. "At Bialik's Home" [Hebrew], *Itoneinu* (1933), 12, in Archive of the History of Jewish and Zionist Education, Tel Aviv University, file 3147/2.

57. R. Alboim-Dror, *Hebrew Education in Eretz Israel* [Hebrew], vol. 1 (Jerusalem, 1986), 352.

58. For the popularity of books on the fallen, see "Give Me a Good Book," *Ba-Machaneh Gadna* 64 (March 1954): 5.

59. Ben-Yehuda, *Foundations and Ways,* 36–37

60. See T. Dolev-Gandelman, "The Symbolic Inscription of Zionist Ideology in the Space of Eretz Israel: Why the Native Israeli is called Tsabar," in *Judaism Viewed from Within and from Without,* ed. H. E. Goldberg (Albany: State University of New York, 1987), 257–85.

61. For the educational importance, see "The JNF Fortieth Anniversary Lecture: The Impact of the Kindergarten," *Hel-Ha-Gan* 9 (1942): 11–17.

62. The description is based on Baruch Ben-Yehuda's account in *Foundations and Ways,* 44–45

63. With thanks to Naomi Meshi of Kibbutz Givat Haim, who provided samples of the JNF certificates.

64. See, for example, "In the Work of the JNF" [Hebrew], in *Of Us—Ha-Shomer Ha-Tza'ir* [Hebrew], Jerusalem chapter house, 5 July 1937, Ha-Shomer Ha-Tza'ir archives, (1) 5.1–3.

65. Quoted in the catalog for the JNF Blue Box Exhibition displayed throughout Israel to celebrate the JNF's ninetieth anniversary.

66. Letter by Ch. Ben-Dor, 25 January 1938, *Selected Letters and Writings* [Hebrew] (1949), 18.

67. O'Day, "Sociological Dilemmas."

68. Y. Ahali, Dafna, 31 December 1947, in Avinoam, *Scrolls of Fire,* 500.

69. M. Salomon, 9 October 1941, in Avinoam, *Scrolls of Fire,* 390.

70. This refers to works by those called "the 1948 generation." See G. Shaked, *Hebrew Fiction 1880–1980* [Hebrew] (Jerusalem, 1978), 1: 62–64; E. Schweid,

Three Watches in Hebrew Literature [Hebrew] (Tel Aviv, 1964), 199. For those who contest the use of the term "writers of the 1948 generation" as a catch-all, see, for example, A. Barteneh, "A Morning without Dawn" [Hebrew], *Masa* (*Davar* literary supplement), 6 July 1984; A. Shoham, "A Generation in Israel: In the Land of Criticism and Distortion" [Hebrew], *Masa,* 17 April 1983. Among the fiercest opponents of the term is Menuha Gilboa in her book *Wounds of Identity* [Hebrew] (Tel Aviv, 1988).

71. Many literary critics and researchers have addressed this point, for example, Z. Shamir, "The Generation of Struggle for Independence and Its Poets" [Hebrew], *Iton 77* 100 (1988): 120–24.

72. G. Shaked, "From the Sea? On the Image of the Hero in Hebrew Literature in the '40s and After" [Hebrew], *Jerusalem Surveys in Hebrew Literature* 9 (1986): 7–22. For poetry, see D. Meron, *Facing the Silent Brother: Studies in the Poetry of the War of Independence* (Jerusalem: Keter, 1992).

73. For this aspect of the 1948 Generation's literature, see Y. Ben-Baruch, "From the Ties of Shared Experience to the Literature of War: The Literature of the Palmach from 1948 to the Present" [Hebrew], *Iton 77* 100 (May 1980): 164–74.

74. S. Kramer, "The Poetry of the Palmach and Its Breaking," *Mozna'im* 20 (1965): 496.

75. For Alterman's enormous influence on Sabra poets, see H. Shaham, "The Influence of Natan Alterman's Early Poems (1938–1944) on Young Hebrew Poetry of the Palmach Generation until the 'Likrat' group (1922–1955)" [Hebrew] (Ph.D. diss., Hebrew University, Jerusalem, 1990).

76. Shamir, "The Generation of Struggle for Independence and Its Poets," 122; also her article in *Al Ha-Mishmar,* 4 May 1979.

77. N. Shein, *A Year since His Death* (Ein Charod: Ha-Kibbutz Ha-Me'uchad, 1947), 165.

78. Z. Levenberg, in Avinoam, *Scrolls of Fire,* 411.

79. Y. Samotritch, "To My Land" [Hebrew], in Avinoam, *Scrolls of Fire,* 46.

80. B. Fachter, "We Are Your Sons" [Hebrew], in Avinoam, *Scrolls of Fire,* 75.

81. N. Arieli, "Homeland" [Hebrew], in Avinoam, *Scrolls of Fire,* 35.

82. U. Fried, 3 September 1936, in Avinoam, *Scrolls of Fire,* 690.

83. I. Golani, 10 December 1947, in *Soul and Abyss* [Hebrew] (Kibbutz Afikim, 1950), 40–41.

84. M. Borenstein, "Sons Are We" [Hebrew], in Avinoam, *Scrolls of Fire,* 13.

85. Letter of 29 March 1938, Ch. Ben-Dor, *Letters and Writings* [Hebrew], 21.

86. See Tzur, *Without a Coat of Many Colors,* 217.

87. Letter of 27 March 1938, Ch. Ben-Dor, *Letters and Writings,* 20.

88. On deserters, see for example the testimony of Rachel Savoray, Haganah Historical Archives, Brigade 25, file 1, and also of Yisrael Gitlick in the same archives, Brigade 15, file 3.

89. E. Peled, letter of 16 November 1945, Ashdot Ya'akov, with my thanks to the writer for providing it.

90. D. Mahancher, letter of 15 July 1948, *Gezer's Day* [Hebrew], 88.

91. This feeling is evidenced by the coining of the word "Negevgrad" (derived from Stalingrad) in the battle diary of the Givati Brigade (Battle Sheet, Southern Front, 13 July 1948, IDF Archives, brigade file).

92. G. Yardeni, ed., *Yermi of the Paratroopers* [Hebrew] (Tel Aviv, 1968), 67.

93. Pa'il, *From the Hagana to the Defense Force.*

94. Y. Livneh, *Simple Words: Poetry of the Heritage* (Tel Aviv: Sifriyat Eleh Ha-Banim, 1950), 71.

95. R. Deutsch, "We Are Coming Back to You, Rafael" [Hebrew], in *Anthology in His Memory* (Mishmar Ha-Eek, 1949).

96. R. Zilberman, *Alon Palmach* 57–59 (January–February 1948): 44.

97. A trickle of this kind of questioning started in the '50s and became a steady flow only some twenty years later. Its apologetic character shows the difference between the two periods.

98. H. Avrech, "Sedom" [Hebrew], 31 May 1948, in Avinoam, *Scrolls of Fire*, 477

99. E. Peled, "We are Always Prepared for Orders: Profile of the Palmach Generation" [Hebrew], lecture given at the Research Center for History of Eretz Yisrael and Its Settlement, Jerusalem, 10 May 1995.

100. From A. Pinkerfeld-Amir, *In Their Lives: Images from the War of Independence* [Hebrew] (Tel Aviv: Amichai, 1961), 121.

101. From *Noam: A Memorial Candle for Noam Grossman, Who Fell in the Judean Mountains* [Hebrew] (Tel Aviv, 1948), 20.

2. The Elect Son of the Chosen People

1. On the concept of the Jewish people as chosen in the Bible, in the words of the sages, and in Jewish prayers, see S. Almog and M. Hed, eds., *The Idea of Chosenness* [Hebrew] (Jerusalem, 1991) .

2. B. Z. Herzl, "My Hopes" [Hebrew], in *Hidden Values or the Discarding of Values* [Hebrew], ed. E. Biltski (Tel Aviv, 1975), 71.

3. N. Syrkin, *Kontres* 19 (1920).

4. B. Katznelson, *Writings* [Hebrew], vol. 6 (Tel Aviv, 1945–1950), 247.

5. E. Shmueli, *Figures and Events in Our History* [Hebrew] (Tel Aviv, 1941), 9.

6. "On the Character of Trumpeldor" [Hebrew], Gymnasia Herzliya newsletter, 1937, Archive of the History of Jewish and Zionist Education, Tel Aviv University, file 3147/1.

7. S. Almog, "Normalization and 'A Light unto the Nations' in Zionism" [Hebrew], in Almog and Hed, *The Idea of Chosenness*, 293.

8. E. Schweid, "Two Approaches to the Idea of Negation of the Diaspora" [Hebrew], *Zionism* 9 (1940): 21–44.

9. On various national religions in the world, see O. Almog, "Secular Religion in Israel" [Hebrew], *Megamot* 37, no. 1 (1996).

10. On the distinction between "Israeli" and "Jew," see S. Herman, *Israelis and Jews* (Philadelphia: Jewish Publication Society of America, 1970).

11. N. Raz, "Diary of a Journey to Poland" [Hebrew], 21 August 1948.

12. For the prominence of the anti-Diaspora ethos in history books, see R. Firer, "Consciousness and Knowledge: The Influence of Zionist Values on Textbooks on Jewish History in the Hebrew Language in the Years 1900–1980" [Hebrew] (Ph.D. diss., Hebrew University, Jerusalem, 1980).

13. Quoted in R. Firer, *Agents of Zionist Education* [Hebrew] (Oranim, 1985), 95.

14. Ibid., 66.

15. Ibid., 73.

16. S. Chernikovsky, *Poems* [Hebrew] (Tel Aviv, 1959).

17. According to Batya Donner (in the catalogue of the "To Live with the Dream" exhibition, Tel Aviv Museum, March 1969), this style was influenced by Soviet propaganda posters and by the nationalistic style of French posters at the beginning of the century, which were also assimilated into German graphics and photography between the two world wars. On the physical image of the pioneer, see G. Efrat, "The Graphic Archetype of the Pioneer" [Hebrew] in the catalogue of the "Image of the Pioneer in Art" exhibition held at the President's Residence, 23 December 1982–30 March 1983, 21.

18. Y. Cohen, "On the Youth of the Homeland" [Hebrew], *Mozna'im,* 4, no. 26 (Kislev 1933): 9–10.

19. N. Shein, *A Year since His Death* [Hebrew] (Ein Charod: Ha-Kibbutz Ha-Me'uchad, 1947), 197.

20. Quoted in the introduction to D. Dayan, *Yes, We Are Youth! The Gadna History Book* [Hebrew] (Tel Aviv: Ministry of Defense, 1977).

21. N. Alterman, "The Silver Tray" [Hebrew], *Davar,* 19 December 1947.

22. Quoted in Y. Tabenkin, *Writings,* vol. 4 (Tel Aviv, 1972), 46.

23. Etta, who served as a driver in the Women's Royal Army Corps in Egypt, letter of 17 April 1945, Kibbutz Geva archives.

24. For the distinction made by Ben-Gurion, in his address to an assembly of youth at Tel Chai (Adar 1943), between "a worthy death," such as those of the Tel Chai heroes, and "an unworthy death," see Y. Weitz, "Aspects of the Yishuv in Relationship to the Holocaust of the Jews in Europe, 1942–43" [Hebrew], in *Observation Points: Culture and Society in Israel* [Hebrew], ed. N. Gretz (Tel Aviv, 1988), 82.

25. See Y. Weitz, "The Youth Movements in the Land of Israel and the Holocaust" [Hebrew], in *The Youth Movements 1920–1960* [Hebrew], ed. M. Na'or, Idan, no. 13 (Jerusalem: Yad Ben-Zvi, 1989), 172–81.

26. Y. Tabenkin, "Lecture at the Sea Company—Kiryat Chayim," in *Devarim,* vol. 4 (Tel Aviv: Ha-Kibbutz Ha-Me'uchad, 1985), 18.

27. Ibid, 32.

28. Y. Rabinowitz, "The Council of Ha-Kibbutz Ha-Me'uchad," Na'an, 10 May 1947, Kibbutz Ha-Me'uchad archives, file 2/11/5.

29. According to Ruth Firer: "The main questions that bothered the writers of school books in the '50s and '60s were: How to regard the six million who had been annihilated?" "How could their passivity be explained?" (Firer, *Agents of Zionist Education,* 70.) She presents several characteristic explanations, one of which is that the Jews were cheated and deceived by the Nazis. Nevertheless, she found the most common approach to be that "the heroic stance of the Jews in the ghettos compensated in a way for the shameful surrender of those who were led to the camps" (71).

30. Order of the day, 16 April 1948, Haganah History Archive, 73/26.

31. Letter written by Elad Peled in 1948.

32. Anita Shapira comments on this: "Intentionally and consciously the legend was cultivated of the brothership in arms between the warriors 'there' and 'here.' The partisans were presented as natural-born Palmachniks. . . . Allon, the Palmach commander, defined this as a meeting 'of brothers in arms and in ideas'" (*The Sword of the Dove: Zionism and Power, 1881–1948* [Hebrew] [Tel Aviv: Am Oved, Ofakim, 1992], 466). This "Israelization" of the revolt has been addressed recently by several historians, including Yechiam Weitz, Yosef Heller, Charles Liebman and Eliezer Don Yechiye, Henry Wasserman, Moshe Tzuckerman and Idith Zertal.

33. *Alon Palmach* 24–25 (December 1944), 35.

34. See A. Chalamish, "The Illegal Immigration: Values, Myth, and Reality" [Hebrew], in Gertz, *Observation Points*, 91.

35. From M. Lissak, "The Image of Immigrants: Stereotypes and Labels during the Mass Immigration of the Fifties" [Hebrew], *Katedra* 43 (1987): 150.

36. See H. Yablonka, *Foreign Brothers: Holocaust Survivors in the State of Israel 1948–52* [Hebrew] (Jerusalem, 1994), 56–57, 69.

37. For an in-depth discussion on the attitude in the Yishuv toward Holocaust survivors who arrived in the country, see T. Segev, *The First Israelis* [Hebrew] (Tel Aviv, 1984); T. Segev, *The Seventh Million: The Israelis and the Holocaust* (New York: Hill and Wang, 1993); A. Shapira, *The Walk to the Horizon* [Hebrew] (Tel Aviv, 1988); Shapira, *The Sword of the Dove*.

38. For examples, see the anthology *In Your Covenant: The Learning Youth in Israel* [Hebrew] (Tel Aviv: Ha-Machanot Ha-Olim, 1937).

39. Y. Frieman, "What the Diaspora Gave Us" [Hebrew], in *Scrolls of Fire: A Collection Including a Selection from the Literary and Artistic Material Left by the Young People Who Fell in the War of Independence and Thereafter* [Hebrew], ed. R. Avinoam (Jerusalem, 1952), 167.

40. B. Tumarkin, "Diary of Beit Ha-Shita" [Hebrew], 19 February 1937, in *The Years of Ha-Machanot Ha-Olim (First and Second Decades)* [Hebrew], ed. Y. Kafkafi (Tel Aviv: Ha-Kibbutz Ha-Me'uchad, 1985), 100.

41. *The Echo of What Was Done* [Hebrew], Kfar Masaryk, 22 November 1947, Kibbutz Ha-Me'uchad archives.

42. *In Memory of Friends* [Hebrew], training bulletin of the Ha-Machanot Ha-Olim in Chulata, 1950, 27–28.

43. Yablonka, *Foreign Brothers*, 135.

44. *Mi-Chaver Le-Chaver* (bulletin of the Yiftach Brigade), January 1949, IDF archives, brigade file.

45. A. Adan, *To the Ink Flag* [Hebrew] (Tel Aviv, 1984), 211–12.

46. Ch. Hazaz, "The Sermon" [Hebrew], in *The Sermon and Other Stories* [Hebrew], new ed. (Tel Aviv, 1991), 139.

47. See S. Veitman, "First Names as Cultural Measurements: Trends in the National Identity of Israelis, 1882–1980" [Hebrew] in Gertz, *Observation Points*, 141–52.

48. M. Yellen-Shtaklis, "Dani the Hero" [Hebrew], *Davar Le-Yeladim* 10, no 8 (20 February 1941): 9.

49. N. Alterman, "Around the Campfire in Cyprus, or Uzi from Mescha Becomes a Displaced Person" [Hebrew], in *Ha-Tor Ha-Shvi'i* (The seventh column),

vol. 4 (Tel Aviv, 1987), 169–71. (First published in "Ha-Tor Ha-Shvi'i"[The seventh column], *Davar*, 21 March 1947.)

50. See G. Turi, "Hebraicization of Family Names in Israel as a Cultural Translation," in Gertz, *Observation Points*, 152–73.

51. See A. Dankner, *Dahn Ben-Amotz: A Biography* [Hebrew] (Jerusalem, 1992).

52. For the ban on Yiddish films, see Ela Shochet, *The Israeli Cinema: History and Ideology* [Hebrew] (Tel Aviv, 1991), 58.

53. The Sabra vernacular included not just special words but also abbreviations, mispronunciations, new verb forms, and deliberate wrong usages. For more details see D. Ben-Amotz and N. Ben-Yehuda, *The World Dictionary of Hebrew Slang* [Hebrew] (Tel Aviv: Zemora-Bitan, 1972), 249–50.

54. N. Gertz, ed., *Statistical Year Book* [Hebrew], Central Bureau of Statistics, 1981 (Tel Aviv: Open University, 1988), table 22B, 56.

55. See Y. Nitzani, *Our Activists and Their Training: On the Way to the Ingathering of the Exiles and the Merging of Tribes* [Hebrew] (Tel Aviv: Histadrut, Dept. of Immigrants from the East and Yemen, 1947), 10–11.

56. See, for example, *Ba-Mivchan* 39 (January 1950).

57. See Segev, *The First Israelis*.

58. For more details on the kibbutz's lack of success among Oriental immigrants, see A. Shamosh, "Be-Zechut Ha-Chikuch" (Thanks to friction), in *Ha-Ma'ayan* (Jerusalem, 1988), 70–88.

59. E. Amir, *Tarnegol Kaparot* (Scapegoat) (Tel Aviv, 1992), 90. (Hereinafter: Amir, *Scapegoat*.) On the feeling that "they simply arrived before us . . . ," see also S. Michael, *Equal and More Equal* [Hebrew] (Tel Aviv, 1976), 35.

60. Firer, *Agents of Zionist Education*.

61. H. R. Turner, "Sponsored and Contested Mobility and the School System," *American Sociological Review* 25, no. 5 (1960).

62. Quoted in U. Ben-Eliezer, "The Palmach 1941–45: A Social Elite in the Construction of Concentrated Power" [Hebrew] (M.A. thesis, Tel Aviv University, 1981), 22.

63. See Na'or, *Youth Movements*, 17. For the common denominator between the kibbutz educational system and elite schools, mainly the British "public" schools, see A. Kahana, "The Influence of Patterns of Kibbutz Socialization on Its Adolescents," *Ha-Kibbutz* 2 (1975): 121–29.

64. Amir, *Scapegoat*, 66.

65. See Y. Sadeh, "A Little History" [Hebrew], in *The Palmach Book* [Hebrew], ed. Z. Gilad and M. Megged (Tel Aviv, 1953).

66. On selectivity in the Palmach, see U. Ben-Eliezer, "The Palmach as the Mirror of Its Generation: Social Sources" [Hebrew], *Medina u-Mimshal* 23 (1984), 29–49.

67. Haganah History Archive, no. 4631. See also the testimony of A. Negev (Haganah History Archive, no. 4676) and of M. Rabinowitz (Haganah History Archive, no. 4147).

68. The hypothesis that those who join a group that requires a severe initiation appreciate and like its members more than those who join a group with easy entrance conditions was proved in a psychological experiment. See E. Aron-

son and J. Mills: "The Effect of Severity of Initiation on Liking for a Group," *Journal of Abnormal and Social Psychology* 59 (1959): 177–81.

69. On the popularity of these tests at the time and on their importance to the image of the officer, see A. Barzel, "To Be or Not to Be . . . an Officer" [Hebrew], *Ba-Machaneh Gadna* 6 (2 December 1956).

70. *Ba-Machaneh* 12 (15 November 1951).

71. See B. Chabas, ed., *The Book of the Second Aliyah* [Hebrew] (Tel Aviv, 1947).

72. Ben-Amotz and Ben-Yehuda, *The World Dictionary of Hebrew Slang*, 84.

73. N. Ben-Yehuda, *Between Calendars — 1948* [Hebrew] (Jerusalem, 1981), 87.

74. Ibid., 87.

75. The "detective" period in Israel started in the '30s. For the development of the local detective story, see Y. Shavit and Z. Shavit, eds., *The Hebrew Detective Returns: Choice Detective Stories from Palestine and the Land of Israel* [Hebrew] (Tel Aviv, 1983).

76. Publication of this tremendously popular series, which had a large youth following, started in 1932. It was based on the real figure of David, a police inspector (of the Mandatory Police) in Jewish Jerusalem and a private detective. For the circumstances surrounding the publication of the series, see D. Tidhar, *In the Service of the Homeland* [Hebrew] (Tel Aviv, 1962), 233–39.

77. The following are a few examples from folk literature about Sabra youth: Jimmy the Palmachnik and his friends organize a fake explosion in their tent, giving everyone a shock and then arousing bellows of laughter (Avneri, *Friends Tell about Jimmy*); Amitai Etzioni's sapper buddies plant a tear gas grenade during a performance at the Kameri Theater (Avneri, *When the Pathbreakers Break Through*, which contains stories about many other pranks); members of Paratrooper Brigade 890 use a smoke grenade to make an unfortunate waiter flee the restaurant so that they don't have to pay the bill (M. Yakobovits, *Gulliver: A Man and a Fighter* [Hebrew] [Tel Aviv, 1973], diary extracts). ("Gulliver" is the nickname for Yitznak Ben Menachem.)

78. All the definitions and examples of slang words are taken from Ben-Amotz and Ben-Yehuda, *The World Dictionary of Hebrew Slang*, 76, 148, 160, 162, 184, 220; D. Ben-Amotz and Ch. Cheffer, *The Complete and Full Bag of Tricks* [Hebrew] (Tel Aviv, 1979), 6, 47.

79. It is interesting to note that the sobriquet "jobnik" has a completely opposite meaning today from what it had originally. In the Palmach it referred to a man sent out to do battle who did a dangerous job and was therefore highly respected. See Ben-Amotz and Ben-Yehuda, *The World Dictionary of Hebrew Slang*, 46.

80. M. Har-Tzion, *Chapters of a Diary* [Hebrew] (Tel Aviv: Levin-Epstein, 1969), 134.

81. "We were a generation that was hooked on the cinema, sometimes going more than once a day," wrote Dan Horowitz in his biography, *Blue and Thorns* [Hebrew] (Jerusalem, 1993). "Our lives were influenced by Gary Cooper. It seems to me that I differentiate between good and bad, and Gary Cooper helped

me to do so," Amos Keinan wrote in his *Beneath the Flowers* [Hebrew] (Tel Aviv, 1979). Similar remarks were made by Chaim Guri in *The Mad One* [Hebrew] (Tel Aviv, 1972). Baruch Nadel's witticism that "Two men created the Palmach— Yitzchak Sadeh and Gary Cooper" is well known. It was no accident that one of the Palmach's urban training camps was called "Hollywood" and its members had nicknames such as Bogart and Tosca. Netiva Ben-Yehuda also used Hollywood terms, in a sort of instinctive Palmach reflex, in describing a battle in which she took part: "One against one. Like in movies of the Wild West" (*Between Calendars*—*1948*).

82. "Kumzitz," *Alon Ha-Palmach* 4 (Tammuz, 1942).

83. The Palmach command's forgiving attitude toward thievery was probably the reason for the increasing number of stolen cars and motorcycles as well as the increasing number of break-ins to supply warehouses during the War of Independence. Stated in the file of the Palmach Military Prosecutor, IDF archives, 2294/50/2951.

84. A. Pinkerfeld-Amir, *In Their Lives: Images from the War of Independence* [Hebrew] (Tel Aviv: Amichai, 1961), 40.

85. It should be pointed out that some of the older generation, mainly journalists and educators and those with a European education, considered that this forgiving attitude went too far, but they were the exceptions. (See, for example, the article by Asher Beilin, "A Crooked Generation," *Davar,* 4 August 1941.)

86. See, for example, Ch. Cheffer, "The Jeep," in Ch. Guri and Ch. Cheffer, *The Palmach Family: Escapades and Song* [Hebrew] (Tel Aviv: Palmach Veterans Organization, 1974), 189.

87. See Uri Avneri's poem, "Samson's Foxes," in *In the Philistine Fields 1948: Battle Diary* [Hebrew], 4th ed. (Tel Aviv, 1950).

88. For example, see "Numbers and Facts" [Hebrew], in Ben-Amotz and Cheffer, *Bag of Tricks,* 89–90.

89. Ben-Amotz and Ben-Yehuda, *The World Dictionary of Hebrew Slang,* 174.

90. See *Palmach, Album* [Hebrew] (Tel Aviv, 1959).

91. Quoted in B. Etzioni, ed., *Tree and Sword: The Battle Road of the Golani Brigade* [Hebrew] (Tel Aviv, 1950), 399.

92. D. Meron, *Against the Silent Brother* [Hebrew] (Jerusalem: Keter, 1982), 18.

93. Y. Lev, "The Bitter Taste" in *From the War: Fiction and Poetry* [Hebrew], ed. U. Ofek (Tel Aviv: Ministry of Defense, 1969), 256.

94. E. Sivan, *The 1948 Generation: Myth, Portrait and Memory* [Hebrew] (Tel Aviv, 1991), 134.

95. Ibid., 150.

96. Ibid., 151.

97. Ibid., 155.

98. Ibid., 134.

99. Ibid., 155.

100. Many articles have been written about the psychological function of idealizing the dead person. For example, G. Tamir, "Long-term Adaptation by Bereaved Parents of War Dead in Israel" [Hebrew], in *Loss and Bereavement in Is-*

raeli Society [Hebrew], ed. R. Melkinson, S. Rubin, and E. Vitstim (Jerusalem, 1993), 217.

101. For the national significance of "The Seventh Column," see D. Miron, *Four Faces of Contemporary Hebrew Literature* [Hebrew] (Jerusalem, 1962).

102. N. Alterman, "The Silver Tray."

103. Grossman, in Avinoam, *Scrolls of Fire*, 19.

104. S. Ben-Yaakov, "Megidulei Artzeinu" (From the produce of our land), in *The Seven: A Year after the Fall of the Seven Guards of Holon* [Hebrew] (Tel Aviv: Achdut, 1949), 150.

105. In A. Pinkerfeld-Amir, introduction to *With Heart and with Logic: Beni (Benjamin) Shapira, Writings and Memories* [Hebrew], ed. A. Pinkerfeld-Amir (Tel Aviv).

106. One of the Sabras wrote in a letter to his girlfriend: "In my letters I'm more handsome than in reality" [Hebrew] (R. Deutsch, Ramat David, 8 December 1947, Mishmar Ha-Emek archive, file 9.21).

107. E. Shmueli, "On the Youth in Israel" [Hebrew], *Carmelit: Literary Year Book* 4–6 (1958), 161–62.

108. Implicit here, apparently, is one of the reasons for the formation of the "destruction of the elite" myth that Emmanuel Sivan refuted some years later (Sivan, *The 1948 Generation*).

109. D. Ben-Gurion, "On the Sons Who Have Fallen" [Hebrew], in *Ba-Machaneh Gadna* 10 (15 April 1956): 2.

110. Y. Karni, "Modest and Great"[Hebrew], in *Little Platform: Prose and Poetry* [Hebrew] (Tel Aviv, 1951), 248.

111. *Sons* [Hebrew] (Ein Charod), 46.

112. Sivan, *The 1948 Generation*, 36–62.

113. For the "civilian" nature of the relationships between commanders and their soldiers in the Palmach and how the system of relationships relied on the commanders' prestige, see also Shapira, *The Sword of the Dove*, 414.

114. Ch. Cheffer, "The Platoon Commander," in Ofek, *From the War*, 26.

115. D. Almagor, "The Commander Who Calls 'Follow Me!'" quoted in *A Man at War: A Selection of Literary Chapters* [Hebrew], comp. and ed. A. Cohen (Tel Aviv, 1975), 213.

116. Y. Zariz, "On the Figure of a Young Commander" [Hebrew], in *C. Poznansky (Poza): Fell in the War of Independence* [Hebrew] (Tel Aviv, 1948), 49.

117. For this period, see B. Morris, *Israel's Border Wars* [Hebrew] (Tel Aviv, 1996).

118. U. Dan, *Ba-Machaneh* 4 (9 September 1956).

119. *Ba-Machaneh* 6 (29 October 1957).

120. *Ba-Machaneh Gadna* 16 (1 May 1956).

121. *Ba-Machaneh* 10 (1 November 1956).

3. Dunce Cap

1. Y. Rimon, "Agudat Dorjev Emet" (The organization of truth-tellers), *Ba-Machaneh Gadna* 11 (15 February 1957).

2. A. Shapira, *The Sword of the Dove: Zionism and Power, 1881–1948* [Hebrew] (Tel Aviv: Am Oved, Ofakim, 1992), 47.

3. This process is extensively described by many researchers from various fields. See, for example, A. Shapira, *The Disillusioned Struggle: Hebrew Labor 1929–1939* [Hebrew] (Tel Aviv, 1977). For an especially colorful description, see A. Elon, *The Israelis: Founders and Sons* [Hebrew] (Tel Aviv: Schocken, 1972).

4. E. Ben-Ezer, *No Tranquillity in Zion: Conversations on the Price of Zionism* [Hebrew] (Tel Aviv, 1986), 159.

5. R. Alboim-Dror, *Hebrew Education in Eretz Israel* [Hebrew], vol. 1 (Jerusalem, 1986), 380.

6. Ibid., 381.

7. D. Meltz, "On the Way to Cultural Experience" [Hebrew], in *Anthology of Ha-Kibbutz Ha-Me'uchad* (Tel Aviv, 1932), 199–203.

8. From the diary of Eliezer Smoli, a teacher at the young kibbutz. E. Smoli, *On the Way to Beit Chinuch: From a Teacher's Diary* [Hebrew] (Tel Aviv, 1953).

9. "The Ha-Shomer Philosophy," in *A Guide for Ha-Shomer Managers* [Hebrew] (Warsaw, 1917), quoted in *The Book of Ha-Shomrim: Anthology for the Twentieth Anniversary of Ha-Shomer Ha-Tza'ir* [Hebrew], ed. Gutthalf and Cohen (Warsaw, 1934).

10. U. Ofek, "The First Hebrew Plays Produced in the Land of Israel" [Hebrew], Bamah 18 (winter 1982): 90–93.

11. *Yediot Le-Madrichei Chagam*, 1 September 1942.

12. D. Dayan, *Yes, We Are Youth! The Gadna History Book* [Hebrew] (Tel Aviv: Ministry of Defense, 1977), 69

13. Ibid., 83.

14. Written on 18 April 1944 and quoted in Z. Dayan, *Poems and Letters* [Hebrew] (Tel Aviv, 1950), 32.

15. Sh. Kramer, *The Changing of the Guard in Our Literature* [Hebrew] (Tel Aviv: Dvir, 1959), 278–79.

16. T. Katriel, *Talking Straight: Dugri Speech in Israeli Sabra Culture* (Cambridge: Cambridge University Press, 1987), 1.

17. D. Zamir, "Where Did the Generals Grow? The Social Origin and Socialization Patterns of the 1948 Generation in Israel's Military Elite" [Hebrew], *Megamot* 25, no. 1 (1979): 88.

18. E. Fried, letter to the scouts in Lintz group, autumn 1935, in *Scrolls of Fire: A Collection Including a Selection from the Literary and Artistic Material Left by the Young People Who Fell in the War of Independence and Thereafter* [Hebrew], ed. R. Avinoam (Jerusalem, 1952), 689.

19. S. Kampinski, letter of 13 February 1948, in Avinoam, *Scrolls of Fire*, 568.

20. Y. Rabin, *Pinkas Sherut* (The Rabin memoirs) (Tel Aviv: Sifriat Ma'ariv, 1979). For other practically identical examples, see Gur, *Company D* [Hebrew], 13; A. Even, *Arik: The Way of a Fighter* [Hebrew] (Tel Aviv, 1974).

21. On this, see Y. Shapira, *Elite without Successors: Generations of Leaders in Israeli Society* [Hebrew] (Tel Aviv: Sifriat Po'alim, 1984).

22. David S., Ein Shemer, "The Moshav Youth Being Tested," *Nativ,* Ha-Shomer Ha-Tza'ir chapter, Petah Tikva, December 1938.

23. *Ba-Ma'aleh* 16, no. 249 (29 August 1941).

24. See Kafkafi, *The Years of Ha-Machanot Ha-Olim* [Hebrew], 77–78, 299, 302, 338, 339.

25. See Y. Shapira, *The Historical Achdut Ha-Avodah and Its Power as a Political Organization* [Hebrew] (Tel Aviv, 1975).

26. S. Kampinsky, letter of 13 February 1948, in Avinoam, *Scrolls of Fire*, 568.

27. The dictionary definitions have been taken from D. Ben-Amotz and N. Ben-Yehuda, *The World Dictionary of Hebrew Slang* [Hebrew] (Tel Aviv: Zemora-Bitan, 1972), 41, 139, 210.

28. D. Mas, Tel Yosef, 9 April 1945, "The Day of Victory," in Avinoam, *Scrolls of Fire*, 612.

29. For the tendency of public officials of the time to use high-flown language, see the article by Y. Zeidman, *The Style of David Remez* [Hebrew], in *Davar Yearbook* (Tel Aviv, 1953), 373–81.

30. S. N. Eisenstadt et al. *The Social Structure of Israel* [Hebrew] (Jerusalem, 1966), 104–5.

31. Rachel, "Niv" (Speech), in *Poems and Letters* [Hebrew] (Kinneret, 1969).

32. M. Duvshani, *Lessons in Hebrew Literature and General Literature for High Schools* [Hebrew] (Tel Aviv, 1960), 2: 81–82.

33. See Segev, *The Seventh Million*.

34. On Israeli anti-intellectualism as provincialism, see Ben-Ezer, *No Tranquillity in Zion*, 162.

35. On the process of severing ties with Jewish heritage and its significance, see E. Schweid, "The Sorrow of Severed Roots" [Hebrew], in *Three Watches in Hebrew Literature* [Hebrew] (Tel Aviv, 1964); Ch. Bartov, "Our Literature between Yesterday and Tomorrow" [Hebrew], *Daf* 28 (June 1966): 13; B. Arpeli, *Webs of Darkness* [Hebrew] (Tel Aviv, 1983), 110–11, 146–54.

36. E. Uchmani, "The Continuity of Judaism on the Path to Compensation" [Hebrew], *Shedemot* 71 (spring-summer 1979): 101.

37. Y. Peres, "The Pioneering Youth Movement" [Hebrew] in Eisenstadt et al., *The Social Structure of Israel*.

38. A. Shapira, "A Generation in the Land" [Hebrew], *Alpa'yim* 2 (1990): 195.

39. T. P. O'Day, "Sociological Dilemmas: Five Paradoxes of Institutionalization," in *Sociological Theory, Values and Change*, ed. E. A. Tiryakian (Glencoe, Ill.: Free Press, 1963), 71–89.

40. Z. Schatz, *On the Edge of Silence* [Hebrew] (Tel Aviv: Davar, 1929), 88.

41. M. Tzur, *Le-Lo Kutonet Pasim* (Without a coat of many colors) (Tel Aviv: Am Oved, 1976), 126.

42. B. Ben-Yehuda, "On the Problem of Youth and their Education" [Hebrew], in *The Ways of Youth: Anthology on Youth Affairs in Zionism* [Hebrew], ed. G. Chanoch (Jerusalem: Youth Division of the Zionist Executive, 1937), 170–71.

43. See, for example, D. Horowitz, *Blue and Thorns: The 1948 Generation, Self-Portrait* [Hebrew] (Jerusalem: Keter, 1993).

44. See Shapira, *Elite without Successors*.

45. Ch. Guri, "We Are the Locals," *Masa* (*Davar* literary supplement), 13 July 1984.

46. On the difficulty of defining the terms "intellectual" and "intellectual strata," see P. Mendes Flohr, "The Jewish Intellectual: Remarks on Clarifying the Term" [Hebrew], *Iyun* 33, part A–B (Teveth-Nissan, 1984).

47. On the question of the education of the 1948 generation, see A. Shapira, "A Generation in the Land"; Horowitz, *Blue and Thorns;* E. Sivan, *The 1948 Generation: Myth, Portrait and Memory* [Hebrew] (Tel Aviv, 1991), in particular, 115.

4. The Stamp of His Country's Landscape

1. See Z. Vilnai, *The Field Trip and Its Educational Value* [Hebrew] (Jerusalem, 1953), 8.

2. A. Gorni, "Landscape, Man, and Earth: The Approach of the Modern Poets in the Thirties and Forties Compared to the Approach of the Poets of the Generation of Revival" [Hebrew], *Iton 77* 44 (1983): 30.

3. See S. Keshet, "From the Expression of Migrants to the Expression of Home Builders: A Study of the Landscape Descriptions of Landscape by Kibbutz Writers from the Third Aliya" [Hebrew], *Mi-Bifnim* 53 (November 1991): 81–86; A. Mahlo, *Between Two Landscapes: Fiction of the Third Aliya between the Landscapes of the Diaspora and Landscapes of the Land of Israel* [Hebrew] (Jerusalem, 1991). On attachment to the landscape in literature of the Third Aliya, see L. Hedomi, *Literary Reflection of Patterns of Systems* [Hebrew] (Jerusalem, 1974). See also G. Ofrat, *Man, Land, Blood—The Myth of the Pioneer and the Rite of the Land in Settlement Drama* [Hebrew] (Tel Aviv: Cherikover, 1980).

4. On the landscape as a central motif in works of painters in Palestine during the twenties and thirties, see Y. Tzalmona, *Landscape in Israeli Art* [Hebrew], catalogue for the exhibition at the Israel Museum, Jerusalem, 1972.

5. On those who contributed to the professional literature, see Y. Bar-Gal, *Homeland and Geography: One Hundred Years of Zionist Education* [Hebrew] (Tel Aviv, 1993), 52.

6. See Z. Zohar, *The Land of Israel in Our Education* [Hebrew], 3d ed. (Jerusalem: Re'uven Mas, 1948), 120, 126.

7. S. Katz, "The Israeli Teacher Guide: The Emergence and Perpetuation of a Role," *Annals of Tourism Research,* vol. 12, 49–72.

8. See M. Rosenstein, "The New Jew: The Link to Jewish Tradition in General Zionist Secondary Education in Eretz Israel" [Hebrew] (Ph.D. diss., Hebrew University, Jerusalem, 1985), 193; and Bar-Gal, *Homeland and Geography.*

9. N. Gabrieli, *Knowledge of the Homeland* [Hebrew], vol. 2 (Tel Aviv, 1935), 57.

10. See U. Praver, "The Way of the Hike in Knowledge of the Land 1888–1918" (M.A. thesis, Hebrew University, Jerusalem, 1992).

11. For further information on this topic, see A. Shtal, "How They Taught Ashkenazis to Love Nature and Hikes" [Hebrew], *Iyyunim Be-Chinuch,* 31 September 1981: 61–71.

12. See R. Alboim-Dror, *Hebrew Education in Eretz Israel* [Hebrew], vol. 2 (Jerusalem, 1990), 364.

13. Sh. Ch. Wilkomitz, "About the Schools in the Moshavot of Our Brothers in Eretz Yisrael" [Hebrew], in *The Teacher: In Memory of Sh. Ch. Wilkomitz* [Hebrew], ed. L. Riklis (Tel Aviv, 1959), 170.

14. See Praver, "The Way of the Hike," 48.

15. M. Michaeli, *The Student Newspaper and Its Educational Value* [Hebrew] (Jerusalem, 1934), 22.

16. See "Discussion on the Next Classes: Members' Discussions at Ein Charod and Tel Yosef," in *Bundle of Letters on Questions of Communal Education* [Hebrew], vol. 1 (1940), 43–44.

17. M. Zaharoni, "Agricultural Education in Eretz Yisrael" [Hebrew], in *Educational Encyclopedia* [Hebrew] (Jerusalem, 1959), 2: 430.

18. D. Dayan, *Yes, We Are Youth! The Gadna History Book* [Hebrew] (Tel Aviv: Ministry of Defense, 1977), supplement no. 6.

19. Praver, "The Way of the Hike," 75.

20. Y. Kafkafi, ed., *The Years of Ha-Machanot Ha-Olim (First and Second Decades)* [Hebrew] (Tel Aviv: Ha-Kibbutz Ha-Me'uchad, 1985), 110.

21. "School Trips" [Hebrew], *Hed Ha-Chinuch*, 13 Iyar 1955, 3.

22. In *With a Pencil of Silver: Shmuel Levin* [Hebrew] (Tel Aviv, n.d.), 11.

23. R. Enis and Y. Ben-Erev, *Gardens and Landscape in the Kibbutz* [Hebrew] (Tel Aviv, 1994), 21.

24. Ibid., 56.

25. Z. Gilad, "Beneath the Lotuses" [Hebrew], in *Chapters of the Palmach: From the Mouths of Fighters* [Hebrew], ed Z. Gilad (Ein Charod: Ha-Kibbutz Ha-Me'uchad), 151.

26. Yigal Allon relates the use of wild plants in Kfar Tabor: Y. Allon, *My Father's House* [Hebrew] (Ein Charod: Ha-Kibbutz Ha-Me'uchad, 1980), 20–21.

27. See Z. Gilad and M. Megged, eds., *The Palmach Book* [Hebrew] (Tel Aviv: Ha-Kibbutz Ha-Me'uchad, 1953), 1: 135.

28. See Shimon Avidan's testimony [Hebrew], Ein Hashofet, 26 August 1984, Kibbutz Movement Archive, Division 48, file 1.

29. See "The Journeys and the Patrols," *Haganah History Book* [Hebrew],3: 445; also Ami Livneh's testimony, "The Reconnaissance of Mishmar Ha-Emek and the Area Around" [Hebrew], 30 October 1991, Mishmar Ha-Emek archive, file 3.63.

30. On reconnoitering in the Palmach, see Y. Eden, *The Reconnaissance Scouts* [Hebrew] (Tel Aviv, 1994).

31. See Vilnai, *The Field Trip and Its Educational Value*, 15.

32. The trips to Masada and the Dead Sea were terminated in 1934 after the death of a pupil during one of them. One hike was documented in Rafi Tehon's book *We Went around the Dead Sea on Foot* [Hebrew] (Tel Aviv, 1978).

33. See D. Bitan, "Masada: The Symbol and the Myth" [Hebrew], in M. Na'or, *The Dead Sea and the Judean Desert 1967–1990* [Hebrew] (Jerusalem, 1990), 227.

34. *The Haganah History Book* [Hebrew], 3: 446.

35. The *Ba-Machaneh Gadna* newspaper used to blazon these marches in enormous headlines, for example: "When Going, Things Start to Move" [He-

brew], 14 (1 April 1957) and "Who Said It's Difficult?" [Hebrew], 15 (15 April 1956).

36. *Alon Ha-Palmach* 24–25 (December 1944): 43.

37. I. Bichosevsky, "In Your Covenant: On Twenty Years of the Movement" [Hebrew], *Ba-Mivchan* 32 (Tishrei, 1947).

38. M. Megged, *Dani's Last Diary* [Hebrew] (Tel Aviv: Am Oved, 1968), 40.

39. A. Bloch, "Exercises and Shared Experience," testimony, 15 November 1949, Labor Party Archive 7/28.

40. For the history of the walks see Dayan, *Yes, We Are Youth!* 202.

41. "The Entire Country Left-Right" [Hebrew], *Ba-Machaneh Gadna*, 15 (13 April 1957): 3.

42. For a description of such a march by three young women, see R. Savorai, "The Trips" [Hebrew], *Me-Bifnim* 1, no. 18 (November 1954): 130–38.

43. M. Har-Tzion, *Chapters of a Diary* [Hebrew] (Tel Aviv: Levin-Epstein, 1969), 53.

5. Uri of Arabia

1. See the research of Ehud Ben-Ezer, especially the introduction to his book *In the Homeland of Contradictory Longings* [Hebrew] (Tel Aviv, 1992).

2. Y. Bergman, "Jewish Folklore and Its Role in the Land" [Hebrew], *Mozna'im* 20 (Elul 1945), 245.

3. This idea was taken from Israel Belkind's book on the Bilu, *The Land of Israel of Our Time* [Hebrew]. See N. Pollak, "The Origin of the Arabs of the Land" [Hebrew], *Molad* 1 (Iyar 1967–Iyar 1968).

4. On the myth of the racial link between Jews and Arabs, see chapter 6 of R. Alboim-Dror, *Hebrew Education in Eretz Israel* [Hebrew], vol. 2 (Jerusalem, 1990).

5. See Y. Goldstein, *The Shepherd Gang: The Idea of the Conquest of Sheepherding in the Second Aliya and Its Realization* [Hebrew] (Tel Aviv: Ministry of Defense, 1993), 12.

6. See Ben-Ezer, *In the Homeland of Contradictory Longings*, 12. See also E. Ben-Ezer, "Where Are the Sons of the Desert?" [Hebrew], *Etmol* 7, no. 2 (1981): 3–5. The theory was also expressed in literature: Amashi, the hero of *The Wanderings of Amashi the Guard* by Ya'akov Rabinowitz [Hebrew] (Tel Aviv, 1929), goes out in search of the lost tribes of Israel among the Bedouin.

7. One of the theory's prominent and energetic supporters was Yitzchak Ben-Zvi. See R. Yanait Ben-Zvi, "Wandering the Land" [Hebrew], *Mozna'im* 16 (1963), 117.

8. See Y. Shavit, "Zionism: Between the Decline of the West and the Revival of the East" [Hebrew], *Mozna'im* 36 (1972), 141.

9. Rabinowitz, *The Wanderings of Amashi the Guard,* 100.

10. Y. Rivkai, *In Our Youth* [Hebrew] (Tel Aviv. 1939), 20–21.

11. R. Benjamin, "Three Who Died as One" [Hebrew], *Ha-Poel Ha-Tza'ir* 12 (April 1910): 7.

12. See David Frishman, "Did You Know the Land?" [Hebrew] in "Impressions from Journeys in Palestine," *Ha-Tzfira* 126 (3–16 June 1911).

13. U. Z. Greenberg, "The Word of the Son of Blood" [Hebrew], in *Shield Area and the Word of the Son of Blood* (Tel Aviv, 1930).

14. Tz. Lieberman, *Oded the Wanderer* [Hebrew] (Tel Aviv, 1930), 50.

15. Ibid, 68.

16. See the poem of A. Pinkerfeld-Amir, "Esau" in *Gadish Poems* (Tel Aviv, 1952), 35.

17. A. Shapira, *The Sword of the Dove: Zionism and Power, 1881–1948* [Hebrew] (Tel Aviv: Am Oved, Ofakim, 1992), 242.

18. M. Regev, "The Arab Problem in Children's Literature" [Hebrew], *Achshav* 230 (1967), 219.

19. Y. Bar-Gal, *Homeland and Geography: One Hundred Years of Zionist Education* [Hebrew] (Tel Aviv, 1993), 178–79.

20. From the newspaper of the scout troupe of Tachkemoni School (Elul 1927), 7.

21. Someone among the Erez group, twelve-year-olds, "The Arab" [Hebrew], articles (draft) for youth movement publications—*El Or, Igeret, Be-Sha'ar*—1937–38, Ha-Shomer Ha-Tza'ir archive, 3.1–3 (3).

22. Bar-Gal, *Homeland and Geography,* 178.

23. R. Firer, "Consciousness and Knowledge: The Influence of Zionist Values on Textbooks on Jewish History in the Hebrew Language in the Years 1900–1980" [Hebrew] (Ph.D. diss., Hebrew University, Jerusalem, 1980), 128.

24. D. Chaviv-Lubman, "Rishon Le-Tzion," *Le-Noar* 4 (1929): 18.

25. For a variety of examples, see Bar-Gal, *Homeland and Geography;* and R. Firer, *Agents of Zionist Education* [Hebrew] (Oranim, 1985).

26. Koestler, *Promise and Fulfilment,* 34.

27. The expression "Muslim gypsies" appears in "Populations of Transjordan" [Hebrew], in *For Youth: Library of the Land of Israel* [Hebrew], ed. A. Epstein, no. 42 (1932), 18.

28. M. Shmueli, "Gedera," in *For Youth: Library of the Land of Israel* [Hebrew], ed. Epstein, no. 9 (1930), 7.

29. See Alboim-Dror, *Hebrew Education in Eretz Israel,* vol. 2, 129.

30. *Generation to Generation* [Hebrew] (Merchavia: Sifriat Po'alim, 1948), 71–72.

31. On this ethos, see Shapira, *The Sword of the Dove,* 324–51.

32. Sashka, *Newspaper of the Negba Group of Children* (no exact date, but from the War of Independence period), Mishmar Ha-Emek Kibbutz archives.

33. See Firer, *Agents of Zionist Education.* On stylized Eastern dress as a fashion, see R. Yanait Ben-Zvi, *We Are Immigrants* [Hebrew] (Tel Aviv: Am Oved, 1962), 131.

34. See I. Even-Zohar, "The Growth and Consolidation of Native and Local Culture in Eretz Israel" [Hebrew], *Katedra* 16 (1980), 161–216.

35. On the Arabic basis of Israeli speech and the idioms that penetrated into modern Hebrew from Arabic, see H. Blank, "On the Arabic Foundation in Israeli Speech" [Hebrew], *Lashon B'nei Adam* (Jerusalem: Bialik Institute, 1989), 135–48; also U. Avneri, *The Conquests of Hebrew in Our Generation* [Hebrew] (Merchavia, 1946), 81–88.

36. See *Janantini! Or Songs of the Finjan of the Arab Division of the Palmach* [Hebrew] (Tel Aviv, 1975).

37. See Battle Sheet, Southern Front, Givati Brigade Headquarters, 9 July 1948, IDF archives, Givati Brigade file.

38. Written by the cultural officer at Combat Headquarters, in Battle Sheet, no. 1 [Hebrew], the Chorev Campaign, Kislev 23 (25 December 1948), IDF Archives, Negev Brigade file.

39. From an announcement by the Safed Governor to Safed residents (undated), IDF Archives, file of leaflets, no. 1.

40. See brigade files and file of leaflets, IDF Archives.

41. A. Kadish, *To Farms and to Arms: The Hachsharot of the Palmach* [Hebrew] (Ha-Merkaz Le-Toldot Ko'ach Ha-Magen, Yad Tabenkin, 1995), 244.

42. "In these trials it was taken into account that most of the accused are in combat units, faithfully carrying out their tasks, and the prison sentence is therefore suspended." (IDF Archives, 2294/50/2951).

43. See Kadish, *To Farms and to Arms,* 245.

44. For more extensive reading, see B. Morris, *The Birth of the Palestinian Refugee Problem, 1947–1949* (Cambridge: Cambridge University Press, 1989); and also Yigal Ilam, *Those Who Carry Out Orders* [Hebrew] (Jerusalem, 1990), 31–52.

45. See Morris, *The Birth of the Palestinian Refugee Problem,* 94, 214, 219.

46. Ilam, *Those Who Carry Out Orders,* 39.

47. Order of the Day, Palmach Bridge 11 (Yiftach), undated, IDF Archives, Yiftach Brigade file.

48. See U. Ben-Eliezer, *Through the Gun Sight: The Creation of Israeli Militarism 1936–1956* [Hebrew] (Tel Aviv, 1995), 312.

49. See, for example, the short stories: *The Prisoner* [Hebrew] by S. Yizhar, *Swearing In* [Hebrew] by Natan Shacham, and *Swimming Competitionm* [Hebrew] by Benyamin Tammuz. All three appeared in *Battleground* [Hebrew], ed. A. Amir (Ministry of Defense Publishing House, 1992). See also S. Levy, "Prisoners in Fiction: The Arabs in the New Hebrew Literature" [Hebrew], *Mozna'im* 57 (1983), 70–73.

6. Monks in Khaki

1. See Y. Ben-David, "Compensations for the Consumption Standard in Kibbutz," *Niv Ha-Kevutza,* 15.3, no. 59 (October 1966): 475–95.

2. See M. Tzur, "Making Do with Little in the Second Aliya" [Hebrew], *Shdemot* 34 (summer 1969): 105–15.

3. G. Gaffner, "Berl's Trousers" [Hebrew], in *Kan al P'nei Ha-Adama* (Here on the ground), ed. M. Tzur (Sifriat Po'alim: Ha-Kibbutz Ha-Me'uchad, 1988). (Hereafter Tzur, *Here on the Ground.*)

4. See C. Adler and Y. Peres, "The Youth Movement and 'Salon Society': A Comparative Analysis of Cultural Patterns of Israeli Youth" [Hebrew], in *Education and Society in Israel: A Reader* [Hebrew], by S. N. Eisenstadt et al. (Jerusalem: Academon, 1968).

5. M. Salomon, 6 March 1948, in *Scrolls of Fire: A Collection Including a Selection from the Literary and Artistic Material Left by the Young People Who Fell in the War of Independence and Thereafter* [Hebrew], ed. R. Avinoam (Jerusalem, 1952), 403. See also N. Ben-Yehuda, *Between Calendars—1948* [Hebrew] (Jerusalem, 1981), 264.

6. Red, which is not in Israel's flag, appears in 80 percent of national flags. See S. Weitman, "National Flags: A Sociological Overview," *Semiotica* 8 (1973).

7. For example, in the paintings of Shalom Sabba and Nachum Gutman, in the caricatures of Arieh Navon, Dan Gelbart, and Dosh, and the sculptures of Natan Rappaport. Likewise in literature—S. Yizhar's *Ziklag Days,* Chaim Guri's poems, and also in films such as *The Sabra, Oded the Wanderer, Hill 24 Doesn't Answer,* and *The Pillar of Fire* series.

8. N. Franko (Kevutzat Ha-Chugim), "Three 'Fashion' Points in Our Favor," in Tzur, *Here on the Ground,* 308.

9. R. Ma'oz, "The Metamorphosis of the Forelock in Israeli Literature," *Mozna'im* 62 (1988): 50.

10. Z. Levenberg, in Avinoam, *Scrolls of Fire,* 411.

11. "Stages of Aliya in the Test of Twenty Years of Immigrants' Camp, C," quoted in Y. Peres, "The Pioneer Youth Movement" [Hebrew], in S. N. Eisenstadt et al., *The Social Structure of Israel* [Hebrew] (Jerusalem, 1966).

12. The students of the Reali School in Haifa were forbidden to go to the cinema, and teachers even took turns waiting outside the cinema to enforce the ban. See M. Rosenstein, "The New Jew: The Link to Jewish Tradition in General Zionist Secondary Education in Eretz Israel" [Hebrew] (Ph.D. diss., Hebrew University, Jerusalem, 1985), 219–20.

13. Ezer Weizman wrote, "I would return from Tel Aviv with a scoop of ice cream and a bottle of brandy. Ice cream they understood. The brandy was inconceivable for them. It was something that aroused amazement and even a certain measure of abhorrence." E. Weizman, *To You the Sky, to You the Land* [Hebrew] (Tel Aviv: Ma'ariv, 1975), 52.

14. Adler and Peres, "The Youth Movement and 'Salon Society,'" 16.

15. Dalia D., "Dance Evenings," *Olamin* [the children's newspaper in Givat Brenner] 6 (1949).

16. N. Dickson, *The Psychology of Sloppiness in the Army* [Hebrew] (Tel Aviv, 1979).

17. Sh. Teveth, *Dayan: Biography* [Hebrew] (Jerusalem: Schocken, 1972), 343.

18. Leah B., "The Mentality of the Small Town Remains," in Tzur, *Here on the Ground,* 177.

19. Y. Ben-Yaakov, "How We Got Through," in Tzur, *Here on the Ground,* 75.

20. "The Connection between a Man and a Woman," in Tzur, *Here on the Ground,* 70.

21. Tz. Ganin, "Kiryat Chaim: All the Children (Nearly) Were in Youth Movements," in *The Youth Movements 1920–1960* [Hebrew], Idan, no. 13, ed. M. Na'or (Jerusalem: Yad Ben-Zvi, 1989), 232.

22. Published by the Hebrew Gymnasium, Jaffa, 1916.

23. For example, the first part of *The Sexual Question* by a Swiss psychiatrist, August Forell, published in 1931 by Ha-Poel Ha-Tza'ir press and the second part in 1946 by the publishing house Mitzpeh; *The Mysteries of Marriage* by a Dutch doctor-sexologist and a sex manual by Prentice Mulford (both published by Ammamit Publishing); a book by Marie Stopes on love and sex; and a book on psychology that included chapters on "hygiene for sex."

24. For example, a booklet by Dr. M. Brachiyahu on adolescence, 1930; a booklet by Y. Norman entitled, *How Will I Tell My Son?* [Hebrew], published by the author (Tel Aviv, 1928); and books on sexual hygiene published by Hadassah Health Publishing (Jerusalem, 1935).

25. Different from all the rest and surprising in its openness and factual tone is the book by Dr. A. B. Matmon, *The Sexual Life of Humans* [Hebrew], which includes a chapter on intercourse and instructs in a contemporary fashion. The first edition was published in 1938 by the Institute for Hygiene and Sexual Science of Tel Aviv, and it was followed by another four editions.

26. An example of the conservative attitude toward sex in the kibbutz movement (until the 1960s) can be found in the opinions of Avraham Aderet, one of the important kibbutz educators: "A full sex life during adolescence without marriage is likely to lead to a debasement of the intimate contact of sexual life by separating it from the deep spiritual connection and mutual responsibility of family life," and "masturbation is fruitless and can be mastered by self-determination." *A Letter on Education* 4, no. 17 (1960): 19, 23.

27. Tz. Zohar and S. Golan, *Sex Education* (Merchavia, 1941), 64.

28. P. Barzak, age eighteen, of Kibbutz Geva, 17 September 1948. My thanks to Mrs. Barzak for providing the letter.

29. Ben-Yehuda, *Between Calendars*, 298–99.

30. See Eliyahu, "On the Erotic Question," in the newspaper of the leadership of the Ha-Shomer Ha-Tza'ir chapter (Tel Aviv, 8 July 1934), archives of the Ha-Shomer Ha-Tza'ir, 3–2.1 (3).

7. Our Gang

1. A. C., "With Yehuda Ya'ari" [Hebrew], *Ha-Poel Ha-Tza'ir* 29 (January 1963).

2. See Y. Ya'ari, "A Path Strewn with Obstacles," *Book of the Third Aliya* [Hebrew] (Tel Aviv, 1964), 889–90.

3. Yosef, Gan Shmuel, draft article for the movement newspapers: *El Or, Igeret, Ba-Sha'ar*, 1937–38, archive of Ha-Shomer Ha-Tza'ir, 3–3.1 (3).

4. See also M. Alon, *Youth in the Kibbutz* [Hebrew] (Tel Aviv, 1975), 45.

5. B. Bettelheim, *The Children of the Dream* (London: Macmillan, 1969), 127–29.

6. Ibid., 87.

7. Ibid., 96.

8. See also "A Longing for a Friend" [Hebrew], in *Youth with Others* [Hebrew], by A. Aderet (Jerusalem: Ministry of Education, 1971).

9. C. Shafroni, "The School in Ein Charod" [Hebrew], in *Anthology of Ha-Kibbutz Ha-Me'uchad* (Tel Aviv, 1932), 313–17.

10. Y. Zak, November 21, 1949, Geva archives, file of letters.

11. Letters of Amnon (no family name given), 1942, Mishmar Ha-Emek archives, file 63.23.

12. *Like a Plant of the Field: Anthology of Ha-Machanot Ha-Olim in Ha-Tenua Ha-Me'uchedet* [Hebrew] (Tel Aviv, 1946), 19.

13. "On the Shared Experience" [Hebrew], in *The Palmach Book* [Hebrew], eds. Z. Gilad and M. Megged (Tel Aviv: Ha-Kibbutz Ha-Me'uchad, 1953), 1: 223.

14. G. Le Bon, *The Crowd* (1895; New York: Viking, 1960).

15. For more on the ecstasy of the hora, see S. D. Yaffe, "From Petach Tikva to the Kinneret" [Hebrew], in *The Book of the Second Aliya,* [Hebrew], ed. B. Habas (Tel Aviv, 1947), 167, 266, 273, 388; and Z. Livneh, *Chapters from the Third Aliya* [Hebrew] (Tel Aviv, 1958), 58, 149.

16. G. Kadman, "Folk Dances as a Revelation of Village Culture in Israel" [Hebrew], *Kama* 4 (1952): 293–94.

17. See also "The Chain of Dances" in *Masada: All the Poems of Yitzchak Lamdan* [Hebrew] (Jerusalem, 1973), 45.

18. See *Cultural Creativity of the Kibbutz: Survey of Spheres, Institutions, and Creators in the Kibbutz Movement* [Hebrew] (Tel Aviv, 1988), 148.

19. A. Shacham, "The Song of Youth, the Song of Our Future: The Place of Singing Songs in the Israeli Youth Movements," in *Shorashim: Collections to Research the Kibbutz and the Youth Movements* (Tel Aviv, 1995), 181.

20. A. Oko, "Songs of the Youth Movement," in *The Youth Movements 1920–1960* [Hebrew], Idan, no. 13, ed. M. Na'or (Jerusalem: Yad Ben-Zvi, 1989), 262.

21. N. Ben-Yehuda, "Autobiography in Poetry and Song," in Na'or, *The Youth Movements,* 153.

22. See C. Guri, "Carrying a World of Hope: Songs of Red Messianism" [Hebrew], *Masa (Davar* literary supplement), 9 December 1990, 14.

23. On the ideological dimension, see N. Shachar, "The Music and Composer in the Kibbutz" (M.A. thesis, Bar-Ilan University, 1981); H. Shmueli, *Israeli Song* [Hebrew] (Tel Aviv, 1971).

24. See A. Shapira, "A Generation in the Land" [Hebrew], *Alpa'yim* 2 (1990): 179. Of 105 popular songs that appear in Ch. Guri and Ch. Cheffer, *The Palmach Family: Escapades and Song* [Hebrew] (Tel Aviv, 1974), about a quarter have Russian melodies.

25. Shacham, *The Song of Youth,* 183.

26. Carmela, "Evenings in Our Movement's Chapter House" [Hebrew], *Afikim,* newsletter of Haifa chapter house, 20 March 1937.

27. *Program for Practical Work (the Amalim Level),* Guidance Department, Ha-Noar Ha-Lomed, Ha-Machanot Ha-Olim, 1947.

28. See *Parties—Additions,* Training Department, Ha-Machanot Ha-Olim, 1948, archives of Yad Tabenkin, brigade 9, series 75.

29. M. Mosinzon, ed. *Let's Sing* [Hebrew] (Tel Aviv, 1949), 1.

30. N. Yonatan, *Landscapes* [Hebrew] (Tel Aviv, 1983), 7.

31. *Ba-Machaneh* 45 (6 July 1950): 6.

32. No systematic, in-depth research on the components of the specific style of Israeli music has yet been carried out, but there have been several preliminary

attempts, such as M. Zemora, "The Biblical Verse in Israeli Song" [Hebrew], *Tatzlil* 3 (1963): 155–57.

33. Told by a veteran member in "This is the History of the Chizbatron" [Hebrew], *Alon Hapalmach* 72 (12 September 1948): 40.

34. The character Amitai Etzioni uses the expression "the coffee ritual" in "His Majesty the Finjan" [Hebrew], in Avneri, *When the Pathbreakers Break Through: From the Diary of a Palmach Soldier* [Hebrew] (1952), 102.

35. For details see M. Tabib, *Dirt Path* [Hebrew] (Tel Aviv, 1961).

36. See M. Tabenkin, "Around the Campfire" [Hebrew], in *From the War: Fiction and Poetry* [Hebrew], ed. U. Ofek (Tel Aviv: Ministry of Defense, 1969), 110.

37. S. Levitan, "We and Our Children" [Hebrew], *Mi-Bifnim* (October 1934): 54.

38. On the Chizbatron's background, see Y. Bar-On, "The Troupe," *Ba-Machaneh* 35–36 (7 May 1986): 49–54.

39. See A. Neder, "On the Army Troupe" [Hebrew], *Ba-Machaneh* 43 (22 June 1960): 11.

40. *Ba-Machaneh* 14 (1 December 1949): 12.

41. Ch. Guri, "Here Our Corpses Are Laid" [Hebrew], in *Flowers of Fire* [Hebrew] (Merchavia, 1949), 79.

42. Ch. Cheffer, "Dudu," in *Light Ammunition: Psalms* [Hebrew] (Tel Aviv, 1955), 89.

43. O. Hillel, "The Friendship of the Fighters," in *The Land of Noon* [Hebrew], 52–53.

44. Horowitz, *Blue and Thorns*, 83.

45. Ch. Guri, "Bab el-Wad" [Hebrew], in Gilad and Megged, *The Palmach Book*, 173.

46. Y. Giladi, Jerusalem, 3 May 1948, in *Scrolls of Fire: A Collection Including a Selection from the Literary and Artistic Material Left by the Young People Who Fell in the War of Independence and Thereafter* [Hebrew], ed. R. Avinoam (Jerusalem, 1952), 508.

47. See R. Dotan, "Girls in the Palmach: Their Roles and Duties" [Hebrew], in *The Battles of the Palmach* [Hebrew] (Tel Aviv, 1989), 35.

48. "Visit to a Palmach Base" [Hebrew], in *Yisrael (Sota) Schwartzman: To His Memory* [Hebrew] (Tel Aviv, 1957), 25.

49. Pinkerfeld-Amir, "The Will of the Youths," in *In Their Lives*, 121.

50. Sh. Elidan, "New 'Headstones,'" *Cherut*, 27 October 1950.

Epilogue

1. Cana'ani, "In the Convoy and to its Side," 62.

2. K. Mannheim, "The Problem of Generation," in *Essays on the Sociology of Knowledge*, ed. P. Kecskemedy (London: Routledge & Kegan Paul, 1952).

3. In A. Ben-Gurion, ed., *Mourning* [Hebrew] (Ha-Va'ada Ha-Beinkibutzit Hvai U-Mo'ed, 1953).

4. On the myth of the European war, see George Mosse, *Fallen Soldiers: Re-*

shaping the Memory of the World Wars (Oxford: Oxford University Press, 1990), 21.

5. Y. Kafri, "The Myth of the Sabra: Was It or Wasn't It" [Hebrew], *Ma'ariv*, 5 December 1986, 27.

6. Uri Zvi Greenberg, "He-Chayyim Be-Zechutam Omrim" (Thanks to them life speaks), quoted in *Memorial Service: Poems about Death and Dying (Appendix to Mourning Anthologies)*, collected by A. Ben-Gurion (Va'adat Chagim Beinkibutzit, 1977).

7. Yisrael Gat, "11 Adar" [Hebrew], in *Like a Plant of the Field: Anthology of Ha-Machanot Ha-Olim in Ha-Tenua Ha-Me'uchedet* [Hebrew] (Tel Aviv, 1946), 162.

8. Vita, "On Accepting New Members" [Hebrew], in *Like a Plant of the Field*, 172.

Glossary

agadim Derogatory term for Holocaust survivors in Israel (from the Hebrew acronym "people of the mournful Diaspora")

aliya (pl. *aliyot*) Immigration to Israel—both individuals and waves of immigrants (lit. "ascent") (see under "First Aliya," etc.)

Amalek The biblical enemy of the Hebrews, who meant to destroy them during their journey from Egypt to Israel. Often used as a simile for any foe of the Jewish people or any anti-Semite.

Amida A central prayer in the Jewish liturgy, recited standing (lit. "standing")

Ashkenazi (pl. *Ashkenazim*) Jew(s) from east and central Europe

Balfour Declaration Official statement (2 November 1917) by the British Foreign Secretary declaring that the British government favored the establishment of a national home for the Jewish people in Palestine

Bar Giora Earlier name of the Ha-Shomer organization

bar mitzvah The Jewish initiation ceremony, traditionally held on a boy's 13th birthday, marking his entry into the Jewish religious community. Secular Zionists created nonreligious bar mitzvah ceremonies, and included girls as well.

beit midrash Center for religious learning, often part of a synagogue, generally for the study of talmudic texts and commentaries (lit. "house of study")

Bilu movement First modern movement for pioneering and agricultural settlement in Palestine, founded in 1882 in Kharkov, Russia (from the Hebrew acronym "House of Jacob, let us arise and go"—Isaiah 2:5)

blorit A waving, uncombed tuft of hair over the forehead, a legendary element of the Sabra countenance

Chagam One of the first premilitary groups organized in the schools; predecessor of the Gadna

chaver Literally "friend," also member, comrade

chevreman Slang for sociable guy, good sport

chizbat (pl. *chizbatim*) A tall story or amusing anecdote, often told around a campfire

Chizbatron Army entertainment troupe

chutzpah Effrontery, impudence

dugri Unpolished, blunt Sabra idiom

dunam Land measure, now equal to one quarter of an acre but with widely varying values before Israeli independence

etrogim An early term for native-born members of the Yishuv (lit. "citrons")

fedayeen Armed Arab infiltrators into Israel after independence

Fifth Aliya A wave of Jewish immigration to Palestine 1932–40, prompted largely by the rise of Nazism in Germany. Often termed a "bourgeois" *aliya*, since many of the immigrants were professionals, arrived with some money and assets, and hoped to maintain a middle-class lifestyle

finjan Sabra term for the pot used to make Arab (Turkish) coffee over an open fire

First Aliya The first wave of modern, nationalist Jewish immigration to Palestine 1882–1903

Fourth Aliya Jewish immigration to Palestine 1924–28, mainly middle-class

gachal Volunteers from overseas who joined the Yishuv's military frameworks (from the Hebrew acronym for "overseas enlistment")

Gadna Youth corps associated with the Haganah; an outgrowth of the earlier Chagam

Gideons Secret defense organization that operated 1913–14

hachshara (pl. *hachsharot*) Agricultural-pioneering training unit; also, the process of being trained for pioneering agricultural work

Haganah Clandestine Jewish organization for armed self-defense in Palestine under the British mandate; became the basis for the IDF

hagshama Realization or consummation of the Zionist mission, also, the personal implementation of pioneering values, in particular those involving manual and agricultural labor and military service

Ha-Kibbutz Ha-Meu'chad A kibbutz movement (see also *Ha-Shomer Ha-Tza'ir*)

Ha-Machanot Ha-Olim Pioneering youth movement, founded in 1926

Ha-Noar Ha-Oved (Ve-Ha-Lomed) Pioneering youth movement (lit: "working [and studying] youth")

Ha-Shomer Early clandestine Jewish self-defense organization in Palestine

Ha-Shomer Ha-Tza'ir Zionist youth movement established in Poland, which later became one of the two kibbutz movements in Palestine (see also *Ha-Kibbutz Ha-Meu'chad*) and one of the three largest Sabra youth movements (together with Ha-Machanot Ha-Olim and Ha-Zofim)

Hasid (pl. *Hasidim*) Follower of Hasidism

Hasidism Religious revivalist movement of the Hasidim founded in the 18th century that emphasized song, dance, and emotional worship

Hatikva The Zionist and Israeli anthem (lit. "The Hope")

Histadrut Early Zionist labor federation established by the pioneers

hora Circle folk dance developed by Zionists

IDF Israel Defense Forces—the Israeli army

Intifada Arab uprising from 1988 until the mid-1990s on the West Bank and Gaza (Judea-Samaria)

JNF Jewish National Fund

jobnik Someone serving in a noncombat position in the army

kafiyyeh Arab headdress made from a diagonally folded square of cloth

kibbutz (pl. *kibbutzim*) Commune, based mainly on agriculture but also engaging in industry

kibbutznik (pl. *kibbutznikim*) Kibbutz member

Kibbutz Brigade Youth movement framework for kibbutz children

kumzitz A get-together, often around a campfire, with songs and *chizbatim*

Lag Be'Omer Festival connected to Bar Kochba's revolt against the Romans when bonfires are lit countrywide (lit. "33rd day of Omer")

Mapai The Socialist-Zionist party (later called the Labor Party) that was the major political force in the Yishuv period and in Israel until 1977 (lit: "Party of Workers in the Land of Israel")

Mistarabim A Palmach unit whose members performed clandestine missions disguised as Arabs

moshav (pl. *moshavim*) Smallholders' cooperative agricultural settlement

moshava (pl. *moshavot*) Village—the first form of Jewish rural settlement in Palestine, with privately owned farms, founded largely during the First Aliya

moshavnik (pl. *moshavnikim*) Member of a moshav

mukhtar The headman of an Arab village or community, generally appointed by the national authorities and serving as a mediating agent between the villagers and the government

muzhik Russian peasant

Nachal Branch of the IDF combining military service with agricultural/community work

Oriental Jew Jew from the Islamic world

Palmach The elite, largely independent strike force of the Haganah, closely associated with the kibbutz and labor movements

Pesach Haggadah The traditional book read aloud at the dinner table on the first evening of the festival of Passover, celebrating the biblical exodus from Egypt

pioneers Collectively, people of the first three *aliyas,* particularly those who worked the land

protektzia Use of connections and patronage, favoritism (from Russian)

Second Aliya A wave of Jewish immigration to Palestine 1904–14, based on pioneering and Socialist-Zionist ideology. They founded the first kibbutzim and moshavim.

Sepharadi (pl. *Sephardim*) Specifically, Jews of Spain and Portugal and their descendants, wherever resident, as contrasted with Ashkenazim, but often used as a synonym for "Oriental Jew"

shaheed Holy martyr, in Arabic

shofar Ram's horn blown like a trumpet on the Jewish penitential holidays of Rosh Ha-Shana and Yom Kippur.

shushu Slang for secret, a secret operation

Third Aliya A wave of Jewish immigration to Palestine 1919–23. In legend, though less so in fact, this was a "socialist" *aliya*.

tzabar Sabra (lit: "cactus pear"); a term used for native-born members of the Yishuv, in particular those born or socialized in the pioneering communities, youth movements, and Palmach

Unit 101 Early, short-lived, but legendary IDF elite commando unit

War of Independence War of 1947–49 when the Jews fought off the invading Arab armies and ensured the establishment of the State of Israel

yeshiva (pl. *yeshivot*) Traditional religious academy devoted primarily to the study of rabbinical literature

Yishuv The Jewish community in pre-state Israel

Yizkor Memorial prayer

Youth Aliya Organization for transferring youngsters to Israel and educating them there

Youth Society Framework in which city children, often from disadvantaged backgrounds, boarded, worked, and studied at kibbutzim

zaks Slang for secret, a clandestine operation

Bibliography

Adler, C. and Y. Peres. "The Youth Movement and 'Salon Society': A Comparative Analysis of Cultural Patterns of Israeli Youth" [Hebrew]. In *Education and Society in Israel: A Reader* [Hebrew], by S. N. Eisenstadt et al. Jerusalem: Academon, 1968.

Avinoam, R., ed. *Scrolls of Fire: A Collection Including a Selection from the Literary and Artistic Material Left by the Young People Who Fell in the War of Independence and Thereafter* [Hebrew]. Jerusalem, 1952.

Bar-Gal, Y. *Homeland and Geography: One Hundred Years of Zionist Education* [Hebrew]. Tel Aviv, 1993.

Ben-Amotz, D. and N. Ben-Yehuda. *The World Dictionary of Hebrew Slang* [Hebrew]. Tel Aviv: Zemora-Bitan, 1972.

Ben-Ezer, E. *No Tranquillity in Zion: Conversations on the Price of Zionism* [Hebrew]. Tel Aviv, 1986.

———. *In the Homeland of Contradictory Longings* [Hebrew]. Tel Aviv, 1992.

Cana'ani, D. "In the Convoy and to Its Side: On the Works of S. Yizhar" [Hebrew]. In *S. Yizhar: A Selection of Critical Articles on His Works* [Hebrew], edited by H. Naggid. Tel Aviv, 1972.

Dankner, A. *Dahn Ben-Amotz: A Biography* [Hebrew]. Jerusalem, 1992.

Dayan, D. *Yes, We Are Youth! The Gadna History Book* [Hebrew]. Tel Aviv, Ministry of Defense, 1977.

Alboim-Dror, R. *Hebrew Education in Eretz Israel* [Hebrew]. 2 vols. Jerusalem, 1986, 1990.

Eisenstadt, S. N. et al. *The Social Structure of Israel* [Hebrew]. Jerusalem, 1966.

Enis, R. and Y. Ben-Erev. *Gardens and Landscape in the Kibbutz* [Hebrew]. Tel Aviv, 1994.

Firer, R. *Consciousness and Knowledge: The Influence of Zionist Values on Textbooks on Jewish History in the Hebrew Language in the Years 1900–1980* [Hebrew]. Ph.D. diss., Hebrew University, Jerusalem, 1980.

————. *Agents of Zionist Education* [Hebrew]. Oranim, 1985.

Gilad, Z. "Beneath the Lotuses" [Hebrew]. In *Chapters of the Palmach: From the Mouths of Fighters* [Hebrew]. Ein Charod: Ha-Kibbutz Ha-Me'uchad, 1950.

Gilad, Z. and M. Megged, eds. *The Palmach Book* [Hebrew]. 2 vols. Tel Aviv: Ha-Kibbutz Ha-Me'uchad, 1953.

Horowitz, D. *Blue and Thorns: The 1948 Generation, Self-Portrait* [Hebrew]. Jerusalem: Keter, 1993.

Ilam, Y. *Those Who Carry Out Orders* [Hebrew]. Jerusalem, 1990.

Kadish, A. *To Farms and to Arms: The Hachsharot of the Palmach.* Ha-Merkaz Le-Toldot Ko'ach Ha-Magen, Yad Tabenkin, 1995.

Kafkafi, V., ed. *The Years of Ha-Machanot Ha-Olim (First and Second Decades)* [Hebrew]. Tel Aviv: Ha-Kibbutz Ha-Me'uchad, 1985.

Kramer, Sh. *The Changing of the Guard in Our Literature.* Tel Aviv: Dvir, 1959.

Like a Plant of the Field: Anthology of Ha-Machanot Ha-Olim in Ha-Tenua Ha-Me'uchedet [Hebrew]. Tel Aviv, 1946.

Livneh, A. Testimony. "The Reconnaissance of Mishmar Ha'Emek and the Area Around" [Hebrew]. 30 October 1991. Mishmar Ha'Emek archive, file 3.63.

O'Day, T. P. "Sociological Dilemmas: Five Paradoxes of Institutionalization." In *Sociological Theory, Values, and Change,* ed. E. A. Tiryakian. Glencoe, Ill.: Free Press, 1963.

Ofek, U. ed. *From the War: Fiction and Poetry* [Hebrew]. Tel Aviv: Ministry of Defense, 1969.

Praver, E. *The Way of the Hike to Knowledge of the Land 1888–1918.* M.A. thesis, Hebrew University, Jerusalem, 1992.

Rosenstein, M. *The New Jew: The Link to Jewish Tradition in General Zionist Secondary Education in Eretz Israel* [Hebrew]. Ph.D. diss., Hebrew University, 1985.

Shacham, O. "The Song of Youth, the Song of Our Future: The Place of Singing Songs in the Israeli Youth Movements." In *Shorashim: Collections to Research the Kibbutz and the Youth Movements.* Tel Aviv, 1995.

Shapira, A. "A Generation in the Land" [Hebrew]. *Alpa'yim* 2 (1990): 178–203.

————. *The Sword of the Dove: Zionism and Power, 1881–1948* [Hebrew]. Tel Aviv: Am Oved, Ofakim, 1992.

Shapira, Y. *The Historical Achdut Ha-Avodah and Its Power as a Political Organization* [Hebrew]. Tel Aviv, 1975.

————. *Elite without Successors: Generations of Leaders in Israeli Society* [Hebrew]. Tel Aviv: Sifriat Po'alim, 1984.

Sivan, E. *The 1948 Generation: Myth, Portrait, and Memory* [Hebrew]. Tel Aviv, 1991.

Tzur, M. *Le-lo Kutonet Passim* (Without a coat of many colors). Tel Aviv: Am Oved, 1976.

————. *Kan al P'nei Ha-Adama* (Here on the ground). Sifriat Po'alim: Ha-Kibbutz Ha-Me'uchad, 1988.

Vilnai, Z. *The Field Trip and Its Educational Value* [Hebrew]. Jerusalem: Youth Department of the Zionist Organization, 1953.

Index

army. *See* IDF
Arnon Canyon (Jordan), 176, 182
"Around the Campfire" (Sadeh), 243
artists, 9, 125, 161, 268n.18
ascent/descent, 21–22
asceticism, 210–14, 217, 218–19
Ashkenazim, xii, 96–103, 295. *See also*
  Diaspora Jews
Ashman, A.: "Blue Box Anthem, The" 51
austerity, 210–11, 212. *See also*
  asceticism
Avigur, Shaul, 7
Avneri, Uri, 6, 10
Avni, Aharon, 268n.18
azov shtuyot, 116

"Bab el-Wad" (Guri), 252
Balfour Declaration (1917), 21, 32, 295
Ba-Ma'aleh, 196
Ba-Machaneh, 12, 33, 133
Ba-Machaneh Gadna, 12, 135–36,
  285n.35
Ba-Machaneh Nachal, 133
Bamat Elef, 7
Barak (Bible), 36
Bardenov, Yermi, 68
bare feet, 212, 213
Bar Giora, 295. *See also* Ha-Shomer
Bar Kochba (Bible), 35, 36, 37, 49, 127,
  244
Bar-Lev, Chaim, 80
bar mitzvah, 46–48, 295
"Barren Woman, The" (Rachel), 92
Bartov, Chanoch, 93
Bas, Schmuel: "Sing, Youth, the Song
  of Our Future," 82
Battalion of Defenders of the Hebrew
  Language, 95
Bazam, Naftali, 268n.18
beauty, male, 78–80
Bedouins. *See* Arabs
Be'ersheva, 119, 204
be-ezrat Ha-Shem (with God's help), 116
be-hayecha, 115
beit midrash, 139, 295
Bellah, Robert, 19, 20
Ben-Amotz, Dahn, 10, 12–13, 95, 198,
  248; *Pack of Lies,* 11–12, 82, 117,
  247, 248
Ben Dor, Chaim, 64–65
Ben-Eliezer, Uri, 156
Ben-Gurion, David, 49, 71, 82, 87, 126,
  214
Benjamin, Rabbi (Yehoshua Radler-
  Feldman), 188
Ben Menachem, Yitzchak (Gulliver), 68,
  129, 279n.77

Ben Shemen, 232
Ben Tardion, Hanina, 126
Ben-Yehuda, Baruch, 27, 28–29, 31, 42,
  50, 156
Ben-Yehuda, Eliezer, 186
Ben-Yehuda, Hemdat, 78
Ben-Yehuda, Netiva, 107, 198, 223–24,
  237, 279n.81
Ben-Yisrael, Shlomo (Gelper): *Detective*
  series, 107, 279n.76
Ben-Zvi, Yitzchak, 286n.7
Berditchewski, Mica Joseph, 139
Bergman, Yehuda, 186
Bernstein, Moshe, 268n.18
betach, 114
Bettelheim, Bruno, 221, 229, 230
Bialik, Chaim Nachman, 29, 49, 60
Biber, Shaul, 11, 12, 248
Bible study, 27–28
bilbul mo'ach, 115
Bilu movement, 49, 295
binding of Isaac, myth of, 39–41
biographies, 14–15
Biram, Arthur, 32, 141–42
blorit, xv, 212, 213–14, 295
"Blue Box Anthem, The" (Ashman), 51
blue boxes, 51–53
blue shirts, 212
Blum, Ludwig, 268n.18
Bograshov, Dr., 174
"Borchi Nafshi," 52
bourgeoisie, 148, 165, 210, 215, 217
Bow of the Writers, The, 14
"Boy Takes Girl," 225
Brenner, Yosef Chaim, 38, 49
British army, 172
British scouts, 163, 166
brotherhood of fighters, 249–53
Buber, Martin, 157
buddy humor, 117–18, 247, 261
Buffalo Bill (William Cody), 249

campfires, 241–44
Cana'ani, David, 258
Canaanite circle, 6–7
capitalism, 210–11
cartoonists, 9
Chagam (Expanded Physical Education
  program), 32–33, 141–42, 295
Charly Kecharly (Horowitz), 17
chaver, 244–45, 295
Cheffer, Chaim, 60, 93, 113, 248, 251;
  "Finjan, The," 243; *Light Ammunition,* 11; *Pack of Lies,* 11–12, 82, 117,
  247, 248; "Platoon Commander, The,"
  130, 132
Cheivar, Jews of, 186

Text: 10/13 Sabon
Display: Mrs. Eaves
Composition: Integrated Composition Systems
Printing and binding: Sheridan Books
Index: Carol Roberts